Elements of ML Programming

ML97 Edition

Jeffrey D. Ullman

An Alan R. Apt Book

Prentice Hall
Upper Saddle River, New Jersey 07458

Library of Congress Cataloging-in-Publication Data

Ullman, Jeffrey D.
     Elements of ML programming/ Jeffrey D. Ullman.
     ML97 Edition
         p. cm.
     "An Alan R. Apt. Book"
     Includes bibliological references and index.
     ISBN: 0-13-790387-1
     1. ML (Computer program language). I. Title.
CIP DATA AVAILABLE

Acquisitions editor: **ALAN R. APT**
Editor-in-chief: **MARCIA HORTON**
Production editor: **IRWIN ZUCKER**
Managing editor: **BAYANI MENDOZA DE LEON**
Director of production and manufacturing: **DAVID W. RICCARDI**
Cover director: **JAYNE CONTE**
Manufacturing buyer: **JULIA MEEHAN**
Editorial assistant: **TONI CHAVEZ**

© 1998, 1994 by Prentice-Hall, Inc.
Simon & Schuster / A Viacom Company
Upper Saddle River, New Jersey 07458

The author and publisher of this book have used their best efforts in preparing this book. These efforts include the development, research, and testing of the theories and programs to determine their effectiveness. The author and publisher make no warranty of any kind, expressed or implied, with regard to these programs or the documentation contained in this book. The author and publisher shall not be liable in any event for incidental or consequential damages in connection with, or arising out of, the furnishing, performance, or use of these programs.

Printed in the United States of America

10 9 8 7 6 5 4 3 2 1

ISBN   0-13-790387-1

Prentice-Hall International (UK) Limited, London
Prentice-Hall of Australia Pty. Limited, Sydney
Prentice-Hall Canada Inc., Toronto
Prentice-Hall Hispanoamericana, S.A., Mexico
Prentice-Hall of India Private Limited, New Delhi
Prentice-Hall of Japan, Inc., Tokyo
Simon & Schuster Asia Pte. Ltd., Singapore
Editora Prentice-Hall do Brasil, Ltda., Rio de Janeiro

Preface

I became interested in ML programming when I taught CS109, the introductory Computer Science Foundations course at Stanford, starting in 1991. ML was used by several of the instructors of this course, including Stu Reges and Mike Cleron, to introduce concepts such as functional programming and type systems. It was also used for the practical purpose of introducing a second programming paradigm, other than the Pascal or C that students learned in the introductory programming course. Reimplementing algorithms and data structures in a significantly different language often is an aid to understanding of basic data structure and algorithm concepts.

I first learned ML from the notes that Reges and Cleron had written for their students. Initially, I was intrigued by the rule system, which gave me much of the power of Prolog, a language with which I had worked for several years. Yet ML did not introduce the semantic complexity that comes from the use of unification and backtracking in Prolog. However, I soon discovered other charms of ML: the type system, the use of exceptions, and the module system for creating abstract datatypes, among others. From the Reges and Cleron notes I also picked up the utility of giving the student a fast overview, stressing the most commonly used constructs rather than the complete syntax.

In writing this guide to ML programming, I have thus departed from the approach found in many books on the language. As an outsider, I had the opportunity to learn the language from the standpoint of the typical programmer. I have tried to remember how things struck me at first, the analogies I drew with conventional languages, and the concepts that I found most useful in getting started. I hope that my selection is accurate, and that the book will facilitate the reader's transition from conventional languages to ML.

The Second Edition

You are reading the second edition of the book. The primary change between the first and second editions is that the second conforms to the new language standard called ML97. All major implementations of ML either have converted, or are in the process of converting, to this standard. For the few matters that are implementation-dependent, such as the choice of diagnostics, the second edition, like the first, follows the Standard ML of New Jersey (SML/NJ) implementation. SML/NJ is the work of Andrew Appel of Princeton University, David MacQueen of Lucent/Bell Labs, and their colleagues.

The following is both a summary of the second edition and a guide to the correspondence between the first and second editions.

- Chapter 1 corresponds to the old Chapter 0.

- Chapter 2 lays the groundwork for ML programming. Sections 2.1 through 2.4 correspond to the old Chapters 1 through 4, respectively.

- Chapter 3 introduces functions in ML. The old Chapter 5 is now Sections 3.1 and 3.2, while the old Chapter 6 appears in Sections 3.3 and 3.6. Old Chapter 7 has become Section 3.4, while Sections 3.5 and much of Section 3.6 are new.

- Chapter 4 covers ML input and output. The old Chapter 9 has been split among Sections 4.1, 4.2, and 4.4, while the new Section 4.3 comes from the old Chapter 22.

- In Chapter 5 we return to the subject of functions in ML, presenting a number of advanced topics. Section 5.1 covers matches and patterns like the old Chapter 19. Section 5.2 covers exceptions, from the old Chapters 8 and 20. Section 5.3 covers polymorphism as in the old Chapter 10. Material on higher-order functions from the old Chapters 11 and 21 is now split among Sections 5.4 through 5.6. The case study in Section 5.7 was originally part of the old Chapter 22.

- Chapter 6 introduces datatypes. The old Chapter 12 is split between Sections 6.1 and 6.2, while old Chapter 13 is now Sections 6.3 and 6.4.

- Chapter 7 presents a number of advanced topics about data structures. Section 7.1 covers record structures, the old Chapter 18. Material on arrays, the old Chapter 16, is now in Sections 7.2 and 7.4. Old Chapter 17, about references, is in Sections 7.3 and 7.5.

- Chapter 8 covers the ML module system. Old Chapter 14 is split among Sections 8.1 through 8.3, and old Chapter 15 is now in Sections 8.4 and 8.5. The case study in Section 8.6 is new.

- Finally, Chapter 9 attempts to summarize the entire language. Some concepts not appearing elsewhere in the book are introduced as well. Section 9.1 on infix operators, corresponds to the old Chapter 24. Sections 9.2 and 9.3 summarize what is called the "top-level environment," the set of features one has in ML without asking for them explicitly. Then Section 9.4 summarizes the "standard basis," or capabilities one can obtain if one calls for them explicitly. Some of the old Chapter 25 is spread among Sections 9.2 through 9.4, but much of these sections is new for ML97.

Section 9.5 corresponds to the old Chapter 23 and covers some important features found only in SML/NJ, involving the creation of executable files. Section 9.6 concludes with syntax diagrams for the entire language and is an updating of the old Chapter 26.

Features of the Book

The test of a language is not the best or most succinct examples of its use. Rather, a language will only be adopted widely if it can handle everyday programming chores well. Thus, I have considered in this book many of the most common data structures, such as trees and hash tables, and many of the most common algorithms, such as sorting or Gaussian elimination. I think the reader will be impressed by how well ML handles these standard tasks that were selected because of their ubiquity, not because they exhibit special features of the language.

To focus the reader's attention, I have inserted boxes at various places in the text. These boxes are interruptions from the main focus of the text, but they are sufficiently important that I want to make sure they are noticed. On the other hand, footnotes are also interruptions to the main thread, but they are there only "for the record" rather than as an aid to understanding.

Exercises

Most of the sections have exercises at the end. In the text, we indicate that an exercise or part of an exercise has a published solution by preceding the exercise or part of an exercise by a star. You can find solutions to exercises with stars at URL http://www-db.stanford.edu/~ullman/emlpsols/sols.html.

Exercises are graded by difficulty. Harder exercises are indicated by an exclamation point in the margin, and a few of the hardest exercises have two exclamation points.

Use of the Book

The book as a whole is a tutorial and reference for the person who wants to program productively in ML. Although there are occasional references to conventional languages like C or Pascal, I believe the book is sufficiently self-contained that it could be used to teach ML as a first programming language.

When we teach students ML in the CS109 course at Stanford, the material covered corresponds closely to what is in Chapters 2, 3, 4.1, 5, 6, and 7. The book can be used as a supplement to a programming language concepts course, in which case Chapter 8 would surely be included.

Acknowledgments

I would like to thank Andrew Appel and David MacQueen, both of whom carefully critiqued the original edition. Matthias Blume was equally a boon for the second edition. They are all three tied for the title of "world's greatest referee."

I value a number of important pointers on ML from John Mitchell. Also, Henry Bauer, Richard LeBlanc, Peter Robinson, and Jean Scholtz have my appreciation for their work as referees of the first-edition manuscript.

Errata from the first edition were found and pointed out to me by Baoquan Chen, Franklin Chen, Martin Erwig, Mark Girod, Naomichi Komuro, Hugh McGuire, Jeffrey Oldham. David Richardson, and Daniel Yankelevich.

Finally, I appreciate the help from several members of the core ML community that kept me informed of changes and encouraged me to keep this book on track. I even got help on the design of the cover for the first edition (see the following note), which has been carried over to the second edition as well.

Cover Art

Special thanks go to Luca Cardelli, who volunteered to create original art for this book. The result is on the cover.

Supplementary Material on the Web

The book's home page is `www-db.stanford.edu/~ullman/emlp.html`. There you can find:

1. Solutions to starred exercises.

2. Code for the major programs in the book.

3. Errata.

4. Notes and exams from Stanford's CS109 involving ML.

5. Links to ML documentation and resources.

J. D. U.
Stanford CA
September, 1997

Table of Contents

Chapter 1

A Perspective on ML and SML/NJ

In this preliminary chapter we shall introduce the reader to the history of ML and the reasons for its existence and popularity. We shall also present the mechanics of using a particular implementation of ML, called Standard ML of New Jersey, which is the implementation used for examples in this book. Finally, some general references on the language are given, including URL's for obtaining ML compilers and on-line documentation.

1.1 Why ML?

ML is a relatively new language that has some extremely interesting features. Its designers incorporated many modern programming-language ideas, yet the language is surprisingly easy to learn and use. In this section we shall enumerate the most important of these features.

A Functional Language

ML is primarily a *functional language*, meaning that the basic mode of computation is the definition and application of functions. Functions can be defined by the user as in conventional languages, by writing code for the function. But it is also possible in ML to treat functions as values and compute new functions from them with operators like function composition.

Side-Effect Freedom

A consequence of the functional style is that computation proceeds by evaluating expressions, not by making assignments to variables. There are ways to give expressions *side-effects*, which are operations that permanently change the value of a variable or other observable object (e.g., by printing output). However, side-effects are treated as necessary aberrations on the basic theme. In contrast, languages like Pascal or C use statements with side-effects as a matter of course. For example, a Pascal assignment like `a := b+c` has a side-effect, since the value of variable `a` is changed after the assignment is executed. In contrast, when ML evaluates an expression like `b+c`, it typically creates an entirely new element with which to associate the result.

Higher-Order Functions

ML supports *higher-order functions* — functions that take functions as arguments — routinely and with great generality. In comparison, languages like Pascal or C support functions as arguments only in limited ways.

Polymorphism

ML supports *polymorphism*, which is the ability of a function to take arguments of various types. For example, in Pascal or C we may have to create different types with similar properties, such as "stack of integers," "stack of reals," "stack of pairs of integers," and so on. We would then have to define operations like "push" and "pop" for each different type of stack. In ML, we can define one notion of a stack, one push function, and one pop function, each of which works no matter what type of elements our stacks have.

Abstract Data Types

ML supports abstract data types through:

1. An elegant type system,

2. The ability to construct new types, and

3. Constructs that restrict access to objects of a given type so all access is through a fixed set of operations defined for that type.

An example is a type like "stack," for which we might define the push and pop operations and a few other operations as the only way the contents of a stack could be read or modified.

These abstract data types, called *structures*, offer the power of "classes" used in object-oriented programming languages like C++, Java, or Smalltalk. They are considered very important for such programming goals as modularity, encapsulation of concepts, and reuse of software. However, the ML notion of a structure also includes and generalizes several other important ideas, such as the libraries of functions provided in many languages and "friend" classes in C++.

Recursion

ML strongly encourages recursion in preference to iterators like for-loops or while-loops that are used commonly in Pascal or C. Recursion generally provides a cleaner expression for computational ideas, especially when coupled with ML's functional programming style. We shall learn a natural, recursive style of programming similar to that used in Lisp or Scheme. However, iterative constructs are available in ML for the times when that style is most appropriate.

Rule-Based Programming

There is in ML an easy way to do rule-based programming, where actions are based on if-then rules. The core idea is a pattern-action construct, where a value is compared with several patterns in turn. The first pattern to match causes an associated action to be executed. In this way, ML has much of the power of Prolog and other languages that are thought of as "artificial intelligence languages."

Strong Typing

ML is a *strongly typed* language, meaning that all values and variables have a type that can be determined at "compile time" (i.e., by examining the program but not running it). A value of one type cannot be given to a variable of another type. For example, the integer value 4 cannot be the value of a real-valued variable, even though the real 4.0 could be the value of that variable. Many other languages allow confusion of types. For example, C allows a value to change its type arbitrarily, through the "cast" mechanism, while Lisp and Prolog do not try to constrain types in general.

Strong typing is a valuable debugging aid, since it allows many errors to be caught by the compiler, rather than resulting in mysterious errors when the program is run. Interestingly, although most other strongly typed languages require a declaration of the type of every variable, ML tries hard to figure out the unique type that each variable may have, and only expects a declaration for a variable when it is impossible for ML to deduce its type.

ML is not the only language to possess these features. For example, Lisp is principally functional, supports higher-order functions, and promotes the use of recursion. Prolog also promotes recursion and supports rule-based programming naturally. Smalltalk and C++ offer powerful abstract-data-type facilities, and so on. However, the combination of features found in ML offers the user a great deal of programming ease. At the same time, ML allows one to use a full palette of modern programming language concepts.

1.2   Standard ML of New Jersey

In this book, we shall assume that the SML/NJ, or "Standard ML of New Jersey," implementation of ML is used. SML/NJ was implemented by David MacQueen of Lucent Bell Laboratories, Andrew Appel of Princeton University, and their colleagues. It is available for most UNIX workstations, for PC's running LINUX, and in an experimental version (at the time of this book's writing) for PC's running Microsoft Windows. There is a Web site at Bell Laboratories from which software and documentation may be downloaded; see the references in Section 1.4. SML/NJ version 109.30, upon which this book is based, has been implemented to conform to the recent ML97 standard.

Interactive Mode

To run SML/NJ in *interactive mode*, in response to the UNIX prompt type

```
sml
```

SML/NJ will respond with:

Standard ML of New Jersey · · ·
–

Here, as throughout this book, we shall use italic font to indicate ML's responses, while text typed by the user will be in the "teletype" font, as `sml` above.

The dash on the second line is ML's prompt. The prompt invites us to type an expression, and ML will respond with the value of that expression. We can make definitions and enter expressions indefinitely, and SML/NJ will respond to each with the resulting value.

- To terminate an SML/NJ session, type <CTRL>d.

Direct Program Execution

It is also possible to get SML/NJ to execute a program in a conventional way. For example, if your ML program is in file `foo`, give the `sml` command with that file as standard input:

```
sml < foo
```

Another option is to issue the `sml` command to UNIX, which gets us started in interactive mode. Then, in response to the prompt, read and execute a file `foo` that contains an ML program. We do so by typing to ML the expression

```
use "foo";
```

Any quoted UNIX path name can appear in place of `"foo"`. This mode is handy when we are debugging a program and want to read in its definitions and then try them in interactive mode.

There is a third way to get an ML program to run using SML/NJ. One can compile an ML program source file into a file that includes the SML/NJ runtime system and thus can be executed directly without invoking command `sml`. This mode of operation is discussed in Section 9.5.

What ML Gives You

When we invoke ML, we are given access to several resources. In ML, all available capabilities — operators like + for addition, functions like `sin`, and some very complex operators not present in other languages — are organized into *structures*, such as `Int` and `Real`, as suggested in Fig. 1.1. The entire collection of capabilities is called the *standard basis*.

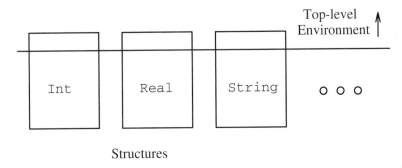

Figure 1.1: Organization of resources in ML

A structure in ML is akin to a library in most other languages. For example, the structure called `Int` contains many functions useful for dealing with integers, such as the arithmetic and comparison operators, but also includes some less typical operators. Thus, ML selects the most important operators from the various structures and puts them in the *top-level environment*. These capabilities are available when we invoke ML. The additional capabilities, those that are found in the various structures but that are not part of the top-level environment, are also accessible if we make a small amount of additional effort. We shall describe how to access those capabilities not in the top-level environment starting in Section 4.1.2.

1.3   Prerequisites for the Reader

We assume the reader is familiar with programming in some conventional language such as Pascal or C. Occasionally, as a matter of interest, we shall compare ML constructs with those of Pascal or C, but familiarity with one or both of these languages is not essential.

It is also assumed the reader is familiar with the process of writing and debugging programs in a conventional language. We expect that the reader has written at least a few recursive programs and has some comfort with that style of programming. However, our first recursive examples will be covered in sufficient detail that the style may be learned here. In addition, we assume the reader is familiar with simple data structures and data structure concepts such as records, pointers, lists, and trees. The author immodestly recommends *Foundations of Computer Science: C Edition* by A. V. Aho and J. D. Ullman, Computer Science Press, New York, 1995 for the reader who desires further background on these subjects.

1.4   References and Web Resources

The original definition of Standard ML is from [3], which evolved into the book [5]. An elaboration of this work is [4]. This version of ML is now given the retronym ML90.

The recent revision, called ML97, is described in the book [6]. An important part of the definition of ML97 is the standard basis, which is obtainable on-line in [1].

The original paper on the Standard ML of New Jersey implementation assumed in this book is [2]. There is an extensive resource library available on-line. The root URL is:

> `http://cm.bell-labs.com/cm/cs/what/smlnj`

A useful on-line document is

`http://cm.bell-labs.com/cm/cs/what/smlnj/top-level-comparison.html`

which explains the difference between earlier versions of SML/NJ and the current, ML97-based versions starting with Version 109.24.

To obtain software to run SML/NJ on various hosts, start at

> `http://cm.bell-labs.com/cm/cs/what/smlnj/software.html`

An important source for non-UNIX implementations of ML is

> `http://www.dina.kvl.dk/~sestoft/mosml.html`

which is the Keldysh Institute of Applied Mathematics in Moscow. Their implementation runs on PC's and MAC's, as well as workstations, and largely conforms to ML97 at the time this book was written.

1. Appel, A. W., N. Barnes, D. Berry, E. R. Gansner, L. George, L. Huelsbergen, D. MacQueen, B. Monahan, C. Müller, J. H. Reppy, J. Thackray, and P. Sestoft, *The Standard ML Basis Library*. Its URL is:

```
http://cm.bell-labs.com/cm/cs/what/smlnj/sml97.html
```

2. Appel, A. W. and D. B. MacQueen, "Standard ML of New Jersey," *International Symposium on Programming Languages, Implementation, and Logic*, pp. 1–13, Springer-Verlag, 1991 is a technical article describing the SML/NJ system.

3. Harper, R. M., D. B. MacQueen, and R. Milner, "Standard ML," ECS–LFCS–86–2, Laboratory for Foundations of Computer Science, Edinburgh University, Dept. of CS, 1986.

4. Milner, R. and M. Tofte, *Commentary on Standard ML*, MIT Press, Cambridge MA, 1991.

5. Milner, R., M. Tofte, and R. M. Harper, *The Definition of Standard ML*, MIT Press, Cambridge MA, 1990.

6. Milner, R., M. Tofte, R. M. Harper, and D. B. MacQueen, *The Definition of Standard ML (Revised)*, MIT Press, Cambridge, MA, 1997.

1.5 Features of ML97

If you are familiar with the earlier version of ML called ML90, then you will notice certain differences between ML90 and the version ML97 covered in this book. If you are not familiar with ML90, then skip this section. The complete list of changes is found in the ML97 source book, reference [6] above. However, for the reader with ML experience, the following is an incomplete list of the changes that are most likely to affect your programming.

1. There is a cleaner organization to features that are available in the top-level basis and features that are available through a library structure.

2. Certain values with unknown type, such as `nil`, are no longer legal expressions. However, polymorphic functions remain a feature of ML.

3. Input/output operators are now defined as part of the standard, rather than being implementation-dependent.

4. Characters are now a separate type, different from strings of length 1.

5. Reals are no longer an equality type; i.e, you cannot test $r = s$ for reals r and s.

6. There is an unsigned integer type called `word`. Both words and ordinary integers may be represented in hexadecimal, if we wish.

7. A datatype called `option` is provided to represent elements that are optionally missing.

8. Requirements to specify types are reduced because there is a default type (integer) for overloaded operators such as + or <.

Chapter 2

Getting Started in ML

In this chapter we shall introduce the reader to the simplest form of programming in ML, where one types expressions to the ML system and receives back values for these expressions. We shall learn how to construct expressions using atomic types such as integers and strings. We shall also discuss expressions involving lists and a simple form of record structure called *tuples*; lists and tuples are both basic ML constructs. The reader will also see an important difference between ML and most other languages: the ML rules regarding types of expressions allow the ML compiler to check at compile time for type errors that in other languages can lead to mysterious run-time bugs.

2.1   Expressions

When we are in interactive mode, the simplest thing we can do is type an expression in response to the ML prompt (–). ML will respond with the value and its type.

Example 2.1: Here is an example of an expression that we may type and the ML response.

    1+2*3;
    val it = 7 : int

Recall from Section 1.2 our convention that we use "teletype" font for things we type and italic font for the response of the ML system. Here, we have typed the expression $1 + 2 * 3$, and ML responds that the value of variable it is 7, and that the type of this value is integer. The variable it plays a special role in ML. It receives the value of any expression that we type in interactive mode. □

Two useful points to observe from Example 2.1 are:

9

- An expression must be followed by a semicolon to tell the ML system that the instruction is finished. If ML expects more input when a \<return\> is typed, it will respond with the prompt = instead of −. The = sign is a warning that we have not finished our input expression.

- The response of ML to an expression is:

  1. The word `val` standing for "value,"

  2. The variable name `it`, which stands for the previous expression,

  3. An equal sign,

  4. The value of the expression (7 in this example),

  5. A colon, which in ML is the symbol that associates a value with its type, and

  6. An expression that denotes the type of the value. In our example, the value of the expression is an integer, so the type `int` follows the colon.

2.1.1   Constants

As in any other language, expressions in ML are composed of operators and operands, and operands may be either variables or constants. At this point, we have not yet discussed the way values may be assigned to variables, so it does not make sense to use variables in expressions. However, syntactically, variables present no surprises. You may think of Pascal identifiers (letters followed by letters or digits) or the identifiers in your favorite language as names for ML variables, although as we shall see in Section 2.3.1, ML identifiers differ somewhat from identifiers in these languages.

ML provides as part of its top-level environment (see Section 1.2) a number of types that are similar to those found in most languages. There is also a way to get from the system some additional types. In this preliminary discussion, we are going to introduce only the most commonly used atomic types and their allowable values. The complete set of types is discussed in Section 9.3.

Integers

Integers are represented in ML as in other languages, with one exception involving the minus sign. A positive integer is a string of one or more digits, such as 0, 1234, or 11111111. A negative integer is formed by placing the unary minus sign, which is the tilde (~), not a dash, in front of the digits, such as ~1234.

Integers may also be represented in *hexadecimal notation*, where the characters `0x` or `0X` are followed by a string of hexadecimal digits. Recall that the hexadecimal digits are 0 through 9 and `A` through `F`, with the letters standing for "digits" with values 10 through 15 (in decimal), respectively. The hexadecimal digits that are letters may be written in either upper or lower case.

Example 2.2: Here are the responses of the ML system to some expressions that are hexadecimal integers.

```
0x1234;
```
val it = 4660 : int

Here, 1234 in hexadecimal, whose decimal value is

$$1 \times 1728 + 2 \times 144 + 3 \times 12 + 4 = 4660$$

is converted to decimal in ML's response. Notice that ML gives you a decimal representation, regardless of whether you write the integer in decimal or hexadecimal.

```
~0xaA;
```
val it = ~170 : int

Here, we notice that either **a** or **A** stands for the hexadecimal digit "10," and upper and lower case can be mixed. We also see that the negation symbol ~ may be used in hexadecimal integers. □

Reals

Reals are also represented conventionally, with the exception that minus signs within reals are represented by ~. An ML constant of type **real** thus consists of

1. An optional ~,

2. A string of one or more digits, and

3. One or both of the following elements:

   (a) A decimal point and one or more digits.

   (b) The letter **E** or **e**, an optional ~, and one or more digits.

As in other languages, the value of a real number is determined by taking the number that appears before the **E** or **e** and multiplying it by 10 raised to the power that is the integer that follows.

Example 2.3: Here are some examples of real numbers:

1. ~123.0 is the negative real that happens to have an integer value -123.

2. 3E~3 has value .003.

3. 3.14e12 has value 3.14×10^{12}.

□

Booleans

There are two boolean values: `true` and `false`. ML is case-sensitive (unlike some other languages such as Pascal or SQL that also use `true` and `false` as boolean constants), so these constants must be written in lower case, never as `TRUE`, `False`, or any other combination involving capitals.

Example 2.4: Here is what happens when we type a boolean value.

```
true;
```
val it = true : bool

Notice that the type of booleans is `bool` in the ML response.   □

Strings

Values of type `string` are double-quoted character strings like `"foo"` or `"R2D2"`. Certain special characters are represented by sequences of characters, as in the language C, where the backslash (\) serves as an escape character. The principal ways to represent characters that cannot be typed on the keyboard, or characters with a special meaning that would confuse the interpretation of strings, are:

1. The two-character sequence \n is used for the "newline" character.

2. \t is used for the tab character.

3. \\ is used for the backslash character.

4. \" stands for the double-quote character, which otherwise would be interpreted as the string ender.

5. A backslash followed by three decimal digits stands for the character whose ASCII code is the number represented by those three digits, in base 10. This convention allows us to type characters for which there is no key on the keyboard. For example \007 is the "character" that rings the bell on the console.

6. Those characters that are control characters can also be written by the three character sequence consisting of a backslash, the caret or uparrow symbol ^, and a character whose ASCII code is in the range 64–95 (decimal), i.e., the capital letters and the five characters [\]^_. The actual character represented is determined by subtracting 64 from the ASCII code for the character typed. For example, \^G stands for <CTRL>G and is the same bell-ringing character that is represented by \007.

There are certain other escape sequences that are less commonly used or that may not be supported by a given ML implementation. See the box on "Other Character Codes."

Example 2.5: The string `"A\tB\tC\n1\t2\t3\n"` is printed as

```
A       B       C
1       2       3
```

Here we see uses of the tab sequence \t and the newline sequence \n. ☐

If a string is too long to be written conveniently on a single line, we may continue it over several lines. We make all but the last line end with a backslash, and all but the first line begin with a backslash.

Example 2.6: The text of item 4 above could be written as a string extending over three lines as follows:

```
"\\\" stands for the double-quote character, \
\which otherwise would be interpreted \
\as the string ender."
```

In the first line, the first quote is not part of the string but indicates that a string follows. The first two backslashes represent the character \. The third backslash and the quote represent the character " (the second character of item 4 above). The backslash at the end of the first line indicates that the string continues on the next line. Note that the space after the comma is shown explicitly on the first line. If that space were missing, the represented string would look like ...`character,which`.... ☐

In general,

- Any sequence of characters beginning and ending with the backslash and containing between the backslashes only "whitespace" characters such as blank, tab, and newline, is ignored in interpretation of strings.

In Example 2.6, we used sequences consisting of a backslash, a newline, and another backslash to make a string break over several lines without the newlines becoming part of the string.

Characters

As in C, there is a distinction between a character string of length one and a single character. ML provides a type `char` for characters. The representation of character values in ML is somewhat unusual: The character # followed by a character string of length one. That is, `#"`x`"` represents the character x.

Example 2.7: Character a is represented by `#"a"`. The tab character is represented by `#"\t"`. ☐

Other Character Codes

ML also provides the following escape sequences: \a, \b, \v, \f, and \r for the ASCII characters 7, 8, 11, 12, and 13, which are the bell-ringing character, backspace, vertical tab, form feed, and carriage return, respectively. In addition, the ML97 standard permits, but does not require, that an implementation support an extended ASCII character set of up to 16 bits, such as the 16-bit character code used in the language Java. If an implementation supports such an extended set (SML/NJ version 109.30 does not), then one can represent such characters by the sequence \u followed by four hexadecimal digits.

2.1.2   Arithmetic Operators

The arithmetic operators of ML are similar to those of Pascal or C. There are:

1. The low-precedence "additive" operators: +, -.

2. The high-precedence "multiplicative" operators: *, / (division of reals), div (division of integers, rounding down toward minus infinity), and mod (the remainder of integer division).

3. The highest precedence unary minus operator, ˜.

However, note the following.

- A unary minus sign is always denoted by a tilde (˜), never by a dash. Thus, we write ˜3*4 and 3-4, but never 3˜4 or -3*4.

- ML is case-sensitive, so the operators mod and div must be written in lower case.

- Associativity and precedence is like Pascal or C; higher precedence operators are grouped with their operands first, and among operators of equal precedence, grouping proceeds from the left. Grouping order can be altered by parentheses in the usual manner.

Example 2.8: Here are some expressions and their responses from the ML interpreter.

        3.0 - 4.5 + 6.7;
        val it = 5.2 : real

Note that grouping of equal precedence operators is from the left. This expression is interpreted as $(3.0 - 4.5) + 6.7$, not $3.0 - (4.5 + 6.7)$, which has value -8.2.

```
43 div (8 mod 3) * 5;
```
val it = 105 : int

All three operators `div`, `mod`, and `*` are of the same precedence, but the parentheses force us to use the `mod` first, then group from the left. Since `mod` calls for the remainder when its left argument is divided by the right, the value of 8 `mod` 3 is 2. We thus evaluate (`43 div 2`)`*5`, or 105. □

2.1.3 String Operators

We may not apply the arithmetic operators to string operands. There is, however, one operator that applies to strings and only to strings. The operator ^ stands for concatenation of strings; it has the precedence of an additive operator. When we *concatenate* two strings s_1 and s_2, we get the string $s_1 s_2$. That is, the resulting string is a copy of string s_1 followed by a copy of s_2.

Example 2.9: Here are some examples of string concatenation.

```
"house" ^ "cat";
```
val it = "housecat" : string

```
"linoleum" ^ "";
```
val it = "linoleum" : string

Notice in the second example that `""` represents the *empty string*, the string with no characters. When we concatenate the empty string with any other string, either on the left or right of the ^ operator, we get the other string as a result. □

2.1.4 Comparison Operators

The six comparison operators that we find in Pascal are also part of the ML repertoire. These are =, <, >, <=, >=, and <>, representing, respectively, the comparisons =, <, >, ≤, ≥, and ≠. They can be used to compare integers, reals, characters, or strings, with one exception:

- Reals may not be compared using = or <>. The other four comparisons of reals, such as <, are permitted, however.

In the case of characters, $c_1 < c_2$ means "lexicographically precedes"; that is, the character code for c_1 is less than the character code for c_2. Similarly, <= means "equals or lexicographically precedes," and so on.

For strings, < is lexicographic order, just as < in Pascal or `strcmp` in C. That is, if s_1 and s_2 are strings, then $s_1 < s_2$ if either

1. s_1 is a proper prefix of s_2, or

Why Can't We Test Reals for Equality?

The policy that forbids testing $r = s$ in ML, when r and s are real quantities, is motivated by the fact that all machines perform real arithmetic only approximately. Thus, in some circumstances, two real-valued expressions that are theoretically equal could turn out, because of rounding error, to be unequal in the machine. If you definitely want to test whether $r = s$, you can test both $r \leq s$ and $s \leq r$, which is the same thing as long as there is no rounding error involved.

---

2. If s_1 and s_2 agree for the first i positions but disagree on the $(i + 1)$st, then the character in the $(i+1)$st position of s_1 precedes the character in the same position of s_2.

Example 2.10:

```
#"Z" < #"a";
```
val it = true : bool

Notice that the value of a comparison expression is a boolean. It may seem surprising that Z precedes a, but remember that in the ASCII code, all capitals precede all lower-case letters.

```
2 < 1 + 3;
```
val it = true : bool

The precedence of the comparison operators is less than that of the arithmetic operators, so $2 < 1 + 3$ is correctly interpreted as $2 < (1 + 3)$.

```
"abc" <= "ab";
```
val it = false : bool

Since ab is a proper prefix of abc, the former precedes the latter in lexicographic order.

```
"abc" <= "ac";
```
val it = true : bool

Now, neither string is a prefix of the other. They first differ in the second position, where the character of abc, which is b, precedes the character c of ac. □

2.1.5   Combining Logical Values

The common logical operations on boolean values may be performed in ML, as in other languages. These logical connectives are similar to the operators AND, OR, and NOT found in Pascal or &&, | |, and ! in C, but with several important differences.

NOT has the usual Pascal meaning, but must be lower case, as not. AND and OR of Pascal are replaced in ML by andalso and orelse. Like C, but unlike Pascal, the right operand of andalso and orelse is evaluated only when the left operand does not determine a value (i.e., only when the left operand of andalso is true, or the left operand of orelse is false).

The precedence of the logical operations in ML agrees with C; not is highest, then andalso, and then orelse. Symbols andalso and orelse are of lower precedence than the comparison or arithmetic operators, but not is higher than any of these.

Example 2.11 : Consider the following expression:

```
1<2 orelse 3>4;
```
val it = true : bool

ML does not evaluate the second condition $(3 > 4)$, since the first being true is sufficient to guarantee that the whole expression is true. Remember that the result of a comparison is a boolean, so it makes sense to connect two comparisons by a logical operation such as orelse.

In the following expression:

```
1<2 andalso 3>4;
```
val it = false : bool

it is necessary to evaluate both conditions. Had the first condition been false, then there would have been no need to check the second, because the whole expression could only be false.   □

Because the symbol not has such high precedence, we must be careful to group its argument properly. Here is an example.

Example 2.12 : The expression not 1<2 is grouped as (not 1)<2, which makes no sense and is a type error in ML. We would have to write not(1<2), although the simpler expression 1>=2 would do as well.   □

Incidentally, one might wonder why it matters whether or not the second operand of a logical operation is evaluated, if the result of the entire expression cannot depend on that operand. The reason is that in some special cases, an ML expression can have a *side-effect*, which is an action whose effect does not disappear after the expression is evaluated. The most common example of a side-effect is when something inside an expression causes information to be printed or read. We have not yet seen any ML operator that has a side-effect, and indeed it is in the ML style to avoid side-effects normally. However, side-effects are possible, as we shall see in Section 4.1 and elsewhere. When they occur, it is essential that we understand the conditions under which part of an expression will not be evaluated and its side-effects consequently not performed.

- Remember to use `andalso` and `orelse`, never `and` and `or`, for the logical operations. There is no special meaning for `or` in ML, but `and` has another meaning entirely, having nothing to do with logical operations.

2.1.6   If-Then-Else Expressions

ML lets us use *conditional expressions* of the form `if` E `then` F `else` G. We compute the value of this expression by first evaluating expression E, which must have a boolean value. If that value is `true`, then we evaluate expression F (and never evaluate G); the value of F becomes the value of the entire if-then-else expression. If the value of E is `false`, then we evaluate only G, which becomes the value of the entire expression.

Example 2.13 : Consider the following conditional expression:

```
if 1<2 then 3+4 else 5+6;
```
val it = 7 : int

We begin by evaluating the expression between the `if` and `then`. In this case, the expression $1 < 2$ evaluates to `true`. Thus, we evaluate the second expression, $3 + 4$. The result, 7, is the value of the entire expression. We do not evaluate the expression $5 + 6$, and if in its place there were an expression with side-effects, those side-effects would not be executed.   □

Here are a few important points about conditional expressions.

- The conditional, or if-then-else operation, is one of the rare operations that takes more than two operands. There is, however, a similar three-operand (*ternary*) operator in C, using the characters ? and : in place of `then` and `else` (nothing in place of `if`).

- If-then-else forms an expression. It is *not* a control-flow construct that groups statements together, as we find in most languages.

- There is no `if` ⋯ `then` construct in ML. Such an expression does not have a value when the condition is false. This point emphasizes the difference between if-then-else as an expression form and as a control-flow construct. There is no harm in having a control-flow construct if-then, since it simply executes no statements if the condition is false. However, an if-then expression might return no value at all and thus could not be used inside larger expressions.

Case Sensitivity in ML

ML is case-sensitive, and operators whose names are composed of letters are written with lower-case letters only. For example, we must be careful to write not, andalso, if, mod, and so on.

There might appear to be an exception concerning letters used in the expression of certain constants. For instance, we saw that either E or e may be used in real constants, and hexadecimal integers can be introduced with either 0x or 0X. In fact, the hexadecimal digits themselves can be written in either upper or lower case. However, this phenomenon is not an exception to case-sensitivity. The ML standard simply allows alternative forms of expression of certain constants.

2.1.7 Exercises for Section 2.1

Exercise 2.1.1: What is the response of ML to the following expressions?

* a) 1+2*3

  b) 5.0-4.2/1.4

* c) 11 div 2 mod 3

  d) "foo"^"bar"^""

* e) 3>4 orelse 5<6 andalso not (7<>8)

  f) if 6<10 then 6.0 else 10.0

* g) 0XAB+123

  h) 0xab<123

Exercise 2.1.2: The following ML "expressions" have errors in them. Explain what is wrong with each.

* a) 8/4

  b) if 2<3 then 4

* c) 1<2 and 5>3

  d) 6+7 DIV 2

* e) 4.+3.5

  f) 1.0<2.0 or 3>4

* g) `#"a"^#"b"`

  h) `123.`

*! i) `1.0 = 2.0`

*! **Exercise 2.1.3:** Write a string that when printed creates the displayed text on lines (3)–(5) of Example 2.6. You may assume that the indentation of the lines is made by a single tab character. Your string should be written over several lines so there are no more than 80 characters appearing on any one line.

Exercise 2.1.4: Express:

* a) *E* `orelse` *F*

  b) *E* `andalso` *F*

as if-then-else expressions. Incidentally, in ML, expressions formed with the symbols `orelse` and `andalso` are actually shorthands for these if-then-else expressions.

2.2 Type Consistency

Having seen some of the important building blocks of expressions, we must now learn what can go wrong when we use expressions built from these operators. ML assigns a unique type to every expression. Operators also have particular types that they require their operands to have. Certain operators take operands of one particular type only. Examples are /, which requires operands of type real, `div`, which requires operands of type integer, and ^, which requires operands of type string. Others, like + or *, can take arguments of different types, e.g., two integers or two reals. As we shall see shortly, it is not possible to mix operands of integer and real types, as it is in C or most other languages. However, ML provides certain operators for converting from a value of one type to an "equivalent" value of another type. We shall also learn a number of these "coercion" operators in this section.

    Let us again remind the reader that there is a purpose to this seeming inflexibility on the part of ML. It enables the ML compiler to type-check programs completely. Thus, no program that can run at all can have a type error. The advantage to the programmer is that what could be a run-time bug in another language's program is caught by the ML compiler.

2.2.1 Type Errors

As we saw in Example 2.1, when an operator is given operands of the proper type, it responds with the result. However, when one or both operands are of the wrong type, we get an error message. The nature of error messages depends on the particular implementation. We shall use the responses from SML/NJ version 109.30 in examples.[1]

Example 2.14: The operator + can take either integer or real arguments. However, both operands must be the same type. When the types of the operands are the same, ML attributes the same type to the result, for instance:

```
1 + 2;
```
val it = 3 : int

```
1.0 + 2.0;
```
val it = 3.0 : real

On the other hand, when the operands are of mixed type, we get an error message, as shown in Fig. 2.1. Let's see what ML is telling us. The first line of the response says that the operator expects operands of types other than what it saw. The second line of the response tells us that the operator + expects an "operand" whose type is a pair of integers. Although + can apply to either integers or reals, the fact that the left argument 1 is an integer suggests that integer addition was meant here.

```
1 + 2.0;
```
Error: operator and operand don't agree [literal]
 *operator domain: int * int*
 *operand: int * real*
 in expression:
  + : overloaded((1 : int),2.0)

Figure 2.1: A type error and its diagnostic message

The * operator in the expression `int * int` is not multiplication, but rather an operator that applies to types and produces a *product type*, that is, the type of a pair, triple, or so on. In particular, `int * int` is the type of any pair of integers, for example, of the pair $(1, 2)$. This response makes us aware of a rather rigid view ML has of operators and operands. Strictly speaking, all operators in ML are *unary*, that is, they take a single argument. A binary (two-argument) operator like + is perceived by ML as taking a single argument that is a pair. In most situations there is no problem with viewing a binary operator as if it had two operands, but there are some differences that we shall address in Section 5.5.

The third line of the response tells us what ML saw as the operand of the operator, namely a pair whose first component (the left operand) is an integer

---

[1] However, SML/NJ also returns a line and column number locating the point at which it detected the error. We do not show this response since it is rarely meaningful out of context.

but whose second component (the right operand) is a real. The final two lines
indicate the expression in which the error occurred. The only additional nuance
is that the operator and operand are shown in the conventional ML prefix form,
with the operator + appearing in front of its operand, which is the pair $(1, 2.0)$.
□

In the fifth line of Fig.. 2.1, we note the use of the term "overloaded" in
reference to +. An operator is *overloaded* if it can apply to two or more different
types, as + can. Notice that the fact + is defined for two integers or two reals
does not mean that it can be applied to one of each. Similar comments apply
to overloaded operators like -, *, <, and the other comparison operators.

If we were to use an operand of the wrong type with an operator that is not
overloaded, we get an error message similar to Fig. 2.1, but without the word
"overloaded." An example follows.

Example 2.15 : The expression

```
#"a" ^ "bc"
```

applies the nonoverloaded operator ^, which concatenates strings, to a character
and a string. The error message would look like:

> *Error: operator and operand don't agree [literal]*
> *operator domain: string * string*
> *operand: char * string*
> *in expression:*
> *^ (#"a","bc")*

□

Another type of error involves applying an operator, overloaded or not, to
operands at least one of which has a type inappropriate for the operator.

Example 2.16 : The division operator / applies only to reals, as we learned
in Section 2.1.2. Here is what happens when this operator is misused.

> ```
> 1/2;
> ```
> *Error: overloaded variable not defined at type*
> *symbol: /*
> *type: int*

Our first observation is that the error message talks about the symbol / and
its application to the type int, which we know is improper. However, what is
the "overloaded variable" in the first line of the error message? ML thinks of /
as a variable. As we shall see in Section 2.3.1, / is a legitimate identifier for a
variable in ML, unlike most languages, where variable identifiers are restricted
to letters and digits plus perhaps a few other symbols. Although we said that
/ applies only to "reals," an implementation of ML may support several kinds
of reals, such as single- and double-precision numbers. Thus, / might indeed
be defined for several different types.   □

Another place where type mismatches may occur through carelessness is in an if-then-else expression. The rules regarding types for this expression are:

- The expression following **if** must have boolean type.

- The expressions following **then** and **else** can be of any one type, but they must be of the same type.

Example 2.17: Figure 2.2 shows what happens when the types of the expressions following **then** and **else** disagree. Here, one is a character and one is a string.

```
if 1<2 then #"a" else "bc";
```
Error: types of rules don't agree [tycon mismatch]
  earlier rule(s): bool → char
  this rule: bool → string
  in rule:
   false ⇒ "bc"

Figure 2.2: A mismatch between the then and else parts

Obviously, ML is telling us something about finding a string (i.e., "bc") when it expected a character to match the character #"a" that followed the **then**. But what's this about "rules"? The explanation lies in the fact that the if-then-else expression is really a shorthand for a more general kind of expression: the case expression. We shall cover the case expression in Section 5.1.4.

For the moment, let us just note that ML's view of the if-then-else is that it involves two "rules," each of which takes a boolean value and produces a value of some one type. The first of these rules associates the boolean value **true** with the character #"a". This rule expresses the principle that if the condition is true, we use the value of the expression that follows the **then**. The second rule associates the boolean value **false** with the value following the **else**, namely "bc" in this case. However, ML expects to find another character-valued expression following **else**, which it will then associate with **false** in the second rule. ML is unhappy that it has found a string-valued expression, because ML will not tolerate groups of rules that produce values of different types. □

- The word "tycon" in the first line of response in Fig. 2.2 is short for "type constructor," that is, a way of constructing types from simpler types. Rules in the sense used in Fig. 2.2 are actually of a function type, mapping booleans to some other type. We discuss function types in Section 3.1.1.

Applying Functions, ML Style

ML offers us a diction for applying a function or operator to an argument that may be unfamiliar to some: $f\ x$ means "apply function f to argument x," just as $f(x)$ does in C or most other languages. Since there is no harm in putting parentheses around an argument, we have used the more conventional style, writing `real(1)` instead of the preferred ML style: `real 1`. By adhering to the more familiar style, with parentheses, we hope to focus attention on the more significant issues of ML, without adding to the "newness" of the language. However, as the book progresses, we shall gradually shift to the ML style of omitting the parentheses around the argument of a function whenever appropriate.

2.2.2   Coercion Between Integers and Reals

Sometimes we have a reason to convert (*coerce*) a value of one type to an "equivalent" value of another type. Thus ML provides certain built-in functions that do the conversion for us. Perhaps the clearest case is when we want to convert an integer to a real with the same value. The function `real` lets us do just that.

Example 2.18 : Applied to an integer, `real` produces the equivalent real value as:

```
real(4);
val it = 4.0 : real
```

As another instance, we can fix Example 2.14, where we tried to add an integer and a real, if we first apply `real` to the integer.

```
real(1) + 2.0;
val it = 3.0 : real
```

shows a correct version of this addition. Of course, there is no point in writing `real(1)` instead of `1.0`, but if we replaced 1 by an integer-valued variable, we would have no choice but to convert the variable by applying the operator `real` to it.   □

When we try to convert a real to an integer, it is not so clear which integer we want, since the real may not equal any integer. ML provides four coercion operators: `floor`, `ceil` (ceiling), `round`, and `trunc` (truncate). Each produces the integer with the same value when given a real that happens to be an integer; for instance, 4.0 is converted to 4 by each of these four functions. In general, given a real number r, `floor` produces the greatest integer that is no larger than r, and `ceil` produces the smallest integer no less than r. Function `round` produces the closest integer, with 0.5 raised to the next highest integer, regardless of whether the real is positive or negative. The `trunc` function drops digits to the right of the decimal point.

Example 2.19: Figure 2.3 shows the effect of these four operators on positive and negative real numbers. We include the special case of a half-integer (3.5 and −3.5), noticing that rounding occurs upward. We also include typical cases where the rounding is to the closest integer. Notice that `floor` and `trunc` do the same thing on positive numbers, but `trunc` agrees with `ceil` on negative numbers. Remember that −3 is "larger" than −3.5 and −4 is "smaller." □

x	floor(x)	ceil(x)	round	trunc(x)
3.5	3	4	4	3
~3.5	~4	~3	~3	~3
3.4	3	4	3	3
~3.6	~4	~3	~4	~3

Figure 2.3: Effect of real-to-integer coercion operators

2.2.3 Coercions Between Characters and Integers

We convert from characters to integers, just as in Pascal, using the `ord` function (which, however, must be lower case in ML). The result of applying `ord` to a character is the integer code for that character. Normally, the character will be one of the ASCII characters, and `ord` will return the ASCII code for that character.

Example 2.20:

```
ord(#"a");
val it = 97 : int
```

```
ord(#"a") - ord(#"A");
val it = 32 : int
```

The latter example computes the difference between the ASCII codes for lower-case `a` and capital `A`. This result is no coincidence. Every lower-case letter has an ASCII code that is 32 more than its corresponding capital letter. □

Similarly, we can convert integers in the range 0 to 255 to characters. The function `chr` performs this task as:

```
chr(97);
val it = "#a" : char
```

2.2.4   Coercions Between Strings and Characters

If we have a character, we can convert it to a string of length one with the operator `str`. That is,

```
str(#"a");
val it = "a" : string
```

However, conversion from strings to characters is not so straightforward. Part of the problem is that we have to deal with strings that are not of length one. ML provides several ways to make the conversion where it makes sense. For example, we shall see the `explode` operator in Section 2.4.5, which converts a string to a list of characters.

2.2.5   Exercises for Section 2.2

Exercise 2.2.1: Write expressions to make each of the following conversions.

* a) Convert 123.45 to the next lower integer.

  b) Convert −123.45 to the next lower integer.

  c) Convert 123.45 to the next higher integer.

* d) Convert −123.45 to the next higher integer.

* e) Convert #"Y" to an integer.

  f) Convert 120 to a character.

*! g) Convert #"N" to a real.

 ! h) Convert 97.0 to a character.

  i) Convert #"Z" to a string.

Exercise 2.2.2: The following expressions contain type errors. What are the errors and how might we fix them?

* a) `ceil(4)`

  b) `if true then 5+6 else 7.0`

* c) `chr(256)`

  d) `chr(~1)`

* e) `ord(3)`

  f) `chr(#"a")`

  g) `if 0 then 1 else 2`

* h) `ord("a")`

2.3 Variables and Environments

In most languages, such as C or Pascal, computing takes place in an *environment* consisting of a collection of "boxes," usually called *variables*. Variables have names and hold values. The name of a box is an *identifier*, which is a string of characters (typically, letters and digits) that the language allows as the name of a variable. There is usually a type associated with a variable, and the contents of a "box" can be any value of the appropriate type. Pascal, C, and most other languages allow variables of types integer, real, and many other types.

At any given time the set of values stored in the variables' boxes constitute the *store*. In conventional languages, computation proceeds by side-effects, that is, by changing the store. One of the interesting things about ML is that it is impossible for the store to change, with a few exceptions, such as arrays and references, that we shall introduce in Chapter 7. Rather, ML does its computing by adding to the environment new *value bindings*, which are associations between identifiers and values. The above brief overview of this section is heady material, so let's start again from the beginning.

2.3.1 Identifiers

Identifiers are character strings with certain restrictions. Most languages allow identifiers that are letters followed by any number of letters and digits. ML allows these too, along with many other strings that are not identifiers in most other languages. In ML, identifiers fall into two classes: alphanumeric and symbolic. There is no difference in their use, with the exception of type variables, as described below, which are alphanumeric identifiers beginning with an apostrophe.

Alphanumeric Identifiers

The *alphanumeric* class of identifiers consists of strings formed by

1. An upper case or lower case letter or the character ' (called apostrophe or "prime"), followed by

2. Zero or more additional characters from the set given in (1) plus the digits and the character _ (underscore).

However, identifiers beginning with the apostrophe ' are *type variables*. They can only refer to types and cannot be bound to ordinary values.

Example 2.21: The following are examples of alphanumeric identifiers:

```
abc
X29a
Number_of_Hamburgers_Served
a'b'c
```

The following is a legal alphanumeric identifier: 'a. However, it cannot be bound to values like 3, 4.5, "six", or any of the values we normally think of as the values of variables. It can only be bound to a type. In fact, ML often chooses the identifier 'a to represent the type of something whose value can be of any type. For instance, 'a might in some contexts be given the type integer as its "value." Note that being bound to the type integer is quite different from being bound to a particular integer like 3. □

Symbolic Identifiers

Of all the characters we can type with a conventional keyboard, there are only ten that cannot appear as part of some sort of identifiers. These ten characters are the three kinds of pairs of parentheses (round, square, and curly), double quote, period, comma, and semicolon. That is, the only characters that always stand alone and cannot be part of an identifier are

```
    ( ) [ ] { } " . , ;
```

Of course the "white space" characters — blank, tab, and newline — also are not part of identifiers. These do not have a meaning by themselves, but they serve to separate the elements of a program.

The remaining 20 keyboard characters that cannot appear in alphanumeric identifiers can be used to form *symbolic identifiers*. To be precise, the set of characters for symbolic identifiers is

```
    + - / * < > = ! @ # $ % ^ & ` ~ \ | ? :
```

Many of these symbols by themselves are names of operators. For example, we have seen the use of +, ^, and several others. ML interprets the identifier + as a special function that adds either two reals or two integers. More precisely, ML initially binds the identifier + to the addition function. Similarly, ML initially binds any other symbolic identifier that stands for an operator to the function implementing that operator.

We are free in ML to form our own identifiers from strings of the 20 characters listed above. These identifiers might be used to name new operators that we define, but they can also be used routinely to name integers, reals, and so on.

Example 2.22 : The following are legal symbolic identifiers: $$$, >>>=, and !@#%. However, !@a is not a legal identifier because it mixes the characters ! and @ (which may only appear in symbolic identifiers) with the character a (which can only be part of an alphanumeric identifier). □

Exercise Care Using Symbolic Identifiers

We advise against using symbolic identifiers to represent values of types such as integers or strings. Besides looking strange, they often cause trouble because they must be surrounded by white space to prevent them from "attaching" to operators like + and forming unintended identifiers that confuse the ML system and cause an error. That is, although `<<` and `a` are both legal identifiers, we must write `<< +a` or `<< + a` to add them. Should we write `<<+a`, we get the error message:

> *Error: unbound variable or constructor:* $<<+$

If we use symbolic identifiers as program variables at all, they should be used as functions, so the above lexical confusion will not occur.

2.3.2   The Top-Level Environment

When we invoke ML, we are given the *top-level environment* (see Fig. 1.1) in which to work. In this environment, the identifiers that have meaning to the ML system are bound to these meanings. The entire contents of the top-level environment is enumerated in Sections 9.2 and 9.3.

In Fig. 2.4 we suggest some of these identifiers. Environments will be represented as a table, with a left column for identifiers and a right column for the associated value. At the bottom of Fig. 2.4 is the top-level environment.[2] We see an entry for the identifier ^ to represent the function that concatenates strings, and we see another named `floor` that represents the floor function discussed in Section 2.2.2. There are other entries for all the operators and functions that we have learned and those we have yet to learn.

In addition, we have shown some other identifiers to which common values have been bound as additions to the top-level environment. In particular, we have the identifier `foo` bound to the integer 3, an identifier `bar` with value equal to the integer 490, and an identifier `pi` that is bound to the real number 3.14159.

2.3.3   An Assignment-Like Statement

It is possible to add an identifier to the current environment and bind it to a value. To do so we use a "statement" called a *val-declaration*, whose simplest form is

---

[2]The top-level environment will always be at the bottom of environment diagrams, which grow upward as new value bindings are made. The term "top-level" is thus unfortunate, but we hope the reader will find the convention of adding new bindings on top of old ones intuitively appealing.

foo	3
bar	490
pi	3.14159
. . .	. . .
^	function to concatenate strings
floor	function to compute the floor of a real
. . .	. . .

Identifier   Value

Figure 2.4: The top-level environment and some added user variables

$$\text{val} \ \langle\text{identifier}\rangle \ = \ \langle\text{value}\rangle$$

That is, we use the keyword val, the identifier for which we wish to create a value binding, an equal sign, and an expression that gives the value we wish to associate with that identifier.[3]

Example 2.23 : Here is an example of how the identifier pi shown in Fig. 2.4 might have been added to the environment.

```
val pi = 3.14159;
val pi = 3.14159 : real
```

Notice that in response to the val-declaration of variable pi, ML responds with the value of pi rather than with the value of it, as was the case in all previous examples. Otherwise, the response to a val-declaration is the same as the response to an expression.

- In general, responses to val-declarations tell us the identifiers that have been bound to values and what those values are.

We might next define an identifier radius as:

```
val radius = 4.0;
val radius = 4.0 : real
```

---

[3]The val-declaration is actually considerably more general, and in place of a single identifier we can have arbitrary "patterns." The matter is discussed further in Section 3.3.4.

Some Points About ML "Assignment"

- Remember to use the keyword `val` to cause a value binding to occur. Assignment statements like `x = y` or `x := y`, familiar from other languages, are errors in ML (with one exception, discussed in Section 7.3.3).

- It is tempting to think of the equal-sign in a val-declaration as equivalent to `:=` in Pascal or `=` in C. However, these assignment operators from other languages cause side-effects, namely the change in the value stored in the place named on the left of the assignment operator. In ML, the val-declaration causes a *new* entry in the environment to be created, associating what is to the left of the equal sign with the value to the right of the equal-sign. Example 2.24 illustrates this point.

Now we have some variables, namely `pi` and `radius`, that we can use along with constants to form expressions. For instance, we can write an expression that is the familiar formula for the area of a circle:

    pi * radius * radius;
    val it = 50.26544 : real

Similarly, we could introduce another identifier, say `area`, and use a val-declaration to give it a value.

    val area = pi * radius * radius;
    val area = 50.26544 : real

Note that in the above example, the expression supplying the value itself involves variables and operators. In previous examples the "expression" was a single constant. □

2.3.4 A View of ML Programming

We now have a rudimentary view of what ML programs look like. They are sequences of definitions, such as the val-declaration that associates values with identifiers (which are loosely the same as "program variables"). So far, we don't have any really interesting assignments to make; we can only bind values of a basic type (e.g., real or string) to identifiers, and we can ask for the value of an expression involving these identifiers and constants, by typing that expression. In Chapter 3 we shall see how to give identifiers values that are functions and how to apply functions to values in order to compute new values. When these functions are recursive, we shall find ourselves programming in a mode that gives us all the power of other programming languages, yet has a distinctive flavor of its own.

It is natural to think of a val-declaration as an assignment, and often we shall not go wrong if we do so. However, there is a subtle but important difference in the way ML views what happens in response to a val-declaration. The next example illustrates some of that difference.

Example 2.24 : Suppose that after issuing the val-declarations of Example 2.23 we "redefine" radius to be equal to 5.0 by:

```
val radius = 5.0;
```
val radius = 5.0 : real

We might imagine that the entry in the environment for radius has had its value changed from 4.0 to 5.0. However, the proper ML view is suggested in Fig. 2.5. Below the top entry is the environment that existed before radius was "assigned" 5.0. We do not show all the identifiers that ML defines for us (e.g., +), but we concentrate on those we have defined: pi, radius, and area.

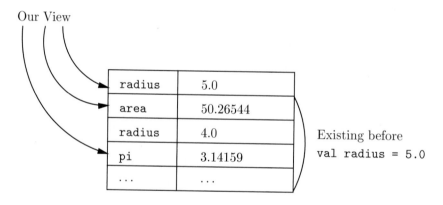

Figure 2.5: The environment after redefining radius

The topmost entry in Fig. 2.5 is an addition to the environment that results from the new val-declaration. We have shown in the current environment two entries that are named by the identifier radius, but only the most recent (upper) one is visible at this time. If we are running ML in interactive mode and simply entering a sequence of val-declarations, then the earlier declaration of radius cannot again become accessible through the current environment. When we discuss functions and their effect on the environment in Section 3.2.1, we shall see that it is sometimes possible to access a "buried" value binding such as the lower entry for radius, just as it is in conventional languages such as C or Pascal.   □

Identifiers Do Not Have Fixed Types

Note that when creating an entry with an old name, as we did in Example 2.24, there is no restriction that the new value be of the same type as the old value. We could just as well have defined `radius` to be an integer in Example 2.24, for instance:

```
val radius = 5;
```

However, we then could not have used this variable `radius` in expressions like `pi * radius * radius`, because of the type mismatch.

2.3.5 Exercises for Section 2.3

Exercise 2.3.1: Tell whether each of the following character strings is (*i*) an alphanumeric identifier suitable for ordinary (nontype) values, (*ii*) a symbolic identifier, (*iii*) an identifier that must represent a type as a value, or (*iv*) not an identifier of ML.

* a) `The7Dwarves`

  b) `7Dwarves`

* c) `SevenDwarves,The`

  d) `'SnowWhite'`

* e) `a<=b`

  f) `hurrah!`

* g) `#1`

  h) `'123`

Exercise 2.3.2: Show the effect on the environment of making the following sequence of val-declarations. Which variables are now accessible?

```
val a = 3;
val b = 98.6;
val a = "three";
val c = a^str(chr(floor(b)));
```

2.4   Tuples and Lists

So far we have seen five types that ML values may have: integer, real, string, character, and boolean. Most languages start with a similar collection of types and build more complex types with a set of operators called *type constructors*, which are dictions allowing us to define new types from simpler types. For example, Pascal has, among other type constructors,

1. The `record...end` notation to build record types, whose fields may be of any type,

2. The ^ operator to build a type whose values are pointers to values of some simpler type, and

3. The array constructor that defines an array type, given a type for elements and an index type.

ML also has a number of ways to define new types, including datatype constructions discussed in Section 6.2 that go beyond what we find in C, Pascal, or most other languages. However, the simplest and possibly most important ways of constructing types in ML are notations for forming tuples, which are similar to record types in Pascal or C, and for forming lists of elements of a given type. In this section we shall learn these notations and also cover the most important operations associated with these types.

2.4.1   Tuples

A *tuple* is formed by taking a list of two or more expressions of any types, separating them by commas, and surrounding them by round parentheses. Thus, a tuple looks something like a record, but the fields are named by their position in the tuple rather than by declared field names.

Example 2.25 : In the following val-declaration we assign to variable `t` a tuple whose first component is the integer 4, whose second component is the real 5.0, and whose third component is the string `"six"`.

```
val t = (4, 5.0, "six");
```
*val t = (4, 5.0, "six") : int * real * string*

Let's try to understand the ML response. It repeats the fact that the value of `t` is the one we just gave it, which should be no surprise. However, it uses terminology we have not seen before in an ML response, as it describes the type of `t`. Recall from Section 2.2.1 that the type `int * real * string` is a product type. Its values are tuples that have three components. The first component is an integer, the second is a real, and the third component is a string. The operator `*` has a different meaning when applied to types than it does when applied to integer or real values. Here `*` has nothing to do with multiplication, but indicates tuple formation.   □

In general, a product type is formed from two or more types $T_1, T_2, \ldots, T_k$ by putting *'s between them, as $T_1 * T_2 * \cdots * T_k$. Values of this type are tuples with k components, the first of which is of type T_1, the second of type T_2, and so on. Example 2.25 showed a case where $k = 3$, T_1 is int, T_2 is real, and T_3 is string.

Example 2.26 : Here are some further examples of tuples and their types.

1. (1,2,3,4) is of type int * int * int * int.

2. (1,(2,3.0)) is of type int * (int * real).

3. (1) is of type int. Strictly speaking, it is not a tuple, just a parenthesized integer.

In (2) the tuple has two components, the first of which is an integer. The second component is itself a tuple with two components: an integer and a real. This grouping is reflected in the type description. ☐

The * operator applied to types is not an associative operator. For example, int * (int * real) is not the same type as (int * int) * real. The latter type describes tuples of two components, the first of which is a pair of integers and the second of which is a single real. For example, ((1,2),3.0) is a value of type (int * int) * real. Neither is the same as the type int * int * real, which describes "flat" tuples like (1,2,3.0).

2.4.2 Accessing Components of Tuples

Given a tuple or a variable whose value is a tuple, we can get any particular component, say the ith, by applying the function #i.

Example 2.27 : In Example 2.25, identifier t was bound to the tuple value

        (4, 5.0, "six")

Now we can obtain its components. For example:

        #1(t);
        val it = 4 : int

        #3(t);
        val it = "six" : string

It is an error to apply a function like #4 that designates a component number higher than the number of components the tuple has. ☐

Tuples can be likened to records whose field names are the numbers $1, 2, \ldots$. In truth, tuples as we have defined them are a special, simplified case of a more general record-structure construct that does allow the programmer to specify names for fields. However, the tuple is adequate and quite convenient for most purposes. We defer the more general case of record structures to Section 7.1.

2.4.3   Lists

ML provides a simple notation for lists whose elements are all of the same type.
We take a list of elements, separate them by commas, and surround them with
square brackets.

Example 2.28: The list of three integers 1, 2, 3 is represented in ML by
[1,2,3]. The response of ML to an expression that is this constant value is

>   [1,2,3];
>   *val it = [1,2,3] : int list*

The response to our list expression is informative. In addition to the usual
repetition of the value in the expression, it assigns the list the type int list,
which is ML's way of saying "list of integers."   □

- In general, "T list" is the type of a list of elements each of which is of
  type T.

Example 2.29: In our second example, the list has a single element that is of
type string.

>   ["a"];
>   *val it = ["a"] : string list*

The type attributed to the list expression is string list, or "list of strings."
The fact that there is only one string in the list is irrelevant. The square brackets
differentiate the expression "a", which is of type string, from the expression
["a"], which is a list of strings that happens to have only one string on the
list.   □

Example 2.30: Finally, here is an example where we erroneously try to mix
the types of elements of a list. We tried to write a list of three characters, but
we forgot the pound sign on the last one, so it became a string of length one,
instead of a character.

>   [#"a", #"b", "c"];
>   *Error: operator and operand don't agree [tycon mismatch]*
>   *operator domain: char * char list*
>   *operand: char * string list*
>   *in expression:*
>   *#"b" :: "c" :: nil*

We shall explain the error message after we have learned some of the notation
of lists in Section 2.4.4.   □

2.4.4   List Notation and Operators

In this section we shall learn several operators that involve lists. These include notation for the empty list, the head and tail of a list, "cons" or construction of a list from a head and tail, and concatenation of lists.

The Empty List

The *empty list*, or list of no elements, is represented in ML by either the name `nil` or by a pair of brackets, `[]`.

Head and Tail

Any list besides the empty list is composed of a *head*, which is the first element, and a *tail*, which is the list of all elements but the first, in the same order.

Example 2.31: If L is the list `[2,3,4]`, then the head of L is 2, and the tail of L is the list `[3,4]`. If M is the list `[5]`, then the head of M is 5, and the tail of M is the empty list, or `nil`. $\square$

We can get the head or tail of a list by applying the function `hd` or `tl` to the list, respectively. The following restates Example 2.31 in a sequence of ML expressions.

Example 2.32: Suppose we define lists L and M by the val-declarations

```
val L = [2,3,4];
```
val L = [2,3,4] : int list

```
val M = [5];
```
val M = [5] : int list

Now we can get the head and tail of each of these lists as follows.

```
hd(L);
```
val it = 2 : int

```
tl(L);
```
val it = [3,4] : int list

```
hd(M);
```
val it = 5 : int

```
tl(M);
```
val it = [] : int list

In the last of these expressions, ML describes the type of `nil` as `int list`. It is possible for `nil` to be of any list type. In this case, since it is the tail of an integer list, it is appropriate to assign it this type.   □

Concatenation of Lists

While `hd` and `tl` take apart lists, there are also two operators that construct lists: concatenation and cons. We consider each in turn.

The *concatenation* operator for lists, which is `@`, takes two lists whose elements are the same type and produces one list consisting of the elements of the first list followed by the elements of the second. Thus

```
[1,2]@[3,4];
```
val it = [1,2,3,4] : int list

- Do not interchange the `^` operator, which is concatenation of strings, with the `@` operator, which is concatenation of lists.

Cons

The *cons* operator, represented by a pair of colons (`::`), takes an element (the head) and a list of elements of the same type as the head, and produces a single list whose first element is the head and whose remaining elements are the elements of the tail. Thus

```
2::[3,4];
```
val it = [2,3,4] : int list

```
2.0::nil;
```
val it = [2.0] : real list

The precedence of the `::` and `@` operators is below that of the additive operators such as `+`, but above that of the comparison operators like `<`. Most unusual is that these operators are *right-associative*, meaning that they group from the right instead of the left as do most operators we have seen.

Example 2.33 : Especially important about right-associativity of these operators is the interpretation of a cascade of cons operators, like

```
1::2::3::nil
```

This expression is grouped from the right, as `1::(2::(3::nil))`. Expression `3::nil` represents the list with head 3 and an empty tail, that is, `[3]`. Next, `2::[3]` is the list whose head is 2 and whose tail is the list whose only element is 3; this list is `[2,3]`. Similarly, the entire expression denotes the list `[1,2,3]`.

Notice that when we have a sequence of cons operators, only the last operand must be a list, such as `nil` in the example above. The other operands must be elements. It would not make sense to group an expression like

---

The Types of Heads and Tails

- Remember that the types of the head and tail are different. If the type of the head is T, then the type of the tail is "list of T," or T list in ML.

- Similarly, the cons operator :: takes a first argument that is of some type T, and a second argument that is of type T list.

- On the other hand, the operator @ takes two arguments of type T list for some type T.

```
1::2::3::nil
```

from the left, as `((1::2)::3)::nil`, because `1::2` is a type mismatch. That is, when the cons operator sees the left operand 1, it expects that the type of the tail will be int list. Since the type of 2 is int, not int list, it is not possible to apply :: to this pair of operands. □

Example 2.34: Let us reprise Example 2.30 and consider the meaning of the error message that we saw there. We repeat the relevant part of Example 2.30 in Fig. 2.6.

```
[#"a", #"b", "c"];
```
1) *Error: operator and operand don't agree [tycon mismatch]*
2) *operator domain: char * char list*
3) *operand: char * string list*
4) *in expression:*
5) *#"b" :: "c" :: nil*

Figure 2.6: Error message from Example 2.30

ML parses lists from the back (i.e., the right end). It starts off assuming a list is empty, i.e., nil. When it sees the last element, "c", it "conses" that element with the list following, i.e., "c" :: nil to get a list of one element, ["c"]. Evidently, the type of this list is string list, since its one element is a string.

Now, ML tries to attach the next-to-last element, #"b", as the head of a list whose tail is ["c"]. But there is a type mismatch in the resulting list #"b" :: ["c"]. That is, since the head is a character, the expected domain of the operator :: is char * char list, i.e., a pair consisting of a character (the head) and a list of characters (the tail).[4] That is what line (2) of the error message is telling us. However, as line (3) states, the actual type of the pair to which the :: operator was applied is `char * string list`, i.e., a head that is a character and a tail that is a list of strings. Lines (4) and (5) of the error message confirm that the problem occurs in the expression #"b" :: "c" :: nil. □

2.4.5 Converting Between Character Strings and Lists

In ML, strings and lists are different types. However, there is a great similarity between a string and a list of characters, and it is possible to convert between the two representations using the built-in functions `explode` and `implode`. The first of these takes a string and converts it to the list of characters appearing in that string, in order.

Example 2.35: Here are two examples of the use of `explode`.

```
explode("abcd");
```
val it = [#"a",#"b",#"c",#"d"] : char list

```
explode("");
```
val it = [] : char list

Notice in the second example that "" is the empty string, which when exploded yields an empty list of characters. □

The function `implode` takes a list whose elements are characters and concatenates all the characters together to form a single string.

Example 2.36: Here are three examples of imploding lists.

```
implode([#"a",#"b",#"c",#"d"]);
```
val it = "abcd" : string

```
implode(nil)
```
val it = "" : string

```
implode(explode("xyz"));
```
val it = "xyz" : string

The second example points out that we can implode the empty list and get the empty string. The third illustrates that implode and explode are inverses of one another, and the effect of explode followed by implode on any string is to return the string itself. □

The Type of the Empty List

Notice that in the second case of Example 2.35, ML deduced that the empty list was of type `char list`, even though there are no elements in the list. ML knows it is an empty list of characters, because `explode` *always* returns a list of characters.

In general, the type of the empty list is `'a list`, i.e., a list of elements of any one type. Recall from Example 2.21 that identifiers beginning with a quote mark denote types. Thus, `'a list` is ML's way of saying "any-type list." However, when the empty list appears as a value, the ML system must be able to discover a concrete type for its elements — the type that the elements would have if there were any elements. We shall have more to say about the need to resolve types in Section 5.3.1.

A third operator, similar to `implode`, works on lists of strings instead of lists of characters. If L is a list of strings, then `concat(L)` produces the string that is the concatenation of all the strings on L, in order.

Example 2.37: Here is an example of `concat` applied to a list of strings.

```
concat(["ab","cd","e"]);
```
val it = "abcde" : string

☐

2.4.6   Introduction to the ML Type System

Every programming language has a *type system*, that is, a collection of types for its values and variables and a way of expressing those types. We have not seen nearly all of the ML type system yet, but it is useful to observe the way types and their representations are constructed. The type system of ML is constructed from a *basis* of elementary types by applying certain *type constructors* recursively. A type constructor is an operator that builds new types from simpler ones. Here is what we have seen so far of the ML type system.

BASIS: We have seen the elementary types `int`, `real`, `bool`, `char`, and `string`.

INDUCTION: We have seen two type constructors:

1. The product-type constructor builds the types of tuples. If $T_1, T_2, \ldots, T_n$ are types, then $T_1 * T_2 * \cdots * T_n$ denotes the type of a tuple whose ith component has type T_i, for $i = 1, 2, \ldots, n$.

---

[4]Recall that all binary operators in ML are perceived as applying to a single pair, rather than to two arguments.

2. The list-type constructor `list` builds list types from element types. If T is a type, then T `list` is the type of lists each of whose elements is of type T.

We may apply these type constructors in any order, as many times as we like, to build new types of increasingly complex structure. In type expressions, `list` is of higher precedence than ∗. Thus, we may need to use parentheses to group operands properly.

Example 2.38 : Here are some examples of constructed types and a typical value for each.

1. Type expression `int list` is a list of integers. It is the appropriate type for values such as `[1,2,3]`.

2. Type expression `string * int list * int` is the type for a tuple with three components, whose types are respectively a string, a list of integers, and a single integer. A typical value of this type is `("ab", [1,2,3], 4)`. Note that in type expressions, `list` has higher precedence than ∗, so this type expression is properly parsed `string * (int list) * int`, rather than `(string * int) list * int`.

3. Type expression `(int * int) list list` is the type of a list of lists of pairs of integers. An appropriate value for this type is

$$[[(1,2),(3,4)], [(5,6)], nil]$$

The list consists of three elements. The first element is the list consisting of the pairs $(1,2)$ and $(3,4)$. The second element is the list with only one element: $(5,6)$. The third element is the empty list.

□

2.4.7   Exercises for Section 2.4

Exercise 2.4.1 : What are the values of the following expressions?

* a) `#2(3,4,5)`

  b) `hd([3,4,5])`

* c) `tl([3,4,5])`

  d) `explode("foo")`

* e) `implode([#"f", #"o", #"o"])`

  f) `"c"::["a","t"]`

* g) ["c","o"]@["b","o","l"]

  h) concat(["c","a","t"])

Exercise 2.4.2: What is wrong with each of the following expressions? If possible, suggest an appropriate correction.

* a) #4(3,4,5)

  b) hd([])

*! c) #1(1)

  d) explode(["bar"])

* e) implode(#"a",#"b")

  f) ["r"]::["a","t"]

* g) tl([])

  h) 1@2

* i) concat([#"a",#"b"])

Exercise 2.4.3: Give the types of the following expressions.

* a) (1.5,("3",[4,5]))

  b) [[1,2],nil,[3]]

* c) [(2,3.5), (4,5.5), (6,7.5)]

  d) ([#"a",#"b"],[nil,[1,2,3]])

*! **Exercise 2.4.4:** Are (1,2) and (1,2,3) the same type? Are [1,2] and [1,2,3] the same type?

Exercise 2.4.5: Give examples of appropriate values for each of the following type expressions. Do not use the empty list as the value for any list component.

* a) int list list list

  b) (int * char) list

* c) string list * (int * (real * string)) * int

  d) ((int * int) * (bool list) * real) * (real * string)

* e) (bool * int) * char.

  ! f) real * int list list list list.

! **Exercise 2.4.6:** Using two of the operators we have learned in this section, it is possible to convert a string of length one into the character of that string. Show how to accomplish this transformation.

Chapter 3

Defining Functions

Now we know everything there is to know about ML, except how to program! In this chapter we shall learn about defining and using functions. Essentially all programming in ML is conducted by the definition of functions and the application of these functions to arguments. As we shall see, ML uses functions in places where more traditional languages use iteration (e.g., while-loops).

3.1 It's Easy; It's `fun`

The keyword `fun` introduces function definitions. In this section we shall see the simplest form of function definitions, which are essentially single expressions that are evaluated for the arguments of the function whenever the function is called. Later sections discuss the more common forms of function definition, involving the matching of arguments to patterns, and the use of temporary definitions in functions. We defer to Chapter 5 some of the more advanced concepts regarding ML functions, such as polymorphic functions (those that can take arguments of different types), higher-order functions (those that take functions as arguments or produce functions as results), and Currying of higher-order functions (writing a function so new functions may be created by instantiating one of its arguments).

The simplest form of function declaration is

fun <identifier>(<parameter list>) = <expression>;

That is, the keyword `fun` is followed by the name of the function, a list of the parameters for that function, an equal-sign, and an expression involving the parameters. This expression becomes the value of the function when we give the function arguments to correspond to its parameters.

Example 3.1: Let us define a function `upper` that converts a lower-case letter to the corresponding upper-case letter.[1] To do so, we need to know that the ASCII code for an upper-case letter is always 32 less than that of the lower-case version. The function `upper` will perform the following steps:

1. A given character is converted to an integer,

2. 32 is subtracted, and

3. The result is converted back to a character.

Here is the definition of function `upper`:

```
fun upper(c) = chr(ord(c)-32);
val upper = fn : char → char
```

There are a number of observations we should make about the function `upper`. First, it has one parameter `c`. The value of `upper` is computed by the expression `chr(ord(c)-32)`. We discuss the ML response to the definition of `upper` in Section 3.1.1.

We may use function `upper` to convert lower-case letters, just as we would in most languages, by applying `upper` to the desired letter. For instance, we can convert `#"a"` to `#"A"` by:

```
upper(#"a");
val it = #"A" : char
```

ML responds to expression `upper(#"a")` as it would to any expression, by assigning its value to `it` and telling the value.   □

3.1.1 Function Types

Notice from Example 3.1 how ML represents function types. The response to the definition of function `upper` was

val upper = fn : char → char

In general, when a function is defined, ML does not respond with the value of that function, which is hard to express other than by repeating the definition of the function. Rather, it responds with the type of the function. The specification of the function type has the form:

`fn` : <domain type> `->` <range type>

That is, the response to a function definition consists of:

---

[1] There is actually a function `toUpper` that is available in a library of functions that ML calls the `Char` "structure." We shall cover structures in Section 8.2 and the particular structure `Char` in Section 9.4.4. Function `toUpper` also has an inverse function, `toLower`, which converts upper-case letters to their corresponding lower-case letters. Moreover, each of the functions `toUpper` and `toLower` leave intact those characters that are not lower- or upper-case letters, respectively, which our simple function `upper` does not do.

Function Parameters and Arguments

In this book we call the variables to which a function is applied in its definition the *parameters*, while the expressions to which the function is applied in a function call are *arguments*. In other literature, one sometimes sees the terms "formal parameters" and "actual parameters" where we use "parameters" and "arguments."

---

1. The keyword `fn`.

2. A colon.

3. The type of the parameter(s), called the *domain type* for the function. This type is `char` in Example 3.1. ML regards each function as having one parameter, but the type of this parameter can be a product type. So in practice there can be any number of parameters for a function.

4. The symbol `->`.

5. The type of the result of the function, that is, the *range type* for the function. In Example 3.1, the range type is also `char`, but it is common for the domain and range types to differ. ML views each function as returning a single value, but since this value may be a tuple, in effect a function can return several items.

The operator `->` is another way to construct types, just like `*` and the word `list`. If T_1 and T_2 are types, then $T_1 \to T_2$ is the type of functions with domain type T_1 and range type T_2, that is, functions which take an argument of type T_1 and return a result of type T_2.

Operator `->` is right-associative, so $T_1 \to T_2 \to T_3$ is interpreted as

$$T_1 \to (T_2 \to T_3)$$

and is the type of a function whose parameter is of type T_1 and whose result is itself a function; that function has domain type T_2 and range type T_3. The notion of a function producing a function as a value may seem strange, but these "higher order functions" are an integral part of ML programming that we shall examine starting in Section 5.4.

3.1.2   Declaring Function Types

It might surprise the reader that we never had to declare the type of the parameter `c` in the function `upper` of Example 3.1 or the type of the value returned by this function. ML deduced that these types are both `char` because of what it knows about the functions `ord` and `chr`. In general ML does not require

---

Don't Confuse `fun` With `fn`

The response in Example 3.1 uses the keyword `fn`, which should not be confused with `fun`, even though both are short for "function." We use `fun` to introduce a declaration of a particular identifier to be a certain function, while `fn` is used in ML to introduce a value that has a function type.

---

declarations for types, although you are free to declare the type if you wish. We shall have more to say about how ML deduces types in Section 3.2.4, and there we shall get a better idea of when we can rely upon ML to deduce types for us.

The most common situation in which we have to declare a type is when ML would use the default rule for an arithmetic or comparison operator to deduce that certain variables were of integer type, and yet we want these variables to be of some other type on which the operator can be used. If we need to, we can follow any variable or expression by a colon and a type. The effect is to declare that variable or expression to have that type. Recall that the colon symbol is also used in ML responses to connect values with their types.

Example 3.2 : Our next example is a function that squares reals.

```
fun square(x:real) = x*x;
val square = fn : real → real
```

The function `square` has one parameter, `x`. By following parameter `x` with a colon and the type `real`, we declare to ML that the parameter of function `square` is of type `real`. ML then infers that the expression `x*x` represents real multiplication, and therefore the value returned by `square` is of type `real`.   □

It is necessary to indicate that `x` is real somewhere. Otherwise, ML will use the default type, integer, for `x`, resulting in a function that can square integers but not reals:

```
fun square(x) = x*x;
val square = fn : int → int
```

We could have attached the `:real` to any or all of the three occurrences of `x` in the definition of `square` in Example 3.2. For example

```
fun square(x) = (x:real)*x
```

is a possibility. However:

- We must be careful to parenthesize the arguments of the colon operator —
  for example, `(x:real)` — because the colon has lower precedence than
  the arithmetic or comparison operators.

Example 3.3: Some care must be exercised in how we specify the types of
variables in a function definition. Here is an example of a surprising error that
can occur if we do not group a variable with its type properly.

```
fun square(x) = x:real * x;
```
Error: unbound type constructor: x

Here, because `*` has higher precedence than `:`, ML has tried to "multiply"
`real` by the third of the three x's before applying the operator `:`. That is not
as strange as it seems. ML knows `real` is a type, and `*` applied to types forms
a product type. That is, ML is trying to form a type consisting of pairs whose
first component is of type `real` and whose second component is of type x. But
it doesn't know about any type named x, so it complains. The solution, which
we used following Example 3.2, is to parenthesize the `x:real` so ML will group
its operators as we intend.   □

3.1.3   Function Application

As an example of the use of the square function, suppose we have defined the
variables `pi` and `radius` to have values 3.14159 and 4.0, as in Example 2.23.
Then we can write

```
pi*square(radius);
```
val it = 50.26544 : real

In this example, function application looks just like it does in Pascal or most
languages; a function is applied to a list of arguments, with parentheses around
the argument list. However, as we discussed in the box on "Applying Functions,
ML Style" in Section 2.2.3, formally, the ML syntax for function application is
simply a pair of expressions standing next to one another, with no intervening
punctuation. That is, F E requires the expression F to be evaluated and
interpreted as a function. Then, expression E is evaluated and function F is
applied to the value of E.

Example 3.4: We could have computed the area of a circle by

```
pi * square radius;
```
val it = 50.26544 : real

Function application has higher precedence than any of the arithmetic operators, so the above expression first applies function `square` to argument `radius`,
and the result is multiplied by `pi`.   □

In principle, it doesn't matter whether or not we put parentheses around a simple argument (i.e., an argument without operators); that is, f x and f(x) are treated the same by ML. However, we advise using the parentheses. Not only do parentheses make the syntax of function application look more familiar, but sometimes they prevent an error such as failure to put parentheses around an operand and its type, to which the operand is connected by the : symbol.

Example 3.5: To underscore the point that function application has higher precedence than the common operators, consider the sequence of statements below, ending in an application of the function square from Example 3.2.

```
val x = 3.0;
val y = 4.0;
square x+y;
val it = 13.0 : real
```

We see from the value produced that ML has grouped the function application (square x)+y; that is, function square is applied to x before the addition with y takes place. If we want to square the sum of x and y, then we are required to use parentheses,

```
square(x+y);
val it = 49.0 : real
```

as we would in most other languages.   □

3.1.4   Functions With More Than One Parameter

We can define a function that has any number of parameters. Normally, we put parentheses around the list of parameters or arguments, both in the function definition and use. The effect is to combine the list of arguments into a tuple, which formally is a single argument but which we may treat as if there were several arguments. It is also possible to write multiparameter functions without parentheses; see Section 5.5.

Example 3.6: Figure 3.1 is another example of a function; it produces the largest of three real numbers. It begins by comparing parameters a and b in line (2). If a is larger, it returns as a result the larger of a and c at lines (3) and (4). If b is larger, then in lines (6) and (7) it returns the larger of b and c. □

Example 3.6 brings up a number of important points about ML types.

- Notice that in Fig. 3.1 ML deduces that b and c are reals, even though only a was declared. One way to make this deduction is to use the fact that the if ··· then ··· else operator must have the same type in both branches. We shall discuss type deduction further in Section 3.2.4.

```
(1) fun max3(a:real,b,c) = (* maximum of three reals *)
(2)     if a>b then
(3)         if a>c then a
(4)         else c
(5)     else
(6)         if b>c then b
(7)         else c;
```
   *val max3 = fn : real * real * real → real*

Figure 3.1: Function computing the maximum of its three arguments

---

Comments

Now that we can write programs of more than one line, we shall have
reason to comment our code. The proper way to do so is shown in line
(1) of Fig. 3.1. The pair of characters (* introduce a comment, which
continues, even across lines, until the matching sequence of two characters
*) is encountered. This convention is similar to most implementations
of Pascal, but in ML it is possible to nest pairs of (*...*), just like
parentheses are nested.

- Also notice that the type of max3 is a function that takes a triple of real
  numbers as its argument and produces a real. That type is shown in the
  response as real * real * real -> real.

- In type expressions * takes precedence over ->. Thus in the type expression above, the domain type is real * real * real, and the range type
  is real.

- If we did not declare the type of any variable in function max3, then ML
  would assume the variables compared by > have the type integer, the
  default type for operator >.

- One advantage of the ML view that functions have only one parameter
  is that a variable whose value is of the appropriate product type can
  be defined and used as the argument of a multiparameter function. For
  example,

```
        val t = (1.0,2.0,3.0);
        max3(t);
```

is correct ML and produces the value 3.0.

3.1.5   Functions that Reference External Variables

The functions illustrated so far use only their parameters in computing their result. Sometimes, we wish to write a function that uses previously defined variables in its body. As in most other languages, the use of a variable x in the definition of a function f "freezes" x as far as the function f is concerned. That is, subsequent redefinitions of x will not affect the function f. A simple example will illustrate the rule.

Example 3.7 : Consider the following sequence of steps:

```
1)  val x = 3;
2)  fun addx(a) = a+x;
3)  val x = 10;
4)  addx(2);
```
val it = 5 : int

A picture of the changes to the environment is shown in Fig. 3.2. At line (1) we create a variable x and give it the value 3. When at line (2) the function addx is defined, its definition uses x. We suggested by an arrow in Fig. 3.2 that the definition of addx refers to this value binding for x. Remember that, as we suggested in Section 2.3.4, the value binding for x, after being added to the environment at line (1), never changes. Thus, we can be sure that the definition of addx will always use 3 as the value of x.[2]

Now, in line (3) we create a new variable, also named x. As we see in Fig. 3.2, the new binding for x goes above the old binding for x and the definition of addx. However, the definition of addx does not change; it continues to refer to the value of x that pertained when the definition of addx was made. Thus, we see that in line (4), addx(2) results in the value 5, not 12, because the value of x in the definition of addx is still 3.   □

3.1.6   Exercises for Section 3.1

Exercise 3.1.1 : Write functions to compute the following:

* a) The cube of a real number x.

 b) The smallest of the three components of a tuple of type int * int * int.

* c) The third element of a list. The function need not behave properly if given an argument that is a list of length 2 or less.

---
[2]You may therefore wonder why we would want to write addx as we did. Indeed, fun addx(a) = a+3 would be a simpler way to write the same function. There are some good reasons to write functions that refer to external variables, however. For example, in Section 8.1.2, we consider a collection of functions that all use the same external variable. If we change this variable, all the functions change in a coordinated way.

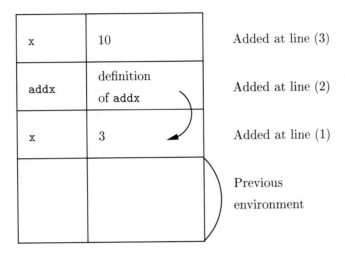

x	10		Added at line (3)
addx	definition of addx		Added at line (2)
x	3		Added at line (1)
			Previous environment

Figure 3.2: Changes to the environment in Example 3.7

   d) The reverse of a tuple of length 3.

* e) The third character of a character string. Your function need not behave well on strings of length less than 3. *Hint*: Use `explode` and your function from Exercise 3.1.1(c).

   f) Cycle a list once. That is, given a list $[a_1, a_2, \ldots, a_n]$, produce the list $[a_2, a_3, \ldots, a_n, a_1]$.

! **Exercise 3.1.2 :** Write functions to do the following.

* a) Given three integers, produce a pair consisting of the smallest and largest.

   b) Given three integers, produce a list of the three in sorted order.

   c) Round a real number to the nearest tenth.

! d) Given a list, return that list with its second element deleted. Your function need not behave well on lists of length shorter than 2.

Exercise 3.1.3 : Suppose we execute the following sequence of definitions:

```
val a = 2;
fun f(b) = a*b;
val b = 3;
fun g(a) = a+b;
```

Give the value of the following expressions:

* a) `f(4)`.

When and Where Function Definitions Occur

The behavior of ML regarding the value of variables used in a function definition is essentially the same as the policy followed by C or Pascal, or most other languages. For example, in C a function's definition can refer to static variables defined prior to the function definition in whatever file the function definition appears. That is, the variables a function definition can use depends on *where* the definition appears in a C program.

It might appear that which variables are usable by a function definition in ML depends on *when* the function is defined. That is, the function can refer to previously defined variables. However, the apparent difference is caused by the fact that we have been thinking of ML programming as done in interactive mode, where steps are entered one at a time. If we think of what we type in interactive mode as a single file of program elements, then we see that ML follows the same rule as C — you may use variables that are located above the function definition in the file. This rule applies exactly if we write ML programs in files and execute them using use, as we discussed in Section 1.2. There are, however, two differences between ML and C in this regard:

1. In C, the value of a variable can change, thus changing what the function does; in ML the value cannot change.

2. In ML, it is possible to make several declarations for the same identifier, external to any function. In C, that would be considered an illegal redefinition.

---

* b) `f(4)+b.`

  c) `g(5).`

  d) `g(5)+a.`

* e) `f(g(6)).`

  f) `g(f(7)).`

3.2   Recursive Functions

It is possible, and indeed frequently necessary, for ML functions to be *recursive*, that is, defined in terms of themselves, either directly or indirectly. In fact, recursive functions in ML substitute for most of the iterations such as while-loops or for-loops than one finds in C, Pascal, and most other languages. Looping statements, while present in ML (See Section 7.3.4), are awkward and generally discouraged.

When writing recursive functions, we must be careful that if a recursive function calls itself, it does so with an argument that is, in some sense chosen by the programmer, smaller than its own argument. For example, if the argument is an integer i, we could safely call the function with argument $i - 1$ or any integer smaller than i. If the argument is a list L, we could call the function on the tail of the list or any shorter list.

Normally, a recursive function consists of

1. A *basis*, where for sufficiently small arguments we compute the result without making any recursive call, and

2. An *inductive step*, where for arguments not handled by the basis, we call the function recursively, one or more times, with smaller arguments.

In this section we shall learn about writing simple recursions. We then introduce two extensions: nonlinear recursion, where the recursive function calls itself several times, and mutual recursion, where several functions are defined recursively in terms of each other. We begin with a simple example of a recursion.

Example 3.8: Let us write a function `reverse(L)` that produces the reverse of the list L.[3] For example, `reverse([1,2,3])` produces the list `[3,2,1]`.

BASIS: The basis is the empty list; the reverse of the empty list is the empty list.

INDUCTION: For the inductive step, suppose L has at least one element. Let the first or head element of L be h, and let the tail or remaining elements of L be the list T. Then we can construct the reverse of list L by reversing T and following it by the element h.

For instance, if L is `[1,2,3]`, then $h = 1$, T is `[2,3]`, the reverse of T is `[3,2]`, and the reverse of T concatenated with the list containing only h is `[3,2]@[1]`, or `[3,2,1]`.

```
(1)  fun reverse(L) =
(2)          if L = nil then nil
(3)          else reverse(tl(L)) @ [hd(L)];
        val reverse = fn : 'a list → 'a list
```

Figure 3.3: A recursive function to reverse a list

In Fig. 3.3 we see the ML definition of **reverse** that follows the basis and inductive step described above. Lines (2) and (3) are the expression that forms

---

[3]ML actually has a built-in function **rev** that performs this operation.

When Does a Function Need to Know Its Type?

Given our discussion in Section 3.1.2, it might surprise you to find that in Example 3.8 it was not necessary for the particular type of elements to be deduced by the ML compiler. The difference between Example 3.8 and previous examples of functions that work on parameters of only one type, is that some functions use an overloaded operator such as + or < that require us to tell ML what type its operands have (or to use the default type for the operator). In Example 3.8, there is no overloaded operator, and thus, we were able to avoid specifying the types of elements of the list. We shall discuss in Section 5.3 more about when a function needs to know the type of its operands and when it can be "polymorphic," working on values of various types.

---

the body of the function definition. In line (2) we handle the basis case: the reverse of the empty list is the empty list. Line (3) covers the inductive step, and we should appreciate how succinctly and naturally it does so. The subexpression `reverse(tl(L))` takes the tail of the given list and reverses it, recursively. We then concatenate this new list with the head element, which is obtained by subexpression `hd(L)`.

- In order to concatenate the reversed tail with the head element, we must place square brackets around the head element, as `[hd(L)]`. Remember that the concatenation operator @ requires two lists as its arguments. If we were to omit the square brackets, we would be concatenating a list and an element, leading to a type mismatch.

The response to the definition of **reverse** in Fig. 3.3 illustrates an interesting point. Unlike our previous examples of functions, ML cannot tell exactly what the type of argument and result is. It can only deduce that these types are both lists of elements of the same type. It calls the element type `'a`, and it calls the argument and result types `'a list`.[4] The type of **reverse** is then a function from `'a` lists to `'a` lists.   □

3.2.1   Function Execution

Whenever a function is called, its arguments are evaluated, and an addition to the environment is created that associates the resulting values with the parameters of the function. This style of argument passing is known as *call-by-value*.

---

[4] Recall that identifiers beginning with a quote are variables denoting types. Actually, the type variable used by ML in this example is `''a` (i.e., two quotes before the a). There is a subtle distinction between `'a` and `''a`, which we shall discuss in Section 5.3.4. Before then, we shall use only `'a`, `'b` and so on as variables denoting types.

It is the same as the manner by which arguments are passed to functions and procedures in C, and the manner in which non-var parameters are handled in Pascal.

When the function is executed, we place on top of the old environment entries that bind the parameters of the function to their associated values. If the function is recursive, new additions are built on top of the old ones for each recursive call. Each addition binds the parameters of the function to the argument values. These bindings intercept any reference to the parameters, thus distinguishing themselves from the entries with the same identifiers in levels below. When a function completes and returns its value, its addition to the environment goes away, but the returned value is available for use in the expression being evaluated.

Example 3.9 : Suppose we are in an environment that has the definition of the function `reverse` from Example 3.8. If we call

```
reverse([1,2,3])
```

then we add to the environment an entry for parameter L and its value. We show this first step above the line in Fig. 3.4.

L	[1,2,3]	Added in call to reverse([1,2,3])
reverse	definition of reverse	Environment before call

Figure 3.4: Environment after the initial call to `reverse`

With this value of L as argument, the condition of line (2) in Fig. 3.3 is false; that is, L is not `nil`. Thus, we must evaluate the expression on line (3), which requires us to evaluate `reverse(tl(L))` or `reverse([2,3])`. Thus we set up another call to `reverse`, adding to the environment a new binding for L that associates L with the value [2,3].

In a similar manner, the new call to `reverse` causes us to make another call, with L bound to [3], and an addition to the environment is set up with this binding. Again a recursive call to `reverse` is necessary, and in the fourth call L is bound to `nil`. The additions to the environment for all four calls are stacked one above the other as suggested in Fig. 3.5. At this point, the identifier L refers to the top binding, with value `nil`.

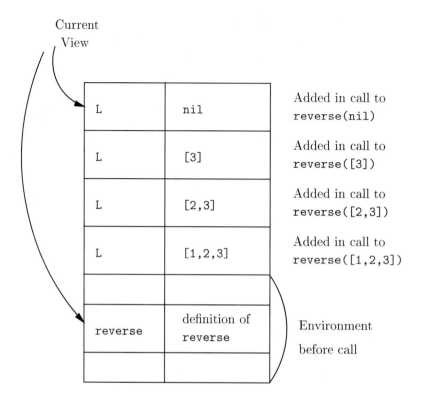

Figure 3.5: Additions to the environment when four calls to reverse are made

Now when we evaluate the body of reverse, the test of line (2) is satisfied, because L has the value nil. The value nil is returned and used in place of reverse(tl(L)) by the call below it — that is, by reverse([3]) — to produce its own answer on line (3). After the return, the top entry for L in Fig. 3.5 disappears, exposing the appropriate value of L, namely [3]. Since hd([3]) is 3, the result produced by reverse([3]) is the empty list concatenated with [3], or just [3].

Now, the addition to the environment for reverse([3]) goes away, and its result is used by the call below it: reverse([2,3]). That, in turn, produces [3,2] as a result and its addition to the environment goes away, leaving the environment that was originally shown in Fig. 3.4. However, the corresponding call, reverse([1,2,3]), now receives the value [3,2], returned from above, to use in place of reverse(tl(L)) in line (3). Thus the original call to reverse is able to produce its value, [3,2,1]. At this point, all bindings for L have disappeared.   □

3.2.2 Nonlinear Recursion

The form of recursion illustrated in Examples 3.8 and 3.9 is relatively simple. Each call either results in one recursive call with a smaller argument, or we reach the basis case and there is no need for a recursion. Now we shall examine a function where the recursion involves more than one recursive call.

The function *combinations of* m *things out of* n or "*n* choose *m*," usually written $\binom{n}{m}$, is the number of ways we can pick a set of m things out of n distinct things. For example, two aces out of the four aces in a card deck can be picked in six possible ways. That is, we can pick any of the four aces first and any of the three remaining aces second. That looks like 12 ways, but in fact we have picked each set in two different orders. For example, the aces of spades and hearts could be picked spade-then-heart or heart-then-spade.

In general, $\binom{n}{m} = n!/((n-m)!m!)$, where $x!$ (*x factorial*) is the product of all the integers from 1 up to x. For instance,

$$\binom{4}{2} = 4!/(2!2!) = 4 \times 3 \times 2 \times 1/(2 \times 1 \times 2 \times 1) = 6$$

Intuitively $n!/(n-m)!$, which equals $n \times (n-1) \times \cdots \times (n-m+1)$, is the number of ways we can select among n things for the first choice, then among the $n-1$ remaining things for the second choice, and so on for m choices. We must divide this number by $m!$ because each set of m elements will have been selected in $m!$ different orders.

There is also a natural recursive way to define $\binom{n}{m}$. Here are the basis and induction rules.

BASIS: There are two parts to the basis. If $m = 0$, then the number of ways to pick 0 things out of n is 1 — don't pick anything. Thus, $\binom{n}{0} = 1$ for any $n \geq 0$. Also, if $m = n$, then there is one way to pick all n things out of n — pick them all. Thus, $\binom{n}{n} = 1$ for all $n \geq 0$.

INDUCTION: If $0 < m < n$, then $\binom{n}{m} = \binom{n-1}{m} + \binom{n-1}{m-1}$. The reason is that if we must select m things out of n, we can either:

1. Reject the first thing and then pick m things out of the remaining $n-1$ things, or

2. Select the first thing and then pick $m-1$ things out of the remaining $n-1$.

Note that $\binom{n}{m}$ makes no sense if $m < 0$ or if $m > n$, so this basis and induction entirely define the function.

Example 3.10 : We can write a function `comb(n,m)` that computes $\binom{n}{m}$. The code appears in Fig. 3.6. Line (2) handles the basis case, and line (3) implements the inductive step. Note that the program will not behave well if the assumption about n and m in the comment of line (1) is violated. We really should test for violations, and there is an important mechanism, the "exception," that allows us to do so and still adhere to the principle that functions return a value of one particular type invariably. We discuss exceptions in Section 5.2.   □

```
(1) fun comb(n,m) = (* assumes 0 <= m <= n *)
(2)            if m=0 orelse m=n then 1
(3)            else comb(n-1,m) + comb(n-1,m-1);
```
*val comb = fn : int * int → int*

Figure 3.6: Function to compute n choose m

The sequence of recursive calls initiated by a single use of function `comb` is rather complex. For example, in the expression

```
comb(4,2);
```
val it = 6 : int

the initial call first calls `comb(3,2)` and later calls `comb(3,1)`. However, before the latter call, `comb(3,2)` calls `comb(2,2)` and `comb(2,1)`, and so on. Figure 3.7 shows the structure of the calls as time progresses from left to right.

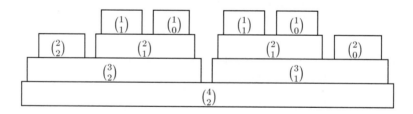

Figure 3.7: Structure of recursive calls for the `comb` function

3.2.3   Mutual Recursion

Occasionally, one needs to write two or more functions that are *mutually recursive*, meaning that each calls at least one other function in the group. Most languages, such as Pascal or C, put some obstacles in the way of writing such functions, but ML has a straightforward mechanism. We shall give an example of mutually recursive functions, first showing the problem that arises if we are not careful. Then, we shall show how ML lets us handle the problem.

Example 3.11 : Suppose we want to write a function that takes a list L as argument and produces a list consisting of alternate elements of L. There are two natural versions of this function. One, which we call `take(L)`, takes the first element of L and alternate elements after that (i.e., the first, third, fifth, and so on). The other, which we call `skip(L)`, skips the first element and takes alternate elements after that (i.e., the second, fourth, sixth, and so on). It is convenient to define these two functions in terms of each other.

BASIS: If L is empty, both functions return the empty list.

INDUCTION: If L is not empty, `take` returns the head element of L followed by the result of applying `skip` to the tail of L. On the other hand, `skip` returns the result of applying `take` to the tail of L.

Figure 3.8 shows a failed attempt to define the functions `take` and `skip`. At the third line of `take`, we assemble the result using the cons operator; the head is the head of L, and the tail is the result of applying `skip` to the tail of L. The problem is that at the third line, the function `skip` is not defined, even though we intend to define `skip` immediately thereafter. Thus, ML responds with an error message. Defining `skip` first would cause a similar error because `take` is used in the third line of `skip`. □

```
fun take(L) =
        if L = nil then nil
        else hd(L)::skip(tl(L));
```
Error : unbound variable or constructor: skip

```
fun skip(L) =
        if L = nil then nil
        else take(tl(L));
```

Figure 3.8: Erroneous attempt to define mutually recursive functions

We can get ML to wait until it has seen both functions `take` and `skip` before trying to interpret variables, if we use the keyword **and** between the function definitions. The general form for defining n mutually recursive functions is shown in Fig. 3.9. There we see the n definitions connected by **and**'s. There is one use of **fun** at the beginning and one use of the semicolon, at the end.

- Do not confuse **and**, which is used to indicate mutual recursions, with `andalso`, which is the logical AND operator in ML.

- It is not necessary to use the **and** construct if there is no mutual recursion. If we define functions $f_1, f_2, \ldots, f_n$, and, for each i, in the definition of f_i we use only functions that appear earlier on the list — that is, $f_1, f_2, \ldots, f_{i-1}$ — then there is no mutual recursion.

Example 3.12 : The correct definition of the functions `take` and `skip` from Example 3.11 is shown in Fig. 3.10. Notice that the response from ML does not

```
fun
    <definition of first function>
and
    <definition of second function>
and

    ...

and
    <definition of nth function> ;
```

Figure 3.9: Form of a mutually recursive function definition

come until after both functions have been seen. Both are identified as functions from lists to lists. The elements of the input and output lists of both functions must be of one type 'a, but ML cannot identify the type.

```
fun
    take(L) =
        if L = nil then nil
        else hd(L)::skip(tl(L))
and
    skip(L) =
        if L = nil then nil
        else take(tl(L));
```
val take = fn : 'a list → 'a list
val skip = fn : 'a list → 'a list

Figure 3.10: Correct definition of mutually recursive functions

Here are two examples of the use of these functions.

```
take([1,2,3,4,5]);
```
val it = [1,3,5] : int list

```
skip([#"a",#"b",#"c",#"d",#"e"]);
```
val it = [#"b",#"d"] : char list

When we use the functions on particular lists, ML can figure out the type of list elements from the argument. Hence, the type of the result list is reported with each use: `int list` in the first case and `char list` in the second. □

3.2.4 How ML Deduces Types

ML is quite good at discovering the types of variables, the types of function parameters, and the types of values returned by functions. The subject of how ML does so is quite complex, but there are a few observations we can make that will cover most of the ways types are discovered. Knowing what ML can do helps us know when we must declare a type and when we can skip type declarations.

1. The types of the operands and result of arithmetic operators must all agree. For example, in the expression (a+b)*2.0, we see that the right operand of the * is a real constant, so the left operand (a+b) must also be real. If the use of + produces a real, then both its operands are real. Thus, a and b are real. They will also have a real value any other place they are used, which can help make further type inferences.

2. When we apply an arithmetic comparison, we can be sure the operands are of the same type, although the result is a boolean and therefore not necessarily of the same type as the operands. For example, in the expression a<=10, we can deduce that a is an integer.

3. In a conditional expression, the expression itself and the subexpressions following the then and else must be of the same type.

4. If a variable or expression used as an argument of a function is of a known type, then the corresponding parameter of the function must be of that type. Similarly, if the function parameter is of known type, then the variable or expression used as the corresponding argument must be of the same type.

5. If the expression defining the function is of a known type, then the function returns a value of that type.

6. If no way to determine the type of a particular use of an overloaded operator exists, then the type of that operator is defined to be the default for that operator, normally integer.

Example 3.13: Consider the function comb(n,m) in Fig. 3.6, which we reproduce here for convenience.

```
(1) fun comb(n,m) = (* assumes 0 <= m <= n *)
(2)          if m=0 orelse m=n then 1
(3)          else comb(n-1,m) + comb(n-1,m-1);
```

In line (2), we see that in one branch of the if-then-else the result is the integer 1. Thus, the expression on line (3) must also be of type integer, and the function comb returns an integer value. In line (3) we also see the expressions n-1 and m-1. Since one operand of each subtraction is the integer 1, the other operands,

n in one case and m in the other, must also be integers. Thus, both parameters
of the function are integers, or strictly speaking, the (one) parameter of the
function is of type int * int, that is, a pair of integers.

Another way we could have discovered that m and n are integers is to look
at line (2). We see m compared with integer 0, so m must be an integer. We also
see n compared with m, and since we already know m is an integer, we know the
same about n.   □

3.2.5   Exercises for Section 3.2

Exercise 3.2.1: Write the following recursive functions.

* a) The factorial function that takes an integer $n \geq 1$ and produces the
product of all the integers from 1 up to n. Your function need not work
correctly if the argument is less than 1.

  b) Given an integer i and a list L, cycle L i times. That is, if

$$L = [a_1, a_2, \ldots, a_n]$$

then the desired result is $[a_{i+1}, a_{i+2}, \ldots, a_n, a_1, a_2, \ldots, a_i]$. You may use
the function cycle defined in Exercise 3.1.1(f).

* c) Duplicate each element of a list. That is, given the list $[a_1, a_2, \ldots, a_n]$,
produce the list $[a_1, a_1, a_2, a_2, \ldots, a_n, a_n]$.

  d) Compute the length of a list.[5]

  e) Compute x^i, where x is a real and i is a nonnegative integer. This function
takes two parameters, x and i, and need not behave well if $i < 0$.

*! f) Compute the largest element of list of reals. Your function need not
behave well if the list is empty.

*! **Exercise 3.2.2:** In the following function definition

```
fun foo(a,b,c,d) =
    if a=b then c+1 else
        if a>b then c else b+d
```

it is possible to deduce that a, b, c, and d are all integers. Explain how ML
makes these deductions.

Exercise 3.2.3: Suppose we define a function f by a statement that begins

```
fun f(a:int, b, c, d, e) = ...
```

---

[5]There is a function length in the ML top-level environment that performs this function;
the exercise asks you to write the function as if it were not already available.

Tell what can be inferred about the types of b, c, d, and/or e if the body of the function is each of the following if-then-else statements:

* a) if a<b+c then d else e.

  b) if a<b then c else d.

* c) if a<b then b+c else d+e.

! d) if a<b then b<c else d.

  e) if b<c then a else c+d.

*! f) if b<c then d else e.

! g) if b<c then d+e else d*e.

Exercise 3.2.4: Consider the factorial function `fact` described in Exercise 3.2.1(a); if you have not written this function, use the published solution. Describe the changes to the environment that occur as a result of a call to `fact(4)`.

3.3 Patterns in Function Definitions

One of the great sources of power in ML is the definition of functions on the basis of the pattern of its parameters. In Sections 3.1 and 3.2 the typical form of a function was "if the argument satisfies a condition then do one thing, else do another." Another way to define functions is to show all the patterns that the argument may have and describe what value to produce in each case.

3.3.1 Patterns as Function Parameters

Each *pattern* is an expression with variables, and when the pattern matches the argument, these variables are given the values that match. The same variables can then be used in the expression that defines the value of the function.

Example 3.14: A common pattern is `x::xs`. Since `::` represents cons, this pattern will match any list that is not empty. In the match, `x` will get the value of the head element, and `xs` will get the value of the tail. For instance, if this pattern is matched to a list L, whose value is `[1,2,3]`, then `x` gets the value 1, and `xs` gets the value `[2,3]`. We can now use `x` in place of the more complicated expression `hd(L)` and `xs` in place of `tl(L)`. □

The general form for a function defined by patterns involves the symbol |, which lets us list alternative forms for the arguments of the function as:

```
fun   <identifier>(<first pattern>)    =   <first expression>
 |    <identifier>(<second pattern>)   =   <second expression>
 |        ...
 |    <identifier>(<last pattern>)     =   <last expression>;
```

The identifiers must all be the same (they are each the name of the function), and the types of the values produced by the expressions on the right of the equal-signs must all be the same. Likewise, the types of the patterns themselves must be the same, but they can differ from the type of the values produced.

As with functions in general, the parentheses around the patterns are optional. However, the juxtaposition of expressions representing application of a function to its arguments has higher precedence than any of the usual operators. Thus it is wise to put parentheses around patterns that are more complex than a single variable. Otherwise, we run the risk that only the first part of the pattern will be treated as the function argument, and an error will result.

ML goes through the various patterns in the order that they appear until it finds one that matches its argument. The first match determines the value produced; other patterns are not considered. Thus, there can be overlap among the various patterns.[6]

- It is also legal to fail to cover all possible cases with the forms. However, you will get the diagnostic

Warning: match not exhaustive

You should then be very sure that the function will be used only with arguments that match one of the patterns.

Example 3.15 : Let us reconsider the function `reverse` from Example 3.8 There are two patterns for the argument L. If L is empty it matches the pattern `nil`. If L is not empty, it will match the pattern `x::xs`. For instance, if the list has a single element, `x` becomes that element and `xs` gets the value `nil`. A nonempty list cannot match `nil`, and `x::xs` does not match the empty list, because there is no head element to give a value to `x`. (It is not possible to give `x` the value `nil` because `x` is an element, not a list). Thus, the following definition works:

```
fun reverse(nil) = nil
  |   reverse(x::xs) = reverse(xs) @ [x]
val reverse = fn : 'a list → 'a list
```

Compare this definition with the equivalent definition in Fig. 3.3.[7] Here, `x` plays the role of `hd(L)` and `xs` plays the role of `tl(L)`. The above function operates by first checking if its argument is `nil` and returning `nil` if so. If the argument is not `nil`, then we can match `x::xs` to the argument; `x` acquires the value of the head and `xs` acquires the value of the tail.

---

[6]However, SML/NJ, as a default, treats completely redundant patterns, that is, patterns that can never be reached when the argument has any value that will match the pattern, as an error.

[7]There is actually a small difference between the two functions we called `reverse`, concerning the types of the elements that may form the lists being reversed. We shall address this distinction in Section 5.3.4.

Names for List Components in Patterns

It is conventional to use a pair of identifiers like x for the head of a list and xs (read "exes") for the tail of the same list. However, beware using a::as. Since as is a keyword in ML (see Section 3.3.2), you will get a strange diagnostic and must find another variable to use in place of as.

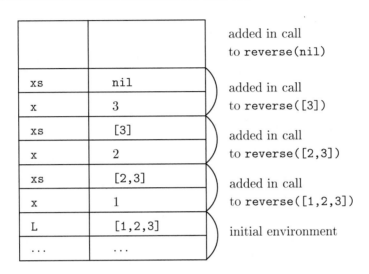

Figure 3.11: Binding values to the identifiers of a pattern

Figure 3.11 suggests the addition to the environment that occurs when reverse(L) is called, where L has the value [1,2,3]. Notice at the last call, to reverse(nil), there are no bindings for x or xs because the pattern nil matches the argument, and we never even try to match the second pattern. All these additions to the environment go away when the initial call to reverse completes.   □

3.3.2 "As" You Like it: Having it Both Ways

It is possible to take a single value and at one time give the value to an identifier and match the value with a pattern. In the match, variables mentioned in the pattern acquire their own values. The form is

<identifier> as <pattern>

Example 3.16: Let us write a function merge(L,M) that takes two lists of integers, L and M, that are sorted lowest-first, and *merges* them. That is, merge produces a single sorted list with all the elements of L and M. The

following recursive definition of `merge` works, assuming that the given lists are sorted. Note that, although no types are specified, integer type is inferred for all values because that is the default type for <.

BASIS: If L is empty, then the merge is M. If M is empty, the merge is L.

INDUCTION: If neither L nor M is empty, compare the heads of L and M. If the head of L, say x, is smaller, then the sorted list is x followed by the merge of the tail of L with all of M. Note that in this case, x is the smallest of all the elements, so x followed by the merge of the other elements will be the proper sorted list.

If instead, the head of M, say y, is at least as small as x, then the merge is y followed by the merge of L and the tail of M. Since y belongs at the head of the result, the complete list will be sorted.

```
(1) fun merge(nil,M) = M
(2)  |   merge(L,nil) = L
(3)  |   merge(L as x::xs, M as y::ys) =
(4)          if x<y then x::merge(xs,M)
(5)          else y::merge(L,ys);
```
   *val merge = fn : int list * int list → int list*

Figure 3.12: Merging two sorted lists

Figure 3.12 defines the function `merge`. Lines (1) and (2) cover the basis cases. Line (3) begins the inductive step. Here each list is nonempty, or the pattern match would have stopped at line (1) or line (2). When we assemble the result in lines (4) or (5), sometimes we want to use an entire list and sometimes only the tail. We also need to refer to the head of each list, to tell which is the smaller on line (4). Thus, in line (3) we express the first argument both as L and as `x::xs`. For instance, if we call `merge` with first argument [1,2,3], L gets the value [1,2,3], x gets the value 1, and `xs` gets the value [2,3]. Similarly, in line (3) we express the second argument both as M and as `y::ys`.

Then on line (4) we compare the heads. If the head of L is smaller, we assemble the output by taking the head of L and following it by the result of merging the tail of L, expressed by `xs`, with the entire list M. On line (5) we cover the case where the head of L is not smaller than the head of M. We assemble the result from the head of M — that is, y — followed by the merge of the entire list L and the tail of M. □

Incidentally, the as-construct in Fig. 3.12 is useful but not essential. We could have used `x::xs` in place of L and `y::ys` in place of M. Lines (3) through (5) of Fig. 3.12 would then look like:

```
|   merge(x::xs, y::ys) =
            if x<y then x::merge(xs,y::ys)
            else y::merge(x::xs,ys);
```

3.3.3 Anonymous Variables

The symbol _ can be used in patterns to stand for an *anonymous* or *wildcard* variable, which is a variable whose name we do not know and do not need to know. We can use _ more than once, but each occurrence refers to a distinct variable not equal to any other occurrence of _ .

```
fun comb(_,0) = 1
|   comb(n,m) =
            if m=n then 1
            else comb(n-1,m) + comb(n-1,m-1);
```
*val comb = fn : int * int → int*

Figure 3.13: A version of `comb` using patterns and an anonymous variable

Example 3.17: Figure 3.13 contains a version of `comb` that makes use of anonymous variables where it can. Like the original in Fig. 3.6, Fig. 3.13 suffers from the fact that if m does not lie between 0 and n, the behavior is wrong.

In Fig. 3.13, the first pattern uses an anonymous variable for the first argument. The first rule says that if the second argument is 0, then the value returned by `comb` is 1 regardless of the first argument. Since the first argument is not needed in the result, we do not have to give it a name, and hence the anonymous variable _ may be used.

In the second pattern, `comb(n,m)`, we need both n and m in the expression that defines the return value. Thus, we cannot use `comb(_,_)` as the second pattern. However, this pattern is legal, and matches exactly the same pairs as `comb(n,m)`. □

3.3.4 What Is and What Isn't a Pattern?

We have seen the following kinds of patterns so far:

1. Constants, for example `nil` or 0.

2. Expressions using the cons operator, such as `x::xs` or `x::y::zs`.

These can appear either as the sole argument of a function, or as one of several arguments of a function, with the tuple of arguments being the entire pattern.

Multiple Uses of a Variable in a Pattern is Illegal

We might be tempted to rewrite the function comb(n,m) of Fig. 3.13 making use of two patterns to handle the two basis cases where $m = 0$ and $m = n$. Our first attempt might be

```
fun comb(_,0) = 1
  | comb(n,n) = 1
  | comb(n,m) = comb(n-1,m) + comb(n-1,m-1);
```

Unfortunately, this code leads to the error message

Error: duplicate variable in pattern(s): n

telling us that we may not use a variable twice in one pattern as we did in pattern comb(n,n) on the second line above. We are forced to combine the last two lines into one pattern and a conditional expression, as we did in Fig. 3.13.

There are actually many other kinds of patterns. For example, instead of a variable as a head element in a pattern, we could have a tuple. We could also have a list as the head element, with this head element expressed in a form such as nil or x::xs. Patterns are discussed more fully in Section 5.1, and the formal definition of patterns is in Figs. 9.14 and 9.15.

Example 3.18: The following function sumPairs takes a list of pairs of integers as argument and sums the integers found in either component of the pairs.

```
fun sumPairs(nil) = 0
  | sumPairs((x,y)::zs) = x + y + sumPairs(zs);
val sumPairs = fn : (int * int) list → int
```

Notice that the type of the argument is (int * int) list, that is, a list of pairs of integers. The head element in the pattern on the second line is (x,y), so x acquires as value the first component of the head pair and y acquires the second component of the head pair. Also, zs in the pattern acquires the tail of the argument as its value. □

Example 3.19: Another similar function is sumLists shown in Fig. 3.14. It takes as argument a list whose elements are themselves lists of integers. The purpose is to sum the integers found among all the lists. Notice that ML finds the type of the argument to be int list list, that is, a list whose elements are of type int list. For example, the value of

```
    sumLists([[1,2], nil, [3,4,5], [6]])
```

is 21. Here, the argument is a list with four elements: the lists `[1,2]`, `nil`, `[3,4,5]`, and `[6]`.

```
(1) fun sumLists(nil) = 0
(2)  |   sumLists(nil::YS) = sumLists(YS)
(3)  |   sumLists((x::xs)::YS) = x + sumLists(xs::YS);
     val sumLists = fn : int list list → int
```

Figure 3.14: Summing the elements of a list of lists

Line (1) of Fig. 3.14 covers the case where the list of lists is empty and the sum is 0. Line (2) covers the case where there is a first element on the list, but that element is itself the empty list. In this case, we can dispense with the head and just sum the integers on the lists of the tail. Line (3) covers the case where there is at least one element on the list that is the head of the list of lists. We take `x`, which is the head of the head, and add to it the result of applying `sumLists` to the list in which the element `x` has been removed from the first list, but all other lists are the same. For instance, if the entire list is `[[1,2], [3,4]]`, then the recursive call's argument is `[[2], [3,4]]`. □

As we learn about constructors and the creation of our own datatypes in Section 6.2, we find there are many other ways to construct data structures besides lists (which are constructed by the cons operator `::`) and tuples (which are constructed by parentheses and commas). All datatypes make patterns of their own. However, there are some other patterns that make sense but are illegal in ML. For example, we might expect to be able to construct patterns using the concatenation operator `@` or arithmetic operators. The next example indicates what happens when we try to do so.

Example 3.20: We might expect to be able to break a list into the last element and the rest of the list. For instance, we might try to compute the length of a list by:[8]

```
    fun length(nil) = 0
     |   length(xs@[x]) = 1 + length(xs);
     Error: non-constructor applied to argument in pattern: @
     Error: unbound variable or constructor: xs
```

However, as we can see, the pattern `xs@[x]` is not legal and triggers two error messages. The first message complains that `@` is not a legal pattern constructor.

---

[8]ML does provide a built-in function **length** that gives the length of a list. It may be implemented by expressing a nonempty list as `x::xs` and returning `1+length(xs)`.

The second message is caused by the fact that, because the pattern is flawed, variable xs does not get bound to a value. Therefore, when we encounter it later, in the expression length(xs), ML has no value to use for xs.

Incidentally, we get a similar pair of error messages if we try to use an arithmetic operator to construct a pattern. For instance,

```
fun square(0) = 0
  | square(x+1) = 1 + 2*x + square(x);
```

is equally erroneous, even though it is based on a correct inductive definition of x^2. □

As a final example of a nonpattern, a real constant cannot appear in patterns. For instance, the following function definition

```
fun f(0.0) = 0
  | f(x) = x;
```

is regarded as syntactically incorrect because a real number is not permitted in a pattern.[9]

3.3.5   How ML Matches Patterns

A pattern, like any expression, can be represented by a tree. The outermost, or highest-level, operator is the root of the tree, and it has one child for each operand. The child for an operand is, in turn, the root of a subtree for that operand. The basis case, an expression or subexpression that is a single constant or variable, is represented by a node labeled by that constant or variable.

Example 3.21 : Consider the pattern expression

```
(x::y::zs, w)
```

This expression has as outermost operator the pair-forming operator, which we shall represent by (,). Its left operand is the subexpression x::y::zs, and the right operand is the subexpression w. The latter is represented by a single node labeled w. The former is grouped x::(y::zs) and is represented by a tree with root operator ::, left child x (a single node) and right child the root of a tree representing subexpression y::zs. The entire expression tree is shown in Fig. 3.15(a); for the moment, ignore the curved lines connecting it to Fig. 3.15(b).

Similarly, Fig. 3.15(b) represents the expression ([1,2,3,4], 5). The root operator is again the pairing operator (,), and the right child of the root represents constant 5. The left operand is the list [1,2,3,4]. We build lists as

---

[9]The reason for this seemingly strange restriction is that ML does not allow equality tests between reals; see Section 2.1.4. Without such a test it is impossible to tell whether a given real constant matches the real constant in a pattern.

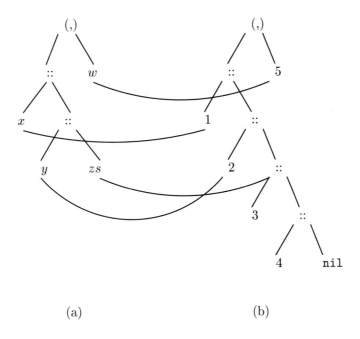

(a) (b)

Figure 3.15: Matching a pattern to an expression

expressions by using the cons operator. Note that the last tail must be nil, not the list consisting of the last element, so there are n uses of the cons operator in a list of length n. □

To match a pattern and an expression, we overlay the pattern's tree and the expression's tree, starting, as a basis step, by matching the roots. For the inductive step, if we have matched nodes N and M of the pattern and expression respectively, then the children of N and M must also be matched in order.

However, sometimes a match will be impossible, and the pattern-match fails. This situation occurs when we try to match a pattern node that is labeled by an operator or constant, and the matching node of the expression has a different label.

Example 3.22: If we try to match the pattern x::xs with the expression nil, we must match operator :: with constant nil at the respective roots, and we fail. If we try to match pattern x::y::zs with [1] (or as an expression: 1::nil), we match the roots with operators :: successfully. However, at the right children we must match the second :: from the pattern with nil from the expression, and thus we fail. □

If we successfully match the pattern with the expression, then any identifiers at the leaves of the pattern tree match nodes that represent subexpressions.

These subexpressions become the values associated with those identifiers.

Example 3.23: Consider again Fig. 3.15. The pattern in Fig. 3.15(a) successfully matches the expression in Fig. 3.15(b); the curved lines indicate the correspondence of the nodes. As a result, the node labeled x in the pattern corresponds to the node labeled 1 in the expression, so x acquires the value 1. The pattern node labeled y corresponds to expression node 2, and pattern node zs corresponds to the expression node representing expression 3::4::nil, or equivalently, the list [3,4]. Finally, the pattern node w corresponds to the expression node 5. □

3.3.6   A Subtle Pattern Bug

Often we wish to use an identifier with a special meaning like nil in our patterns. At this point we have few such special words. But beginning in Section 6.2 we shall see that words of this type, called "data constructors," can be created by the programmer and used in patterns. Such a misspelled word is usually a legal identifier and looks like a pattern that matches anything. SML/NJ treats completely redundant patterns as an error, but other ML compilers may issue only a warning and allow the function to be used.

```
(1) fun reverse(niil) = nil
(2)  | reverse(x::xs) = reverse(xs) @ [x];
(3) Error: match redundant
(4)          niil ⇒ ...
(5)    →    x :: xs ⇒ ...
```

Figure 3.16: The reverse function with a misspelling

Example 3.24: In Fig. 3.16 is the reverse function of Example 3.15, in which we have misspelled nil as niil on line (1). We see in lines (3) through (5) the SML/NJ response. The system has detected the pattern niil will match any argument, and therefore the pattern x::xs on line (2) can never be reached. The single arrow at the beginning of line (5) indicates which pattern is redundant. □

3.3.7   Exercises for Section 3.3

Exercise 3.3.1: Write the following functions from previous exercises, using two or more patterns in each.

* a) The factorial function of Exercise 3.2.1(a).

  b) The function from Exercise 3.1.1(f) that cycles a list one position. If the list is empty, return the empty list.

c) The function from Exercise 3.2.1(b) that cycles a list i times, where i, as well as the list, is a parameter.

* d) The function from Exercise 3.2.1(c) that duplicates each element of a list.

e) The function from Exercise 3.2.1(d) that computes x^i.

* f) The function of Exercise 3.2.1(e) that computes the largest of a list of reals.

! **Exercise 3.3.2:** Write a function that flips alternate elements of a list. That is, given a list $[a_1, a_2, \ldots, a_n]$ as argument, produce $[a_2, a_1, a_4, a_3, a_6, a_5, \ldots]$. If n is odd, a_n remains at the end.

! **Exercise 3.3.3:** Write a function that, given a list L and an integer i, returns a copy of L with the ith element deleted. If the length of L is less than i, return L.

Exercise 3.3.4: Show the sequence of calls to `sumLists` (as defined in Fig. 3.14) and the bindings to variables of patterns that occur when we call

```
sumLists([[1,2],nil,[3]])
```

Exercise 3.3.5: Does the pattern of Fig. 3.15(a) match the following expressions? If so, give the value bindings for each of the variables x, y, zs, and w.

* a) (["a","b","c"],["d","e"])

b) (["a","b"],4.5)

* c) ([5],[6,7])

Exercise 3.3.6: Draw trees as in Fig. 3.15 to show how the pattern

```
[(x,y),zs]
```

matches the expression [((1,2),3)].

* **Exercise 3.3.7:** There is a recursive definition of the square of a nonnegative integer: $0^2 = 0$ (basis), and $n^2 = (n - 1)^2 + 2n - 1$ (inductive step for $n > 0$). Write a recursive function that computes the square of its argument using this inductive formula.

* **Exercise 3.3.8:** Write a function that takes a list of pairs of integers, and orders the elements of each pair such that the smaller number is first. Use the as construct, so you can refer to the pair as a whole when it is not necessary to change it.

Exercise 3.3.9: Write a function that takes a list of characters and returns `true` if the first element is a vowel and `false` if not. Use the wildcard symbol `_` whenever possible in the patterns.

!! Exercise 3.3.10: The simple rule for translating into "Pig Latin" is to take a word that begins with a vowel and add `"yay"`, while taking any word that begins with one or more consonants and transferring them to the back before appending `"ay"`. For example, `"able"` becomes `"ableyay"` and `"stripe"` becomes `"ipestray"`. Write a function that converts a string of letters into its Pig-Latin translation. *Hint:* Use `explode` and the function from Exercise 3.3.9 that tests for vowels.

Exercise 3.3.11: Suppose we represent sets by lists. The members of the set may appear in any order on the list, but we assume that there is never more than one occurrence of the same element on this list. Write functions to perform the following operations on sets.

* a) `member(x,S)` returns true if element x is a member of set S; that is, x appears somewhere on the list representing S.

  b) `delete(x,S)` deletes x from S. Remember that you may assume that x appears at most once on the list for S.

* c) `insert(x,S)` puts x on the list for S if it is not already there. Remember that in order to preserve the condition that there are no repeating elements on a list that represents a set, we must check that x does not already appear in S; it is not adequate simply to make x the head of the list.

*! Exercise 3.3.12: Write a function that takes an element a and a list L of lists of elements of the same type as a and inserts a onto the front of each of the lists on the list L. For example, if $a = 1$ and L is `[[2,3],[4,5,6],nil]`, then the result is `[[1,2,3],[1,4,5,6],[1]]`.

*! Exercise 3.3.13: Suppose sets are represented by lists as in Exercise 3.3.12. The *power set* of a set S is the set of all subsets of S. A set of sets can be represented in ML by a list whose elements are lists. For example, if S is the set $\{1,2\}$, then the power set of S is $\{\emptyset, \{1\}, \{2\}, \{1,2\}\}$, where $\emptyset$ is the empty set. This power set can be represented in ML by the list of lists `[nil,[1],[2],[1,2]]`. That is, the elements of the lists are themselves lists, each representing one of the subsets of S. Write a function that takes a list as argument, representing some set S, and produces the power set of S. *Hint:* Recursively construct the power set for the tail of the list and use the function from Exercise 3.3.12 to help construct the power set for the whole list.

*! Exercise 3.3.14: Write a function that, given list of reals $[a_1, a_2, \ldots, a_n]$, computes

$$\prod_{i<j}(a_i - a_j)$$

That is, we compute the product of all differences between elements, with the element appearing later on the list subtracted from the element appearing first. If there are no pairs, the "product" is 1.0. *Hint*: Start by writing an auxiliary function that, given a and $[b_1, b_2, \ldots, b_n]$, computes $\prod_{i=1}^{n}(a - b_i)$.

* **Exercise 3.3.15:** Write a function to tell whether a list is empty. That is, return `true` if and only if the argument is an empty list.[10]

Exercise 3.3.16: Explain how ML deduces that the function `sumPairs` of Example 3.18 has domain type `(int * int) list`.

3.4 Local Environments Using `let`

Sometimes we need to create some temporary values — that is, local variables — inside a function. The proper way to do so is with a `let` $\cdots$ `in` $\cdots$ `end` expression. A simplified form of this expression, where only val-declarations are used, is shown in Fig. 3.17.

```
let
    val <first variable> = <first expression>;
    val <second variable> = <second expression>;
        ...
    val <last variable> = <last expression>
in
    <expression>
end
```

Figure 3.17: Simple form of the "let" construct

That is, following the keyword `let` is a list of one or more val-declarations, just like those introduced in Section 2.3.3. These are followed by the keyword `in`. Following `in` is an expression that may use the variables defined after `let`. This expression may also use any other variables accessible in the environment in which the function using `let` is defined, provided their identifiers are not redefined by the temporary declarations between `let` and `in`. The keyword `end` completes the expression. Here are a few important points to remember about `let` expressions:

- Semicolons following the declarations are optional. We shall adopt Pascal style and follow each but the last by a semicolon.

- Just as for val-declarations in the top-level environment, don't forget to use the keyword `val`.

---

[10]There is a built-in ML function `null` that does this task. We should not use this function in the solution.

- We must not omit the keywords in and end, which are as essential as the let.

- In truth, the let expression is more general than is suggested by Fig. 3.17, and any "declaration" can appear where we have shown val-declarations. So far, we have not seen any other kinds of declarations besides val-declarations and function declarations (with the keyword fun). However, there are several others; for example, we shall meet exception declarations in Section 5.2. The complete syntax for declarations is in Fig. 9.19.

- As another generalization, a pattern may appear in place of a single identifier in any val-declaration. Also, more than one expression may appear after the let, although the utility of an expression list will not become apparent until we study side-effects in Section 4.1.3.

3.4.1   Defining Common Subexpressions

One use of a let expression is to allow us to use common subexpressions. The following example illustrates the technique.

Example 3.25 : Suppose we want to compute the hundredth power of a number x. We could write the expression x*x* $\cdots$ *x(100 x's) if we had the patience, but it is less tedious and less prone to error if we write the function in Fig. 3.18.

```
fun hundredthPower(x:real) =
        let
            val four = x*x*x*x;
            val twenty = four*four*four*four*four
        in
            twenty*twenty*twenty*twenty*twenty
        end;
val hundredthPower = fn : real → real


hundredthPower(2.0);
val it = 1.2675060022823E30 : real


hundredthPower(1.01);
val it = 2.70481382942153 : real
```

Figure 3.18: Raising a number to the 100th power

In Fig. 3.18 we define two local variables, four and twenty (no jokes about blackbirds, please). We first define four to be x^4, and then define twenty to be four raised to the fifth power, or x^{20}. Finally, we use twenty in the final expression after the keyword in, which is twenty raised to the fifth power, or x^{100}.

We then see two uses of this function, first computing 2^{100}, which is about 10^{30}, and then computing $(1.01)^{100}$. The latter value is close to $e = 2.718\cdots$, as it must be because e is the limit as n goes to infinity of $(1 + 1/n)^n$.   □

3.4.2   Effect on Environments of let

When we enter a let expression, an addition to the current environment is created, adding value bindings for all the identifiers defined between the let and the in.

twenty	1048576.0
four	16.0
x	2.0

added for
let-expression

added on call
to hundredthPower

environment before call
to hundredthPower

Figure 3.19: Additions to environment when hundredthPower is called

Example 3.26 : In Fig. 3.19 we see the situation when the function of Fig. 3.18 is called. The first addition is for the function call; it is a binding for the parameter x. The next additions are for the let expression and include bindings for the local variables four and twenty. We have shown x bound to the value 2.0 in the call and the local variables bound to their consequent values. As always, when the function call returns, the additions to the environment disappear. However, the returned value is made available as the value of the function in the environment that results after the return.   □

Example 3.27 : We can rewrite Fig. 3.18 to use x not only as the argument of the function hundredthPower, but also as both local variables. The function then appears as in Fig. 3.20. It behaves exactly like the function of Fig. 3.18. However, the additional bindings in Fig. 3.21 each associate the variable x with a value.   □

```
fun hundredthPower(x:real) =
        let
            val x = x*x*x*x;
            val x = x*x*x*x*x
        in
            x*x*x*x*x
        end;
```
val hundredthPower = fn : real → real

Figure 3.20: Repeat of Fig. 3.18 with x used for all variables

x	1048576.0	added for second val-declaration
x	16.0	added for first val-declaration
x	2.0	added on call to hundredthPower
		environment before call to hundredthPower

Figure 3.21: Additions to environment corresponding to Fig. 3.20

3.4.3   Splitting Apart the Value Returned by a Function

Another important use of `let` expressions is when the result of a function has
components or parts that we want to separate before we use them. In particular,
when the type of the value returned by a function is a tuple, we can get at the
components by a more general form of val-declaration than we suggested was
possible in Fig. 3.17. Instead of a single identifier following the word `val`, we
can have any pattern. For instance, if a function f returns a three-component
tuple, we could write

```
val (a,b,c) = f(...
```

and have the three components of the result of f bound to variables a, b, and
c respectively. This approach is often more convenient than writing

```
val x = f(...
```

which associates the entire tuple with x, and then extracting the individual
components with #i operators in subsequent val-declarations such as

---

Patterns for Lists of Length 1

Note that the way we express "list of length 1" as a pattern is to put square brackets around a single identifier, like [a] in line (2) of Fig. 3.22. Such a pattern can only match a list with a single element, and variable a acquires that element as its value.

Another way to express "list of length 1" is with the pattern a::nil. Again, a acquires the lone element as its value.

```
val a = #1(x);
```

Example 3.28: Let us implement a function split(L) that takes a list L and splits it into two lists. One list consists of the first element, third element, fifth element, and so on; the other list consists of the second element, fourth element, sixth element, and so on. This function has an important application. In tandem with the function merge of Fig. 3.12, it lets us write a function mergeSort that is an efficient sorter of lists. We shall cover mergeSort next, in Section 3.4.4.

We want the function split to produce a pair of lists. The recursion consists of two basis parts and an inductive part.

BASIS: If L is empty, then produce a pair of empty lists. If L has a single element, the first list of the pair produced has that element and the second list is empty.

INDUCTION: If the given list has two or more elements, let the first two elements be a and b. Recursively split the remaining elements into a pair of lists (M, N). The desired result is the pair of lists $(a :: M, \, b :: N)$. That is, the first list has head a and tail equal to the first of the returned lists, and the second has head b and tail equal to the second of the returned lists.

An ML implementation of split is shown in Fig. 3.22. Line (1) implements the first part of the basis: return a pair of empty lists in response to the empty list. Line (2) implements the second part of the basis, where the given list has length 1.

Lines (3) through (5) handle the inductive case. The pattern a::b::cs in line (3) can only match a list with at least two elements; a acquires the first element as value, b acquires the second, and cs acquires the list of the third and subsequent elements as its value. In line (4), we apply split recursively to the third and subsequent elements; the result is bound to the pair (M,N). That is, M is bound to the first component of the result, which is the elements in positions 3, 5, 7, and so on of the original list. N acquires the second component of the return value, which is the elements in positions 4, 6, 8, and so on from the original list.

```
(1) fun split(nil) = (nil,nil)
(2)  |   split([a]) = ([a],nil)
(3)  |   split(a::b::cs) =
             let
(4)               val (M,N) = split(cs)
             in
(5)               (a::M, b::N)
             end;
```

val split = fn: 'a list → 'a list * 'a list

```
split([1,2,3,4,5]);
```

val it = ([1,3,5],[2,4]) : int list * int list

Figure 3.22: Splitting lists

Finally, in line (5) we construct the return value for the present call to split. The first component has head a — that is, the first element of the given list — followed by M, the list of all the other odd-position components. Thus, the first component is the odd-position elements in order. Similarly, the second component b::N is all the even-position elements.   □

3.4.4   Mergesort: An Efficient, Recursive Sorter

We can combine the functions merge of Fig. 3.12 with split of Fig. 3.22 to sort lists of integers. This algorithm is one of the simplest ways to sort n elements in time proportional to $n \log n$ steps. We shall not develop the analysis of this algorithm here, but we shall complete the specification of the algorithm in ML. The idea behind the mergesort algorithm is expressed in the following induction.

BASIS: If the given list L is empty or consists of a single element, then L is surely sorted already, so just return L.

INDUCTION: If L has at least two elements, split L to produce the (approximately) half-size lists M and N. Recursively mergesort M and N. Then merge the sorted lists M and N to produce the sorted version of L.

The function mergeSort is shown in Fig. 3.23. It must be preceded by the functions merge and split to form the complete implementation of the mergesort algorithm. Incidentally, ML discovers that mergeSort works only on integer lists because it uses merge, which we wrote to work only for integer lists.

Lines (1) and (2) implement the basis; the remaining lines are for the inductive step. Line (4) splits the given list. Lines (5) and (6) sort the half-sized lists, and the result is produced by merging the sorted lists in line (7). Incidentally,

```
(1) fun mergeSort(nil) = nil
(2)  |   mergeSort([a]) = [a]
(3)  |   mergeSort(L) =
             let
(4)               val (M,N) = split(L);
(5)               val M = mergeSort(M);
(6)               val N = mergeSort(N)
             in
(7)               merge(M,N)
             end;
```
val mergeSort = fn : int list → int list

Figure 3.23: Mergesort

we could also have combined some steps by eliminating lines (5) and (6) and replacing line (7) by merge(mergeSort(N),mergeSort(M)).

3.4.5   Exercises for Section 3.4

* **Exercise 3.4.1:** Write a succinct function to compute x^{1000}.

Exercise 3.4.2: Rewrite Fig. 3.22 so line (4) does not use a pattern in the val-declaration. That is, replace line (4) by val x = split(cs), and obtain the components of pair x as needed.

* **Exercise 3.4.3:** Improve upon the power-set function of Exercise 3.3.13 by using a let expression and computing the power set of the tail only once.

Exercise 3.4.4: Improve upon the function of Exercise 3.2.1(e), to compute the maximum of a list of reals, by using a let expression. *Hint*: Compute the maximum of the tail of the list first.

*! **Exercise 3.4.5:** Write a function to compute x^{2^i} for real x and nonnegative integer i. You should make only one recursive call in your function. *Hint*: Note that we can start with x and apply the squaring operation i times. For example, when $i = 3$, we compute $((x^2)^2)^2$.

Exercise 3.4.6: Write a version of sumPairs of Example 3.18 that sums each component of the pairs separately, returning a pair consisting of the sum of the first components and the sum of the second components.

Exercise 3.4.7: Write a function that takes a list of integers as argument and returns a pair consisting of the sum of the even positions and the sum of the odd positions of the list. You should not use any auxiliary functions.

3.5   Case Study: Linear-Time Reverse

We have seen two versions of a function to reverse lists: first in Fig. 3.3 and
then in Example 3.15. These functions each seem simple enough, but they
suffer from a common flaw that they take time proportional to n^2 to reverse
lists of length n. In comparison, a well-designed reverse function, such as the
function `rev` in the ML top-level environment, can reverse lists of length n in
time proportional to n. In this section, we shall see how to write a list-reverse
function that is efficient and learn a general technique for programming with
lists as we do.

3.5.1   Analysis of Simple Reverse

Let us begin by understanding why a function like that of Example 3.15 takes
time proportional to n^2. The function is reproduced here for reference:

```
fun reverse(nil) = nil
  | reverse(x::xs) = reverse(xs) @ [x];
```

Suppose $T(n)$ is the time it takes `reverse` to work on a list of length n. We
can develop a *recurrence* relation, where $T(n)$ is defined in terms of $T(n-1)$
and then "solve" the equation for $T(n)$, to get an expression for $T(n)$ in terms
of n alone (not T).

BASIS: The basis case is when $n = 0$; that is, the list is empty. In this case the
first pattern, `nil`, matches, and `nil` is returned. The whole process takes only
some constant amount of time, so we shall say $T(0) = a$ for some constant a.

INDUCTION: Suppose $n \geq 1$. There are a number of steps that the program
will go through to process a list of length $n \geq 1$:

1. The first pattern doesn't match, and it takes some constant amount of
   time for the ML system to determine that `nil` doesn't match the argument.

2. It takes another constant amount of time to match the pattern `x::xs` and
   assign the head of the list to `x` and the tail to `xs`.

3. It takes time $T(n-1)$ to compute the value of `reverse(xs)`. The reason
   is that `xs` is surely a list of length $n-1$ if `x::xs` is of length n.

4. To compute the return value `reverse(xs) @ [x]` requires that we copy
   the list `reverse(xs)` and append the final element `x` as we do. This
   process takes time proportional to n, the length of the resulting list.

The constant time taken by the first two steps is dominated by the linear
time taken by the last step. Thus, $T(n)$ is approximately $T(n-1) + bn$ for
some constant b; the $T(n-1)$ represents the time for the recursive call and bn
represents the time for the other steps. The recurrence equation is thus:

$$T(0) = a$$
$$T(n) = T(n-1) + bn \text{ for } n = 1, 2, \ldots$$

There are several ways to solve this equation. Perhaps the simplest to to check that $T(n) = a + bn(n+1)/2$ satisfies the equations and is therefore the solution. Since $a + bn(n+1)/2$ is proportional to n^2 as n gets large, we see the justification for our claim that **reverse** takes time proportional to n^2 on lists of length n.

A more intuitive argument is to observe that on a list of length n, **reverse** gets called recursively on lists of length $n-1$, $n-2$, and so on, down to 0. Each call on a list of length i results in work bi for some constant b, except the call on a list of length 0, which results in work a. The total work is thus

$$a + \sum_{i=1}^{n} bi = a + bn(n+1)/2$$

which, as we observed, is proportional to n^2.

3.5.2   ML's Representation of Lists

A better function for reversing lists can be designed if we use the cons operator, `::`, instead of the concatenation operator `@`. It may not be obvious, but while it takes time proportional to the length of the first list to concatenate lists, we can cons a head and a tail in constant time. Thus, before giving the proper design for **reverse**, we must understand something of how ML represents lists internally.

Lists are represented in a conventional, linked list fashion, as suggested by Fig. 3.24. Cells consist of a pair of pointers, the first to an element of the list and the second to the next cell. If a list is bound to a variable L, then in the ML environment there is an entry in which the identifier L is associated with a pointer to the first cell of the list.

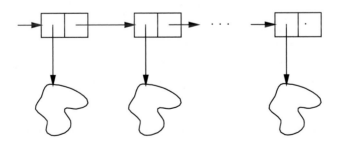

Figure 3.24: Representing a linked list

Suppose we wish to construct the list `x::xs` given values of head `x` and tail `xs`. We have only to create a new cell C. The first pointer of C points to the head of the list, that is, to the value of `x`, and the second pointer in C points to the value of xs. In this way, C becomes the first cell on the linked list that represents the value of x::xs. The process is suggested by Fig. 3.25. Notice that creating cell C and setting its pointers to refer to the values of x and xs takes a constant amount of time, independent of how big the value of x or xs is. There is no need for ML to "look inside" the values of the head or tail. Similarly, we can invert this process. In constant time we can find the head and tail of a list. No copying is necessary.

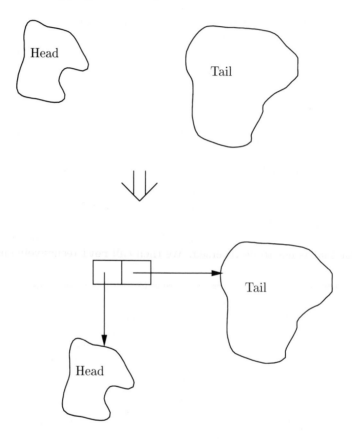

Figure 3.25: Applying the cons operator

3.5.3   A Reversal Function Using Difference Lists

There is a trick known to LISP programmers as *difference lists,* in which one manipulates lists more efficiently by keeping, as an extra parameter of your function, a list that represents in some way what you have already accomplished. The idea comes up in a number of different applications; we hope that seeing it used to reverse lists will illustrate the technique sufficiently that its use will be apparent when you need it.

We design an auxiliary function `rev1(L,M)` whose job is to return $L^R M$, that is, the reverse of list L followed by the list M (not reversed). Note that we use the superscript R as a convenient way to indicate the reverse of a list. If we wish to reverse list L, we have only to call `rev1(L,nil)`. The result is L^R concatenated with the empty list, which is just L^R.

```
(1) fun rev1(nil, M) = M
(2)  |   rev1(x::xs, ys) = rev1(xs, x::ys);
    val rev1 = fn : 'a list * 'a list → 'a list


    fun reverse(L) = rev1(L,nil);
    val reverse = fn : 'a list → 'a list
```

Figure 3.26: List reversal using difference lists

Figure 3.26 shows the function `rev1` and its use to define a linear-time list-reversal function. Line (1) of `rev1` handles the basis case, when there is nothing left to reverse. Then, the result is just a copy of the second argument.

Line (2) handles the inductive case, where we need to reverse a list of one or more elements. We move the head of the list we need to reverse to the beginning of the list that is not to be reversed. We then call `rev1` recursively on the new pair of lists. Eventually, all the elements of the first list are moved to the front of the second list, in reverse order. At that point, the basis case applies and the recursion ends.

To see why the technique works, suppose we call

$$\text{rev1}([a_1, a_2, \ldots, a_n], \ [b_1, b_2, \ldots, b_m])$$

Then the desired output is the list $[a_n, a_{n-1}, \ldots, a_1, b_1, b_2, \ldots, b_m]$. When we move the head of the first list to the second, we call

$$\text{rev1}([a_2, a_3, \ldots, a_n], \ [a_1, b_1, b_2, \ldots, b_m])$$

The result of this call is $[a_n, a_{n-1}, \ldots, a_2]$ followed by the element a_1, followed by $[b_1, b_2, \ldots, b_m]$, which is the result desired for the original call to `rev1`.

Example 3.29: Here is the sequence of calls that results when we try to reverse the list `[1,2,3]`:

```
reverse([1,2,3])
rev1([1,2,3], nil)
rev1([2,3], [1])
rev1([3], [2,1])
rev1(nil, [3,2,1])
```

At this point, the basis applies, and the result `[3,2,1]` is produced. □

3.5.4   Analysis of Fast Reverse

We can argue that the reversal program of Fig. 3.26 takes time proportional to
the length of the list, as follows.

1. Function `rev1` calls itself with a first argument that is shorter by 1 than
   its parameter, so with a first argument of length n, `rev1` makes n recursive
   calls.

2. Each recursive call to `rev1` takes a constant amount of time to break apart
   a head and tail and then cons a head and tail, until we get to the basis
   case at line (1) of Fig. 3.26. The basis case also takes constant time.

3. Thus, `rev1` takes time proportional to the length of its first argument.

4. The time taken by `reverse` on a list of length n is essentially the time
   taken by `rev1` when given a first argument of length n. Thus, `reverse`
   takes time proportional to the length of the list it is to reverse.

3.5.5   Exercises for Section 3.5

*! Exercise 3.5.1: Write a function `cat(L,M)` that produces the concatenation
`L@M` of the lists L and M. However, your function should not use the `@` operator;
only the cons operator `::` should be used. Your function must run in time
proportional to the length of L, independent of M.

!! Exercise 3.5.2: Write a function `cycle(L,i)` that cycles list L by i positions,
as in Exercise 3.2.1(b). However, your function must take time proportional to
the length of L (which we assume is at least i). *Hint:* You need to break this
function into a sequence of steps performed by auxiliary functions.

3.6   Case Study: Polynomial Multiplication

In this section we shall show one useful way to represent polynomials in a single
variable. We shall consider ways to perform polynomial multiplication, which is
also the important signal-processing operation known as convolution. We begin
with some simple functions that get the job done, but take time proportional to
n^2 to multiply polynomials of length n. Then, we exhibit a more complicated
algorithm that multiplies polynomials in time proportional to $n^{1.59}$. We do not
show the algorithm that is asymptotically most efficient — the "Fast Fourier
Transform" approach. That algorithm takes time proportional to $n \log n$.[11]

---

[11] See Aho, Hopcroft, and Ullman, *Design and Analysis of Computer Algorithms*, Addison-
Wesley, 1974, for a discussion of efficient polynomial multiplication, including both the FFT
and the Karatsuba-Ofman approach discussed in Section 3.6.5.

3.6.1   Representing Polynomials by Lists

We shall use lists of reals to represent polynomials by their coefficients, lowest degree first. For instance, the polynomial $x^3 + 4x - 5$ is represented by the list [~5.0, 4.0, 0.0, 1.0]. In general, the polynomial $\sum_{i=0}^{n} a_i x^i$ is represented by the list of $n + 1$ elements $[a_0, a_1, \ldots, a_n]$. Conventionally, we shall take the empty list to represent the polynomial 0, but this polynomial also has other representations such as [0.0] and [0.0, 0.0].

An important observation is that if L is a list representing polynomial P, and L is of the form $a :: M$ (that is, L has head a and tail M), and the tail represents polynomial Q, then $P = a + Qx$. That is, multiplication by x in effect shifts the elements of the corresponding list one position right. For instance, if

$$P = x^3 + 4x - 5$$

then we observed that the representing list is [~5.0, 4.0, 0.0, 1.0]. Thus, a is ~5.0 and M is [4.0, 0.0, 1.0]. M represents the polynomial $Q = x^2 + 4$. Note that $P = a + Qx$, that is, $P = -5 + (x^2 + 4)x$.

3.6.2   A Simple Polynomial-Multiplication Algorithm

In Fig. 3.27 we see three functions that perform common operations on polynomials in this representation. The first, padd(P,Q), adds polynomials P and Q. We recursively define the sum of two lists P and Q that represent polynomials by:

BASIS: If either P or Q is the empty list, then the sum is the other. Note that if both are empty, the result is the polynomial 0 represented by the empty list.

INDUCTION: For the induction, assume that neither list is empty. Suppose P has head p and a tail representing polynomial R, while Q has head q and a tail representing polynomial S. Then the sum $P + Q$ is the list with head element $p + q$ and tail equal to the result of applying padd to the two tails. The correctness of this rule is seen as follows. If $P = p + Rx$ and $Q = q + Sx$, then

$$P + Q = (p + q) + (R + S)x$$

In line (1) of Fig. 3.27 we see one part of the basis. Whenever the second polynomial is the empty list, the result is the first polynomial. Line (2) handles the other part of the basis. If the first polynomial is empty, the result is the second.

If neither of the first two patterns match the arguments, then it must be that both polynomials are nonempty lists. Thus, in line (3) the pattern p::ps is sure to match the first argument, and q::qs will surely match the second argument. Notice we have attached type **real** to the variable p of this pattern. That is enough for ML to figure out the type of all variables and to disambiguate the use of + in line (3).

As a result of the match, p acquires the value of the first element of the first polynomial, and q acquires the value of the first element of the second polynomial. Their sum becomes the first element of the result, and padd is applied to the tails to get the tail of the result.

```
       (* padd(P,Q) produces the polynomial sum P+Q *)

(1)  fun padd(P,nil) = P
(2)    |   padd(nil,Q) = Q
(3)    |   padd((p:real)::ps, q::qs) = (p+q)::padd(ps,qs);


       (* smult(P,q) multiplies polynomial P by scalar q *)

(4)  fun smult(nil,q) = nil
(5)    |   smult((p:real)::ps,q) = (p*q)::smult(ps,q);


       (* pmult(P,Q) produces PQ *)
(6)  fun pmult(P,nil) = nil
(7)    |   pmult(P,q::qs) = padd(smult(P,q), 0.0::pmult(P,qs));
```

Figure 3.27: Polynomial addition and multiplication

In lines (4) and (5) of Fig. 3.27 we see the function smult that multiplies a polynomial P by a scalar q. That is, each term in the polynomial is multiplied by q. The recursive definition of this operation is:

BASIS: If P is empty, then the product is the empty list representing 0.

INDUCTION: If P has head p, then the head of the result is pq. The tail of the result is found by recursively applying smult to the tail of P and the scalar q.

Line (4) handles the basis and line (5) handles the inductive step. The justification for this algorithm is that if $P = p + Rx$, then $Pq = pq + Rqx$.

Now let us consider the function pmult of lines (6) and (7) of Fig. 3.27. This function multiplies polynomials P and Q using a recursion on the length of the second polynomial.

BASIS: If the second polynomial is empty, then the result is empty.

INDUCTION: If the second polynomial Q can be written as $q + Sx$, then

$$PQ = Pq + PSx$$

The product Pq is a scalar multiplication. PS is a recursive application of the polynomial multiplication with a smaller second argument.

The basis is implemented by line (6). In line (7) we see the inductive step; `smult(P,q)` produces Pq, while `pmult(P,qs)` produces the polynomial product we called PS in the inductive formula above. To multiply this product by x, we "shift" the terms right by inserting an element 0 in front of the list that represents PS. That shift is the purpose of the subexpression `0.0::pmult(P,qs)`. Finally, we use `padd` to add the lists representing Pq and PSx.

3.6.3   Analysis of Simple Multiplication

Let us analyze the running time of each of the three functions in Fig. 3.27.

Analysis of `padd`

First, we claim that the function `padd` takes time proportional to the shorter of its two arguments. To see why, observe that both arguments decrease in length by 1 at each recursive call on line (3) of Fig. 3.27. When either argument reaches length 0, line (1) or (2) will stop the recursion. Thus, the number of recursive calls equals the length of the shorter argument.

However, the work done at each call, exclusive of the recursive call, takes only a constant amount of time independent of the lengths of the lists. As we discussed in Section 3.5.2, each of the pattern-matching steps is done without looking past the first cons operator, and building the result in line (3) by applying the cons operator likewise takes a constant amount of time. Finally, the addition $p + q$ at line (3) also takes constant time independent of the list lengths.

Our conclusion is that `padd` takes time that is a constant per call times the number of calls, which is the length of the shorter list. That is, the time for `padd` is proportional to the length of the shorter list.

Analysis of `smult`

The number of recursive calls is equal to the length of the list in the first argument, because the length decreases by one at each call, and when the length reaches 0, the first pattern, in line (4), matches and the recursion stops. As for `padd`, it is easy to see that the only steps performed at each call, other than the recursive call, are constant-time operations of matching a cons operator or `nil`, applying a cons operator, and an arithmetic step, multiplying two integers. The running time of `smult` is thus proportional to the length of its first argument — the polynomial being scalar-multiplied.

Analysis of `pmult`

Suppose we execute `pmult(P,Q)`, where P and Q are polynomials (lists) of length n and m, respectively. Since the recursion is on the second argument, whose length decreases by 1 at each call, the number of recursive calls is m. We must calculate the work done at each call, exclusive of the recursive call.

1. The pattern matching at lines (6) and (7) takes constant time.

2. The call to smult at line (7) takes time proportional to n.

3. The cons with head 0.0 at line (7) takes constant time.

4. The application of padd at line (7) takes time proportional to its shorter argument. The first argument is always of length n (it is a scalar multiplication of polynomial P), while the second argument is never shorter than n. Thus, the application of padd takes time proportional to n.

The calls to smult and padd dominate the work, which is thus proportional to n at each call. Since there are m recursive calls to pmult, the total work is nm for polynomials of length n and m, respectively, or n^2 if the polynomials are of the same length n.

3.6.4   Auxiliary Functions for a Faster Multiplication

It turns out that polynomial multiplication of length-n polynomials does not have to take time proportional to n^2. If we use the "fast Fourier transform," we can actually do the job in time proportional to $n \log n$. We shall not give this algorithm here. Rather, we shall show an intermediate approach that takes time proportional to $n^{1.59}$ (the constant 1.59 approximates $\log_2 3$) called the Karatsuba-Ofman algorithm. To begin, there are a number of auxiliary functions that we shall need. We show them first and analyze their running times. The functions are shown in Fig. 3.28.

The Function psub

The purpose of psub(P,Q) is to compute $P - Q$ for polynomials P and Q. It does so by negating Q, i.e., scalar-multiplying it by -1, and then adding. The running time of this function is no greater than the length of the longer polynomial, since the call to smult takes time proportional to the length of Q and the call to padd takes time proportional to the shorter length.

The Function length

This function, taking the length of a list, is actually a built-in function of ML. However, we write it here so we can confirm its running time. Notice that the number of recursive calls equals the length of the list to which it is applied, and the work done at each call is a constant, independent of the list. Thus, length requires time proportional to the length of its argument.

The Function bestSplit

This function serves a technical purpose that will become clear when we see how the Karatsuba-Ofman algorithm works. The arguments n and m are the

```
(* psub(P,Q) computes the difference of polynomials P-Q *)

fun psub(P,Q) = padd(P,smult(Q,~1.0));


(* length(P) computes length (degree+1) of polynomial P *)

fun length(nil) = 0
|   length(p::ps) = 1+length(ps);


(* bestSplit(n,m) computes an appropriate size for the
   low-order "half" of polynomials of length n and m.
   It is the smaller of n and m should one be less than
   half the other.  If they are approximately the
   same size, then it is half the larger. *)

fun bestSplit(n,m) =
        if 2*n <= m then n
        else if 2*m <= n then m
        else if n <= m then m div 2
        else (* n/2 < m < n *) n div 2;


(* shift(P,n) computes P times x^n, for polynomial P(x) *)

fun shift(P,0) = P
|   shift(P,n) = 0.0::shift(P,n-1);


(* carve(P,n) returns a pair of polynomials.  The first is
   the low-order n terms of P and the second is what remains
   of P, divided by x^n *)

fun carve(P,0) = (nil,P)
|   carve(p::ps,n) =
        let
            val (qs,rs) = carve(ps, n-1)
        in
            (p::qs, rs)
        end;
```

Figure 3.28: Auxiliary functions used for Karatsuba-Ofman multiplication

lengths of two lists, and our goal is to find a length that is approximately half the lengths of the lists. What `bestSplit` actually does is take the smaller of n and m in cases where these two lengths are not similar — one is at least twice the other. If the two numbers are within a factor of 2 of each other, then it takes half the larger. Since `bestSplit` is not recursive, its running time is seen to be some constant.

The Function `shift`

The purpose of `shift(P,n)` is to put n 0's in front of polynomial P. The effect of this operation is to multiply $P(x)$ by x^n. The running time of `shift` is easy to analyze. There are n recursive calls, and each call takes a constant time, exclusive of the recursive call. Thus, the total time is proportional to n.

The Function `carve`

The purpose of `carve(P,n)` is to break polynomial P into two polynomials Q and R, such that Q is the n low-order terms of P and R is the remainder, divided by x^n. That is, as polynomials, $P = Q + x^n R$. As lists, the process is straightforward: the first n elements of the list representing P become the representation of Q, and the remaining elements represent R.

The operation of `carve` is a simple induction on n. For the basis, when $n = 0$, Q is empty and R is P. For the induction, we set aside the first element of P, call `carve` recursively to take $n - 1$ elements from the front of P, and then put the first element of P at the head of the list formed for Q. A `let` expression allows us to receive a pair of lists from the recursive call and to manipulate them to form the answer.

To analyze the running time of `carve`, observe that the number of recursive calls is n, the value of the second argument. The work at each call is constant, exclusive of the time spent in the recursive call. Thus, the total time is proportional to n.

3.6.5   The Karatsuba-Ofman Algorithm

Another approach to multiplying polynomials is to think of each polynomial as two half-sized polynomials. Figure 3.29 shows two polynomials P and Q, broken into their s low-order terms and a remainder. That is, we can write:

$$P = T + x^s U$$
$$Q = V + x^s W$$

If we use these formulas in the product PQ we get

$$PQ = TV + x^s(TW + UV) + x^{2s}UW \qquad (3.1)$$

On the assumption that the high-order pieces U and W are themselves no larger than s, we have broken the multiplication PQ into four half-sized multiplications TV, TW, UV, and UW, plus some shifts and additions. By the analysis

---

Incomplete Matching in Function `carve`

When we compile `carve`, we get a warning:

Warning: match nonexhaustive
(P,(0 : int)) ⇒ ...
(p :: ps,n) ⇒ ...

The compiler has correctly pointed out that we have made an assumption about the relationship between the arguments P and n of `carve(P,n)`: n will never be greater than the length of P. Thus, the first pattern looks for $n = 0$, and the second pattern assumes that if $n > 0$, then P must not be `nil`. If we were to call `carve(nil,n)`, where $n > 0$, then neither pattern would match and the function would fail. Fortunately, when we use `carve` in the Karatsuba-Ofman algorithm, our assumptions are certain to be met. However:

- It is generally a bad practice to write functions whose patterns do not cover all possible cases, even cases for which the function was not intended.

---

of Section 3.6.3, the shifts and additions take time that is linear in the size of the polynomials. That is, we can write a recurrence equation for $T(n)$ the time it takes to multiply polynomials of length n using Formula 3.1 directly:

$T(1) = a$
$T(n) = 4T(n/2) + bn$

The solution to this equation is

$T(n) = (a + b)n^2 - bn$

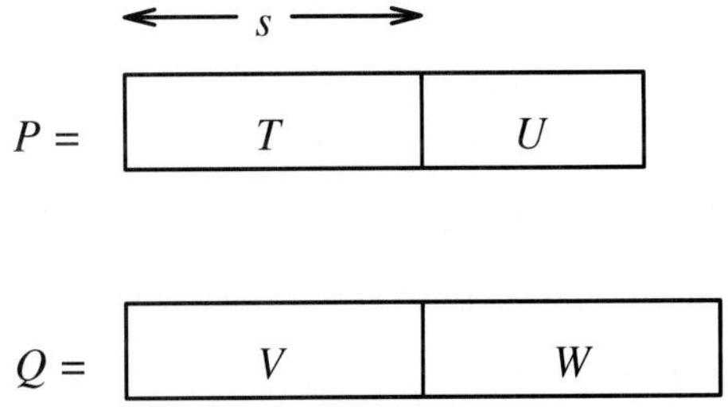

Figure 3.29: Breaking polynomials into half-sized pieces

That is, $T(n)$ is proportional to n^2, exactly as for the straightforward polynomial multiplication method.

To design a faster algorithm, we need to reduce the number of times we multiply half-sized polynomials. We can do so even at the expense of an increased number of operations that take time linear in the size of the polynomials, such as adding or subtracting polynomials, "shifting" (multiplying by a power of x), or "carving" polynomials into two.

We can reduce the number of half-sized multiplications to three if we compute TV and UW as in Formula 3.1, but write the middle term as:

$$TW + UV = (T + U)(V + W) - TV - UW \qquad (3.2)$$

Since TV and UW are already computed, Formula 3.2 uses only one additional half-sized multiplication, $(T+U)$ times $(V+W)$, rather than the two additional multiplications needed if we computed $TW + UV$ directly. Notice that the fact Formula 3.2 uses two additions and two subtractions in place of a single addition is not a real problem. Intuitively, multiplication takes time that grows faster than linear in n, so the cost of the multiplications swamps out the cost of the additions for large n.

```
      (* komult(P,Q) computes the product of polynomials PQ using
         the Karatsuba-Ofman method that only calls itself three
         times rather than four on half-sized polynomials. *)

 (1) fun komult(P,nil) = nil
 (2)  |   komult(nil,Q) = nil
 (3)  |   komult(P,[q]) = smult(P,q)
 (4)  |   komult([p],Q) = smult(Q,p)
 (5)  |   komult(P,Q) =
              let
 (6)              val n = length(P);
 (7)              val m = length(Q);
 (8)              val s = bestSplit(n,m);
 (9)              val (T,U) = carve(P,s);
(10)              val (V,W) = carve(Q,s);
(11)              val TV = komult(T,V);
(12)              val UW = komult(U,W);
(13)              val TUVW = komult(padd(T,U), padd(V,W));
(14)              val middle = psub(psub(TUVW,TV), UW);
              in
(15)              padd(padd(TV,shift(middle,s)), shift(UW,2*s))
              end;
```

Figure 3.30: The Karatsuba-Ofman multiplication algorithm

Figure 3.30 implements this idea in a recursive ML function. Lines (1) and (2) handle the basis cases where one of the polynomials is the empty list. In these cases, the empty list is returned. Lines (3) and (4) handle additional bases cases where one of the polynomials is of length 1. Such a polynomial is a constant, so we can use the linear-time scalar multiplication algorithm to handles these cases.

Line (5) begins the inductive case. We use each of the auxiliary functions from Fig. 3.28 at least once in a sequence of val-declarations. Lines (6) and (7) compute the lengths of the two polynomials, and line (8) picks the value of s using the `bestSplit` function. The role of s, the length of the low-order pieces T and V, was illustrated in Fig. 3.29.

Then, lines (9) and (10) divide the two polynomials into low-order and high-order pieces, as suggested by Fig. 3.29. Line (11) computes the first half-sized product, TW, and line (12) computes the second: UW. Lines (13) and (14) implement the expression of Formula 3.2. That is, line (13) computes $(T + U)(V + W)$, and line (14) subtracts from this expression the terms TV and UW.

Finally, the result of the function is computed in line (15). This expression implements Formula 3.1. However, the middle term, $TV + UW$, has been computed by Formula 3.2, rather than directly.

3.6.6 Analysis of the Karatsuba-Ofman Algorithm

We can show that the dominant cost of the algorithm of Fig. 3.30 is the three half-sized multiplications. Let $T(n)$ be the running time of this function on two polynomials of length n. For the basis, where $n = 1$, one of the basis cases of lines (3) or (4) applies. The running time is thus some constant, say $T(1) = a$.

For the induction, let $n > 1$. Then the inductive case starting at line (5) applies. The following is a list of the running times for each of steps (6) through (15):

6: Proportional to n.

7: Proportional to n.

8: Constant.

9: Proportional to n.

10: Proportional to n.

11: $T(n/2)$.

12: $T(n/2)$.

13: A term proportional to n for the calls to `padd` plus $T(n/2)$ for the call to `komult`.

14: Proportional to n.

15: Proportional to n.

The sum of the times is thus $3T(n/2)$ plus a term that is proportional to n. We may write the recurrence equation as:

$$T(1) = a$$
$$T(n) = 3T(n/2) + bn$$

The solution to this equation is

$$T(n) = (a + 2b)n^{\log_2 3} - 2bn$$

as you may check by substitution in both equations. Thus, the running time of the Karatsuba-Ofman algorithm is proportional to $n^{\log_2 3}$, or $n^{1.59}$, significantly less than the n^2 of more straightforward algorithms.

3.6.7   Exercises for Section 3.6

Exercise 3.6.1 : Write a function `genPoly(n)` that generates a polynomial of length n (degree $n - 1$), all of whose coefficients are 1.0. Measure the running time of the straightforward algorithm `pmult` of Fig. 3.27 and the algorithm of Fig. 3.30 with its attendant auxiliaries from Figs. 3.27 and 3.28. The code can be downloaded from the book's web site. Consider polynomials of length n ranging from 1 to about 1000, generated by `genPoly`. For what value of n does the running time of `komult` drop below the running time of `pmult`?

! Exercise 3.6.2 : One problem with `komult` is that for small n it wastes time, compared with the straightforward approach to polynomial multiplication. Rewrite `komult` so it calls `pmult` to multiply polynomials whose length is below some limit. Experiment with running times as in Exercise 3.6.1 to find the limit below which it makes sense to use `pmult`, and adjust your function accordingly.

! Exercise 3.6.3 : Write a function to evaluate a polynomial at a given real value a. That is, define a function `eval(P,a)` that takes a list (polynomial) P and a real number a, and computes $P(a)$.

*! Exercise 3.6.4 : Given a list of reals $[a_1, a_2, \ldots, a_n]$, find the polynomial whose roots are $a_1, a_2, \ldots, a_n$. *Hint*: Note that this polynomial is the product of $(x - a_i)$ for $i = 1, 2, \ldots, n$.

!! Exercise 3.6.5 : We can represent polynomials in two variables, x and y, by a list of lists. Think of such a polynomial as a polynomial in x, whose coefficients, instead of being real numbers, are polynomials in y. Represent these polynomials in y by lists as we did in Section 3.6.1. Then use the lists representing these polynomials as the elements of a list representing the polynomial in x. For example, the polynomial $1 + 2xy + 3xy^2 + 4x^3y$ can we written as $1 + (2y + 3y^2)x + (4y)x^3$. The polynomial $2y + 3y^2$ is represented by the list [0.0, 2.0, 3.0] and the polynomial $4y$ is represented by [0.0, 4.0]. Thus, the polynomial in x can be written

```
[[1.0], [0.0,2.0,3.0], [], [0.0,4.0]]
```

Write functions to add polynomials in two variables, scalar-multiply such polynomials, and polynomial-multiply these polynomials. You need not use a "Karatsuba-Ofman" type trick to improve efficiency.

Chapter 4

Input and Output

In this chapter we shall learn how to read and write information from files. ML offers us a number of tools, ranging from a simple function that prints strings to the standard output to more complex functions that perform UNIX-style input/output and more.

Our study of input and output forces us to learn a number of additional features of ML. In this chapter we shall find discussions of the following topics in addition to input/output:

1. The unit type, which is similar to "void" in C.

2. The type constructor `option`, which allows us to express values that are either present or absent.

3. Lists of statements.

4. A way to access functions that are in the standard basis of ML but not in the top-level environment.

4.1 Simple Output

ML provides a `print` operator that writes a character string to the standard output. This function is simple to use and can do most of what we need for typical output operations. Thus, it is a good point to begin our study of I/O.

4.1.1 The Print Function

The expression `print(x)` causes the value of a character string `x` to be printed on the "standard output," which would be the terminal unless you have called SML/NJ with another standard output designated (via the UNIX > operator). The value returned by the `print` function is the *unit* (). This symbol, which we have not seen before, is the lone value of the type `unit`, which we have also not encountered previously.

One purpose of the unit is to serve as the value returned by a function, such as `print`, that does its work by a *side-effect*. Notice that unlike all expressions of ML encountered so far, `print` has an effect on more than the ML environment; it changes the external world: either what appears on the user's terminal or the contents of the file that is the current standard output.

- Note that `print` does *not* return the value printed as its own value.

Example 4.1 : In Fig. 4.1 is a function called `testZero`, which tests whether or not its integer argument is 0 and prints one of the strings `"zero"` or `"not zero"` as appropriate. Notice that ML responds by saying that `testZero` is a function from the type integer to the type unit, because the unit is the "value" produced by the `print` function. The fact that a string is produced as a side-effect is not reflected in the type of the function.

```
fun testZero(0) = print("zero\n")
|    testZero(_) = print("not zero\n");
```
val testZero = fn : int → unit

```
testZero(2);
```
not zero
val it = () : unit

Figure 4.1: A function that uses the print function

We also see in Fig. 4.1 a use of `testZero(2)` and ML's response. We first see the printed response `not zero` on the standard output. Following immediately is the normal response of ML after evaluating a function:

val it = () : unit

Notice that the value of the expression `testZero(2)` is the unit (). That is what `print` returns, and therefore that is what `testZero` returns. □

- Remember from Section 2.1.1 that in strings we can use the sequence \n to represent a newline. Had we omitted printing this character in the print statements of Fig. 4.1, the output would have run together, as

    not zeroval it = () : unit

The Type unit

The unit type is another of the basic types of the ML system, like int. In a sense it is like the C type void. However, while there is no value for a "void" in C, the ML unit type has exactly one value, ().

The unit appears in a surprising place in ML: as the argument of a seemingly zero-argument function. Thus, if we were to write a zero-argument function that when called returns the string hello world, it would appear as follows:

```
fun hello() = "hello world"
```
val hello = fn : unit → string

That is, function hello has an argument after all; the unit. It would be called by applying it to the unit, as:

```
hello();
```
val it = "hello world" : string

4.1.2 Printing Nonstring Values

It is possible to print values other than strings if we first convert the value to a string. For example, we learned in Section 2.2.4 that the function str will change a character into a string of length 1. Thus, we could write

```
val c = #"a";
print(str(c));
```

to print an a on the standard output.

However, printing characters as strings is not very interesting. More often, we would like to print integers or real numbers, or perhaps values of other types. There is a function toString associated with integers, reals, and some other types that converts values of those types to appropriate character strings. The identifier toString denotes one of several rather different functions, and in order to tell which one is meant, it is necessary to prefix the identifier toString by the name of the "structure" to which it belongs, and a dot. We shall take up structures, both user-defined structures and structures provided by ML, in Section 8.2. However, roughly, for each type there is a structure with the same name but with the first letter capitalized. For example, the structures Int, Real, and Bool are associated with the types int, real, and bool, respectively.

Example 4.2 : Here is an example of printing the value of a real number as a string:

```
val x = 1.0E50;
```

val x = 1e50 : real

```
print(Real.toString(x));
```

1e50val it = () : unit

Notice that ML selects a representation for our chosen real number that is equivalent to, but not exactly the way we typed it. Also observe that there is no newline character printed, so the standard "`val =`" response of ML follows the printed value on the same line, with no intervening space.

Similarly, we can print integers or booleans by

```
print(Int.toString(123));
```

123val it = () : unit

```
print(Bool.toString(true));
```

trueval it = () : unit

In each of these cases, we have used the integer or boolean value as an argument directly, rather than "assigning" the value to a variable. In practice, there would be little point in writing an integer or boolean and converting it to a string, rather than printing the resulting string directly, provided we knew the value to be printed in advance. We would only use these conversion functions if we wished to print some value that was calculated at run time.   □

4.1.3   "Statement" Lists

It is often useful to execute a sequence of two or more "statements" with side-effects, such as `print` expressions.[1] The syntax for doing so in ML is

$$(<\text{first expression}>; \cdots ; <\text{last expression}>)$$

That is, a list of expressions is separated by semicolons and surrounded by parentheses. The construct is like **begin** $\cdots$ **end** in Pascal or { $\cdots$ } in C.

Each expression is evaluated in turn. However, the list of expressions is itself an expression and produces a value. The value produced by a list of expressions is the value produced by the last of the expressions.

---

[1] Technically, there is no such thing as a "statement" in ML, only expressions. However, expressions that cause side-effects behave much like statements of ordinary languages. We shall informally refer to them as statements.

Example 4.3: The function `printList` in Fig. 4.2 prints each element of an integer list in order and in a vertical column. Line (1) handles the case where the list is empty. Nothing is printed, and the unit is returned. Note that we do not care what `printList` returns since, unlike most ML functions, `printList` does its job by its side-effects, not by its returned value. However, like all functions, `printList` must return one type of value, unit in this case.

```
(1) fun printList(nil) = ()
(2)  |   printList(x::xs) = (
(3)          print(Int.toString(x));
(4)          print("\n");
(5)          printList(xs)
        );
```
  val printList = fn : int list → unit

```
printList([1,2,3]);
```
  1
  2
  3
  val it = () : unit

Figure 4.2: Printing a list as a side-effect

Lines (2) through (5) handle the case where the list is not empty. We see, beginning at line (3), a sequence of three expressions, each of which causes a printing side-effect. Line (3) prints the head element of the list. Since the function `Int.toString` is applied to the head element x, this element must be an integer. Line (4) prints the newline character, thus skipping to the next line of output. Line (5) is a recursive call to `printList` on the tail of the list. That expression causes the rest of the list to be printed and returns the unit. The unit thus becomes the value of the list of statements and the value returned by the function. The ML response confirms that `printList` is a function that takes an integer list as argument and returns a unit.

In Fig. 4.2, this function is used to print the list `[1,2,3]`. The initial call to `printList([1,2,3])` prints 1, then prints a newline (i.e., it skips to the next output line), and last calls `printList` recursively on the tail `[2,3]`. That call results in the printing of the elements 2 and 3 on separate lines. Finally, since `printList([1,2,3])` is an expression, ML responds with the value of this expression, which is the unit. □

Opening Structures

It is possible to give an identifier such as `toString` that is defined within one or more structures its meaning within that structure, without requiring that the structure name be prefixed. To do so, we `open` the structure, for example,

    `open Int;`

to open the structure for integers. ML responds with a long list of functions that are available in this structure. The names of these functions are now part of the ML environment and can be referred to without prefixing `Int`. to those names. For example, `print(toString(123))` is now legal. However, the `toString` functions from other structures still must be referred to with their structure name as a prefix; e.g., `print(toString(12.34))` is illegal.

    Figure 1.1, which we repeat here as Fig. 4.3, suggests the situation regarding structures. The entire content of all these structures is called the *standard basis*. The top-level environment of ML, which is available when the ML compiler is invoked, gives the user certain functions from various structures, such as the operators discussed in Sections 2.1 and 2.2. Other functions of the standard basis are available "below the surface," if we refer to these functions by a *long identifier* that includes the structure name. However, an entire structure can be "raised" to the surface by the `open` command.

4.1.4   Statement Lists Versus Let-Expressions

You may have noticed a similarity between the list of statements mentioned above and the let-expression from Section 3.4. Each involves a sequence of steps that are evaluated or executed in turn, and the result is the value returned by the last expression. However, different kinds of expressions are allowed between the `let` and `in` keywords than are allowed in statement lists or are allowed between the `in` and `end`.

    Between `let` and `in` we must find *declarations* such as val-declarations, function definitions, and a few more kinds of declarations that we shall learn later (see Fig. 9.19 for a summary of declarations). Intuitively declarations are the kinds of expressions that evoke a response other than *val it* = $\cdots$ when you type them in the top-level environment. For example, they may result in ML telling the value of some identifier other than `it`.

    On the other hand, the "ordinary" expressions that can appear in an expression list (or after the `in` of a let-expression) are characterized by an ML response in which the identifier `it` has its value told. See Fig. 9.13 for the com-

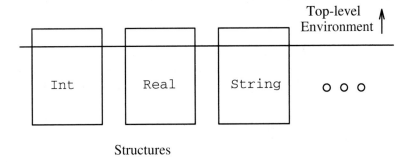

Figure 4.3: Parts of structures of the standard basis appear in the top-level environment; the remainders are also available

plete structure of expressions. Another way to look at the distinction is that let-expressions make significant alterations to the environment through their declarations, while expressions leave the environment unchanged. Note that side-effects such as printing or reading input do not change the environment as far as ML is concerned, although they do change the state of the surrounding file system.

- Although we have not yet seen an example, an expression list can appear between the in and end in a let-expression, in place of a single expression. The surrounding parentheses are unnecessary in such a list.

4.1.5 Exercises for Section 4.1

* **Exercise 4.1.1:** If we were to change line (1) of Fig. 4.2 to

```
fun printList(nil) = 0
```

and leave the rest of printList as it is, would there be a type error in the function printList?

Exercise 4.1.2: Write the function comb, computing $\binom{n}{m}$, in such a way that when we call comb(n,m) it prints n and m before printing the result. Print out suitable words so n, m, and $\binom{n}{m}$ are clearly distinguishable from one another.

*! **Exercise 4.1.3:** Write a function that, given integer n, prints 2^n X's, using n recursive calls. *Hint*: Compute the desired string recursively before printing it.

!! **Exercise 4.1.4:** Write a function that, given n, prints 2^n X's using only $\log_2 n$ recursive calls.

Should We Open Structures?

There is a school of thought that one should never open a structure. One reason is that it is hard to remember exactly which functions are brought into the current environment when a given structure is opened. Should we open a structure, we might absent-mindedly replace some function we needed by a function of the same name in the structure, with unpredictable results. However, for succinctness, in the balance of this chapter we shall asume that the `TextIO` structure is open.

4.2   Reading Input From a File

ML's approach to reading and writing files will be familiar if you have used UNIX file reading and writing commands from C or another language. In this section we shall cover file reading, while writing files is treated in Section 4.3.

4.2.1   Instreams

The ML type `instream` is a source of characters that may be read by certain functions that we are about to learn. If you are familiar with file input/output in UNIX, you will see an analogy between an instream and the file-ID of a file that is opened for reading. The necessary functions are found in a structure called `TextIO`. If we wish, we may issue the command:

```
open TextIO;
```

ML responds with a list of the functions available in the `TextIO` structure. We may now refer to these functions without prefixing them with `TextIO` and a dot. Had we not opened the `TextIO` structure, we could still use its functions if we prefixed them by `TextIO` and the dot.

Our first step in reading a file is to obtain a value of type `instream` that is associated with the file, opened for reading. We issue the command:

```
openIn("<file name>")
```

This expression causes the file named by the quoted string to be opened for reading. It returns a "token," or internal value, of type `instream`. This token must be used to read from the file in the future.

Example 4.4:

```
val infile = openIn("foo");
```
val infile = − : instream

opens the file named `foo` in the directory in which the ML program is running. To read from the file subsequently, we refer to it by the identifier `infile`, not `foo`.

The argument to `openIn` may be any legal path name. For instance, the expression

```
val infile2 = openIn("/usr/spool/mail/ullman");
val infile2 = - : instream
```

opens the author's mail file for reading. In the future, this file must be referred to by the identifier `infile2`. □

4.2.2 Reading Characters From a File

Once we have opened the file, we can read characters from it. There are several different functions that can read different amounts of the opened file. Let us begin by using a simple approach involving the following two functions:

1. `endOfStream(<file>)` is a *predicate* (function that returns a boolean) that tells whether we are at the end of the file. The value of `<file>` must be an `instream`, that is, a token returned by `openIn`. Function `endOfStream` returns `true` if this instream currently has no input waiting. If the instream refers to a standard file, then the end-of-file has been reached. However, if the instream is a special file, such as a terminal, then `endOfStream` might return `true` at one time and later return `false` when more input had been typed at the terminal.

2. `inputN(<file>,n)` reads the next n characters from the file named `<file>`. What is read is returned as a string. Again, `<file>` is an `instream` or internal token used to designate an opened file. If there are fewer than n characters remaining in the file, then only what remains is read, and fewer than n characters are returned. However, if the "file" is actually a source like an input terminal, then `input` will wait until n characters appear or an explicit end of file is seen. There will be an indefinite wait if these characters never arrive.

Example 4.5 : Figure 4.4 shows a function `readList` that opens a file, reads it character-by-character, and returns the list whose elements are the characters of the file, in order. Each element is a string of length 1.

Line (2) says that if we have reached the end of the file, then we return the empty list. Line (3) handles the case where the file is not empty. We use the `inputN` function to read a string of length one from the file, and this string becomes the head of the list being formed. The tail of the list is constructed by a recursive call to the function `readList`. ML deduces that `infile` must be of type `instream`, because function `inputN` requires that type for its first argument.

```
(1) fun readList(infile) =
(2)          if endOfStream(infile) then nil
(3)          else inputN(infile,1) :: readList(infile);
```
   val readList = fn : instream → string list


```
(4) readList(openIn("test"));
```
   val it = [”1”,”2”,”\n”,”a”,”b”,”\n”] : string list

Figure 4.4: Reading a file and turning it into a list of characters

We also see in line (4) of Fig. 4.4 the application of `readList` to a file named `test` that holds the six characters shown in Fig. 4.5. Note that two of the characters in the file are newline characters, one after each line.


```
12
ab
```


Figure 4.5: The file `test`

In the expression `readList(openIn("test"))` of line (4), `openIn` opens the file `test` and produces a token of type instream representing this file. We never see the value of this token, but it immediately becomes the argument of `readList`; that is, the parameter `infile` of `readList` gets this instream as its value for the call.

Finally, we see the response of ML to this expression; it ascribes to identifier `it` the list of characters of the file `test`. Note that we have, in effect, "dropped the list on the floor." In a more realistic example, we would pass the list as an argument to another function, which would perform some useful computation on the list.   □

4.2.3   Reading Lines of a File

The function `inputLine(<file>)` is applied to an instream. It returns a string consisting of the characters on the first unread line of the instream, that is, all characters up to and including the next newline character. If there are one or more characters remaining on the instream, but there is no newline character, then the characters up to the end of file are returned with a newline character appended.

Example 4.6: Suppose we open the file of Fig. 4.5 with:

```
val infile = openIn("test");
```

In Fig. 4.6 are three consecutive uses of the `inputLine` function; in each case the string returned is "thrown on the floor."

```
inputLine(infile);
```
val it = "12\n" : string

```
inputLine(infile);
```
val it = "ab\n" : string

```
inputLine(infile);
```
val it = "" : string

Figure 4.6: Uses of `inputLine`

Note that the two lines of the file are returned by the first two calls, and since the end of file has then been reached, the third call returns the empty string, not a newline. However, had the final newline been omitted, and the file `test` composed of the five characters 12\nab, the responses would have been exactly the same as Fig. 4.6, including the newline character following b in the second use of `inputLine`. □

4.2.4 Reading Complete Files

We can read an entire text file with the function `input(<file>)`. Again, the file is an instream. The result of this call is a character string consisting of all the remaining characters of the instream.

Example 4.7 : If we open the file from Fig. 4.5 as we did in Example 4.6, then

```
val s = input(infile);
```

binds s to the string "12\nab\n". Among other possibilities, we could apply the `explode` function to s, producing a list of characters. We could then process this list character by character in a variety of ways. □

4.2.5 Reading a Single Character

Yet another function to read text files is `input1(<file>)`. This function reads from the instream `<file>` a single character. However, the value is returned in a form we have not seen before, involving the type constructor `option`. That is, the type of the value returned by `input1` is `char option`, whose values are either of the form

1. SOME c, where c is a character, or

2. NONE.

If SOME c is returned by input1, then c is the character read. If NONE is returned, then no character remained on the instream.

Example 4.8 : Suppose infile is an instream opened for reading the file test of Fig. 4.5. Here is the first call to input1 on this instream.

```
input1(infile);
```
val it = SOME #"1" : char option

Notice that the first character of the file is returned as an option; its type is char option. The next five calls return SOME #"2", SOME #"\n", SOME #"a", SOME #"b", and SOME #"\n". The seventh and subsequent calls return NONE. □

The fact that the character is returned as an option is actually convenient, since it lets us gracefully handle the situation where there are no more characters on the instream. We use SOME and NONE in patterns, thereby distinguishing the end of file without having to use endOfStream to test the end explicitly.

Example 4.9 : In Fig. 4.7 we see another way to read a file and turn it into a list of characters. The work is done by the auxiliary function makeList1, which takes an instream called infile and a character option and returns the list consisting of the character in the option (if there is one) and all the characters remaining on the instream.

```
fun makeList1(infile, NONE) = nil
|   makeList1(infile, SOME c) =
        c :: makeList1(infile, input1(infile));
```
*val makeList1 = fn : instream * char option → char list*

```
fun makeList(infile) = makeList1(infile, input1(infile));
```
val makeList = fn : instream → char list

Figure 4.7: Converting a file into a list of characters

The first line of makeList1 handles the case where the option is NONE. This case occurs when there were no more characters on the instream when we tried previously to read the instream using input1. Since we have no more characters available, we return the empty list.

Some Operators for Options

There are two useful operators on options. Given a value x whose type is T `option` for some type T, we can say:

1. `isSome(x)` to get a boolean value that is `false` if the value of x is `NONE` and `true` if the value of x is `SOME` y for some value y.

2. `valOf(x)` returns y if x is of the form `SOME` y. If x is `NONE`, then a runtime error occurs.

For instance, we could write the function `makeList1` of Fig. 4.7 as:

```
fun makeList1(infile, c) =
        if isSome(c) then
            valOf(c)::makeList1(infile,input1(infile))
        else nil;
```

The remainder of `makeList1` handles the case where we have successfully read a character c from the instream, and `SOME` c is the second argument of `makeList1`. We extract the character c itself from the pattern `SOME` c and make this character the head of the list being formed. The tail of the list is what we get by applying `input1` to get a character option from the instream and recursively calling `makeList1` with the instream and this character option as arguments.

The function `makeList`, also defined in Fig. 4.7, Simply applies `input1` to its instream and calls `makeList1` with the instream and this first character option as arguments. Function `makeList1` will read character after character, until `NONE` is returned by `input1`. □

4.2.6 Lookahead on the Input

The function `lookahead(<file>)` is similar to `input1`, but `lookahead` does not consume the character read from the input. It returns a character option, just as `input1` does.

Example 4.10: Let us again assume that `infile` is an instream opened for reading the file of Fig. 4.5. Here are the responses to a use of `lookahead` followed by a use of `input1`:

```
lookahead(infile);
```
val it = SOME #"1" : char option

A Comparison Between Options and Lists

The type constructors `option` and `list` have certain similarities. In each case, there are two identifiers, called *value constructors*, that are used to build values of these types. The value constructor `NONE` is a value by itself, just as `nil` is a value by itself. And just as the type of `nil` is `'a list` (a list of any type), the type of `NONE` is `'a option` (an option of any type).

Each has a second value constructor: `::` in the case of lists and `SOME` in the case of options. However, `::` is a binary, infix operator and can be used recursively to create lists of arbitrary length. `SOME` is a unary, prefix operator and may not be used recursively. That is, while a value like `1::2::3::nil` is of type `int list`, value `SOME SOME 1` is not of type `int option`. Rather, it is a value of type `int option option`.

We shall learn more about type constructors like these in Section 6.2, when we take up the matter of datatypes. Both `list` and `option` are actually examples of datatypes that are provided by the ML system, rather than being defined by the user, as most datatypes are.

```
input1(infile);
```
val it = SOME #"1" : char option

Notice that while `lookahead` reports the first character on the instream, that character is not read from the instream. Rather, it remains to be consumed by the later call to `input1`. A following call to either `lookahead` or `input1` would return the second character, `SOME 2`. Of course `lookahead` would leave 2 on the instream; `input1` would not. □

The function `canInput(f,i)` is a predicate that returns `true` if there are at least *i* characters currently available on the instream *f*. For instance,

```
canInput(infile,1)
```

returns `false` exactly when `lookahead(infile)` returns `NONE`.

4.2.7   Closing Instreams

We may close a file that has been opened for reading with the command

```
closeIn(<file>)
```

Here, the file argument is an instream that was returned by `openIn`. It is generally not essential that files be closed. The ML system will handle files correctly when the program terminates.

4.2.8 Exercises for Section 4.2

Exercise 4.2.1: Write expressions that will do the following.

* a) Open file `zap` for reading.

* b) Close the file whose instream is `in1`.

  c) Read 5 characters from the instream `in2`.

* d) Read a line of text from the instream `in3`.

  e) Read the entire file from instream `in4`.

  f) Find the first character waiting on the standard input without consuming it.

*! g) Find how many characters are presently waiting on the standard input.

Exercise 4.2.2: Suppose we have a file with the characters

```
abc
de
f
```

Suppose the file has been opened for reading and `infile` is a variable whose value is the instream for this file. Tell what happens if the following commands are executed repeatedly.

* a) `val x = input(infile);`

  b) `val x = input1(infile);`

* c) `val x = inputN(infile,2);`

  d) `val x = inputN(infile,5);`

* e) `val x = inputLine(infile);`

  f) `val x = lookahead(infile);`

Exercise 4.2.3: Give the types of the following expressions:

* a) `SOME ()`

  b) `SOME 123`

* c) `SOME NONE`

  d) `fun f() = SOME true;`

* e) `fun f(NONE) = 0 | f(SOME i) = i;`

* **Exercise 4.2.4 :** Read a file of characters, treating it as a sequence of *words*, which are sequences of consecutive non-white-space characters. Each word is followed by either a single white space character or the end-of-file, so two or more consecutive white spaces indicate there is an empty word between them. Return a list of the words in the file.

! **Exercise 4.2.5 :** Design the following calendar-printing function. Take as input a month, the day of the first of that month, and the number of days in the month. Months and days are abbreviated by their first three letters. The month, day, and number of days are each separated by a single white-space character. For example, a request to print the calendar for a September in which the first of the month is on a Thursday would be

```
Sep Thu 30
```

Print the calendar as:

1. A row with the month (full name) indented by three tabs.

2. A blank row.

3. A row with the names of the days (three-letter abbreviations) separated by tabs.

4. As many rows as necessary, with the days printed in the proper columns.

For example, Fig. 4.8 shows the calendar desired for September when Sept. 1 falls on a Thursday.

			September			
Sun	Mon	Tue	Wed	Thu	Fri	Sat
				1	2	3
4	5	6	7	8	9	10
11	12	13	14	15	16	17
18	19	20	21	23	24	25
26	27	28	29	30		

Figure 4.8: Example calendar page

4.3   Output to Files

We saw in Section 4.1 how to print output on the standard output file. In this section we shall learn more about output, including the type `outstream`, which is the analog of an instream. We shall also study commands to write to any of several outstreams.

4.3.1 Outstreams

We met the type `instream` in Section 4.2.1. Normally, an instream represents a file of characters that has been opened for input. We may imagine an instream to be represented by the token (normally an integer) used by the operating system to refer to that file. However, we are not allowed by ML to see this token or even to compare it to another instream value.

Similarly, there is a type `outstream` that normally represents a file of characters that has been opened for output. We may also think of an outstream as the internal token representing this file. We create an outstream when we open a file for writing. While there is only one reading mode — read a file from the beginning — there are two output modes:

1. Function `openOut(<file>)` opens a file for writing. The file is first made empty, and a token of type `outstream` is returned.

2. Function `openAppend(<file>)` opens a file for appending. This function does not empty the file; it leaves the file as it is. An `outstream` is returned, and future output operations on this outstream are added to the end of the file.

These functions, like all the functions introduced in this section, are found in the structure `TextIO`. Thus, we must either open `TextIO` or prepend `TextIO` and a dot to the names of these functions. We continue to assume that `TextIO` is opened.

Example 4.11 : Here is an example of a file-opening statement.

```
val outfile = openOut("/u/ullman/foo");
```
val outfile = – : outstream

Notice that the value of `outfile` is not shown; it is represented by a dash, because it is an internal token whose value we are not allowed to know. Its type is identified as `outstream`.

The effect of this `openOut` statement is to empty the file /u/ullman/foo. An outstream is returned and bound to the identifier `outfile`. In the future, we can write characters onto the end of file /u/ullman/foo by referring to `outfile`. □

4.3.2 Closing Outstreams

After writing to an outstream f, we can close the file by `closeOut(f)`. Here f is the outstream token that we received from `openOut` or `openAppend` when we opened the file. Any characters waiting in the buffer for the file are written, and the file is closed to further writing. Should we later try to write to an outstream that has been closed (or try to read from a closed instream) we get an error condition called an "exception" (see Section 5.2).

Flushing the Output

The function flushOut(<file>) "flushes" the outstream to which it is applied. We would normally use flushOut if the outstream were a terminal or other device whose output is buffered. This command assures that any characters waiting in the buffer are written at the time flushOut is executed, even if we do not immediately close the outstream.

Example 4.12: We close the file /u/ullman/foo mentioned in Example 4.11 with closeOut(outfile). We refer to the file by outfile because that identifier was bound to the outstream for the file /u/ullman/foo in the call to openOut that created outstream outfile. □

4.3.3   The output Command

Function output(f,s) appends the string s to the end of the outstream f. Unlike input, which has a variety of functions that obtain various prefixes of an instream, essentially all output is done either with the output function or the print function described in Section 4.1.

Example 4.13: Let us consider an example using function output to the standard output stdOut (see the box on "Standard Input and Output"). In Fig. 4.9 we see a version of the comb function that with each call prints a line of X's of length equal to the value of n in that call. The output helps us picture the sequence of calls made by an initial call to comb(n,m).

Lines (1) and (2) are the function put(n), which prints n X's and then a newline on the standard output. We see in line (1) the basis case, where $n = 0$ and we print just the newline. In line (2) is the case where $n > 0$. We print one X, then recursively print $n - 1$ more X's and the newline.

Lines (3) through (6) are the modified function comb. On line (4) n X's are printed. Then, lines (5) and (6) do the normal recursion for comb. Finally, line (7) is an example call to comb(5,2). The original call of line (7) and each recursive call it makes is reflected by a line of X's, and at the end is ML's response to the original call. Note that because put prints to the standard output, the X's appear on the terminal mixed with ML's own responses, which also go to the terminal. □

- Note that Example 4.13 uses only single characters as output strings in lines (1) and (2) of Fig. 4.9. In general, strings of any length may be used.

4.3.4   Exercises for Section 4.3

Exercise 4.3.1: Write expressions that will do the following.

```
(1) fun put(0) = output(stdOut,"\n")
(2)  |   put(n) = (output(stdOut,"X"); put(n-1));
```
val put = fn : int → unit

```
(3) fun comb(n,m) = (
(4)          put(n);
(5)          if m=0 orelse m=n then 1
(6)          else comb(n-1,m) + comb(n-1,m-1)
    );
```
*val comb = fn : int * int → int*

```
(7) comb(5,2);
```
XXXXX
XXXX
XXX
XX
XX
X
X
XXX
XX
X
X
XX
XXXX
XXX
XX
X
X
XX
XXX
val it = 10 : int

Figure 4.9: Printing a profile of calls to comb

Standard Input and Output

UNIX has a notion of a "standard" input, output, and error file for a process, normally the terminal or window in which the process originates. Structure `TextIO` provides names for these three standard files:

1. `stdIn` is an instream, the standard input.

2. `stdOut` is an outstream, the standard output.

3. `stdErr` is an outstream, the standard error file.

None of these instreams and outstreams need to be opened. You may refer to them, knowing that the surrounding operating system will direct the characters to or from the appropriate place, such as your terminal.

Standard Input Can Interact With the `sml` Command

When using standard input, we must be careful how we call ML. If we use the UNIX command `sml <foo`, then file `foo` becomes the standard input, and `inputN(stdIn,i)` will read i characters from file `foo`, not from the terminal. If we want to read from the terminal, we need to invoke `sml` without an input file, and then get the file `foo` by `use "foo"`. Now, the terminal will be referred to by `stdIn`.

---

    a) Open file `baz` for writing.

 * b) Open file `/usr/spool/mail/fred` for appending.

    c) Close the file whose outstream is `out1`.

 * d) Write the string `"super"` to the outstream `out2`.

*! **Exercise 4.3.2:** Write a function to read integers i and b separated by a single nondigit and print the representation of i in base b. If $b > 10$, then represent digits ten and above by their decimal representation surrounded by parentheses. For example, 570 in base 12 is 3(11)6; that is, $570 = 144 \times 3 + 12 \times 11 + 6$. You should read from an instream `infile` and write to outstream `outfile`.

! **Exercise 4.3.3:** Write a function that, given i prints 2^i X's, using i recursive calls. *Hint*: Use an auxiliary function that computes the desired string before the string is printed.

4.4 Case Study: Summing Integers

In this extended example, the problem we shall address is how to read a list of integers from a designated file and compute their sum. The following restrictions are assumed.

1. Integers are positive only.

2. Integers are separated by one or more characters that are not digits.

3. The last integer may or may not be followed by one or more nondigits before the end of the file is reached.

The entire program appears in Fig. 4.10. In line (1), we open the `TextIO` structure so that the file-reading functions will be available to us. Line (2) defines a symbolic constant `END`, whose value is -1. This constant is a convenient way for the various functions in Fig. 4.10 to signal that they have failed to find any more integers on the instream and are ready to complete the sum.

Function `digit` in line (3) checks whether its argument lies between the characters `"0"` and `"9"` in lexicographic order. Note that in the ASCII code, the digits have consecutive codes.

Now, let us divide the task into some components. Our initial sketch of the program, in a "Pidgin-Pascal" notation, is shown in Fig. 4.11.

Getting the next integer from the file is itself a complex task. First, there may not be any more integers, since no digits may remain on the file. We shall handle this situation by producing the integer -1. Note we can do so here because of the assumption that there are no negative integers. Thus there can be no ambiguity whether -1 is a legitimate integer — it cannot be. However, to make the role of -1 more transparent, we use `END`, the variable defined on line (2), in place of -1.

If there is an integer to be found, we can divide the process into two steps:

1. Skipping over characters to find the first digit, and

2. Reading subsequent digits until either a nondigit or the end of file is encountered, computing the value of the integer as we go.

4.4.1 The Function `startInt`

The first of these operations is performed by the function `startInt` shown in lines (4) through (8) of Fig. 4.10. Function `startInt` is mutually recursive with an auxiliary function `startInt1` that does most of the work. In line (4), `startInt` gets the first character (as a character option) from the input file and passes that character and the file to `startInt1`. The latter function first checks on line (5) if the optional character is not present (i.e., the `char option` is `NONE`). In that case the end of file has been reached and the special constant `END` is returned to signal that there are no more integers.

```
(1) open TextIO;

(2) val END = ~1;

(3) fun digit(c) = c >= #"0" andalso c <= #"9";

(4) fun startInt(file) = startInt1(file, input1(file))

(5) and startInt1(file, NONE) = END
(6)  |   startInt1(file, SOME c) =
(7)          if digit(c) then ord(c)-ord(#"0")
(8)          else startInt(file);

(9) fun finishInt(i,file) =
(10)         if i = END then END
(11)         else finishInt1(i,file,input1(file))

(12) and finishInt1(i, file, NONE) = i
(13)  |   finishInt1(i, file, SOME c) =
(14)         if digit(c) then
                     finishInt(10*i+ord(c)-ord(#"0"), file)
(15)         else i;

(16) fun getInt(file) = finishInt(startInt(file), file)

(17) fun sumInts1(file) =
             let
(18)             val i = getInt(file)
             in
(19)             if i = END then 0
(20)             else i + sumInts1(file)
             end;

(21) fun sumInts(filename) = sumInts1(openIn(filename));
```

Figure 4.10: ML Code to read a file and sum all the integers found on that file

---

Using Boolean Expressions Succinctly

If you are like the author, you are tempted to write a predicate like `digit` as

```
fun digit(c) =
        if c>= #'0' andalso c <= #'9' then true
        else false;
```

This code is correct but "illiterate." When we write a function that returns a boolean, we can use the test as the return value itself.

> **if** there are no more integers on the file **then**
>   return 0
> **else begin**
>   get an integer from the file;
>   recursively sum the rest of the file;
>   return the sum of the first integer and
>   the rest of the file
> **end**

Figure 4.11: Sketch of integer-summing program

If the character is present, then `input1` returns SOME c for some character c. In that case, at lines (6) through (8) `startInt1` first checks if c is a digit. If so, then the value of that digit is returned at line (7) by subtracting the ASCII code for 0 from the ASCII code for the digit. The difference is the integer value of the digit. But if the character c is not a digit, then `startInt1` instead ignores this character and calls `startInt` to get the next character from the file.

4.4.2 The Function `finishInt`

Now we have a way to find the first digit of an integer and return the value of that digit. Next, we need a function `finishInt(i,file)` that takes an integer i, which represents the value of digits read so far, and reads as many more consecutive digits as there are in the instream named `file`. Eventually the value of the integer represented by this entire sequence of digits is produced by `finishInt`. The key arithmetic point to remember is that if i is the value of digits read so far, and we read one more digit, say d, then the value of the integer up to the newly read digit is $10i + d$.

Completing the integer that was begun by `startInt` is the task of function `finishInt` and its mutually recursive auxiliary function `finishInt1`. At

Signaling the End of the File

Admittedly, the style we have adopted for signally that no integers remain on the file — returning −1 when no integer is found — is fraught with danger and should be avoided. We shall learn two safer ways to represent the end of file. One is Exercise 6.2.4, where we consider the use of datatypes, and another is Exercise 5.2.3, where we consider exceptions and their handling. Still another way (discussed in Exercise 4.4.1) would be to return an `int option`, which would either be `NONE` if there were no integer remaining on the input or `SOME` i, if integer i were found.

line (10) of Fig. 4.10, `finishInt` tests if we are already at the end of file, because `startInt` has returned the special integer `END`. If so, then `finishInt` also returns `END` to signal that there is no integer and the end of file has been reached.

If the integer was successfully started by `startInt`, then `finishInt` reads the next character from the instream and calls `finishInt1` with this character and the integer i read so far. If the next character is not there, because the end of file has now been reached, then at line (12) `finishInt1` returns i, the integer found so far. But if there is another character c on the input, then `finishInt1` tests if c is a digit at line (13). If so then on line (14) `finishInt1` multiplies the integer i by 10, and adds the value of the digit read, to get a new integer, which we may call j. Also on line (14), `finishInt1` calls `finishInt` recursively with integer j and the same file.

If, on the other hand, the character passed to `finishInt1` is not a digit, then the integer being read is finished. Function `finishInt1` return the integer i on line (15), and the recursion ends.

4.4.3 The Function `getInt`

The functions `startInt` and `finishInt` are combined as one function `getInt` on line (16) of Fig. 4.10 that either reads the next integer from a file or returns `END` if the end-of-file is encountered before any digits. If there are one or more digits in the file, `startInt` will get the value of the first, and `finishInt` will repeatedly multiply its integer argument by 10 and add in the value of the next digit, eventually returning the value of the entire string of consecutive digits. This value is returned by `getInt`.

Should `getInt` be called when there is no integer left on the file, then `startInt` will return `END`; so will `finishInt`, and therefore `getInt` returns `END`.

Using Auxiliary Functions

Contrast the approach used in Example 4.9, where we designed a recursive auxiliary function `makeList1` that was called once by its primary function `makeList` with the approach used in Fig. 4.10, where the auxiliary functions `startInt1` and `finishInt1` were mutually recursive with their corresponding primary functions. Either style could be used in either example. For instance, on line (8) of Fig. 4.10 we could have `startInt1` call itself with

```
else startInt1(file, input1(file));
```

The code would then look more like that of Example 4.9. We would follow the definition of `startInt1` by the definition of `startInt`, and the two functions would no longer be mutually recursive. Which approach is preferable is a matter of taste.

4.4.4 The Function sumInts

Finally, we see in lines (17) through (21) of Fig. 4.10 the functions that do the summing of integers. The work is really done by `sumInts1`, which at line (18) reads an integer off the instream. If the integer is END (i.e., -1), then we have reached the end of the file and found no integer, so the sum of integers found is 0. We handle this case in line (19). If a nonnegative integer is found, then on line (20) we recursively call `sumInts1` to sum the rest of the integers on the file, and add the integer found first, to produce the correct sum.

The final touch is the function `sumInts` of line (21). This function takes a string `filename`, which is the name of the file whose integers we must sum, and applies `openIn` to it. The result is an instream representing the file. This instream is passed to `sumInts1` and, through it, to the other functions of Fig. 4.10 that read from the file.

4.4.5 Eager Evaluation

One might wonder whether all the complexity of Fig. 4.10 is really necessary. For example, we could have converted the file into a string in one step, using function `input`. We could then use `explode` to create a list of characters and process this list. It might well be more convenient to process the list than to read characters directly from the input file, as we did.

However, there is a disadvantage to doing so, because of ML's method of parameter passing, which is call-by-value (recall Section 3.1). That is, the first thing that would happen if we used `input` is that the entire file would be turned into a string. But suppose we had agreed to terminate the list of integers not by the end of the file, but by some special character like `#"e"`, which could appear in the middle of the file. In that case, we would not need to read the part of the file beyond the first `#"e"`. However, should we start by using functions `input` and `explode` to convert the file to a list of characters, we would wind up reading the entire file whether or not we needed it. This style of computing values is called *eager evaluation*. Its opposite, where parts of an argument such as a list or file are evaluated only as needed, is called *lazy evaluation*.

ML follows the eager evaluation approach because of the call-by-value semantics associated with its function arguments. However, by careful programming, we can have a measure of lazy evaluation. Notice in particular that the program of Fig. 4.10 reads one integer at a time, and it never creates a list of all the integers before it sums them. More to the point, if we had used a marker like `#"e"` to indicate the end of the group of integers to be summed, and suitably modified the program of Fig. 4.10 to look for `#"e"` instead of the end-of-file, the program would never even read the file beyond the first `#"e"`.

In truth, it should be pointed out that while ML argument evaluation is "eager," there are other aspects of the language design that are "lazy." For instance, we mentioned that the second argument of `andalso` or `orelse` is evaluated "lazily," that is, only if needed.

4.4.6   Exercises for Section 4.4

! **Exercise 4.4.1:** Generalize the program of Fig. 4.10 to allow negative integers on the input. We assume that negative integers are preceded by the minus sign (-) rather than the tilde (~). Note that we not only have to recognize negative integers, but we can no longer use -1 as a convenient value to indicate that the end of file has been reached. *Hint*: Return an integer option that tells whether the end of file has been reached.

Exercise 4.4.2: Rewrite `makeList` and `makeList1` of Example 4.9 so the two functions are mutually recursive.

Exercise 4.4.3: Rewrite functions `startInt` and `startInt1` of Fig. 4.10 so they are not mutually recursive. Do the same for functions `finishInt` and `finishInt1`.

Chapter 5

More About Functions

This chapter continues the study of ML functions that we began in Chapter 3. First, we introduce the "match," a special kind of expression similar to the pattern-matching diction that we studied in connection with function definitions in Section 3.3. In fact, we shall see that function definitions using **fun** are really a shorthand for a match.

Then we introduce the "exception," a mechanism that lets us deal with those functions for which certain values of its argument(s) do not allow the function to return a sensible value. Then, we discuss two of the things that distinguish ML from other programming languages: the ease with which one can write

1. Polymorphic functions — functions that accept arguments of different types — and

2. Higher order functions — functions that take functions as arguments and/or produce functions as return values.

We conclude the chapter with a discussion of ways to construct new functions from old, especially the technique known as "Currying," where we bind some of the arguments of a function to make a new function.

5.1 Matches and Patterns

Patterns and the matching of patterns to expressions play a central role in ML programming. In this chapter we look at some additional ways that patterns are used.

1. We use patterns in *matches*, which resemble the sequence of patterns and associated expressions that appear in function declarations using the keyword **fun**. In turn, matches are essential components of

(a) *Function expressions.* These allow us to define functions as values, by using the keyword `fn`. An important use of these expressions is to define anonymous functions that can be used as arguments to higher-order functions without giving them a name; see Section 5.1.3.

(b) *Case expressions.* These are similar to the case-statements of Pascal or the switch-statements of C.

(c) *Exception-handlers*, which we shall cover in Section 5.2.3. These allow us to handle error conditions gracefully.

2. We use patterns in val-declarations, which we shall find are really much more general than the bindings of values to single variables that we have been using almost exclusively.

5.1.1   Matches

A *match* expression consists of one or more *rules*, which are pairs of the form

<pattern> => <expression>

The rules are separated by vertical bars, so the form of a match is:

<pattern 1> => <expression 1> |
<pattern 2> => <expression 2> |
              . . .
<pattern *n*> => <expression *n*>

Each of the expressions following the `=>`'s must be of the same type, since any one of them could become the value of the match.

The match is applied to a value *v*. We compare each pattern of the match with *v* in order, until we find a pattern that matches *v*, say the *i*th pattern. This match of a pattern with *v* binds values to each of the identifiers in the pattern, in the manner discussed with regard to functions in Section 3.3.5. Identifiers in the *i*th expression are then replaced by their associated values, and the resulting value of the *i*th expression becomes the value of the match.

5.1.2   Using Matches to Define Functions

An alternative way to define a function *f*, without using the keyword `fun`, is

val rec f = fn <match>

The keyword `rec`, short for "recursive," is necessary only if the function *f* is recursive, that is, if the identifier *f* appears in one or more expressions of the match. This keyword informs ML that any uses of *f* in the match refers to the function *f* being defined recursively and is not an undefined or previously defined variable.

Matches That Don't Cover All Possibilities

If there exist values that match none of the patterns, then ML will issue a warning:

Warning: match not exhaustive

when the match is compiled. If the match is actually applied to a value that does not match any of the patterns, then the exception `Match` is raised and computation halts, unless the program has been designed to "handle" the error as discussed in Section 5.2.3.

Example 5.1: Another way to write the definition of the function **reverse** of Example 3.15 is

```
val rec reverse = fn
        nil => nil |
        x::xs => reverse(xs) @ [x];
val reverse = fn : 'a list → 'a list
```

Here the keyword **rec** is necessary because **reverse** appears in the match itself. In a function definition like

```
val rec addOne = fn x => x+1;
```

the keyword **rec** is legal. However, it is unnecessary, and possibly confusing, since the match consisting of a single pattern x and expression x+1 does not mention the name addOne. □

As a general rule, any function definition using **fun** that has the form

$$\text{fun } f(P_1) = E_1 \mid f(P_2) = E_2 \mid \cdots \mid f(P_n) = E_n;$$

is a shorthand for the val-declaration

$$\text{val rec } f = \text{fn } P_1 \Rightarrow E_1 \mid P_2 \Rightarrow E_2 \mid \cdots \mid P_n \Rightarrow E_n;$$

5.1.3 Anonymous Functions

We can also use a match, preceded by the keyword **fn**, as an anonymous function that is used once and thrown away. That is, if M is a match, then (**fn** M) is a function without a name. It may be applied to an argument E by writing (**fn** M)(E).

Example 5.2: Consider the expression

```
(fn x => x+1)(3);
val it = 4 : int
```

Here, we use the simple one-pattern match of function `addOne` in Example 5.1, but without giving it a name. It is applied to the argument 3, and produces the value 4. □

The example above may be an uninteresting use of anonymous functions, since its effect can be simulated more simply. However, in Section 5.4 we shall see many places where anonymous functions are useful as arguments of higher-order functions.

5.1.4   Case Expressions

The form of a *case expression* is

$$\text{case } <\text{expression}> \text{ of } <\text{match}>$$

The value of a case expression is found by matching, in order of appearance, each pattern in the match against the value of the expression. As soon as a matching pattern is found, the corresponding expression in the match is evaluated and becomes the value of the case expression. If there is no pattern matching the expression, then the exception `Match` is raised.

Example 5.3 : One use of a case expression is to replace an auxiliary function that has no use besides supporting some "primary" function. Since the case expression has all the power of a match, it can easily replace one use of a function. In Fig. 5.1 we see a rewrite of the pair of mutually recursive functions `startInt` and `startInt1` from Fig. 4.10. We have used the case statement to replace `startInt1` entirely.

```
(1) fun startInt(infile) =
(2)         case input1(infile) of
(3)             NONE => END |
(4)             SOME c =>
(5)                 if digit(c) then ord(c) - ord(#"0")
(6)                 else startInt(infile);
```

Figure 5.1: Function `startInt` using a case statement

In line (2), the expression for the case statement is given; it is `input1(file)`, which we should recall gets a character option from the instream. There are two possible cases. In line (3) we handle the case where `NONE` was returned by `input1`; i.e., the end of file has been reached and there is no character. In this case, `startInt` must return the special value `END` to signal the end of file.

Lines (4) through (6) handle the case where a character was returned. The pattern `SOME c` allows us to extract the character. If it is a digit, then the value of that digit is returned on line (5). If the character is not a digit, then on line (6) we call `startInt` recursively to search further on the file for the first digit. □

5.1.5   If-Then-Else Expressions Revisited

The if-then-else expression, which we introduced in Section 2.1.6, is actually a shorthand for a case expression. That is,

$$\text{if } E_1 \text{ then } E_2 \text{ else } E_3$$

stands for

$$\text{case } E_1 \text{ of true => } E_2 \text{ | false => } E_3$$

And in turn, a case expression `case` E `of` M, where M is a match, is equivalent to the function application `(fn` M`)(`E`)`.

Example 5.4: One place where the underlying meaning of the if-then-else expression needs to be understood is if we make an error and get a diagnostic from the ML compiler. Without understanding what is going on, the response of the compiler can seem rather mysterious. Suppose we confuse characters with strings in the following expression:

```
if x<y then #"a" else "b"
```

The above expression is equivalent to the case expression

```
case x<y of
    true => #"a" |
    false => "b"
```

In the case expression above, the rules of the match, `true => #"a"` and `false => "b"`, do not produce values of the same type. The first rule tells ML to expect character results. Thus, when the second rule is encountered, the error message

> *Error: types of rules don't agree [tycon mismatch]*
> *earlier rule(s): bool $\rightarrow$ char*
> *this rule: bool $\rightarrow$ string*
> *rule:*
> *false $\Rightarrow$ "b"*

is produced. □

5.1.6   Exercises for Section 5.1

Exercise 5.1.1: Rewrite the functions `finishInt` and `finishInt1` from Fig. 4.10 to use a single function with a case statement.

Exercise 5.1.2: Write the following functions as values, using `fn` and a match.

* a) Function `padd` of Fig. 3.27.

   b) Function `smult` of Fig. 3.27.

   c) Function `pmult` of Fig. 3.27.

   d) Function `sumPairs` of Example 3.18.

* e) Function `printList` of Example 4.3.

   f) Function `merge` of Fig. 3.12.

   g) Function `comb` of Fig. 3.13.

*! **Exercise 5.1.3:** A year is a leap year if and only if it is divisible by 4, but not by 100, unless it is also divisible by 400. Write a case expression that tells whether year y is a leap year.

Exercise 5.1.4: Recall from Exercise 2.1.4 that expressions using `orelse` and `andalso` can be rewritten as if-then-else expressions. We now find that if-then-else expressions can be rewritten as case expressions. Write:

* a) E `orelse` F

   b) E `andalso` F

as case expressions.

5.2   Exceptions

Many functions are *partial*, meaning that they do not produce a value for some of the possible arguments of the function's domain type. It is essential that we be able to catch such errors, but the constructs given so far do not let us do so. The canonical example of an erroneous argument is division by 0. We have claimed that in ML an expression like `a div b` must invariably produce a value of type integer. But what if `b` has the value 0? Will ML in fact produce an integer as a result?

The fact is that, as in other languages, division by 0 produces an error. If we do nothing to handle the error, it will stop the computation with an "uncaught exception" message.

Example 5.5: Here are some of the operators we have seen and their response when given operands for which they have no defined value.

Real Arithmetic in ML

Real arithmetic in ML avoids raising exceptions by using two special constants `inf` (infinity), and `nan` ("not a number"). For example, `5.0/0.0` produces the value `inf`, `~5.0/0.0` produces the value `~inf`, and `0.0/0.0` and `inf-inf` both produce the value `nan`.

```
5 div 0;
```
uncaught exception Div


```
hd(nil: int list);
```
uncaught exception Empty


```
tl(nil : real list);
```
uncaught exception Empty


```
chr(500);
```
uncaught exception Chr

The first example is an integer division by zero, and the system raises the exception `Div`. Note that the `Div` exception will be raised and will halt the entire program whenever integer division by zero occurs. The division might be explicit, as in these examples, or it may be a division by some expression that happens to evaluate to 0. However, as we shall see in Section 5.2.3, it is possible to turn an exception into an appropriate value; this process is called "handling" exceptions. Handling the exception `Div` keeps the computation going by providing a value for the expression with denominator 0.

The next two examples apply the operators `hd` and `tl` to get the head and tail, respectively, of the empty list. Since the empty list has neither a head nor a tail, both of these exceptions raise the built-in exception `Empty`. Note that an expression consisting of a function like `hd` or `tl` applied to nil, is illegal unless we pick a type for the result, as we have done here.[1] We shall have more to say about the rationale for this requirement in Section 5.3.1.

The last example applies the built-in operator `chr` to an integer that is too big to represent a character; `chr` requires an integer in the range 0 to 255. Thus, the exception `Chr` is raised. □

---

[1] Older versions of ML allowed such function applications in situations where it was not necessary to know the type of the result.

5.2.1 User-Defined Exceptions

We may also define our own exceptions and "raise" them in code we write when an exceptional condition is discovered. The simplest form of an exception declaration is

```
exception Foo;
```
exception Foo

Foo is thus declared to be the name of an exception. In the definition of a function f, we can use an expression

```
raise Foo
```

to raise exception Foo when we find an erroneous input or other condition that we associate in our minds with "Foo."

If function f raises exception Foo during the running of a program, then f returns no value at all. Rather, ML will halt execution and print the message

```
uncaught exception Foo
```

Note that the type of Foo is "exception," written exn. The range type of function f is generally *not* exn, but rather whatever type the function f returns when no exception is raised.

Example 5.6: Reconsider the comb(n,m) function of Fig. 3.6 that computes $\binom{n}{m}$. This function is

```
fun comb(n,m) = (* assumes 0 <= m <= n *)
        if m=0 orelse m=n then 1
        else comb(n-1,m) + comb(n-1,m-1);
```
*val comb = fn : int * int → int*

We pointed out in Example 3.10 that this function was not designed to work correctly in situations where either n was negative or m was outside the range 0-to-n. One approach to the problem is to define some exceptions and rewrite comb to raise them when the input is improper. Figure 5.2 shows this modification.

We begin by defining two exceptions, BadN and BadM. It is possible to define several exceptions at one time as

```
exception BadN and BadM;
```

or more generally, any list of exceptions separated by the keyword and.

These exceptions are used in lines (2) and (3) of the function comb to check for the erroneous input possibilities. The expressions raise BadN and raise BadM, when executed, cause the function comb to terminate abnormally, without returning an integer.

```
      exception BadN;
```
exception BadN

```
      exception BadM;
```
exception BadM

```
(1)  fun comb(n,m) =
(2)          if n<0 then raise BadN
(3)          else if m<0 orelse m>n then raise BadM
(4)          else if m=0 orelse m=n then 1
(5)          else comb(n-1,m) + comb(n-1,m-1);
```
val comb = fn : int * int → int

```
      comb(5,2);
```
val it = 10 : int

```
      comb(~1,0);
```
uncaught exception BadN

```
      comb(5,6);
```
uncaught exception BadM

Figure 5.2: Using exceptions to catch error conditions in comb

- Note that this situation violates the principle that a function invariably returns a value of its range type. However, exceptions are the only violation of this principle in ML.

The rest of the function, in lines (4) and (5), can assume the inputs satisfy $0 \leq m \leq n$. The first use of the function, comb(5,2), returns an integer, normally. The last two examples of use have improper inputs. Their result is that an exception is raised, and the function comb does not return an integer. Since these exceptions are not caught ("handled"), they result in an error message and termination of the computation. □

5.2.2 Expressions With Parameters

When we declare an exception, we can give it an associated type. The form of the declaration is:

```
exception <identifier> of <type>
```

The identifier is an *exception constructor*, essentially the name of an exception. When we raise the exception, it takes an argument of this type.

Example 5.7: Let us define an exception constructor Foo that takes an argument of type string. The declaration is:

```
exception Foo of string;
```

exception Foo of string

When we raise exception Foo, it must take a string as argument. For instance, if a function contains the phrase

```
raise Foo("bar")
```

and this portion of the function is executed, we get from the ML runtime system the message

uncaught exception Foo

On the other hand, if we do not provide the string argument, just saying:

```
raise Foo
```

then we get an error message from the ML compiler when we try to compile the function containing this phrase. The message is:

> *Error: argument of raise is not an exception [tycon mismatch]*
>   *raised: string → exn*
> *in expression:*
>   *raise Foo*

In its response, ML indicates that it does not even regard Foo by itself as an exception. In the second line of the response it notes that the type of Foo is string -> exn, that is, a function from strings to exceptions.   □

5.2.3   Handling Exceptions

Raising an uncaught exception always stops computation. We may prefer that when an exception is raised, there is an attempt to produce an appropriate value and continue the computation. We can use an expression of the form

<expression> handle <match>

to help in this process. Here, the expression E before the `handle` keyword is one in which we fear that one or more exceptions may be raised. The match takes exceptions as patterns and associates them with expressions of the same type as E.

If E produces a value v and does not raise an exception, then the match is not applied to v, and v is the result of the `handle` expression. However, if E raises an exception, perhaps with arguments, then the match is applied. The first pattern that matches the exception causes its associated expression to be evaluated, and this value becomes the value of the `handle` expression. If none of the patterns match, then the exception is uncaught at this point. The exception may be handled by another, surrounding `handle` expression, or it may remain uncaught, percolate up to the top level, and stop the computation.

Example 5.8 : Let us reconsider the function `comb` of Fig. 5.2, where we attempted to compute $\binom{n}{m}$ and catch situations where $n \leq 0$, $m < 0$, or $m > n$. In Fig. 5.2, our only response when we found an error in the arguments was to raise one of two exceptions `BadN` and `BadM` and cause computation to halt.

A better approach is to declare an exception `OutOfRange`, which takes a pair of integers as parameters. When we raise this exception, we let the function arguments n and m be the arguments of the exception as well. We can then handle the error as follows. For $n = m = 0$, we shall treat the value of $\binom{0}{0}$ as 1. Otherwise, we print an error message telling the user what values n and m had when the error occurred. However, we let `comb` return the value 0 in the hope that it will be possible for computation to proceed.[2]

Figure 5.3 shows the program. Line (1) declares the exception constructor `OutOfRange` and says that its argument type is `int*int`, that is, a pair of integers. Lines (2) through (6) define the function `comb1`, which is like `comb` in Fig. 5.2. However, lines (3) and (4) detect possible errors and raise the exception `OutOfRange(n,m)` so the arguments that caused the error will be transmitted with the exception when it is raised.

In line (7) we define the function `comb`, which calls `comb1` and then handles the exceptions that are raised by `comb1`. Line (8) shows the first rule of the match, where both arguments are 0, and the result is 1. Lines (9) through (15) handle all other cases of the exception. We print the message "out of range" and the values of n and m as a side-effect.

The last expression, on line (15), is 0. Recall it is the value of the final expression in a list of expressions that is returned. Thus the value returned by `comb` is 0 in all exceptional cases besides $m = n = 0$.

Line (16) shows a correct use of `comb`. Here, `comb1` returns the value 6 and raises no exception. There is no exception to handle, so 6 is produced by `comb`, and ML tells us that 6 is the value of `it`.

Line (17) shows an erroneous use of `comb`, where `comb1` raises the exception `OutOfRange(3,4)` at line (4). This exception fails to match the pattern on

---

[2]We should be very sure that no unexpected errors will be introduced by the chosen value 0, or hard-to-diagnose bugs may result.

```
(1)  exception OutOfRange of int*int;
```
*exception OutOfRange of int * int*

```
(2)  fun comb1(n,m) =
(3)          if n <= 0 then raise OutOfRange(n,m)
(4)          else if m < 0 orelse m > n then
                      raise OutOfRange(n,m)
(5)          else if m=0 orelse m=n then 1
(6)          else comb1(n-1,m) + comb1(n-1,m-1);
```
*val comb1 = fn : int * int → int*

```
(7)  fun comb(n,m) = comb1(n,m) handle
(8)          OutOfRange(0,0) => 1 |
(9)          OutOfRange(n,m) => (
(10)                 print("out of range: n=");
(11)                 print(Int.toString(n));
(12)                 print(" m=");
(13)                 print(Int.toString(m));
(14)                 print("\n");
(15)                 0
                );
```
*val comb = fn : int * int → int*

```
(16)  comb(4,2);
```
val it = 6 : int

```
(17)  comb(3,4);
```
out of range: n=3 m=4
val it = 0 : int

```
(18)  comb(0,0);
```
val it = 1 : int

Figure 5.3: Combinatorial function handled by an exception

line (8), but matches the pattern of line (9), which gives n the value 3 and m the value 4. We see two lines of response. The first is the side-effect resulting from the sequence of print-expressions in lines (9) through (14). The second is the value of it, which is 0. This integer is the value returned by comb because 0 is the last expression on line (15).

Finally, line (18) shows an erroneous situation where the pattern of line (8) is matched. The exception OutOfRange(0,0) is raised on line (3). It matches the pattern on line (8), and the value 1 is produced. Thus, 1 becomes the value of it in the ML response. There is no side-effect as there was when the pattern of line (9) was the correct match. □

5.2.4 Exceptions as Elements of an Environment

Let us trace the effect on the environment of the sequence of declarations in Fig. 5.2 where we declared BadN and BadM to be exceptions. These effects are shown in Fig. 5.4. Each of the two exception declarations adds to the environment. We show identifiers BadN and BadM bound to unidentified values. That is, the associated values are internal symbols that are never seen by the user; only identifiers declared to be exceptions are printed when an exception is raised.

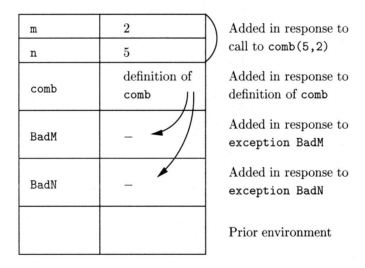

Figure 5.4: Additions to environments for exceptions

When we define the function comb, its binding is a further addition to the environment. Since the definitions of the two exceptions sit below it, comb has access to these exceptions for its own code, as suggested by the arrows in Fig. 5.4. We then show the further additions that occur when the call to comb(5,2) is made. It adds boxes for its parameters as usual; these boxes will disappear when the call returns.

5.2.5   Local Exceptions

It is not necessary to declare exceptions outside a function. We can declare them inside the function, using a `let` expression, so we know they will make sense any time the function is used, regardless of whether or not the exceptions are declared outside the function.

There is, however, a problem with locally defined exceptions. If we try to handle them, the function that does the handling will not be in the scope in which the exceptions were defined, and thus the match used by the handler will not recognize the local exceptions, even if it uses the same identifier in one of its patterns. The following example illustrates the problem.

```
fun comb2(n,m) =
        let
            exception OutOfRange of int*int
        in
            if n <= 0 then raise OutOfRange(n,m)
            else if m<0 orelse m>n then
                    raise OutOfRange(n,m)
            else if m=0 orelse m=n then 1
            else comb2(n-1,m) + comb2(n-1,m-1)
    end;

fun comb(n,m) = comb2(n,m) handle
        OutOfRange(0,0) => 1 |
        OutOfRange(n,m) => (
                print("out of range: n=");
                print(Int.toString(n));
                print(" m=");
                print(Int.toString(m));
                print("\n");
                0
            );
```

Error: nonconstructor applied to argument in pattern: OutofRange

Figure 5.5: Function `comb2` raises an exception that cannot be handled by `comb`

Example 5.9 : Suppose we try to write `comb1` of Fig. 5.3, but with exception `OutOfRange` local to `comb1`. We would find that we cannot handle this exception in function `comb` when it is raised. Figure 5.5 illustrates this erroneous way to use exceptions. We have omitted the global definition of `OutOfRange` that appeared in line (1) of Fig. 5.3. In its place, function `comb2`, which replaces `comb1` of Fig. 5.3, declares a local exception with name `OutOfRange`.

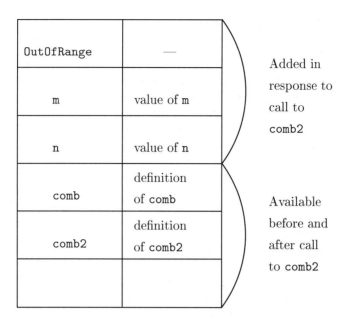

Figure 5.6: Local exceptions cannot be used after their function returns

Figure 5.6 suggests what would be the situation before, during, and after the call of comb2 by comb. Before the call, the definitions of comb and comb2 are available. When comb2 is called, it creates new bindings for its parameters n and m and its local exception OutOfRange. These bindings are available during the execution of comb2, but when comb2 finishes, then the bindings for n, m, and OutOfRange go away and are not available to comb. In particular, when comb of Fig. 5.3 tries to handle exception OutOfRange, the identifier OutOfRange is not defined.

In fact, the code of Fig. 5.5 is illegal. In response to the definition of comb we get from the ML compiler the error message:

Error: non-constructor applied to argument in pattern: OutOfRange

as seen in Fig. 5.5. □

5.2.6   Exercises for Section 5.2

Exercise 5.2.1: Write a function to return the third element of a list. Define suitable exceptions to tell what is wrong in the cases that the response of the function is not defined. Raise the appropriate exception in response to erroneous inputs.

* **Exercise 5.2.2:** Write a factorial function that produces 1 when its argument is 0, produces 0 for a negative argument while printing an error message, and

produces $n!$ for a positive argument n. Organize your code so a function `fact1` does the work of computing $n!$ and raises an exception `Negative(n)` if n is a negative integer.

*! Exercise 5.2.3: In Fig. 4.10 we wrote a program to read nonnegative integers and signal the end of file with the integer -1. It is better to handle this signal with an exception. Modify Fig. 4.10 by declaring an exception `Eof` and raising it in function `startInt` when the end of file is found. Modify function `sumInts1` to handle `Eof`. Other functions can ignore `Eof`, passing the problem to `sumInts1`.

*!! Exercise 5.2.4: We can represent a matrix of reals by a list of lists. Each list on the "main" list represents one row of the matrix. It is possible to compute the determinant of a matrix by *pivotal condensation*, a technique where we recursively eliminate the first row and the first column.[3] The method can be described as follows.

BASIS: If there is one row and column, then return the one element.

INDUCTION: If there are more than one row and column,

  i. Normalize the first row by dividing each element by the first element, say a, in the row.

  ii. For each element M_{ij} not in the first row or column, subtract from M_{ij} the product of the first element in row i and the jth element in row 1. These are the elements furthest above, and furthest to the left of M_{ij}.

  iii. Recursively compute the determinant of the matrix formed by eliminating the first row and first column. The result is a times this determinant. Recall a is the constant from step (i) that was originally in the upper left corner of the matrix.

Write a collection of functions that implement the pivotal condensation algorithm. Define suitable exceptions to catch errors, including

  1. The case where $a = 0$ in step (i) and division by a would therefore yield infinity in step (ii), and

  2. Cases where the matrix is not originally square. That is, there are not as many rows as columns, or there are unequal-length rows.

Hint: It helps to take this one in easy stages. Start with a function that normalizes a row (list) by dividing each element by a given constant. Also, write a function to subtract a multiple of one row from another. Then, write

---

[3]This method is not often preferred for computing determinants, since when followed blindly it can result in failure even in cases where the determinant is not zero (i.e., where the matrix is nonsingular). It can be improved by permuting the rows at each recursive step so the *pivot* (element in the upper left corner) has as large a magnitude as possible.

a function that takes a list of rows and subtracts from the tail of each row the product of the head of the row and a given list. The latter is the heart of the pivotal condensation process. The given row is the normalized tail of the first row. When we multiply it (as a vector) by the head of a row and then subtract the result from the tail of the same row (again, thinking of lists as vectors), we are performing the basic operation required by the pivotal condensation algorithm.

Exercise 5.2.5: Consider the following function:

```
fun myFavoriteException("sally") = Div
|   myFavoriteException("joe") = Match;
```

* a) What is the type of this function?

! b) Both `myFavoriteException("joe")` and `myFavoriteException("zzz")` seem to produce `Match` as the answer. What is the difference between the results of these two calls?

5.3 Polymorphic Functions

We saw in previous chapters that sometimes a function requires arguments of a particular type. Other times, arguments are not restricted to a type, or they are partially restricted. For example, an argument might have type `'a list`, meaning a list of any one type of element is required. The ability of a function to allow arguments of different types is called *polymorphism* ("poly" = "many"; "morph" = "form"), and such a function is called *polymorphic*.

In this section, we study what makes a function polymorphic, or conversely, what forces an argument to be restricted to a single type. Before proceeding, it is useful to remember some points about ML types.

- ML is strongly typed, meaning it is possible to determine the type of any variable or the value returned by any function by examining the program, but without running the program. Put another way, an ML program for which it is not possible to determine the types of variables and function return-values is an incorrect program.

- The algorithm whereby ML deduces the types of variables is complex and beyond the scope of this book. In practice, it is usually easy to see what ML is doing to discover types, as we discussed informally in Section 3.2.4.

- Although we must be able to tell the types of all variables in a complete program, we can define functions whose types are partially or completely flexible; these are the polymorphic functions.

Example 5.10: The extreme example of a polymorphic function is the *identity* function, which we can define by

```
fun identity(x) = x;
```
val identity = fn: 'a → 'a

This function simply produces its argument as its own result, and the argument can be of any type whatsoever. ML observes that the type of the argument and the result are the same, and so designates the type of the identity function as `'a -> 'a`.

We can use the identity function with anything as an argument. For instance:

```
identity(2);
```
val it = 2 : int

Here the type of the result is found to be an integer.

We can even give the identity function a function as an argument; it will produce that function as result.

```
identity(ord);
```
val it = fn : char → int

Although ML does not tell us specifically what function is returned, the fact that the result is `ord` is suggested by the description of the type of the result, a function from characters to integers.

We can even apply the function `identity` twice in the same expression, using it on values of different types, as long as no type error is thereby introduced.

```
identity(2) + floor(identity(3.5))
```
val it = 5 : int

Here, `identity` has been applied to a value of type `int` and another value of type `real` in one expression. □

Example 5.11: Suppose we have defined the function `identity`, as above. Here is a new function f that is polymorphic to an extent:

```
fun f(x) =
        if x<10 then identity
        else rev;
```
val f = fn : int → 'a list → 'a list

Note that `rev` is the built-in list-reversal function provided by ML. It is essentially the function `reverse` from Fig. 3.26. Because `rev` requires an argument that is a list of some type, its type is `'a list -> 'a list`. Since f, like all ML functions, must have a unique range type, the function `identity` within f must also be applied only to types of the form `'a list`, even though `identity` could otherwise be applied to a more general type: `'a`. □

5.3.1   A Limitation on the Use of Polymorphic Functions

A type variable, such as 'a actually has two meanings that differ subtly.

1. A type variable 'a can say "for every type T, there is an instance of this object with type T in place of 'a." Such a type variable is called *generalizable*. The primary example of such a use is in descriptions of the type of polymorphic functions. For instance, the type 'a->'a used to describe the type of the function identity in Example 5.10 represents such a *type schema*, where the function identity can be used with any type, even in the same expression, as we saw in that example.

2. A type variable 'a can represent any one type that we choose. However, once that type is selected, the type cannot change, even if we reuse the object whose type was described using the type variable 'a. A type variable of this kind is *nongeneralizable*. We shall defer an example of a nongeneralizable type variable to Example 5.16.

Versions of ML prior to ML97 did not always distinguish between the two meanings for type variables, and often there is little harm in blending the two. However, because of certain technical problems that prevent compile-time determination of types, which we recall is an essential feature of ML, the ML97 specification requires that expressions at the top level (i.e., expressions that are not subexpressions of another expression) be such that the generalizable interpretation is appropriate. Moreover, ML97 is conservative about allowing the generalizable interpretation for type variables. As a result, only certain kinds of expressions at the top level can have types involving type variables. These expressions, called *nonexpansive expressions*, include function definitions as a common case. In general, we can build nonexpansive expressions by the following rules:

1. A constant or a variable is nonexpansive.

2. A function definition is nonexpansive.

3. A tuple (or more generally a record structure as described in Section 7.1) of nonexpansive expressions is nonexpansive.

4. A nonexpansive expression may be preceded by a "constructor" that is either an exception constructor or a data constructor belonging to a datatype. The latter constructors are covered Section 6.2, but we give a simple example of this form of nonexpansive expression in Example 5.14.

In addition, we can attach types to nonexpansive expressions with a colon and a type expression, and we can use the keyword op where appropriate in nonexpansive expressions.

Expressions that are not of these forms are *expansive* and not allowed to have type variables. The error message that we get when, at the top level, we write an expansive expression with a type variable, accuses that type variable of being "nongeneralizable," i.e., of not having the first interpretation given at the beginning of this section.

The matter of which expressions are permitted to have types with type variables and which are not is complex. However, a few examples should suffice to cover the cases that are likely to surface in practice.

Example 5.12: If we apply a function to an argument, and the type of the result has type variables, then these type variables are nongeneralizable and the expression is illegal. A simple example is:

```
identity(identity);
```
Error: nongeneralizable type variable
val it = 'Z → 'Z

Here, ML has recognized that the result is a function whose domain and range types are arbitrary but the same (represented by 'Z here). However, it does not accept the expression, because it is expansive and has a type variable.

We can apply the identity to itself only if we provide a concrete type for the domain and range. For instance:

```
identity(identity: int -> int);
```
val it = fn: int → int

Now the resulting expression, which is the identity function on integers only, has a type with no type variables, so the fact that the expression is expansive becomes irrelevant. □

Example 5.13: We can safely build tuples of nonexpansive expressions. For example:

```
(identity, identity);
```
*val it = <poly-record> : ('a → 'a) * ('b → 'b)*

Here, we have constructed an expression consisting of a pair of identity functions. Notice that the type of the pair involves two distinct type variables 'a and 'b, because each of the identity functions could apply to a different type.

In contrast to tuple-formation, list formation is considered to build an expansive expression. Thus, an expression like [identity, identity] is illegal in ML. □

Example 5.14: Another way to build nonexpansive expressions is with the data constructors that are associated with datatypes. We have not yet covered the subject of datatypes (see Section 6.2), but we have met one example of a datatype that ML provides for us in the top-level environment: the option. That is, the names SOME and NONE are actually treated by the ML system as data constructors of the datatype option. Thus, for example, the following expression is legal.

When Does a Type Problem Arise?

Remember that the problem leading to the "nongeneralizable type variable" error that we have been discussing in this section can arise only when all three of the following conditions are met by an expression:

1. The expression is at the top level; that is, the expression is not a subexpression of some larger expression.

2. The type of the expression involves at least one type variable.

3. The form of the expression does not meet the conditions for it to be nonexpansive.

If even one of these conditions is not met, we need not worry about the type of the expression.

```
SOME identity;
```
val it = SOME fn : ('a → 'a) option

Here, we have applied the data constructor `SOME` to a nonexpansive expression — the variable `identity` that represents the identity function. The response tells us that the result is an option of a function of the type of the identity function, `'a->'a`. □

Example 5.15 : Next, let us observe that we can use expressions that would be illegal at the top level inside another expression, as long as the resulting expression is legal. Consider the expression of Fig. 5.7.

```
let
    val x = identity(identity)
in
    x(1)
end;
```
val it = 1 : int

Figure 5.7: A nongeneralizable type variable for a subexpression

Here, we have defined x to be the identity applied to itself. We saw in Example 5.12 that such an expression is illegal at the top level. However, here `identity(identity)` is a subexpression, so we do not yet trigger the objection that there is a nongeneralizable type variable, even though the type variable `'a` in the type `'a->'a` for `x` is indeed nongeneralizable. Since the one type to

which x applies is found in the expression x(1) to be int, ML finds no problem
with the expression as a whole. In fact, the complete expression of Fig. 5.7
has no type variables in its type, so the issue of nongeneralizable type variables
does not come up.   □

```
let
     val x = identity(identity)
in
     (x(1), x("a"))
end;
```
Error: operator and operand don't agree [literal]
  operator domain: int
  operand: string
  in expression
   x ("a")

Figure 5.8: Trying to reuse a nongeneralizable type variable

Example 5.16: The variable x in Fig. 5.7 is nongeneralizable. That is, the
interpretation of its type variable is that one and only one type may ever be
substituted for that variable. We can see in Fig. 5.8 the effect of the nongener-
alizability of the type of x. There, we try to use x twice to stand for the identity
applied to different types. That is, the variable 'a in the type 'a->'a of x is
bound to int when ML encounters the expression x(1). When x is next applied
to the argument "a" it is too late to change the value of 'a, so we are trying
to apply the identity function on integers to a string and get the error message
shown in Fig. 5.8.

To further emphasize the difference between generalizable and nongeneralizable type variables, consider that the following expression:

```
(identity(1), identity("a"));
```
*val it = (1,"a") : int * string*

is legal. The difference between this expression and the almost-identical Fig. 5.8
is that when we defined x in Fig. 5.8, even though the value of x is the identity
function, ML converted the interpretation of the type variable in x's type from
generalizable to nongeneralizable. True, the system might have realized that x
was just the identity function, and allowed it to retain the generalizable interpretation for its type variable. However, as we mentioned at the beginning of
this section, ML must be conservative about using the generalizable interpretation, or it will be impossible for the system to guarantee correct compile-time
type checking.   □

5.3.2 Operators that Restrict Polymorphism

Most of the operators that we have met prevent polymorphism in functions where they are used. These "polymorphism-destroying" operators include:

1. Arithmetic operators: `+`, `-`, `*`, and `~`.

2. Division-related operators such as `/`, `div`, and `mod`.

3. The inequality comparison operators: `<`, `<=`, `>=`, and `>`. Note we exclude `=` (equal-to) and `<>` (not-equal-to) from this group. They behave differently from the inequality comparisons as far as polymorphism is concerned. We shall discuss this matter in Section 5.3.4.

4. The boolean connectives: `andalso`, `orelse`, and `not`.

5. The string concatenation operator: `^`.

6. Type conversion operators such as `ord`, `chr`, `real`, `str`, `floor`, `ceiling`, `round`, and `truncate`.

All but groups (1) and (3) force their argument(s) and result to be of one specific type. Groups (1) and (3) include operators that apply to several different types, but ML requires that the type be known from inspection of the program. Thus, operators in groups (1) and (3) not only restrict their arguments and results to one type, they frequently require us to indicate with a colon what that type is.

5.3.3 Operators that Allow Polymorphism

We have seen several operators that allow polymorphism, although they somewhat restrict the types of their results and/or arguments. Three classes of operators in this category are:

1. Tuple operators, such as the tuple-forming operator, consisting of parentheses and commas, as $(,,\ldots,)$. Also in this group are the component-reading operators, `#1`, `#2`, and so on.

2. The list operators `::`, `@`, `hd`, and `tl`, the list constant `nil`, and brackets used as the list-former $[\cdots]$.

3. The *equality* operators `=` and `<>`.

When we apply a tuple constructor, we get a tuple type of some sort. When we apply a list-building operator, we are restricted to create a list type of some sort. When we apply an equality operator, we restrict the arguments to be of the same "equality type," a concept we shall discuss shortly, in Section 5.3.4. However, there are no other constraints forced on the types of operands or results.

Let us consider why list operators do not prohibit polymorphism. A similar explanation applies to the tuple-forming operators. First, consider an expression like $x + y$. ML implements the addition operator by computing a new value, the sum of x and y. To compute the sum, ML needs to know whether to add integers or reals.

In contrast consider the cons operator :: . ML represents lists internally in the conventional, linked-list fashion that we discussed in Section 3.5.2. Cells consisting of a pair of pointers, the first to an element and the second to the next cell, represent the list.

To apply the cons operator, the ML runtime system creates a new cell, puts a pointer to the head in the first field of the cell, and puts a pointer to the tail in the second field of the cell. Notice that with this scheme, the operation is performed in exactly the same way regardless of the types of the head and tail. Of course, ML requires that it be able to deduce the types of head and tail before running the program and requires that they be compatible types (i.e., if the head is of type T, then the tail is of type T list).

5.3.4   The Equality Operators

Now let us look at the *equality operators* = and <>. ML defines a class of types called *equality types*, which are those that allow equality to be tested among values of that type. Most basic types — integer, boolean, character, and string — are equality types.[4] Two ways to form more equality types are:

1. Forming products of equality types (for tuples).

2. Forming a list whose elements are of an equality type.

Note that rules (1) and (2) can be applied recursively. So, for example, int * int is an equality type, (int * int) list is an equality type,

```
    int list * string
```

is an equality type, and so on. We shall also see user-defined datatypes in Section 6.2, and some of these new types will be equality types as well.

Example 5.17: Let us define two variables to be pairs of integers.

```
    val x = (1,2);
    val x = (1,2) : int * int
```

```
    val y = (2,3);
    val y = (2,3) : int * int
```

---

[4]Remember, however, that the reals are not an equality type, for reasons we discussed in Section 2.1.4.

Then we can compare these values, for instance:

```
x=y;
```
val it = false : bool

```
x = (1,2);
```
val it = true : bool

Similarly, we could define and compare lists, as:

```
val L = [1,2,3];
```
val L = [1,2,3] : int list

```
val M = [2,3];
```
val M = [2,3] : int list

Then we can compare as follows:

```
L <> M;
```
val it = true : bool

```
L = 1::M;
```
val it = true : bool

Notice in the last example that ML evaluates expressions before testing for equality, so it discovers that the expression `1::M` denotes the same list as is denoted by the variable L. □

On the other hand, functions cannot be compared for equality even though we might think that two functions should be equal if they do exactly the same thing on all inputs. Any type involving a function is not an equality type.

Example 5.18: Suppose we write an expression such as

```
identity = identity;
```

where `identity` is the function defined in Example 5.10. Then we get the error message shown in Fig. 5.9.

Line (1) of Fig. 5.9 says that the type of the operator (the = sign) does not agree with the type of its operand (the pair of identity functions). The problem is that equality or inequality can only be tested among pairs of the same equality type, and no function type is an equality type. Thus, even though the two uses of `identity` as a function name obviously denote the same function, the comparison is not legal in ML.

Line (2) further explains that the operator = requires arguments of the same equality type, here denoted by ''Z.

(1)   *Error: operator and operand don't agree [equality type required]*
(2)   *operator domain: "Z * "Z*
(3)   *operand: ('Y → 'Y) * ('X → 'X)*
(4)   *in expression:*
(5)   *= (identity, identity)*

Figure 5.9: Functions cannot be compared for equality

- Remember that type variables whose values are restricted to be an equality type are distinguished by having names that begin with two quote marks rather than only one.

Line (3) points out that the actual pair of arguments given is two polymorphic functions. One function is from some type 'X to the same type, and the second is from some type 'Y to that same type.

- Note that there is no reason to believe that 'X and 'Y are the same type. As with polymorphic functions in general, two uses of the identity function need not apply to the same type.

Finally, lines (4) and (5) indicate that the error was in the expression

```
identity = identity
```

However, it gives the operator and operands in prefix form, where the operator is applied in the same way a function is applied to its argument.   □

Example 5.19 : To explore further the effect of an = or <> comparison on the set of permissible types, let us reconsider the two versions of the function `reverse` that we developed in Examples 3.8 and 3.15. These are repeated in Fig. 5.10(a) and (b), as functions `rev1` and `rev2`, respectively. However, here we have used the correct type variable name ''a (with two quotes) that ML uses to describe the type of the function in Fig. 5.10(a). This type name tells us that any type can be used, provided it is an equality type.

   In Fig. 5.10(b), we see the ML response telling us that the function `rev2` can take an argument of any type whatsoever, regardless of whether it is an equality type. If we give each of these programs a list whose elements are from one equality type, both functions produce the same answer. The difference shows up, however, if we apply each function to a list whose elements are chosen from one non-equality type. For instance, consider a function call of the form

```
reverse([floor, trunc, ceil]);
```

where `reverse` can be either `rev1` or `rev2`. Each of the elements on the list are functions from reals to integers that we discussed in Section 2.2.2. Thus, the type of elements on the list is

```
(1) fun rev1(L) =
(2)         if L = nil then nil
(3)         else rev1(tl(L)) @ [hd(L)];
```
   val rev1 = fn : "a list → "a list

(a) Reversal using an equality comparison

```
(4) fun rev2(nil) = nil
(5) |   rev2(x::xs) = rev2(xs) @ [x]
```
   val rev2 = fn : 'a list → 'a list

(b) Reversal without using an equality comparison

Figure 5.10: Two functions for reversing a list

```
fn : real -> int
```

If we use **rev2**, the function of Fig. 5.10(b), then the list will be reversed normally, which yields the list [ceil, trunc, floor]. The ML response is:

   rev2([floor, trunc, ceil]);
   val it = [fn,fn,fn] : (real → int) list

That is, ML tells us that the result is a list of three functions, each from reals to integers.

```
(1)   Error: operator and operand don't agree [equality type required]
(2)   operator domain: "Z list
(3)   operand: (real → int) list
(4)   in expression:
(5)       rev1 floor :: trunc :: ceil :: nil
```

Figure 5.11: Error response when list reversal requires an equality type

However, if we use **rev1**, the function of Fig. 5.10(a), then we get the error message in Fig. 5.11. This message is similar to that in Fig. 5.9. Line (2) refers to the operator **rev1**, which takes as an argument a ''Z list, that is, a list whose elements are from any one equality type. Line (3) says that the argument actually found, which is [floor, trunc, ceil], is a list of functions from reals to integers. This type, being a function type, is not an equality type and therefore is not suitable as the type ''Z. Lines (4) and (5) indicate the offending expression. Note that lists are represented by `::` and `nil` rather than by square brackets. □

We may well wonder why the function `rev1` of Fig. 5.10(a) requires an equality type. The reason is found in line (2), where the comparison `L=nil` occurs. If list L is to be tested for equality to something, then surely L must be of an equality type, which means its elements must be chosen from an equality type.

In contrast, line (4) in Fig. 5.10(b) makes essentially the same test by matching L to the pattern `nil`. Recalling the discussion in Section 3.3.5 about how ML matches patterns, we see that here we are not testing for equality of L to `nil`. Rather, we are matching the expression tree for the value that L currently has, to the one-node tree for the expression `nil`. ML can match trees without testing for equality of anything except constants of the basic types and identifiers.

You may think that there is something wrong with this analysis and observe that in line (2) of Fig. 5.10(a) we don't really need to test equality of elements to compare a list L with `nil`. That is quite true, although if we had replaced the test of line (2) by a test for equality to a list other than `nil`, for instance `L=[1,2]`, then L would surely have to be of an equality type. The designers of ML have chosen to infer that an equality type is needed by the presence of an operator `=` or `<>`, and they have chosen not to consider equality to `nil` as a special case. You may regard that choice as either "a bug or a feature" of ML, as you wish.

- ML has a built-in function `null` that tests whether a list is empty without requiring that list to be of an equality type. We could write line (2) of Fig. 5.10(a) as

  ```
  (2) if null(L) then nil
  ```

  and then the function `rev1` of Fig. 5.10(a) would not require an equality type. Its type would be `'a list -> 'a list`, just like Fig. 5.10(b).

5.3.5   Exercises for Section 5.3

Exercise 5.3.1: Let `rev1` be the function of Fig. 5.10(a) and `rev2` the function of Fig. 5.10(b). What is the result of the following calls?

* a) `rev1([(rev1: int list -> int list), rev1])`

  b) `rev2([(rev1: int list -> int list), rev1])`

  c) `rev1([rev1,rev1])`

* d) `rev2([rev2,rev2])`

  e) `rev1([chr,chr])`

* f) rev2([chr,chr])

g) rev1([chr,ord])

h) rev2([chr,ord])

Exercise 5.3.2: We can restrict polymorphic types (type expressions with variables) by: (*i*) equating type variables, (*ii*) replacing a type variable by a constant type, or (*iii*) replacing a type variable by a nonconstant expression. Give an example of each kind of restriction for the following type expressions.

* a) 'a * 'b * int

b) ('a list) * ('b list)

! **Exercise 5.3.3:** Suppose $f(x, y, z)$ is a function. Give an example of a definition of f that would cause the argument of f to have each of the following types.

* a) 'a * ''b * ('a -> ''b)

b) 'a * 'a * int

* c) 'a list * 'b * 'a

d) ('a * 'b) * 'a list * 'b list

Exercise 5.3.4: Tell whether or not each of the following types is an equality type.

* a) int * string list

b) (int -> char) * string

* c) int -> string -> unit

* d) real * (string * string) list

Exercise 5.3.5: Let L have the value [(1,2), (3,4)], let M have the value (1,2), and let N have the value (3,4). Which of the following equality tests have the value true?

* a) L = M::[N]

b) M::L = L@[N]

* c) [(1,2)]@[N] = L@nil

d) N::L = (3,4)::M::N::nil

```
fun f(nil) = nil
|   f([x]) = [x]
|   f(x::y::zs) = [x,y];

fun g(x,y) = (f(x), f(y));

fun h(x,y) =
        let val v = f(nil) in (x::v, y::v) end;
```

Figure 5.12: Functions for Exercise 5.3.7

* Exercise 5.3.6: If the ML runtime system applies the cons operator without looking at the elements of the list, how can it be sure the types of the head and tail are compatible?

! Exercise 5.3.7: In Fig. 5.12 are three functions, f, g, and h. Function f takes any list and returns the list with the third and subsequent elements, if they exist, deleted. Function g applies f to a pair of arguments and returns the pair of results. Function h computes a local value v by applying f to nil (which returns an empty list) and then conses the two arguments of h to v. For each of the expressions below, indicate whether it is legal, and if not, what is the error?

* a) g([1,2,3], ["a"]).

* b) g([1,2,3], nil).

   c) g([f,f], [1]).

   d) g([1], [1.0]).

* e) h(1, 2).

   f) h(1, "a").

* g) h(nil, nil).

   h) h([1], nil).

5.4 Higher-Order Functions

A typical function has parameters that represent "data." That is, the parameters are of some basic type like real, or they are lists or tuples of basic types, lists or tuples of those, and so on. However, it is also possible for parameters or results of functions to have function types. In Section 5.3, we met some functions that can take arguments of other types, including function types. Examples are the identity function, which can take an argument of any type, or `rev2` of Fig. 5.10(b), which is able to reverse a list of functions.

Functions that take functions as arguments and/or produce functions as values are called *higher-order functions*. ML makes it easy to define higher-order functions. In contrast, the mechanisms in conventional languages for defining and using higher-order functions tend to be cumbersome, and there may be some limitations on the power of these mechanisms. For example, it may not be possible to define a function like `identity` that works on values of any type whatsoever.

Example 5.20: Let us consider a higher-order function that is often used as an example for conventional programming languages: numerical integration by the trapezoidal rule. The idea is to compute the (approximate) integral of some function $f(x)$ between limits a and b — that is, $\int_a^b f(x)dx$ — by dividing the line from a to b into n equal parts for some n. We then approximate the integral as the sum of the areas of the n trapezoids that are suggested by Fig. 5.13 for the case $n = 3$.

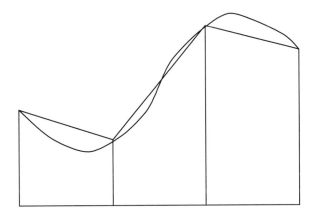

Figure 5.13: Integration by the trapezoidal rule

In more detail, let $\delta = (b - a)/n$. Then the ith trapezoid has width δ and runs from $a + (i - 1)\delta$ to $a + i\delta$. The area of the ith trapezoid is δ times the average of the two vertical sides, that is:

$$\delta\Big(f\big(a + (i - 1)\delta\big) + f(a + i\delta)\Big)/2$$

Figure 5.14 shows the function `trap(a,b,n,F)` that takes two real numbers, the limits a and b, an integer n (the number of trapezoids to use), and a function F to be integrated. As we cannot easily iterate from 1 to n and thereby sum the areas of all the trapezoids, our ML function will use an equivalent recursive strategy. The function `trap` computes the area of the first trapezoid only. It

---

The Order of a Function

Technically, the order of a function is defined by the following induction.

BASIS: A function is "first-order" if its arguments and result are all "data," that is, not functions.

INDUCTION: A function is of order one more than the largest of the orders of its arguments and result. Note that there are some functions, like the identity function, that do not get an order by this induction, and are therefore of "infinite order."

---

then computes a new lower limit that is one trapezoid's width to the right of the old lower limit a, and decreases n by 1. A recursive call with the new values of a and n sums the areas of the remaining trapezoids.

```
        fun trap(a,b,n,F) =
(1)             if n<=0 orelse b-a<=0.0 then 0.0
                else
                    let
(2)                     val delta = (b-a)/real(n)
                    in
(3)                     delta*(F(a)+F(a+delta))/2.0 +
(4)                         trap(a+delta,b,n-1,F)
                    end;
        val trap = fn : real * real * int * (real → real) → real
```

Figure 5.14: Function implementing the trapezoidal rule

In line (1) of Fig. 5.14 we test for the basis case, where $n = 0$ and $b = a$. Then the value of the integral is 0. However, at the same time we handle data errors, where n or $b - a$ is negative, or where one of n and $b - a$ but not the other is 0. These errors can only occur on the initial call to `trap`, and we really should catch them with exceptions, rather than by returning 0 as we do.

If we are not at the basis case, then in line (2) we compute the local variable `delta` to be $1/n$th of the width of the range of integration; that is, `delta` is the width of each trapezoid.[5] Lines (3) and (4) evaluate the integral. In line (3) we compute the area of the first trapezoid, multiplying `delta` by the sum of the heights of the sides — `F(a)` and `F(a+delta)` — and then dividing by 2.

---

[5]The value of `delta` should be the same at each call to `trap`, and we leave it as an exercise to rewrite the function so it evaluates `delta` only once. However, reevaluating `delta` for each trapezoid does have the advantage of preventing the accumulation of roundoff errors in situations where the value of `delta` cannot be represented precisely in the computer.

Simulating Iterations by Recursions

The reader should examine the "trick" of Fig. 5.14 carefully, because it is a common way to convert from a loop in an iterative language to a recursive function in a functional language. The general idea is to write a function that, as a basis case, tests if the loop is done. For the induction it does one iteration of the loop and then calls itself recursively to do whatever iterations of the loop remain. The arguments of the function are the loop index and any other variables that are needed in the loop. The hard part in designing the function often is deciding how to express the result of the loop as a value to be returned by the function.

Line (4) adds to this area the result of the recursive call on the range that excludes the first trapezoid.

Note the type of the function `trap` as described in the ML response. It is a function that takes a 4-tuple for an argument; the four components (a, b, n, and F) are respectively of types `real`, `real`, `int`, and `real -> real`. The result of the function `trap` is a real.

As an example of a use of the function `trap`, let us define a suitable function F, such as

```
fun square(x:real) = x*x;
val square = fn : real → real
```

Then, we can call, for instance,

```
trap(0.0, 1.0, 8, square);
val it = .3359375 : real
```

This call asks for the integral $\int_0^1 x^2 dx$, whose exact value is $1/3$. We divide the range into 8 parts, and the result is high by less than 1%.   □

5.4.1   Some Common Higher-Order Functions

We shall now introduce three useful higher-order functions. The first two are actually present as ML built-in functions, although they appear in a form somewhat different from the form we use here.

1. The *map* function takes a function F and a list $[a_1, a_2, \ldots, a_n]$, and produces the list $[F(a_1), F(a_2), \ldots, F(a_n)]$. That is, it applies F to each element of the list and returns the list of resulting values. This function is known to Lisp users as *mapcar*. Since there is in ML a function `map` that is similar in spirit but different in type, we shall use `simpleMap` for our initial version of map. In Section 5.6.3 we cover the ML version of map.

2. The *reduce* function takes a function F with two arguments and a list $[a_1, a_2, \ldots, a_n]$. The function F normally is assumed to compute some associative operation such as addition, that is, $F(x, y) = x + y$. The result of `reduce` on F and $[a_1, a_2, \ldots, a_n]$ is

$$F(a_1, F(a_2, F(\cdots, F(a_{n-1}, a_n) \cdots)))$$

Thinking of F as an associative binary infix operator, we have the simpler expression $a_1 F a_2 F \cdots F a_n$. For example, if F is the sum function, then $reduce(F, [a_1, a_2, \ldots, a_n])$ is $a_1 + a_2 + \cdots + a_n$, the sum of the elements on the list. ML has two functions `foldl` and `foldr` (fold from the left or right) that are similar in spirit to the function `reduce` that we shall design. The latter functions are covered in Section 5.6.4.

3. The function *filter* takes a predicate P, that is, a function whose value is boolean, and a list $[a_1, a_2, \ldots, a_n]$. The result is the list of all those elements on the given list that satisfy the predicate P.

5.4.2   A Simple Map Function

We can define a simple version of the map function as follows.

```
fun simpleMap(F,nil) = nil
|   simpleMap(F,x::xs) = F(x)::simpleMap(F,xs)
```
*val map = fn : ('a → 'b) * 'a list → 'b list*

In the first line we see that if the list is empty, then there are no elements to apply the function F to, so `simpleMap` returns the empty list. The second line covers the inductive case, where we apply F to the head of the list and then recursively apply `simpleMap` to the same function F and the tail of the list. The result is assembled by taking $F(x)$, that is, F applied to the head element, and following it by the result of applying F to all the other elements of the list.

Notice the type of `simpleMap`. It has two parameters, the first of which is a function F from some type `'a` to a possibly different type `'b`. The second parameter is a list of elements of the type `'a`, which is the type F expects for its argument. The result of `simpleMap` is of type `'b list`, that is, a list of elements of the range type of function F. We see that `simpleMap` is as polymorphic as it can be; it only requires that the list elements be of the type that the function F expects.

Example 5.21: Let us define the function `square` to produce the square of a real, as

```
fun square(x:real) = x*x;
```
val square = fn : real → real

Then we may apply `square` to each element of a list of reals by using `simpleMap` as follows.

```
simpleMap(square, [1.0, 2.0, 3.0]);
```
val it = [1.0,4.0,9.0] : real list

That is, `simpleMap` applies `square` to each of 1.0, 2.0, and 3.0 in turn and produces the list of their squares. □

Example 5.22 : The function to which `simpleMap` is applied need not be something we write; it could be a suitable built-in function. For instance, ˜, the unary minus operator, has the form we expect for a function used as an argument of `simpleMap`. We can write

```
simpleMap(~, [1,2,3]);
```
val it = [˜1,˜2,˜3] : int list

This application of `simpleMap` has negated each element of the given list. □

If we want to apply `simpleMap` to a function that we must define, we need not write the definition of that function separately and give it a name as we did for `square` in Example 5.21. Just as we may write the value of an integer, say 23, without giving it a name, we may express the value of a function anonymously. We saw how to do so in Section 5.1.2. We write the function as the keyword **fn** (not to be confused with **fun**) followed by a match. Recall that a match is written as one or more groups consisting of a pattern, the symbol => (not to be confused with ->), and an expression that is the value of the function for inputs that match the pattern. If there is more than one group, the groups are separated by vertical bars.

Example 5.23 : We can apply `square` to each member of a real list without actually defining `square` to be the name of the function, as follows.

```
simpleMap(fn x => x*x, [1.0, 2.0, 3.0]);
```
val it = [1.0,4.0,9.0] : real list

This anonymous function uses only one pattern, x, and the result of the function for this pattern is x^2.

Notice that in the definition of the squaring function as a value,

```
fn x => x*x
```

we did not have to declare x to be real. ML was able to figure out that * represents real multiplication from the fact that the second parameter of `simpleMap` is a real list. □

5.4.3   The Function reduce

Another useful higher-order function is one we shall call reduce. It is related to, but different from, functions foldl and foldr in the ML top-level environment; we discuss the latter functions in Section 5.6.4. Our function reduce takes a function F of two arguments and a nonempty list $[a_1, a_2, \ldots, a_n]$. A recursive definition of the result of reducing the list by function F is:

BASIS: If $n = 1$, that is, the list is a single element a, then the result is a.

INDUCTION: If $n > 1$, then let b be the result of reducing the tail of the list, which is $[a_2, a_3, \ldots, a_n]$, by function F. Then the reduction of the whole list $[a_1, a_2, \ldots, a_n]$ by F is $F(a_1, b)$.

Example 5.24: Usually the function F defines an associative operator, in which case it does not matter in what order we group the list elements. For instance:

1. The reduction of a list with F equal to the addition function produces the sum of the elements of the list.

2. The reduction by the product function produces the product of the elements of the list.

3. The reduction by the logical AND operator produces the value true if all the elements of a boolean list are true and produces false otherwise.

4. The reduction by the function max (larger of two elements) produces the largest element on the list.

□

```
    exception EmptyList;
    exception EmptyList

(1) fun reduce(F,nil) = raise EmptyList
(2) |   reduce(F,[a]) = a
(3) |   reduce(F,x::xs) = F(x, reduce(F,xs));
    val reduce = fn : ('a * 'a → 'a) * 'a list → 'a
```

Figure 5.15: The function reduce

An implementation of the function reduce is shown in Fig. 5.15. Since reduce does not make sense on the empty list, we create an exception EmptyList and raise it at line (1) if the second argument of reduce is nil. Next, line (2) says that if the list has a single element a, then that element is the value of reduce regardless of the function used.

- By intercepting lists of length 1 at line (2), we avoid ever calling `reduce` recursively on an empty list, which would cause an error.

Finally, line (3) implements the inductive step. We reduce the tail of the given list, using the function F, and then apply F to the head and the result of this reduction.

Notice the type of `reduce`. It is a function that takes as first parameter a function F, both of whose parameters are of the same type `'a` and whose result is also of this type. The second parameter of `reduce` is a list of elements of type `'a`, and the result of `reduce` is also of type `'a`.

These equalities of type are inferred by ML as follows. F is used with the result of `reduce` as its second argument in line (3), so the result of `reduce` and the second parameter of F must be of the same type, say `'a`. In line (2) we see that the elements of the list can be the result of `reduce`, which says that the element type is also `'a`. We see in line (3) that elements of the list can also be the first argument of F, which tells us that the first parameter of F is also of type `'a`. Finally, from line (3) we see that the result types of `reduce` and F are the same, so F produces a value of type `'a` as well.

Example 5.25: This example illustrates the use of function `reduce`. It also uses `simpleMap` and in general illustrates how one can program using higher-order functions effectively.

The *variance* of a list of reals $[a_1, a_2, \ldots, a_n]$ is the average of the squares minus the square of the average. More precisely, one formula for the variance is

$$\left(\sum_{i=1}^{n} a_i^2\right)/n - \left(\left(\sum_{i=1}^{n} a_i\right)/n\right)^2 \tag{5.1}$$

The variance is a measure of the amount by which the elements of a list differ from their average value. In fact, an equivalent formula for the variance is the average of the squares of the differences between each element and the average element. In other words, the variance may also be written $\left(\sum_{i=1}^{n} (a_i - \bar{a})^2\right)/n$, where $\bar{a}$ is the average element, or $\bar{a} = \left(\sum_{i=1}^{n} a_i\right)/n$.

The square root of the variance, called the *standard deviation*, represents the amount by which a typical element differs from the average. For example, if all the elements are the same then the variance and standard deviation are 0. If half the elements are 10.0 while the other half are 20.0, then each element differs from the average (15.0) by 5.0, so the variance is 25.0 and the standard deviation is 5.0.

We can evaluate Formula (5.1) for the variance using the higher-order functions `simpleMap` and `reduce` as follows. Suppose we have function `square` to take the square of a real and function `plus` to sum two reals. We can obtain the sum of the squares of the elements of a list L by the expression `reduce(plus, simpleMap(square,L))`. That is, `simpleMap(square,L)` produces the list of squares, and `reduce` with first argument `plus` sums these squares. We divide this result by n, the length of the list L, to get the average square. Then we can get the average by reduce(plus,L)/n, and we can apply square to get the square of the average. The necessary functions, assuming that reduce and simpleMap are as previously defined, are shown in Fig. 5.16.

```
(1)  fun square(x:real) = x*x;
     val square = fn : real → real


(2)  fun plus(x:real,y) = x+y;
     val plus = fn : real * real → real


     fun variance(L) =
             let
(3)                  val n = real(length(L))
             in
(4)                  reduce(plus,simpleMap(square,L))/n -
(5)                      square(reduce(plus,L)/n)
             end;
     variance = fn : real list → real


(6)  variance([1.0, 2.0, 5.0, 8.0]);
     val it = 7.5 : real
```

Figure 5.16: Computing the variance using higher-order functions

In lines (1) and (2) of Fig. 5.16 we define the functions square and plus. Then we see the definition of function variance. At line (3) it computes n, the list length, which is a common subexpression, as a real number. Recall that ML provides a built-in function length at the top level, to compute the length of a list (as an integer), as well as a function real to convert an integer to an equivalent real number. Lines (4) and (5) are Formula (5.1).

Finally, in line (6) we see a use of the function variance on the list of elements $[1, 2, 5, 8]$. Here, $n = 4$. The sum of the squares is $1 + 4 + 25 + 64 = 94$, so the average square is $94/4 = 23.5$. The average element is 4, so the square of the average is 16. Since $23.5 - 16 = 7.5$, the variance is 7.5, as we see in the ML response.

Another way to compute the variance is to take the average of the squares of the differences between the elements and the average. In this case, we would average $(1-4)^2$, $(2-4)^2$, $(5-4)^2$, and $(8-4)^2$, or $(9+4+1+16)/4 = 7.5$. □

5.4.4 Converting Infix Operators to Function Names

We might expect that we could use the operator + in place of the function plus of Example 5.25. For example, can we write reduce(+,L) in line (5) of Fig. 5.16. Should we do so, we get the error message:

> *Error: expression or pattern begins with infix identifier: "+"*

The problem is that ML, like most languages, defines the usual arithmetic operators to be infix. That is, they appear between their operands. However, the function F in the definition of reduce is expected, as are all functions, to precede its operands.

To allow an infix operator to be used as the name of a function, we precede it by the keyword op. For example, we may write

```
op + (2,3);
val it = 5 : int
```

In effect, op + is the same function as the function plus defined in Fig. 5.16, except that the latter is restricted to reals and the former needs to have its parameter type determined. As another example, line (5) of Fig. 5.16 can be written

```
square(reduce(op +, L)/n)
```

with no change in the behavior of the program.

5.4.5 The Function Filter

Another useful higher-order function is filter, which appears in Fig. 5.17. This function takes a predicate P and a list L, and produces the list of elements of L that satisfy the predicate P. In line (1) we see the basis case: if the list L is empty then filter produces the empty list regardless of P. Lines (2) through (4) cover the inductive case. We test at line (3) whether $P(x)$ is true for the head element x of the list L. If so, the resulting list is x followed by whatever we get by filtering the tail of the list with predicate P. On line (4) we see that if $P(x)$ is false then x is not selected and the result is whatever we get by filtering the tail.

Notice the type of filter. It has two parameters, the first of which is a function of type 'a -> bool. This type indicates that the argument corresponding to the first parameter of filter can be a predicate with any domain type. The second argument is a list of elements of the type 'a to which the predicate applies. The result of filter is another list of elements of this type.

In line (5) of Fig. 5.17 we see an example of the use of filter. The first argument is a description of the boolean-valued function that is true when its argument is greater than 10. We use the keyword fn and a one-pattern match to describe this function. The second argument is a list of integers, and the result is those integers greater than 10, in the order of their occurrence on the list.

```
(1) fun filter(P,nil) = nil
(2)  |   filter(P,x::xs) =
(3)           if P(x) then x::filter(P,xs)
(4)           else filter(P,xs);
```
      *val filter = fn : ('a → bool) * 'a list → 'a list*


```
(5) filter(fn(x) => x>10, [1,10,23,5,16]);
```
      val it = [23,16] : int list

Figure 5.17: The function filter

5.4.6 ˙ Exercises for Section 5.4

* **Exercise 5.4.1:** Write a function `tabulate` that takes as arguments an initial value a, an increment δ, a number of points n, and a function F from reals to reals. Print a table with columns corresponding to values x and $F(x)$, where $x = a, a + \delta, a + 2\delta, \ldots, a + (n-1)\delta$.

Exercise 5.4.2: *Simpson's rule* is a more accurate way to integrate functions numerically. If we evaluate a function F at $2n + 1$ evenly spaced points,

$$a, a + \delta, a + 2\delta, \ldots, a + 2n\delta$$

then we may estimate the integral $\int_a^{a+2n\delta} F(x)dx$ by

$$\delta\Big(F(a) + 4F(a + \delta) + 2F(a + 2\delta) + 4F(a + 3\delta) + 2F(a + 4\delta) + \cdots$$
$$+ 2F(a + (2n - 2)\delta) + 4F(a + (2n - 1)\delta) + F(a + 2n\delta)\Big)/3$$

That is, the even-position terms all have a coefficient of 4, while the odd position terms have coefficient 2, except for the first and last, which have coefficient 1. Write a function `simpson` that takes starting and ending points a and b, an integer n (such that the evaluation is to use $2n + 1$ points as above), and a function F to integrate by Simpson's rule. Try out your function on polynomials x^2, x^3, and so on. What is the smallest integer i such that Simpson's rule fails to get the exact integral of x^i with $a = 0.0$, $b = 1.0$, and $n = 1$?

Exercise 5.4.3: When implementing either the trapezoidal rule or Simpson's rule, it is possible to compute δ once and for all, rather than at each recursive call (although as explained in the text, this strategy may cause roundoff errors to accumulate). Reimplement

* a) The function `trap` of Fig. 5.14.

   b) Your function `simpson` from Exercise 5.4.2.

in such a way that δ is computed once.

Exercise 5.4.4: Improve the function `trap` of Fig. 5.14 by printing an appropriate error message and then raising an exception when the input is bad (as detected by line (1) of Fig. 5.14).

Exercise 5.4.5: Use the function `simpleMap(F,L)` to perform the following operations on a list L.

* a) Replace every negative element of a list of reals by 0, leaving nonnegative elements as they are.

   b) Add 1 to every element of an integer list.

* c) Change every lower-case letter in a list of characters to the corresponding upper-case letter. Do not assume that only lower-case letters appear in the list.

! d) Truncate each string in a list of strings so it is no more than 5 characters long. That is, delete the sixth and subsequent characters while leaving shorter strings alone.

Exercise 5.4.6: Use the function `reduce` to perform the following operations on a list L.

* a) Find the maximum of a list of reals.

   b) Find the minimum of a list of reals.

* c) Concatenate a list of characters (i.e., the function `implode`).

   d) Find the logical OR of a list of booleans.

Exercise 5.4.7: Use the function `filter` to perform the following operations on a list L.

* a) Find those elements of a list of reals that are greater than 0.

   b) Find those elements of a list of reals that are between 1 and 2.

*! c) Find those elements of a list of strings that begin with the character `#"a"`.

 ! d) Find those elements of a list of strings that are at most 3 characters long.

 ! **Exercise 5.4.8:** What is the effect on a list L of `reduce(op -, L)`?

*! **Exercise 5.4.9:** Write a function `lreduce` that takes a two-parameter function F and a list $[a_1, a_2, \ldots, a_n]$ and produces

$$F\Big(\cdots F\big(F(a_1, a_2), a_3\big) \cdots, a_n\Big)$$

That is, this function is like `reduce`, but it groups the elements of the list from the beginning of the list instead of the end.

Exercise 5.4.10: What is the effect of `lreduce(op -, L)`?

* **Exercise 5.4.11:** Another version of `reduce` takes a basis constant g of some type `'b`, a function F of type `'a * 'b -> 'b`, and a list of elements of type `'a`. The result applied to a list $[a_1, a_2, \ldots, a_n]$ is

$$F\Big(a_1 \cdots F\big(a_{n-1}, F(a_n, g)\big) \cdots\Big)$$

Write a function `reduceB` that performs this operation.

* **Exercise 5.4.12:** Use the function `reduceB` from Exercise 5.4.11 to

  ! a) Compute the length of a list.

  !! b) Compute the list of suffixes of a list. For example, given the list `[1,2,3]`, produce `[[1,2,3], [2,3], [3], nil]`.

*! **Exercise 5.4.13:** Another use of polymorphic functions is to allow *late binding* of overloaded symbols such as `+` or `*`. That is, instead of using these symbols in a function f, we invent names for them such as `plus` and `times`, and we let these names be parameters of the function f. Then, we can call f with appropriate definitions for the parameters, thus binding the names to the correct meanings as late as possible. As an exercise:

  a) Write a function `eval` that takes as parameters functions representing scalar addition and multiplication, as well as taking a polynomial (represented as a list in the manner of Section 3.6) and a value at which to evaluate the polynomial.

  b) Show how to call your function from (a) to evaluate the integer polynomial $4x^3 + 3x^2 + 2x + 1$ at the point $x = 5$.

5.5 Curried Functions

Until now, we have considered only functions that have a single parameter, although that parameter often is a tuple written with parentheses and commas. Thus, we have written many ML functions that looked like multiparameter functions of languages like C or Pascal. Technically, these ML functions really have a single parameter, of a product type, but in practice there is little harm in pretending they are ordinary multiparameter functions.

However, ML provides a more general way to connect a function name to its parameters or arguments. It is sometimes useful to express multiparameter functions in *Curried form*,[6] where the function name is followed by the list of its parameters, with no parentheses or commas. The following example illustrates the difference between the Curried and uncurried form of functions. We shall be introduced to the important advantage of the Curried form when we discuss partially instantiated functions in Section 5.5.1.

Example 5.26 : Let us write a two-parameter function that computes x^y. In lines (1) and (2) of Fig. 5.18 we see such a function `exponent1` in the style we have been using. This function takes a parameter that is a pair consisting of a real x and an integer y, and returns x^y. It is not carefully designed because it loops forever on a negative integer y.

```
(1) fun exponent1(x,0) = 1.0
(2)  |   exponent1(x,y) = x * exponent1(x,y-1);
     val exponent1 = fn : real * int → real


(3) fun exponent2 x 0 = 1.0
(4)  |   exponent2 x y = x * exponent2 x (y-1);
     val exponent2 = fn : real → int → real


(5) exponent1(3.0,4);
     val it = 81.0 : real


(6) exponent2 3.0 4;
     val it = 81.0 : real
```

Figure 5.18: Two styles for exponentiation functions

The Curried function `exponent2` in lines (3) and (4) of Fig. 5.18 does exactly the same computation as the uncurried function `exponent1`. The parameters of `exponent2` are not surrounded by parentheses or separated by commas, either in the definition on lines (3) and (4) or in the recursive use on line (4).

Lines (5) and (6) show appropriate calls to the two functions. Each computes $3^4 = 81$. □

5.5.1 Partially Instantiated Functions

Curried functions are useful because they allow us to construct new functions by applying the function to arguments for some, but not all, of its parameters.

---

[6]Named after the mathematician Haskell Curry, who investigated this form of function definition.

Precedence of Function Application

The parentheses around `y-1` on line (4) are necessary for ML to group arguments properly. Without parentheses around `y-1`, the second argument in the recursive call to **exponent2** will be regarded as y. Constant 1 will be subtracted from the result of the call, leading to a type error. The reason for this interpretation is that juxtaposition of expressions, which is function application in ML, is an operator of higher precedence than the arithmetic operators.

To begin our exploration of this matter, notice the subtle difference between the responses to the two functions in Fig. 5.18. ML finds the type of `exponent1` to be a function that takes a pair of type `real * int` as parameter and returns a real. However, the type of `exponent2` is given as `real -> int -> real`. Remembering that the `->` operator associates from the right, we interpret this type as `real -> (int -> real)`, that is, a function taking a real as argument and returning a function from integers to reals.

This type suggests how the function `exponent2` is interpreted. In the call of line (6) in Fig. 5.18, the first argument, 3.0, is given to the function `exponent2`, resulting in a new function g. This function, of type `int -> real`, takes an exponent y as its argument and produces the result $g(y) = 3^y$. The function g is a value in its own right and can, under the right circumstances, be isolated and bound as the value of an identifier.

The process of forming new functions by binding one or more of the parameters of an existing function is called *partial instantiation*. In the general mathematical setting, we can take a function f of n arguments, say $f(x_1, x_2, \ldots, x_n)$. We bind the first k of those arguments to constants $a_1, a_2, \ldots, a_k$ to form a new function, which we may call $f_{a_1, a_2, \ldots, a_k}(x_{k+1}, x_{k+2}, \ldots, x_n)$. The definition of function $f_{a_1, a_2, \ldots, a_k}$ is as expected:

$$f_{a_1, a_2, \ldots, a_k}(x_{k+1}, x_{k+2}, \ldots, x_n) = f(a_1, a_2, \ldots, a_k, x_{k+1}, x_{k+2}, \ldots, x_n)$$

In ML, Curried functions can be partially instantiated by applying them to values, one for each of the first k parameters. It is only possible to instantiate the parameters from the left, not in any order.

Example 5.27: Having made the definition of `exponent2` in Example 5.26, we can proceed to create a new function by instantiating its first argument. An example is

```
val g = exponent2 3.0;
```
val g = fn : int → real

Now g is a function that takes an integer y as argument and returns 3^y. Figure 5.19 suggests what has happened. Identifier g has been bound to a value that is a notation representing the function `exponent2` applied to 3.0.

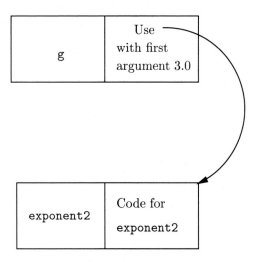

Figure 5.19: Partially instantiating a function

We can use g like any other function if we provide its proper argument. For example,

```
g 4;
```
val it = 81.0

applies g to the integer 4, producing 3^4, or 81. □

Here are a number of points about partial instantiation and the Curried form of functions.

- Note that we are not restricted to the no-parentheses form. We could have written $g(4)$ instead of g 4, and we could have defined new functions from `exponent2` with parentheses. For instance,

  ```
  val h = exponent2(10.0)
  ```

  makes h a function that computes powers of 10.

- As discussed in Section 3.1.5, the value of the function g does not change if we define a new function called `exponent2`, because the definition of g refers to the specific value shown in Fig. 5.19.

- We can partially instantiate a function by binding arguments other than in left-to-right order of appearance, but to do so we need to define a new function using `fun`. For example, we could bind the second argument of `exponent2` to the value 3, producing a function that cubes a real number, by:

```
fun cube x = exponent2 x 3;
```

This approach to partially instantiating functions works even if the function definition was not written in Curried form.

5.5.2   The ML Style of Function Application

As we learned in Example 5.26, parentheses around arguments of ML functions are optional in many cases. The only time they are essential is when the argument has components that are kept together with an operator whose precedence is below that of function application. Unfortunately, function application is almost the highest-precedence operator of all. Thus, for instance, the following give us errors.

1. `fun f c:char = 1.0` is grouped `(f c):char = 1.0`. To ML, it appears as if we are trying to say that the *result* of f is a character, when in fact it is defined to be a real. Thus, we need to write `fun f(c:char) = 1.0`.

2. `fun f x::xs = nil` is grouped `(f x)::xs = nil`, which is not likely to be what we intended. We need to write `fun f(x::xs) = nil`.

3. `print Int.toString 123` is grouped `(print Int.toString) 123` and leads to a type error since `Int.toString` (the function that converts integers to strings from the structure `Int`) is not itself a string, which the function `print` requires. Thus, we need one pair of parentheses: `print(Int.toString 123)`.

On the other hand, there are many places where the parentheses around arguments are superfluous, and we shall start omitting parentheses in safe situations. Here are some of the places where we can avoid parentheses.

1. `f [1,2,3]` or even `f[1,2,3]` means the same as `f([1,2,3])`. In general, if the argument of a function is already bracketed so it cannot be split apart by the function application, then no parentheses are needed.

2. `chr 100` means the same as `chr(100)`. In general, operators are functions, and the same rules as apply to functions apply to operators.

3. `open TextIO` is not only permitted, it is necessary. The keyword `open` is not a function, and we cannot put parentheses around the structure name when we open a structure like `TextIO`.

5.5.3 Exercises for Section 5.5

*! **Exercise 5.5.1:** Write, in Curried form, a function `applyList` that takes a list of functions and a value and applies each function to the value, producing a list of the results.

*! **Exercise 5.5.2:** Write, in Curried form, a function `makeFnList` that takes a function F whose domain type is D and whose range type R is a function type $T_1 \to T_2$. The result of `makeFnList` is a function G that takes a list of elements $[d_1, d_2, \ldots, d_n]$ of type D and produces a list of functions $[f_1, f_2, \ldots, f_n]$ of type R, such that $f_i = F(d_i)$.

* **Exercise 5.5.3:** Write a function `substring`, either Curried or not, that takes two parameters and tests whether the first is a substring of the other. String x is a *substring* of string y if we can write y as the concatenation of strings w, x, and z. It is permissible for any of the strings to be empty. For example, `"abc"` has substrings including `""`, `"b"`, and `"ab"`. Using `makeFnList` of Exercise 5.5.2, construct a function f that takes a list of strings $[s_1, s_2, \ldots, s_n]$ and produces a list of functions $[F_1, F_2, \ldots, F_n]$, such that $F_i(x)$ tells whether s_i is a substring of x.

*! **Exercise 5.5.4:** From f of Exercise 5.5.3, create a list of functions that, respectively, check whether one of the words `"he"`, `"she"`, `"her"`, `"his"` is a substring of a given string.

* **Exercise 5.5.5:** Apply your list from Exercise 5.5.4 to the string `"hershey"`, using function `applyList` from Exercise 5.5.1. What is the result?

! **Exercise 5.5.6:** Repeat Exercise 5.5.3 for *subsequences* in place of substrings. String x is a subsequence of string y if x is formed by striking out zero or more positions of y. For example, `"ac"` is a subsequence of `"abc"` but is not a substring. Then, as in Exercise 5.5.4, create a list of functions that test whether the following strings are subsequences of a given string:

$$["ear", "part", "trap", "seat"]$$

Finally, apply your list of functions to the string `"separate"`.

Exercise 5.5.7: It is actually quite easy to convert an n-parameter function, for fixed n, from Curried to uncurried form. Write the following higher-order functions that perform the translations.

* a) Given a function F that takes one parameter whose type is a product type with n components, the function `curry` applied to F produces a function G that takes n arguments in Curried form. $G\ x_1\ x_2\ \cdots\ x_n$ produces the same value as $F(x_1, x_2, \ldots, x_n)$.

   b) Given a Curried function F that takes n parameters, the function `uncurry` applied to F produces a function G that takes one parameter that is a tuple with n components. $G(x_1, x_2, \ldots, x_n)$ produces the same value as $F\ x_1\ x_2\ \cdots\ x_n$.

5.6 Built-In Higher-Order Functions

ML provides certain higher-order functions in the top-level environment. In several cases these functions are similar to functions such as `simpleMap` and `reduce` that we studied in Sections 5.4.2 and 5.4.3, respectively. In this section, we shall introduce these functions and their use. We shall also give definitions of these built-in ML functions in terms of simpler constructs, both to help the reader see the meaning of these functions and to illustrate some useful function-writing ideas.

5.6.1 Composition of Functions

We shall now study a problem that is of intrinsic importance and that also encourages us to view functions as values disembodied from any arguments to which they might be applied. The *composition* of functions F and G is that function C such that for any argument x, $C(x) = G\big(F(x)\big)$.

Example 5.28: Let $F(x) = x + 3$, and let $G(y) = y^2 + 2y$. Then the composition of F and G, or $G\big(F(x)\big)$, is $(x+3)^2 + 2(x+3)$, or $x^2 + 8x + 15$. We get this formula by substituting $F(x)$ for y in the formula for G and then expanding the formula.   □

We can define a higher-order function `comp` that takes two functions as arguments and applies them to a third argument. The ML code is simple:

```
fun comp(F,G,x) = G(F(x));
val comp = fn : ('a → 'b) * ('b → 'c) * 'a → 'c
```

Notice the type of this function. First, recall that `*` takes precedence over `->`, so the type expression is grouped

```
(('a -> 'b) * ('b -> 'c) * 'a) -> 'c
```

Thus, the function `comp` has three parameters, the first of which (F) is a function from some type `'a` to some (possibly different) type `'b`. The second parameter, G, takes a value of the type `'b` and produces a value of some (possibly different) type `'c`. The third parameter is of the type `'a` to which F applies, and the result is of the type `'c` that G produces.

Example 5.29: We can use `comp` to compute the composition of the two functions from Example 5.28 on a particular value of x, for instance:

```
comp(fn x => x+3, fn y => y*y+2*y, 10);
val it = 195 : int
```

Here we have defined the first argument of `comp` to be the function $x+3$ and the second to be the function $y^2 + 2y$. The composition of these functions, which we discovered in Example 5.28 was the polynomial $x^2 + 8x + 15$, is then applied to 10, and produces the correct result, $10^2 + 8 \times 10 + 15 = 195$.   □

5.6.2   The ML Operator o For Composition

However, Example 5.29 is somehow unsatisfactory. It is true that we can apply the composition of any two functions to an argument, as long as the types match properly. Yet we cannot address the question of Example 5.28: "what function is the composition of functions $x + 3$ and $y^2 + 2y$?" Function comp as we defined it is relatively useless. It is a "shorthand" for $G(F(x))$, but it even fails to save us keystrokes.

What we really want is a function that takes only the two functions F and G as its arguments and produces the function C that is the composition of F and G. For instance, in the case of Example 5.28, we would like the composition function to return the function $x^2 + 8x + 15$ itself, rather than returning the value of this function for a particular value of x. In ML, there is an operator o (lower-case "Oh") that composes functions.

Example 5.30 : If we defined

```
fun F x = x+3;
```

```
fun G y = y*y + 2*y;
```

then the function $G(F(x)) = x^2 + 8x + 15$ can be obtained by

```
val H = G o F;
```

which makes H the desired function.   □

Let us write a function comp that behaves like the ML operator o, but our function will not be an infix operator, as o is. A useful technique for defining higher-order functions is to describe, within a let-expression what the effect of the function is supposed to be, giving the function so described a name, say f. Then, between the in and end place f by itself.

For the function comp, we use a let-expression to define, in terms of a parameter x, what the function that is the composition of F and G does. The expression that follows the keyword in is just the name of the defined function. The proper definition appears in Fig. 5.20.

Line (2) defines a function C to have the desired behavior; it is the composition of F and G. In line (3) we see that the value of the function comp, which is what we are defining with the let-expression, is the function C itself. The type of comp confirms that we are on the right track. It takes two arguments:

1. A function F from some type 'a to some type 'b, and

2. A function G from type 'b to some type 'c.

The result of comp is a function of type 'a -> 'c, that is, a function from type 'a to type 'c.[7] This function is the composition of F and G.

---

[7]To parse this type expression, remember that -> groups from the right. Thus, the proper grouping is ('a -> 'b) -> (('b -> 'c) -> ('a -> 'c)).

```
(1) fun comp F G =
            let
(2)               fun C x = G(F(x))
            in
(3)               C
            end;
```
$val\ comp = fn : ('a \rightarrow\ 'b) \rightarrow ('b \rightarrow\ 'c) \rightarrow\ 'a \rightarrow\ 'c$

```
(4) fun F x = x+3;
```
$val\ F = fn : int \rightarrow int$

```
(5) fun G y = y*y+2*y;
```
$val\ G = fn : int \rightarrow int$

```
(6) val H = comp F G;
```
$val\ H = fn : int \rightarrow int$

```
(7) H 10;
```
$val\ it = 195 : int$

Figure 5.20: Computing the composition of two functions

Next, we see in Fig. 5.20 a definition of the function F to be $x + 3$ and the function G to be $y^2 + 2y$. Then we define the function H to be comp F G, that is, the composition of F and G. We now have a name H that we can use to refer to the function that is the composition of F and G, that is, the function whose expression as a polynomial is $x^2 + 8x + 15$. This function can be applied to any integer argument; we show it in Fig. 5.20 applied to argument 10.

5.6.3 The "Real" Version of Map

As we mentioned in Section 5.4.2, the top-level environment of ML has a function map that is similar to the function simpleMap that we defined there. However, instead of taking both the function and list as arguments, map takes only a function F as an argument. The result of map is a function that takes a list of elements and returns the list that is the result of applying F to each element of the list.

Figure 5.21 is a definition of the ML built-in function map. Of course, this definition is unnecessary, as one can use map in programs without it. In line (1),

---

Defining `comp` Via Currying

The same function `comp` that we constructed in a let-expression in Fig. 5.20 can also be written as a 3-argument Curried function:

```
fun compC F G x = G(F(x));
```

It may seem strange that a function that takes x as an argument could be the same as the two-argument function `comp` in Fig. 5.20. However, the two functions have the same type, and they behave the same way. For example, `compC F G` is surely a function of x, while `comp F G` seems to have no argument. However, since the result of `comp F G` is a function, it can be applied to an argument of the domain type of G, just like `compC F G` can. That is, an expression like

```
comp (fn x=>x+3) (fn y=>y*y+2*y) 10
```

makes sense, and gives the answer 195 that we saw in Fig. 5.20, even though `comp` was not defined to have a third argument.

---

we see that `map` takes one argument, a function F. In a let-expression, we define a function M that takes a list and applies F to each element. Line (2) says that M applied to the empty list is the empty list. Line (3) says that for nonempty list, M applies F to the first element and calls itself recursively on the tail to apply F to the remaining elements. Finally, at line (4) we say that this function M is the result of `map` when it is applied to F.

```
(1) fun map F =
            let
(2)             fun M nil = nil
(3)             |   M(x::xs) = F x :: M xs
            in
(4)             M
            end;
    val map = fn : ('a → 'b) → 'a list → 'b list
```

Figure 5.21: The ML function `map`

Notice the type of `map` in the ML response. Remembering that `->` groups from the right, this type is `('a -> 'b) -> ('a list -> 'b list)`. That is, `map` is a function that takes as its argument a function F from type `'a` to type `'b`. Then, `map` returns a function M that takes a list of elements of type `'a` and

---

Representing a Composition

It is useful to consider the way the values of F, G, and H are represented by ML, if H is the composition of F and G. Since functions are defined by code, the identifiers F and G are bound to a value that is code. However H, being defined by a composition, is bound to a value that is a notation saying it is the composition of F and G. The situation is suggested in Fig. 5.22.

Note that the value for H refers to the values bound to F and G in the current environment, not to the names F and G. The distinction becomes important if we bind identifier F or G to a new value. Since H is bound to the particular environment entries suggested in Fig. 5.22, and entries in an environment do not change their values, the value of H does not change.

---

produces a list of elements of type 'b.

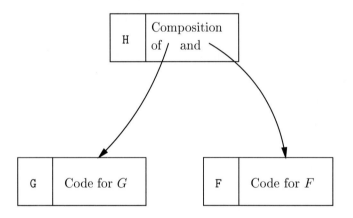

Figure 5.22: Representing function values in an environment

Example 5.31 : If map is as defined in Fig. 5.21, and square is the function that squares reals, then map(square) is the function that takes a list of reals and squares each one. We could create this function by

```
val squareList = map square;
val squareList = fn : real list → real list
```

Then, we can use this function as

```
squareList [1.0, 2.0, 3.0];
```

val it = [1.0,4.0,9.0] : real list

to square each element of a particular list. □

5.6.4 Folding Lists

ML provides the user a pair of functions called `foldr` and `foldl`. Both functions perform a variety of the *fold* operation, which takes a list $L = [a_1, a_2, \ldots, a_n]$ and treats each element a_i as if it were a function; call this function F_{a_i}. When we apply a folding operation to L, we construct the function that is the composition of all the functions $F_{a_1}, F_{a_2}, \ldots, F_{a_n}$, that is, $F_{a_1} \circ F_{a_2} \circ \cdots \circ F_{a_n}$.

Example 5.32: Many operations on lists can be specified by folding, using an appropriate definition of the functions F_{a_i} and also choosing the right constant to which the composition of functions is applied. For instance, suppose $L = [a_1, a_2, \ldots, a_n]$ is a list of integers, and the function F_{a_i} is the function that multiplies its argument by a_i. Then the function $F_{a_1} \circ F_{a_2} \circ \cdots \circ F_{a_n}$ multiplies its argument by the product of the elements of the list L, that is, $a_1 \times a_2 \times \cdots \times a_n$. If we apply this function to 1, we can compute the product of the elements of a list.

As another example, suppose instead that F_{a_i} is the function that adds 1 to its argument, regardless of what a_i is. Then the function $F_{a_1} \circ F_{a_2} \circ \cdots \circ F_{a_n}$ adds n to its argument. In particular, applied to 0 it computes the length of the list L. Thus, folding also lets us define the length function if we correctly specify the functions F_{a_i}. □

The missing element in Example 5.32 is the method of going from a_i to the proper F_{a_i}. In effect, we need to reverse the effect of partial instantiation of these functions, by writing one function $F(a, x)$ such that $F(a, x)$ equals $F_a(x)$ for all a and x.

Example 5.33: Let us consider the two problems in Example 5.32. If F_{a_i} is to multiply its (integer) argument x by a_i, then we want $F(a, x) = ax$, or in ML:

```
fun F(a,x) = a*x;
```
*val F = fn : int * int → int*

In the second problem, where we want each F_{a_i} to add one to its argument, we define $F(a, x) = x + 1$, or:

```
fun F(a,x) = x+1;
```
*val F = fn : 'a * int → int*

in ML.   □

The difference between `foldr` and `foldl` is that `foldr` composes the functions F_{a_i} starting from the end (i.e., from the right), and `foldl` composes them starting from the left. That is, `foldr`, given list $[a_1, a_2, \ldots, a_n]$ and initial value b, computes

$$F_{a_1}(F_{a_2}(\cdots (F_{a_n}(b)) \cdots))$$

while `foldl` computes

$$F_{a_n}(F_{a_{n-1}}(\cdots (F_{a_1}(b)) \cdots))$$

A definition for function `foldr` is shown in Fig. 5.23. Again, let us emphasize that `foldr` is a primitive of ML, and we do not need to define it. However, seeing a definition in terms of more elementary operations is instructive. The definition of `foldl` is similar, and we leave it as an exercise.

```
(1) fun foldr F y nil = y
(2) |    foldr F y (x::xs) = F(x, foldr F y xs);
```
   val foldr = fn : ('a * 'b) → 'b → 'b → 'a list → 'b

Figure 5.23: Definition of `foldr`

We define `foldr` in Curried form, with three parameters.

1. Function F is of type `'a * 'b -> 'b`. Type `'a` is the type of list elements, and `'b` is both the range type of F and the type of the result of applying `foldr`.

2. Value `y` is of type `'b`. It is the initial value associated with the empty list.

3. List L is a list of elements of type `'a`.

Line (1) of Fig. 5.23 covers the case of an empty list. Then we just return the initial value y. Line (2) covers the inductive case, where the list $L = [a_1, a_2, \ldots, a_n]$ has a head element `x` and a tail `xs`. That is, `x` is a_1 and `xs` is $[a_2, \ldots, a_n]$. To compute the result we do the following:

a) Apply `foldr` to function F, the initial value y, and the tail of the list. The result is computed recursively by applying the functions

$$F_{a_n}, F_{a_{n-1}}, \ldots, F_{a_2}$$

associated with the elements of the tail, in turn, to the initial value y.

b) Apply the function F to the list head x and the result of (a). This step has the effect of composing function F_{a_1} with the other functions $F_{a_2}, \ldots, F_{a_n}$ that have already been applied to y. As a result, all the functions associated with the entire list L are applied to the initial value y. They are applied in the reverse of the order in which they appear on the list, with the last element's function applied first.

Example 5.34: If we want to take the product of the elements of list of integers L, we can use `foldr` with a suitable product function, such as that in Example 5.33 and initial value 1. That is, we may write

```
val L = [2,3,4];
foldr op * 1 L;
```
val it = 24 : int

Note that in order to use the multiplication function as the first argument of `foldr`, we need `op` to make it a prefix operator. The arguments of `foldr` are grouped as `foldr (op *) 1 L`.

- But beware putting those optional parentheses in exactly that way, because *) is interpreted as a comment-ender, and an error will result. In this special case we would need to write `fold (op * ) 1 L`.

□

Because `foldr` is defined in Curried form, we can partially instantiate `foldr` with a function F and an initial value b and get another function that takes a list L and "folds" L according to F and b.

Example 5.35: We can write a function that takes the product of the elements on any integer list by:

```
val prod = fold op * 1;
```
val prod = fn : int list → int

```
prod [2,3,4];
```
val it = 24 : int

□

5.6.5 Exercises for Section 5.6

Exercise 5.6.1: Use the higher-order functions `map`, `foldr`, and `foldl` described in this section to build the following functions on lists. You should write anonymous functions that operate on list elements only.

* a) A function that turns an integer list into a list of reals with the same values.

b) A function that turns an integer list L into a list of reals, each of which is the absolute value of the element on L.

*! c) The function `implode`, which turns a list of characters into a single string with those characters in order.

d) The function `concat`, which turns a list of strings into the concatenation of all those strings.

*! e) A function that turns a list of integers $[a_1, a_2, \ldots, a_n]$ into the alternating sum $a_1 - a_2 + a_3 - a_4 + \cdots$.

f) A function that computes the logical AND of a list of booleans.

* g) A function that computes the logical OR of a list of booleans.

! h) A function that computes the *exclusive or* of a list of booleans. The exclusive or of $a_1, a_2, \ldots, a_n$ is `true` if an odd number of the a_i's are `true` and `false` if an even number of the a_i's are `true`.

*! Exercise 5.6.2: Write a definition for the function `foldl` analogous to the definition of `foldr` in Fig. 5.23. *Hint*: Recompute the initial value in the recursion.

Exercise 5.6.3: Since the function `comp` of Fig. 5.20 was written in Curried form, we can bind the first argument F to a function to get a new function that takes a function G as argument and produces the function G o F. However, if we write an expression such as

```
val I = comp (fn x => x+3);
```

we get an error message saying there is a "nongeneralizable type variable," namely the unknown type that is the range type for I and the function to which I will be applied.

*! a) We can fix the definition of I above if we give it a type. If we want the range type of I to be `string`, what is a suitable type declaration to add to the definition of I?

b) Having defined I as in part (a), show how to use I to create a function that given an integer x returns a string consisting of the digits of $x + 3$.

c) Use your answer to (b) to create a function that, given an integer x prints $x + 3$.

*! Exercise 5.6.4: Suppose we define `comp` as in Fig. 5.20 and

```
fun add1 x = x+1;
```

Give the type and value for each of the following functions or constants. To avoid a nongeneralizable type variable error as discussed in Exercise 5.6.3, you should declare all unknown types to be integers.

a) `val compA1 = comp add1;`

!! b) `val compCompA1 = comp compA1;`

c) `val f = compA1 add1;`

d) `f(2);`

!! e) `val g = compCompA1 compA1;`

f) `val h = g add1;`

g) `h(2);`

! Exercise 5.6.5: Repeat Exercise 5.6.4 for the following expressions. The functions `compA1` and `compCompA1` are as defined in Exercises 5.6.4(a) and (b). However, you should redeclare their type for the uses described below.

a) `val f = compA1 real;` where `real` is the built-in function that converts integers to equivalent reals.

b) `val compT = comp trunc;` where `trunc` is the built-in function that converts a real to an integer, rounding towards 0 if necessary.

!! c) `val g = compCompA1 compT;`

d) `val h = g real;`

e) `f(2);`

f) `h(3.5);`

g) `h(~3.5);`

Exercise 5.6.6: Write a version of the function `filter` from Section 5.4.5 that takes only a predicate P as argument and produces a function that takes a list of elements of suitable type and returns those elements on the list that satisfy P.

!! **Exercise 5.6.7:** Using `foldr` and an anonymous function, write a function that takes a list of reals $[a_0, a_1, \ldots, a_{n-1}]$ and produces a function that takes an argument b and evaluates the polynomial

$$a_0 + a_1 x + a_2 x^2 + \cdots + a_{n-1} x^{n-1}$$

at $x = b$; that is, it computes $\sum_{i=0}^{n-1} a_i b^i$.

! Exercise 5.6.8: Write the two-argument function `simpleMap` of Section 5.4.2 in Curried form. Show that its behavior is exactly the same as that of the one-argument function `map` of Fig. 5.21.

5.7   Case Study: Parsing Expressions

In this section we shall look at one of the fundamental parts of a compiler, a parser for expressions. In so doing we shall review some of the ideas introduced in this chapter: case statements and exceptions. We also see an interesting application of several "old" ideas: the lookahead operator for reading an instream, a mutual recursion involving five functions, wildcards in patterns, and the use of statement lists, including the addition of a final "statement" to return the proper value.

The problem we shall address is how to read arithmetic expressions from the input and compute their value. The operands of these arithmetic expressions are integers, and the operators used are *, +, -, and /.[8] For simplicity, we assume there are no blanks or other white space between characters of the expression. It is easy to ignore white space or other characters should we wish; the case study of Section 4.4 showed how.

5.7.1   The Grammatical Structure of Arithmetic Expressions

We shall describe the structure of expressions using a graphical notation equivalent to context-free grammars; it is illustrated in Fig. 5.24. Each *syntactic category* is named on the left; we have in Fig. 5.24 four syntactic categories: INTEGER, ATOM, TERM, and EXP (expression). A syntactic category represents a set of sequences of elements. Each element can be a string of characters or it can be another syntactic category. The possible instances of a syntactic category are indicated by the possible paths from the left end of its graph to the right end; each path represents a sequence of elements that is an instance of the syntactic category named at the left.

For instance, in Fig. 5.24(a) the graph for INTEGER requires us to go through DIGIT once. Then we can continue to the right end or we can cycle back to pass through DIGIT any number of additional times. That is, an INTEGER is a string consisting of one or more DIGIT's. The syntactic category DIGIT is not defined by a graph, but we define it to consist of any of the digits 0 through 9.

In Fig. 5.24(b) we see that an ATOM is defined to be either an INTEGER or a sequence consisting of a left parenthesis, an EXP, and a right parenthesis. That is, an ATOM is an integer or a parenthesized expression.

Next we see that a TERM is an ATOM followed by zero or more additional elements, each element consisting of either a multiplication or a division sign, followed by another ATOM. That is, a TERM is a sequence of one or more ATOM's separated by multiplication and/or division signs. Similarly, an EXP is a sequence of one or more TERM's separated by plus and/or minus signs.

---

[8]Of course, ML would use `div` for integer division, but that is unimportant because we are not reading ML programs in this example.

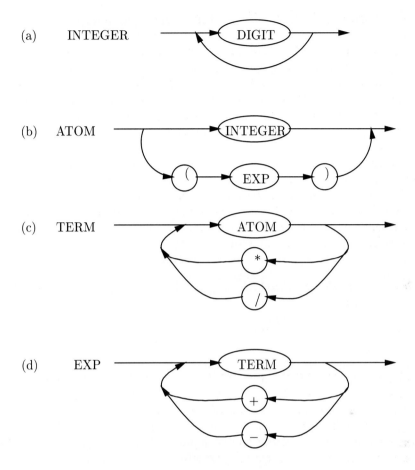

Figure 5.24: The structure of arithmetic expressions

5.7.2 Structure of the Parsing Program

Figures 5.25 and 5.26 together show a program that computes the value of an expression.[9] Its functions carefully choose between the `lookahead` operator and the `input1` operator to make sure that input characters are consumed only at the appropriate time.

Let us examine the statements and functions in Fig. 5.25. Line (1) opens the `TextIO` structure, which we shall need to perform input operations on the file. Line (2) is the definition of an exception `Syntax` that will be raised when an ill-formed input is found. Line (3) is the familiar function `digit` that tests whether a character is a digit.

---

[9]This program implements a parsing method called "recursive descent." The reader may consult *Compilers: Principles, Techniques, and Tools*, A. V. Aho, R. Sethi, and J. D. Ullman, Addison-Wesley, Reading MA, 1986 for an explanation of this technique.

Then come six functions — the last five are mutually recursive — that collectively implement the diagrams of Fig. 5.24. Each takes a parameter IN that is the instream on which the expression appears. Some functions take an additional parameter that helps the function return the integer value of some portion of the input. This additional parameter, if present, will be referred to as "the parameter" or "the argument" of the function, even though IN is also a parameter.

We shall introduce the functions, and then later return to the details of their implementation. The six functions, each of which returns the value of whatever input it consumes, are:

1. integer consumes whatever prefix of the current input is a sequence of digits. The parameter i is the integer value of any digits that have been seen and consumed on the input immediately before the current call to integer. The result returned is the value of the digits seen so far (as represented by i) and any further digits found consecutively on the input. An initial call to integer with $i = 0$ implements the diagram of Fig. 5.24(a) and returns the value of the digits read.

2. atom looks on the input for either

   (a) An integer or
   (b) A left parenthesis, followed by any expression, followed by a right parenthesis.

   It thus implements the diagram of Fig. 5.24(b).

3. term looks for an atom on the input and, after consuming one, calls termTail. The argument i for termTail is the value of the atom found. Together, term and termTail implement the diagram of Fig. 5.24(c).

4. termTail looks for and consumes from the input zero or more groups consisting of a * or / sign and an atom. It takes a parameter i, which is the value of all atoms found so far, multiplied or divided as dictated by the signs that connect them. If termTail finds a * or / as the next input character, it consumes it and calls atom. The value i is multiplied or divided, as appropriate, by the value of the atom found. The result becomes the argument of a recursive call to termTail. If termTail does not find a * or / as the next input character, it does nothing but return its argument i.

5. expression looks for a term on the input and, after consuming one, calls expTail with argument i equal to the value of the term found. Together, expression and expTail implement the diagram of Fig. 5.24(d).

6. expTail looks for and consumes from the input zero or more groups consisting of a + or - sign and a term. It takes a parameter i, which

```
(1)  open TextIO;

(2)  exception Syntax;

(3)  fun digit(c) = (#"0" <= c andalso c <= #"9");

(4)  fun integer(IN,i) =
(5)        case lookahead(IN) of
(6)           SOME c =>
(7)              if digit(c) then (
(8)                  input1(IN); (* consume character c *)
(9)                  integer(IN, 10*i+ord(c)-ord(#"0"))
                  )
(10)             else i (* if c is not a digit, return i
                           without consuming input *)
                  |
(11)          NONE => i (* ditto if end of file is reached *)

(12) fun atom(IN) =
(13)       case lookahead(IN) of
(14)          SOME #"(" => (
(15)                 input1(IN); (* consume left paren *)
                      let
(16)                     val e = expression(IN)
                      in
(17)                     if lookahead(IN)=(SOME #")") then
                           (
(18)                           input1(IN); (* consume
                                 right parenthesis *)
(19)                           e (* return expression *)
                           )
(20)                    else raise Syntax
                      end
                   )
                   |
(21)          SOME c =>
(22)              if digit(c) then integer(IN,0)
(23)              else raise Syntax
                  |
(24)          NONE => raise Syntax
        and
```

Figure 5.25: Parser for arithmetic expressions (beginning)

is the value of all terms found so far, added or subtracted as dictated
by the signs that connect them. Its operation is analogous to that of
`termTail`.

5.7.3   Detailed Explanation of the Parser Code

Let us now examine the code of Fig. 5.25 in more detail.

The Function `integer`

Function `integer` is in lines (4) through (11). Line (5) uses `lookahead` to obtain
a character-option from the instream. That is, the expression `lookahead(IN)`
evaluates to either `NONE` if there is no more input, or `SOME` c, if c is the first
character remaining on the input. Nothing is consumed from the input, however.

Lines (6) through (10) cover the case when a character c is present. Line (7)
tests if c is a digit, and if so, this digit is consumed from the instream at line (8).
At line (9) `integer` is called recursively with an argument that represents the
effect of appending the digit c to the integer read so far. The formula used on
line (9) is the same one that was used in Fig. 4.10. Line (10) covers the case
when c is not a digit. In this case, the integer i has ended, and its value is
returned by `integer`.

The second and final case of the case statement is handled by line (11).[10]
Here, there is no more input, so the integer i has ended and is returned. Note
that `integer` is only called on line (22), where we have already determined that
at least one digit waits on the input. Thus `integer` properly implements the
diagram of Fig. 5.24(a), which requires that at least one digit be consumed.

The Function `atom`

The function `atom` appears in lines (12) through (24). A case statement starts on
line (13), and the first case is when the next character waiting on the instream
is a left parenthesis. If so, then the input must begin with a parenthesized
expression. Line (15) consumes the left parenthesis from the input, and line (16)
calls `expression` to consume an expression from the input. At this point we
expect a right parenthesis to follow, and line (17) checks the right parenthesis
is there. If so, the parenthesis is consumed from the input at line (18), and
the value of the expression between the parentheses is returned at line (19).
However, if after reading the expression at line (16), the following character is
not a right parenthesis, then there is a syntax error, and the exception `Syntax`
is raised at line (20).

- Notice that the reason for the let-in-end construct in lines (16) through
  (20) is because we cannot return the value e of the expression read on

---

[10]Notice that we have put the vertical bars separating cases on a line of their own to make
it easier to separate complex cases visually.

line (16) immediately. We need to hold it and check that there is a right parenthesis following.

Lines (21) through (23) handle the second case, where there is a character waiting on the input, but it is not a left parenthesis. We test if it is a digit at line (22), and if so we conclude that the atom is an integer and call `integer` to consume the integer from the instream. Using argument 0 in this call is correct, since there are no previous digits when the initial call to `integer` is made. Recursive calls to `integer` from itself will increase the value of the argument. If the character is neither a digit nor a left parenthesis, then there is a syntax error, which is reported at line (23).

The final case is when there is no character on the input. Since we are expecting an atom, there must be a syntax error, which is reported at line (24).

The Function `term`

Line (25) in Fig. 5.26 is the entire function `term`. It first calls `atom` to consume an atom from the input and return the value of that atom. This value becomes the argument of `termTail`, which multiplies or divides the value of the first atom by the sequence of zero or more atoms it finds on the input.

We have used a succinct but subtle style in designing the function `term`. The call to `atom` occurs within a call to `termTail`, so the call to `atom` is executed first. We could have separated the two steps more transparently, but less succinctly by code such as

```
let val i = atom(IN) in termTail(IN,i) end
```

The Function `termTail`

Function `termTail` appears in lines (26) through (34) of Fig. 5.26. On line (27) it looks at the next input, which becomes the basis of a 3-way case-statement. Lines (28) through (30) cover the case where the next character is `*`. This character is consumed on line (29). Then `atom` is called on line (30) to read and evaluate the next atom on the input. The value of this atom is multiplied by i, which is the value of the argument to `termTail`, and this product becomes the argument in a recursive call to `termTail`.

Lines (31) through (33) handle the case where the next character is `/` analogously to lines (28) through (30). Line (34) handles all other possible values of the next character. If the next character is other than `*` or `/`, the term is complete. In this case, `termTail` returns its own argument as the value of the entire term that has just been seen on the input.

Functions `expression` and `expTail`

Finally, lines (35)–(44) are functions `expression` and `expTail`. Their workings are analogous to those of `term` and `termTail`, and we omit the details.

```
(25)           term(IN) = termTail(IN,atom(IN))
      and
(26)         termTail(IN,i) =
(27)               case lookahead(IN) of
(28)                     SOME #"*" => (
(29)                             input1(IN); (* consume * *)
(30)                             termTail(IN,i*atom(IN))
                              )
                          |
(31)                     SOME #"/" => (
(32)                             input1(IN); (* consume / *)
(33)                             termTail(IN,i div atom(IN))
                              )
                          |
(34)                     _ => i
      and
(35)         expression(IN) = expTail(IN,term(IN))
      and
(36)         expTail(IN,i) =
(37)               case lookahead(IN) of
(38)                     SOME #"+" => (
(39)                             input1(IN); (* consume + *)
(40)                             expTail(IN,i+term(IN))
                              )
                          |
(41)                     SOME #"-" => (
(42)                             input1(IN); (* consume - *)
(43)                             expTail(IN,i-term(IN))
                              )
                          |
(44)                     _ => i;

(45) val infile = openIn("test");

(46) expression(infile);
```

Figure 5.26: Parser for arithmetic expressions (end)

An Example Use of the Parser

On line (45) we begin to use the functions we have written. Identifier `infile` is bound to an instream representing the opened file `test`; this file contains an expression that we wish to evaluate. A call to `expression(infile)` on line (46) results in the value of the expression in file `test` being returned by ML.

5.7.4   Exercises for Section 5.7

! **Exercise 5.7.1:** Give the grammatical diagram(s) for the form of real constants of ML as described in Section 2.1.1.

! **Exercise 5.7.2:** ML allows us to construct values from integers using list-formation (with square brackets) and tuple-formation (with parentheses). An example is `[(1,2),(3,4)]`.

    a) Give grammatical diagrams for the set of values that can be formed by these two construction rules. You do not need to enforce the ML requirement that list elements have the same type.

    b) Implement a parser for this class of character strings. You should read the input from an instream `IN`. The response of your parser is a boolean indicating whether the input is or is not of the proper form. Your program should allow white space among the integers, parentheses, commas, and brackets, but not in the middle of an integer. The entire value will be terminated by the character `$`.

Chapter 6

Defining Your Own Types

In this chapter we shall learn ways to extend the type system of ML with user-defined types. There are two ways to make type extensions:

1. *Type definitions* are shorthands or macros for previously defined type expressions.

2. *Datatype definitions* are rules for constructing new types with new values that are not the values of previously defined types.

6.1 Defining New Types

As in Pascal or C, it is possible to define new types in ML. However, ML has a more powerful *type system* (rules for defining types) than these languages. In ML, types can take one or more type-valued variables as parameters. It is also possible in ML to create types whose values are built in more complex ways than is possible in the type systems of most languages.

6.1.1 Review of the ML Type System

Before proceeding, let us review what we know about the type system of ML. Types in ML are defined recursively, with a basis of primitive types and rules for constructing more complex types from these.

BASIS: The basic types we have met are `int`, `real`, `string`, `char`, `bool`, `unit`, `exn` (exception), `instream`, and `outstream`. In addition, a type variable such as `'a` or `''a` can serve in place of a constant type such as `int`. These variables represent values of any type or any equality type respectively.

INDUCTION: We can build new types from old types T_1 and T_2, as follows.

1. $T_1 * T_2$ is a "product" type, whose values are pairs. The first component of the pair is of type T_1 and the second is of type T_2. More generally,

$T_1 * T_2 * \cdots * T_n$ is the type for a tuple of n components, the ith component of which is of type T_i, for all $i = 1, 2, \ldots, n$.

2. $T_1 \rightarrow T_2$ is a "function" type, whose values are functions with domain type T_1 and range type T_2.

3. We may create new types by following a type such as T_1 by certain identifiers that act as *type constructors*. So far, we have met:

   (a) The `list` type constructor. That is, for every type T_1, there is another type T_1 `list`, whose values are lists all of whose elements are of type T_1.

   (b) The `option` type constructor. For every type T_1 there is a type T_1 `option` whose values are `NONE` and `SOME` x where x is any value of type T_1.

We shall meet additional type constructors `ref`, `array`, and `vector` later. In this section we learn that the user can define any identifier to be a type constructor by making the appropriate type declaration.

The expressions defined inductively as above are called *type expressions*.

6.1.2   New Names for Old Types

To begin, we shall learn the use of the keyword `type`, which defines a new type in a simple way — as an abbreviation for other types. The simplest form of an abbreviation is

$$\texttt{type} \ \langle\text{identifier}\rangle \ \texttt{=} \ \langle\text{type expression}\rangle$$

That is, the keyword `type` is followed by the name we choose for the new type, an equal sign, and an expression involving existing types.

Example 6.1: We might define the type `signal` to be a list of reals by

```
type signal = real list;
```
type signal = real list

We can then give a value of the appropriate form this new type as

```
val v = [1.0, 2.0] : signal;
```
val v = [1.0, 2.0] : signal

Notice that following a value by a colon and a type name declares the value to be of the given type.

The type `signal` is nothing more than an abbreviation. For instance, we can define:

```
val w = [1.0, 2.0];
```
val w = [1.0, 2.0] : real list

Here, ML is given a real list and is not told to regard it as of type `signal`. However, if we compare *v* and *w* as in

```
v=w;
```
val it = true : bool

ML recognizes that *v* and *w* have the same value and does not complain that one is a `signal` while the other is a `real list`. Rather, it recognizes that these are two designations for the same type. □

6.1.3 Parametrized Type Definitions

More generally, we can define a family of types with one or more type variables (identifiers beginning with a quote mark) as parameters. The syntax is

type (<list of type parameters>) <identifier> = <type expression>

That is, following the keyword `type` is a list of type variables serving as type parameters. If there is only one type variable, the parentheses are optional. The parameters are followed by an identifier, which is the type constructor for the type. Finally comes an equal sign and a type expression, which may involve the parameters.

Types in the defined family are described by providing type expressions corresponding to the type parameters and following the type expressions by the type constructor for the type. An example should help to make these ideas clearer.

Example 6.2: A useful data structure for remembering and retrieving an association between data of two types is the *mapping* (not to be confused with the "map" function of Sections 5.4.2 or 5.6.3. In ML, we can think of this structure as a list of pairs. The first component of each pair is of some type `'d`, called the *domain type*, and the second component is of some type `'r`, called the *range type*.[1] In a mapping we do not expect to see two pairs with the same domain element, although there is nothing in the type definition that requires uniqueness of domain elements.

For instance, we might wish to store a count of words in a document as a list of pairs of the type (`string * int`). The first component is a word, and the second component is the number of times the word occurs. The counts for the first paragraph of Section 6.1 would include such pairs as

---

[1]Note that the terms "domain" and "range" are used in connection with both mappings and functions. There is no coincidence; the mapping and function describe similar mathematical objects. A mapping associates pairs of values by listing the pairs, while a function is a program that computes the second component of a pair from the first component.

```
[("in",6), ("a",1), ("as",2), ("types",4), ("ML", 4),...]
```

We can see such a set of pairs as assigning an integer value to each domain element (a word) that is mentioned. Mathematicians would say that words are thereby "mapped" to integers.

Here is a definition of the parameterized type constructor `mapping`.

```
type ('d, 'r) mapping = ('d * 'r) list;
```
*type ('a, 'b) mapping = ('a * 'b) list*

A few important points about this type definition:

- SML/NJ uses `'a`, `'b`, and so on for type variables, regardless of the type variables chosen by the programmer.

- Note that the list of type parameters `'d` and `'r` is separated by commas after the keyword `type`, as if they were parameters of a function. However, in the type expression `('d * 'r) list`, we represent the type of a pair whose components are respectively of types `'d` and `'r` by separating the types with the product-type operator `*`.

We can now stipulate that a certain value is of a particular mapping type. For example, the "assignment"

```
val words = [("in",6), ("a",1)] : (string, int) mapping;
```
val words = [("in",6), ("a",1)] : (string, int) mapping

declares identifier `words` to have a particular value of the type

```
(string, int) mapping
```

That type is an instance of the parameterized type `mapping` formed by choosing the appropriate types for the type parameters `'d` and `'r` in the definition of `mapping`. □

6.1.4   Exercises for Section 6.1

Exercise 6.1.1: Give type definitions (abbreviations) for the following types.

* a) A set of sets, where the type of elements is unspecified and sets are represented by lists.

 b) A list of triples, the first two components of which have the same type and the third component of which is of some (possibly) different type.

Exercise 6.1.2: Give a value of type `(real, real) mapping`, where the type mapping is defined in Example 6.2. Your value should have 3 pairs.

6.2   Datatypes

Since the `type` declaration is limited to definitions of "abbreviations," it is of limited power. Often, we want to create types whose values are new structures. For instance, with the types learned so far we cannot express the notion of a tree.

ML has a very powerful mechanism for defining new types called *datatypes*. A datatype definition involves two kinds of identifiers:

1. A *type constructor* that is the name of the datatype. The type constructor is used to buld types just as type names like `mapping` of Example 6.2 are used.

2. One or more *data constructors*, which are identifiers used as operators to build values belonging to a new datatype.

6.2.1   A Simple Form of Datatype Declaration

The concept of datatypes generalizes such ideas as enumerated types in Pascal and C or union types in these languages, but it goes far beyond these. Thus, we shall take the datatype concept in easy stages. In our first example we see a rather simple use of datatype definition corresponding to an enumerated type. The datatype declaration consists of the keyword `datatype`, a name for the datatype, and a list of data constructors separated by vertical bars.

Example 6.3 : Let us define the datatype with name `fruit` to consist of the three values `Apple`, `Pear`, and `Grape`.

```
datatype fruit = Apple | Pear | Grape;
```
datatype fruit = Apple | Grape | Pear

Identifier `fruit` is the type constructor for the datatype. The names `Apple`, `Pear`, and `Grape` are the data constructors for the datatype `fruit`. Note that SML/NJ alphabetizes lists of data constructors; they do not necessarily appear in the order in which they were declared.

We can use the new datatype in a function or other expression. For instance, we can write

```
fun isApple(x) = (x=Apple);
```
val isApple = fn : fruit → bool

The function `isApple` returns true if its argument is `Apple` and false for any other fruit. The function `isApple` equates its parameter x to a value `Apple` of type `fruit`. Thus, the ML compiler will infer that the argument type of `isApple` is `fruit`. It is an error to pass as an argument anything that is not one of the data constructors for the datatype `fruit`. For instance, `isApple` makes the following responses.

Capitalization Convention

There is a common ML convention regarding the capitalization of the first letter in an identifiers.

1. Capitalize the first letter of:

   (a) Data constructors.

   (b) Exception names (often called *exception constructors*).

   (c) Structure names. We have seen a few built-in structure names such as `TextIO` or `Int`, but we shall not cover user-defined structures until Section 8.2.

   (d) Functors (covered in Section 8.3).

2. Do not capitalize the first letter of:

   (a) Variables.

   (b) Function names.

   (c) Type constructors.

3. Spell "signatures" with all capitals. We shall introduce signatures in Section 8.2.1; they are essentially the type of a structure.

Some ML programmers absolutely refuse to start any variable or function name with a capital. We shall not be so strict, since it is often convenient to remind the reader of a variable's type by a capital. For instance, we have found it useful to distinguish a list L from its elements, whose names are uncapitalized, or to distinguish a polynomial P from an uncapitalized coefficient.

```
isApple(Pear);
```
val it = false : bool

```
isApple(Apple);
```
val it = true : bool

```
isApple(Banana);
```
Error: unbound variable or constructor: Banana

The last response indicates that `Banana` is not an acceptable argument for the function `isApple`. □

We may observe from Example 6.3 something about the form of datatype definitions that serve as enumerated types. The keyword `datatype` is followed by the name of the type, an equal sign, and a list of the data constructors separated by vertical bars.

- Remember that type abbreviations are introduced by the keyword `type`, but datatypes with data constructors require the keyword `datatype`.

- Notice that `datatype` definitions, even in the simple case of Example 6.3, define a new type that is not an abbreviation for any other type.

- For each type there is a set of values. We know, for instance, that the values for the type `int` are the integers. Data constructors are used to build the expressions that are the values for user-defined datatypes. In Example 6.3, the data constructors *are* the values. We shall see that data constructors for more complex datatypes may be combined in powerful ways to build the set of possible values for a type.

6.2.2 Using Constructor Expressions in Datatype Definitions

Now we take up the more general form of datatype definition, where

1. Type variables can be used to parameterize the datatype, just as they can for type definitions.

2. The data constructors can take arguments.

This form of a datatype declaration is

```
datatype   (<list of type parameters>) <identifier>  =
           <first constructor expression>            |
           <second constructor expression>           |
                        ...                           |
           <last constructor expression>
```

That is, we use the keyword `datatype` followed by a list of zero or more type variables used as parameters in the type expressions that follow. Parentheses are optional if there is one type parameter, and illegal if there are zero type parameters, as in the datatype of Example 6.3. The type parameters are followed by an identifier, which is the type constructor for the datatype. Finally come the equal sign and one or more constructor expressions separated by vertical bars.

A *constructor expression* consists of a constructor name, the keyword `of`, and a type expression. A simple example is

```
Banana of int
```

This constructor expression says that values of the datatype being defined can have the form Banana(23), or in general, Banana(i) for any integer i. Some important points to remember are:

- Notice that the data constructor is used to "wrap" the data with (optional) parentheses. In an expression like Banana(23), we not only get an integer value, 23, but we are told by the data constructor Banana something about the form, meaning, or origin of this value; perhaps a bunch with 23 bananas is represented.

- Thus, data constructors are "applied" to data as if they were functions, but they are not functions. Rather, we use constructors to form symbolic expressions whose appearance is similar to that of an expression involving function applications.

- Do not confuse data constructors with type constructors. Data constructors are used to build expressions that are values for the type. Type constructors are used in expressions that denote types themselves.

Example 6.4: The next example is one in which the datatype capability of ML is used in a manner similar to the union types found in Pascal or C, among other languages. The idea is to manufacture a type whose elements are formed from either of two previously defined types. We use two data constructors, each of which wraps elements of one of the two types, and thus tells us which of the two types is found inside the wrapping.

We want to deal with "elements" that may be *pairs* or *singles*. The first component of each element will be of some type 'a, and the second component, if it exists, will be of some type 'b. We shall call the datatype element. It will have two data constructors, P, which forms a pair, and S, which forms a single. In effect, the first type of the union is 'a and the second type is 'a * 'b. The declaration and ML response are shown in Fig. 6.1.

```
(1) datatype ('a, 'b) element =
(2)     P of 'a * 'b |
(3)     S of 'a;
     datatype ('a,'b) element = P of 'a * 'b | S of 'a
```

Figure 6.1: Datatype that is the union of singles and pairs

In line (1) of Fig. 6.1 we see that a datatype is being declared; it has two type variables as parameters, 'a and 'b. The name of the datatype is "('a, 'b) element." The identifier element becomes a binary type constructor, that is, a type constructor that applies to a pair of types, just like the type constructor mapping of Example 6.2. Line (2) tells us about the data constructor P, which takes as data a pair consisting of an 'a value and a 'b value and "wraps" them in the symbol P. Similarly, line (3) tells us about the data constructor S, which takes an 'a value and wraps it with an S. Note that the type produced is an ('a, 'b) element, even though the data itself does not involve a value of type 'b in this case.

Now let us see how the element datatype can be used. We can let the type parameters 'a and 'b be anything we choose, but for an example let 'a be string and 'b be int. To get concrete, we might wish to extend the word-count problem of Example 6.2 to allow the list to include some words that are not present (represented by "singles"), while pairs represent a word that is present, along with its count of occurrences. For instance, a list of elements representing the first paragraph of Section 6.1 might include

```
[P("in",6), S("function"), P("as",2),...]
```

Suppose we want to take a list of (string, int) element's and sum the integers in the second components of those elements that have second components. The function sumElList in Fig. 6.2 does this task.

```
(1) fun sumElList(nil) = 0
(2)  |    sumElList(S(x)::L) = sumElList(L)
(3)  |    sumElList(P(x,y)::L) = y + sumElList(L);
```
     val sumElList = fn : ('a, int) element list → int

Figure 6.2: Summing second components of element's

Line (1) handles the basis case; when the list is empty the sum is 0. Line (2) handles the case where the first element is a single. Then, there is no contribution to the sum from the head element, so the result is obtained by a recursive application of sumElList to the tail. Line (3) handles the case where the head element is a pair. We recursively apply the function to the tail and then add to the resulting sum the second component of the pair at the head.

- The function sumElList does not constrain the type for first components of pairs. However, line (1) tells us the result of sumElList is an integer. The addition on line (3) must therefore be integer addition, so the second components of pairs are integers. Thus, the domain type for the function sumElList is ('a, int) element list.

- In lines (2) and (3), we use the data constructors P and S as part of the pattern to distinguish the two cases of elements. This style is very common when we program with datatypes. We use one pattern for each data constructor, so each kind of value belonging to the datatype is handled appropriately.

Finally, we can apply function sumElList to a particular list as

```
sumElList [P("in",6), S("function"), P("as",2)];
val it = 8 : int
```

When we apply the function `sumElList` to this particular list, we deduce that the type `'a` for this list is `string`. Notice that we have safely omitted the parentheses around the argument of `sumElList`, since the square brackets around a list guarantees that the argument cannot be misinterpreted. □

6.2.3 Recursively Defined Datatypes

The datatype `element` of Example 6.4 did not involve nesting of constructors to build values. Rather, we only applied each constructor to appropriate values to form the values of the new type. In many interesting and important examples, values are built by applying the data constructors recursively to build arbitrarily large expressions.

Example 6.5 : A (*labeled*) *binary tree* is defined recursively as follows.

BASIS: The *empty tree* is a binary tree.

INDUCTION: If T_1 and T_2 are binary trees, and a is a label, then we may form another binary tree T by creating a *node* with label a, *left subtree* T_1, and *right subtree* T_2. The new node is the *root* of T.

We represent the empty tree by the absence of any mark. A node is represented by its label, a line to the lower left running to the root of its left subtree, and a line to its lower right running to the root of its right subtree. If either subtree is empty, we omit the line to that subtree. Figure 6.3 shows an example binary tree with strings as labels.

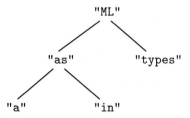

Figure 6.3: An example of a binary tree labeled by strings

Figure 6.4 is a datatype declaration for a binary tree with a type parameter `'label` representing the type of labels in the tree. The type constructor for this datatype is `btree`. In any use, the variable `'label` would be replaced by the actual type. For instance, the binary tree of Fig. 6.3, having string labels, is a value of type `string btree`.

Line (1) of Fig. 6.4 declares the name of the datatype, `btree`, and its type parameter `'label`. Since there is only one type parameter, we have exercised

```
(1) datatype 'label btree =
(2)      Empty |
(3)      Node of 'label * 'label btree * 'label btree;
```
*datatype 'a btree = Empty | Node of 'a * 'a btree * 'a btree*

Figure 6.4: Datatype definition for binary trees

our option to omit parentheses around the parameter. Line (2) gives `Empty` as a data constructor. This constructor takes no argument and will appear only as an identifier, just as the fruit names used as data constructors in Example 6.3 appear by themselves. Line (3) introduces the data constructor `Node`, which is applied to a triple of values. The first is of type `'label` and the second two are of type `'label btree`; that is, they are of the same type as the type being defined. The response of ML repeats these points.

The values of type `'label btree` are defined recursively as follows.

BASIS: The data constructor `Empty` is a value.

INDUCTION: An expression of the form $Node(a, L, R)$ is a value, if a is of the `'label` type and L and R are `'label btree`'s, that is, binary trees with appropriately typed labels.

- In general, the values for a datatype are those that are constructed by applying the data constructors to values of the appropriate types, as many times as we wish.

For instance, consider the tree of Fig. 6.3. First, we note that the labels are strings, so `'label` must have the value `string`, and this tree is a `string btree`. The leaves (nodes with two empty subtrees) are represented by an expression of the form $Node(a, Empty, Empty)$, where a is the label of the node. For instance, the node labeled `"types"` is represented by the expression `Node("types", Empty, Empty)`.

Then we can work up the tree, constructing the expression for a node after the expressions for its two subtrees have been constructed. Thus, after handling all three leaves, we can work on the node labeled `"as"`. This node has the expression

```
Node("as", Node("a",Empty,Empty), Node("in",Empty,Empty))
```

That is, the first component is the label, `"as"`. The second component is the expression for the left subtree, which consists of the leaf labeled `"a"`; this tree has the expression `Node("a", Empty, Empty)`. The third component is a similar expression for the leaf labeled `"in"`.

Finally, the expression for the root uses the expression for the node labeled `"as"` for its left subtree and the expression for the leaf labeled `"types"` as its right subtree. When combined with the label at the root, we find that the expression for the entire tree is that shown in Fig. 6.5.   □

```
Node("ML",
    Node("as",
        Node("a",Empty,Empty),
        Node("in",Empty,Empty)
    ),
    Node("types",Empty,Empty)
)
```

Figure 6.5: A value of type `string btree`

6.2.4 Mutually Recursive Datatypes

Occasionally we need to define two or more datatypes in a mutually recursive way. We can do so by connecting the definitions with the keyword **and**. Type, as well as datatype, definitions may also be connected with **and**, but there is less need to do so.

Example 6.6 : We can define an *even tree* to be a binary tree in which each path from the root to a node with one or two empty subtrees has an even number of nodes. As a special case, the empty tree, whose paths we may regard as having length 0, is an even tree. Similarly, an *odd tree* is a binary tree all of whose paths from the root to a leaf or to a node with one empty subtree have an odd number of nodes. The tree of Fig. 6.3 is neither even nor odd, because there is an even-length path from the root to leaf `"types"` and there are odd-length paths from the root to the other two leaves.

There is a simple, mutually recursive definition of the datatypes `evenTree` and `oddTree`.

BASIS: The empty tree is an even tree.

INDUCTION: A node with a label of type `'label` and two subtrees that are odd trees is the root of an even tree. A node with a label of type `'label` and two subtrees that are even trees is the root of an odd tree.

Lines (1) through (4) of Fig. 6.6 show this mutually recursive definition in ML. Line (1) makes `Empty` a constructor for even trees, and line (2) makes `Enode` be a constructor that takes a label and two odd trees to construct an even tree. Similarly, line (4) makes `Onode` the only constructor of odd trees, taking a label and two even trees.

Lines (5) through (9) use the data constructors `Onode` and `Enode` to build some odd and even trees. Line (5) creates an odd tree consisting of a single

```
      datatype
(1)      'label evenTree = Empty |
(2)          Enode of 'label * 'label oddTree * 'label oddTree
      and
(3)      ·'label oddTree =
(4)          Onode of 'label * 'label evenTree * 'label evenTree;
```

*datatype 'a evenTree = Empty | Enode of * 'a oddTree * 'a oddTree*
*datatype 'a oddTree = Onode of 'a * 'a evenTree * 'a evenTree*

```
(5) val t1 = Onode(1,Empty,Empty);
```

val t1 = Onode(1,Empty,Empty) : int oddTree

```
(6) val t2 = Onode(2,Empty,Empty);
```

val t2 = Onode(2,Empty,Empty) : int oddTree

```
(7) val t3 = Enode(3,t1,t2);
```

val t3 = Enode(3, Onode(1,Empty,Empty),
*   Onode(2,Empty,Empty)) : int evenTree*

```
(8) val t4 = Onode(4,t3,Empty);
```

val t4 = Onode(4, Enode(3, Onode #, Onode #), Empty) :
*   int oddTree*

```
(9) val t5 = Enode(5,t4,t4);
```

val t5 = Enode(5, Onode(4, Enode #, Empty),
*   Onode(4, Enode #, Empty)) : int evenTree*

Figure 6.6: Mutually recursive datatype definitions

node labeled 1. Note that ML now deduces that for this tree the type `'label` is integer. Line (6) similarly creates a node labeled 2. It, like all single-node trees, is an odd tree.

Line (7) uses the two odd trees from the previous two lines to create an even tree whose root has label 3, whose left subtree is the single node labeled 1, and whose right subtree is the single node labeled 2. Notice ML's response, which gives the expression for this tree and identifies its type as an `int evenTree`.

Line (8) builds another odd tree by taking a root node with label 4, the even tree `t3` from line (7), and an empty even tree as left and right subtrees.

Finally, line (9) takes a root node labeled 5 and two copies of the odd tree `t4` from line (8) and creates another even tree. Each # in the response to line (9) represents the tree `t3`. Figure 6.7(a) shows the complete expression for `t5` expanded out, while Fig. 6.7(b) is a picture of this even tree. Note that each root-to-leaf path has an even number of nodes.   □

The reader familiar with a language like Pascal or C that uses pointers as a type constructor may have seen trees constructed by pointers in records that represent nodes. Notice that the ML approach is somewhat different. The value of the tree is represented in ML programs by an expression built from data constructors applied to arguments. For example, the value of `t3` printed after line (7) of Fig. 6.6 does not involve any pointers to the values of `t1` or `t2`.

The distinction is seen if identifiers such as `t1` or `t2` are redefined. Then, the value of `t3` does not change. However, had a tree like `t3` been constructed in Pascal or C, with pointers to the trees represented by `t1` and `t2`, the value of tree `t3` would change as a side-effect of the change to trees `t1` or `t2`.

6.2.5   Exercises for Section 6.2

* **Exercise 6.2.1:** Give an example of a value of type `int btree`, where `btree` is the datatype defined in Example 6.5. Your tree should have 3 nodes.

*! **Exercise 6.2.2:** Define a type (not a datatype) `mapTree` that is a specialization of the `btree` datatype to have a label type that is a set of domain-range pairs. Then, define a tree `t1` that has a single node with the pair (`"a"`,1) at the root.

Exercise 6.2.3: Write a function that takes a `btree` as its argument and returns a pair consisting of the left and right subtrees. Define an exception for the erroneous case where the tree is empty.

*! **Exercise 6.2.4:** In Fig. 4.10 we wrote a program to read and sum integers, using the awkward convention that −1 represented the situation where the end of file had been reached and no integer was available. A better approach is to define a datatype `intOrEof` that has one data constructor `Eof` to represent the absence of an integer and another data constructor `Integer` that wraps an integer. Rewrite Fig. 4.10 to use this strategy and avoid the use of −1, which was represented there by the identifier `END`.

```
Enode(5,
    Onode(4,
        Enode(3,
            Onode(1,Empty,Empty),
            Onode(2,Empty,Empty)),
        Empty
    ),
    Onode(4,
        Enode(3,
            Onode(1,Empty,Empty),
            Onode(2,Empty,Empty)),
        Empty
    )
)
```

(a) Nested expression for tree t5

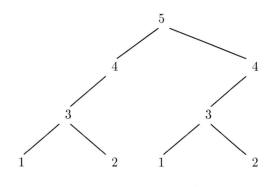

(b) Picture of tree t5

Figure 6.7: Representations of the tree t5 from Fig.6.6

Eliding Parts of Values

Notice in the response that SML/NJ only shows complicated expressions for a fixed number of levels and elides deeper structure with the # sign. For instance, in the response to line (8) of Fig. 6.6 the first # stands for the tree `t1`, or `Onode(1,Empty,Empty)`, and the second # stands for `t2`, or `Onode(2,Empty,Empty)`.

Options as a Datatype

Notice that the `option` type constructor first introduced in Section 4.2.5 is actually a built-in datatype, with constructors `NONE` and `SOME of 'a` for any type `'a`. Its uses are similar to that of the datatype `intOrEof` in Exercise 6.2.4. In fact, if we don't mind the less descriptive data constructors `NONE` and `SOME`, we can use `option` in place of `intOrEof`, with data constructor `NONE` replacing `Eof` and `SOME of int` replacing `Integer of int`.

! **Exercise 6.2.5:** Tell whether a type or a datatype declaration would be more suitable for the following. Give the appropriate declaration.

* a) A type whose values are the suits of a card deck.

  b) A type whose elements are either lists of (only) integers or lists of (only) reals.

* c) A type whose values are "things," where a "thing" is either an integer or a list of "things."

  d) A (parameterized) type whose values are pairs whose components can be of any type, as long as they are of the same type.

! **Exercise 6.2.6:** Define mutually recursive datatypes `zeroTree`, `oneTree`, and `twoTree` to be those binary trees whose every path from the root to a node with at least one empty subtree has length whose remainder when divided by 3 is 0, 1, or 2 respectively.

*! **Exercise 6.2.7:** We can define a graph with nodes of some type `'node` as a list of pairs. Each pair consists of a node of type `'node` and a list of its successor nodes.

  a) Write this type definition.

More Equality Types

Both types and datatypes may be used to define more equality types.

- A type is an equality type if the type that it stands for is an equality type.

- A datatype is an equality type if its constructor expressions, if any, involve only equality types or the datatype itself.

- A mutually recursive collection of datatypes are equality types if their constructor expressions involve only equality types and the datatypes in the collection.

b) Write a function `succ(a,G)` that produces the set (represented by a list) of successors of node a in graph G. If a is not a node of G, then raise the exception `NotANode`.

!! c) Write a function `search(a,G)` that finds the set of nodes reachable from node a in graph G, including a itself. *Hint*: It helps to write an auxiliary function `search1(L,R,G)` that finds all the nodes that are reachable from one or more of the nodes on list L in graph G, without going through a node on the list R. Function `search1` then returns all the nodes it has reached plus all the nodes on R. We may use parameter R of `search1` to keep track of nodes we have already reached in our search. We thus avoid getting trapped in infinite loops, even if the graph G has cycles.

! **Exercise 6.2.8 :** In propositional logic, statements are represented by *propositional variables*, which we may think of as identifiers. Logical expressions can be built from propositional variables by applying a number of logical operators. In our exercise, we shall define logical expressions and their truth values in a simple but useful form as follows.

BASIS: A propositional variable is a logical expression. Its truth value may be assigned to be either true or false.

INDUCTION: If E_1 and E_2 are logical expressions, then

1. `AND`(E_1, E_2) is a logical expression, and its value is true if and only if both E_1 and E_2 have the value true.

2. `OR`(E_1, E_2) is a logical expression, and its value is true if either E_1 or E_2 or both have the value true.

3. `NOT`(E_1) is a logical expression whose value is true if and only if the value of E_1 is false.

An example of a propositional expression is $\text{AND}\big(\text{OR}(p,q),\ \text{NOT}(p)\big)$. Do the following:

a) Devise a datatype whose values represent logical expressions as described above. You may assume that propositional variables are represented by strings.

b) Write a function eval(E,L) that takes a logical expression E and a list of true propositional variables L, and determines the truth value of E on the assumption that the propositional variables on L are true and all other propositional variables are false.

6.3   Case Study: Binary Trees

In this section, we shall solidify our familiarity with datatypes by writing a number of functions on binary trees, using the datatype btree introduced in Example 6.5. Most of these functions involve the "binary search tree" described below.

6.3.1   Binary Search Trees

Binary search trees are binary trees whose labels obey a particular property called the *binary search tree property*, or *BST property*, which we shall define shortly. The BST property only makes sense if there is an ordering relation, often referred to as $<$, that allows us to compare values of the label type. For example, the types int, real, char, and string have this ordering. To be more general, we shall only assume that there is a predicate lt(x,y) obeying the important properties of $<$ on integers, reals, or strings. These properties are:

1. *Transitivity.* That is, $lt(x,y)$ and $lt(y,z)$ imply $lt(x,z)$, just as $x<y$ and $y<z$ tell us that $x<z$.

2. *Comparability.* If $x \neq y$, then exactly one of $lt(x,y)$ and $lt(y,x)$ is true.

3. *Irreflexivity.* $lt(x,x)$ is never true for any x.

Note that, like transitivity, (2) and (3) are obeyed by the conventional $<$. We never have $x<x$, and if $x \neq y$, then either $x<y$ or $y<x$ will be true, but never both.

Now we can state the BST property with regard to a given comparison operator $<$:

- *BST property*: If x is the label of any node n in a binary search tree, then for every label y in the left subtree of n we have $y<x$, and for every label y in the right subtree of n we have $x<y$.

Example 6.7: The tree of Fig. 6.3, which we reproduce here as Fig. 6.8, is a binary search tree if we take the ordering to be the usual lexicographic order on strings but first convert capital letters to lower case.[2] Our desired `lt` function requires first converting capitals to lower case, and then doing the standard comparison.

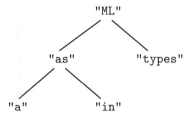

Figure 6.8: A binary search tree

Here is a function `lower` that converts a list of characters by replacing the upper-case letters by the corresponding lower-case letters.

```
fun lower(nil) = nil
|   lower(c::cs) = (Char.toLower c)::lower(cs);
```
val lower = fn : char list → char list

It makes use of a function `toLower` in the structure `Char`, which contains many useful functions on characters; see Section 9.4.4. The effect of `toLower(c)` is to return the character *c* unless *c* is a capital letter, in which case it returns the corresponding lower-case letter. For instance, `toLower(#"A")` and `toLower(#"a")` both have value `#"a"`, while `toLower(#"1")` has the value `#"1"`. The operation of `lower` is quite simple; it applies `toLower` to each character on the list, in turn.

Now we can use `lower` to define a suitable function `strLT` that compares strings as we wish, treating upper- and lower-case letters as identical. This function:

1. Explodes its two argument strings,

2. Converts each character to lower case using `lower`,

3. Implodes the resulting character list back into a string, and

4. Compares the results using the built-in `<` comparison operator for strings.

---

[2] Remember that in ASCII, a capital letter has a code 32 less than its corresponding lower-case letter, and therefore precedes all lower-case letters according to the $<$ relationship defined for ML strings. By converting to lower case before comparing strings, we avoid unintuitive comparisons such as `"Zap"<"abcd"`.

The function `strLT` is shown below. Notice that we have omitted the unnecessary parentheses around the arguments in the two uses of `explode`. However, the remaining parentheses are necessary.

```
fun strLT(x,y) =
        implode(lower(explode x)) <
            implode(lower(explode y));
```

*val strLT = fn : string * string → bool*

Let us verify that the tree of Fig. 6.8 is a binary search tree when we use the function `strLT` as < in comparisons of labels. First consider the root of Fig. 6.8, whose label is "ML". The three words in the left subtree — "a", "as", and "in" — each precede "ML" in the order defined by function `lt` above. The one word "types" in the right subtree follows "ML". These observations tell us the BST property is satisfied at the root.

In order to verify the BST property for the tree as a whole, we must consider all the nodes. For the node labeled "as", we find only "a" in the left subtree and "in" in the right subtree. Since `lt("a","as")` and `lt("as","in")` are both true, the BST property holds at this node. The other three nodes have only empty subtrees, so they cannot violate the BST property. We conclude that Fig. 6.8 satisfies the BST property.   □

6.3.2   Lookup in Binary Search Trees

Binary search trees are useful because they let us search for elements at the nodes, insert new elements, and delete elements in time that is usually much less than the number of nodes in the tree. In particular, we only have to follow one path in the tree, starting at the root and heading down the tree. The BST property helps us find a particular label x if it exists somewhere in a binary search tree. We start at the root and progress down the tree in the only direction that could hold x, until we either find x or come to an empty tree.

The following recursive algorithm assumes we have some tree T to search and directs us in the proper way. In practice, we look for an element x by starting our search at the root of the entire binary search tree, although as we proceed, T could be any of the subtrees encountered during our search.

BASIS: If we are at an empty tree, then fail; x is not in the tree. If we are at a tree with root n and the label of n is x, then our search for x succeeds.

INDUCTION: If we are at the root of some nonempty tree, the label of the root is y, and $x \neq y$, then

1. If $lt(x,y)$, then recursively search only the left subtree.

2. Otherwise (i.e., $lt(y,x)$), search only the right subtree.

```
datatype 'label btree =
    Empty |
    Node of 'label * 'label btree * 'label btree;
```
*datatype 'a btree = Empty | Node of 'a * 'a btree * 'a btree*

```
fun lower(nil) = nil
|   lower(c::cs) = (Char.toLower c)::lower(cs);
```
val lower = fn : char list → char list

```
fun strLT(x,y) =
        implode(lower(explode x)) <
            implode(lower(explode y));
```
*val strLT = fn : string * string → bool*

```
(1) fun lookup lt Empty x = false
(2) |   lookup lt (Node(y,left,right)) x =
(3)         if lt(x,y) then lookup lt left x
(4)         else if lt(y,x) then lookup lt right x
(5)         else (* x=y *) true;
```
*val lookup = fn : ('a * 'a → bool) → 'a btree → 'a → bool*

```
(6) val t = Node("ML",
                Node("as",
                    Node("a",Empty,Empty),
                    Node("in",Empty,Empty)
                ),
                Node("types",Empty,Empty)
            );
```
val t = Node ("ML",Node ("as",Node #,Node #),
Node ("types",Empty,Empty)) : string btree

```
(7) lookup strLT t "function";
```
val it = false : bool

Figure 6.9: Lookup in a binary search tree

In Fig. 6.9 we see the definition of the datatype `btree`, repeated from Fig. 6.4, and the definitions of the functions `lower` and `strLT` from Example 6.7. Then comes the definition of function `lookup`. This function is written in Curried form and has three arguments:

1. A "less-than" function whose type is `'a * 'a -> bool`,

2. A `'a btree`.

3. An element of type `'a`, and

The range type of `lookup` is `bool`. We designed `lookup` so that it could be partially instantiated with a particular less-than function to create a two-parameter function that looks up an element in a binary search tree, using this less-than function.

Now, let us study how `lookup` works. Line (1) of Fig. 6.9 handles one of the basis cases, where the tree is empty. Line (2) provides the pattern that matches all other cases. Variable x matches the value being searched for, and `Node(y,left,right)` matches the expression for any binary tree except the empty tree. In the match, `y` acquires the value of the label, `left` gets the value of the left subtree, and `right` gets the value of the right subtree.

Line (3) handles the case where the desired label is less than the label at the root; we must then search only the left subtree. Line (4) handles the opposite case, where the desired label is greater than the label at the root and we must search the right subtree. The only remaining case, in line (5), is when x and y are equal. Then, x has been found, which is the second basis case. Function `lookup` thus returns `true` at line (5).

Line (6) defines a variable t to be the specific tree of Fig. 6.5. Then, at line (7), we call `lookup`, searching for the word `"function"` in the tree t, using the specific comparison function `strLT`. We first compare `"function"` with `"ML"`, and at line (3) go to the left subtree, rooted at `"as"`. There we find `"function"` follows `"as"`, so we go to the right, the tree rooted at `"in"`. Next, we find `"function"` precedes `"in"`, so we go to the left subtree. This tree is empty, so at the next call the pattern of line (1) applies, and we return `false`. The desired label `"function"` is not in the tree.

- Notice how pattern matching is used in the function `lookup` to determine which data constructor is used at the outermost layer of the expression representing the binary tree.

- Pattern matching is also used to pick apart the structure of the tree and allow us to attack pieces of the expression recursively.

6.3.3 Insertion into Binary Search Trees

Next, let us look at a similar function `insert` to insert an element into a binary search tree in the appropriate place. The function `insert lt T x` returns

---

Avoiding Equality Tests in Searches

We have been very careful in `lookup` not to assume that the type of labels is an equality type. We use *only* the given `lt` comparison function to compare elements x and y, and we discover $x = y$ when we determine that both $x < y$ and $y < x$ are false (equality must follow if the $<$ relationship is a total order). Had we done the test $x = y$ explicitly on line (5) of Fig. 6.9 or earlier, then the type `'a` in the description of `lookup`'s type would appear as `''a`, and the type of labels would have to be an equality type for `lookup` to work.

---

the tree that results when x is inserted into tree T using the function `lt` for comparisons. The facts that a modified tree is returned and that the tree T itself is unchanged are essential points in understanding how **insert** works. The recursive algorithm can be described as follows.

BASIS: To insert x into the empty tree, return the tree with one node, labeled x. To insert x into a tree whose root is labeled x, return the given tree. In the latter case, no modification is necessary.

INDUCTION: To insert x into a tree with root labeled y, where $x \neq y$, recursively insert x into the left subtree if $x < y$ and into the right subtree otherwise. Return a copy of the tree, with its left or right subtree modified, respectively.

Figure 6.10 is ML code to execute this algorithm. It uses the auxiliary definitions for datatype `btree`, comparison function `strLT`, and tree t from Fig. 6.9.

```
(1) fun insert lt Empty x = Node(x,Empty,Empty)
(2)   |   insert lt (T as Node(y,left,right)) x =
(3)           if lt(x,y) then Node(y,(insert lt left x),right)
(4)           else if lt(y,x) then Node(y,left,(insert lt right x))
(5)           else (* x=y *) T; (* do nothing; x was
                                     already there *)
```

*val insert = fn : ('a * 'a → bool) → 'a btree → 'a → 'a btree*

```
(6) insert strLT t "function";
```

val it = Node ("ML",Node ("as",Node #,Node #),
*   Node ("types",Empty,Empty)) : string btree*

Figure 6.10: Insertion into a binary search tree

Line (1) handles the case of insertion into an empty tree, where a one-node tree is returned. Line (2), like the same line in Fig. 6.9, matches any nonempty tree and breaks it into its important components. However, the whole tree is also matched to the identifier T at line (2), using the keyword as.

In line (3), we are directed to insert into the left subtree. We return a tree whose root label is the same as it was: y. The right subtree is also the same as it was, but the left subtree is modified to be whatever the recursive call to insert lt left x produces. That will be the left subtree, modified to include a node labeled x at the appropriate place. Line (4) does the symmetric thing when x must be inserted into the right subtree. Finally, line (5) handles the remaining case, where the element x to be inserted is at the root of the tree T. Since x is already in the tree, we need make no change and can just return T.

Line (6) shows a call to insert with first argument "function", second argument the tree t defined in Fig. 6.9, and the comparison function strLT from that figure. We eventually find our way to the empty tree that is the left subtree of the node labeled "in". In the tree constructed as the return value, that empty subtree is replaced by a tree with one node labeled "function". The resulting two-node tree replaces the one-node tree whose node is labeled "in", yielding a four-node tree to replace the three-node tree whose root is labeled "as". Figure 6.11 shows the tree returned by the original call to insert.

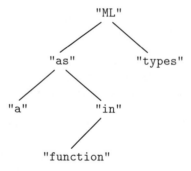

Figure 6.11: Binary search tree after insertion of "function"

6.3.4 Deletion from Binary Search Trees

We can delete a specified element x from a binary search tree, but the strategy is a bit more complicated than lookup or insertion. As for insertion, we leave the given tree intact but return a modified version of the tree in which x does not appear. The idea is expressed by the following recursive algorithm, which curiously has most of the effort in the basis case where the targeted element is found at the root of the tree.

BASIS: Nothing needs to be done to delete x from an empty tree; x is not there anyway. Just return the given tree. To delete x from a tree whose root has label x, modify the tree to remove x and maintain the BST property as follows.

1. If the root has at least one empty subtree, replace the tree by the other subtree.

2. If the root has two nonempty subtrees:

   (a) Find the least element in the right subtree,

   (b) Delete it from the right subtree (which is always an example of case (1) above, since the least element in a binary search tree must have an empty left subtree), and

   (c) Make the least label be the label of the root, replacing x.

   Return the resulting tree.

INDUCTION: To delete x from a tree whose root has label y, where $x \neq y$, recursively delete x from the left subtree if $x < y$ and from the right subtree if $y < x$.

Figure 6.12 gives the necessary code to implement this algorithm. To understand it, start with the function `delete` of lines (7) through (16). Line (7) handles the first part of the basis, where we try to delete x from the empty tree and simply return the empty tree. In line (8) we handle all other cases, where we need to dissect it into its important components as we did for `lookup` and `insert`.

Lines (9) and (10) cover the inductive cases, where we must delete from the left or right subtree. For instance, in line (9) we must delete from the left. To do so, we assemble the result by taking the original label y, the original right subtree, and the left subtree that we get by deleting x from the original left subtree.

Lines (11) through (16) handle the hard basis case, where x has been found at the root and we must rearrange the tree. Line (11) is the beginning of a case statement, in which we consider whether one or both of the left and right subtrees are empty. Lines (12) and (13) are for the case where one of the subtrees is empty and we return the other.

If neither subtree is empty, then the case of line (14) applies. We call the function `deletemin` (to be described next) on the right subtree at line (15). This function returns a pair:

1. z, the smallest label in the right subtree, and

2. `r1`, the tree that results from deleting z from the original right subtree.

```
(1) exception EmptyTree;
    exception EmptyTree


    (* deletemin(T) returns a pair consisting of the least
       element y in tree T and the tree that results if we
       delete y from T.  It is an error if T is empty *)

(2) fun deletemin(Empty) = raise EmptyTree
(3)  |   deletemin(Node(y,Empty,right)) = (y,right) (* The
                  critical case.  If the left subtree is empty,
                  then the element at current node is min. *)
(4)  |   deletemin(Node(w,left,right)) =
             let
(5)               val (y,L) = deletemin(left)
             in
(6)               (y, Node(w,L,right))
             end;
    val deletemin = fn : 'a btree → 'a * 'a btree



(7) fun delete lt Empty x = Empty
(8)  |   delete lt (Node(y,left,right)) x =
(9)          if lt(x,y) then Node(y,(delete lt left x),right)
(10)         else if lt(y,x) then Node(y,left,(delete lt right x))
             else (* x=y *)
(11)            case (left,right) of
(12)                (Empty,r) => r |
(13)                (l,Empty) => l |
(14)                (l,r) =>
                      let
(15)                       val (z,r1) = deletemin(r)
                      in
(16)                       Node(z,l,r1)
                      end;
    val delete = fn : ('a * 'a → bool) → 'a btree → 'a → 'a btree
```

Figure 6.12: Deletion from a binary search tree

In line (16) we assemble the result, which has z in place of x at the root, the original left subtree, and the revised right subtree r1. Note that because z is the least label of the right subtree, the BST property is satisfied with z at the root. It surely precedes anything in tree r1, and because $x < z$, it must be that anything in the left subtree precedes z as well as x.

Now let us consider the function deletemin. This function is only called on nonempty trees, so we use the exception EmptyList in line (1) and raise it in line (2) if somehow the function is called on an empty tree. Note that, unlike the functions insert, delete, and lookup, function deletemin does not need the comparison function lt as an argument.

The least label in a binary search tree is found by following left branches until we reach a node that has an empty left subtree. The situation is suggested in Fig. 6.13. Thus line (3) handles the case where we are at a tree with an empty left subtree. We return the pair consisting of:

1. The label of this node, which must be the least element, and

2. The right subtree, which is what is left when we delete the node with the least element.

Notice that this deletion is an easy basis case, where one of the subtrees is empty.

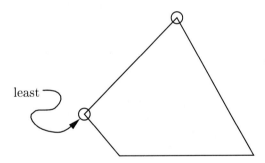

Figure 6.13: Locating the least label in a tree

Lines (4) through (6) handle the case where the left subtree is not empty and we must search further. In line (5) we recursively apply deletemin to the left subtree, obtaining a pair (y, L) consisting of the least label y and what remains of the left subtree after deleting y. In line (6) we assemble the desired result, a pair with y as the first component. For the second component we construct a tree with the original label w, the new left subtree L, and the original right subtree.

6.3.5 Some Comments About Running Time

We can, and shall, demonstrate that the operations of lookup, insert, and delete on binary search trees take time proportional to the length of the path followed.

A path in a "typical" binary search tree will have length that is logarithmic in the number of nodes in the tree. So, binary search trees are a very efficient way to represent large sets if we only want to perform these three operations. We shall not try to prove the contention that the typical path is logarithmic in length; the reader may rely on this observation if he or she is unfamiliar with the lore surrounding binary trees.

However, it is useful to verify the fact that the time taken by these algorithms is proportional to the length of the path traversed. Function `lookup` in Fig. 6.9 is the easiest to analyze. Line (1) takes a constant amount of time, independent of the size of the tree, to test whether the second argument is `Empty` and return `false` if so. Line (2) takes a constant amount of time to examine the root node of the tree and match variables `x`, `y`, `left`, and `right` in the pattern. Line (5) takes a constant amount of time to return `true` if we reach that line.

Lines (3) and (4) require constant time to apply function `lt`.[3] We must also consider the time consumed in line (3) or (4) by the recursive call to `lookup`. However, whether we call `lookup lt left x` or `lookup lt right x`, we have moved one node down the tree. Thus as we follow our path down the tree, we spend only a constant amount of time at each node and then move down. Hence the total amount of time spent is proportional to the length of the path followed.

The argument about `insert` in Fig. 6.10 is similar. The only difference is that after making the recursive call to `insert` at line (3) or (4), we have to assemble a new tree, for example by evaluating the expression

```
Node(y,(insert lt left x),right)
```

in line (3). Is it possible that we have to copy the tree produced by

```
insert lt left x
```

in this situation?

Fortunately, it is not. ML is implemented in such a way that this value-construction is done by pointers, just as it is typically done by programmers using conventional languages. In ML, these pointers are "behind the scenes," and the user may imagine that the trees themselves are manipulated. In practice, the construction of a tree from given trees — or in general, any fixed number of steps of value-construction using data constructors — takes a constant amount of time, independent of the size of the values being manipulated.

Interestingly, we avoid copying values even in situations where it appears to be necessary. For example, consider line (11) of Fig. 6.6, where we construct the value of `t5` from two copies of the value of `t4`. In ML implementations, the value of `t5` can have two pointers, each to the value of `t4`. Because values of variables do not change in ML, we can rely on the value of `t4` remaining the

---

[3]Technically, `lt` could be any function that returns a boolean, no matter how complicated. But `lt` does not get the tree as an argument, and so its running time could not depend on the size of the tree.

same should we ever need the value of t5. In other languages, we normally could not take this risk.

6.3.6   Visiting All the Nodes of a Binary Tree

The previous examples each have the property that we follow one path down a binary tree from the root to a leaf. There is another class of functions that operate on a tree by visiting each node in a systematic order. We shall give two simple examples.

Example 6.8 : Let us write a function `sum(T)` that takes a binary tree (not necessarily a binary search tree), defined by the `btree` datatype of Fig. 6.4, and sums the labels of all the nodes, which we shall assume are integers. The function `sum` is written below:

```
fun sum(Empty) = 0
|   sum(Node(a,left,right)) = a + sum(left) + sum(right);
```
*val sum = fn : int * int btree → int*

That is, the sum over an empty tree is 0, and the sum over any other tree is the label at the root plus the sums over the left and right subtrees. As we see from the ML response, the label type is forced to be integer because of the 0 on the first line.   □

6.3.7   Preorder Traversals

Our second example of a function that visits all the nodes of a binary tree concerns "preorder traversals." A *preorder traversal* of a tree is a listing of the node labels by the following recursive algorithm.

1. List the label of the root.

2. In order from the left, list all the nodes of each subtree in preorder.

Example 6.9 : Consider the tree of Fig. 6.8. To list its labels in preorder, we first list the label at the root, `"ML"`. Then we work on the 3-node subtree rooted at `"as"`. We list `"as"`, next work on the left subtree `"a"` and finally work on the right subtree `"in"`. Any 1-node tree is listed in preorder by listing the label alone, so we follow `"as"` by `"a"` and then `"in"`.

Last, we return to the root, having listed its left subtree but not its right subtree. The right subtree, being a 1-node tree, is listed by listing its label `"types"`. Thus

```
["ML", "as", "a", "in", "types"]
```

is the complete preorder listing.   □

Here is a function `preOrder(T)` that lists a binary tree in preorder.

```
fun preOrder(Empty) = nil
|   preOrder(Node(a,left,right)) =
        [a] @ preOrder(left) @ preOrder(right);
```
val preOrder = fn : 'a btree → 'a list

This function follows the definition of preorder in a straightforward way. An empty tree yields nothing, while any other tree yields the label of its root, followed by the preorder listings of its left and right subtrees. Note that if either or both of those subtrees is empty, it will not produce any contribution to the preorder listing.

6.3.8   Exercises for Section 6.3

Exercise 6.3.1: Write functions to list the nodes of a binary tree in:

a) *Postorder*, in which the label at the root follows the postorder traversals of the left and right subtrees.

b) *Inorder*, in which the label of the root is in between the inorder traversals of the left and right subtrees.

Exercise 6.3.2: Suppose we define the type `mapTree` as in Exercise 6.2.2 (see the solutions if you have not worked this exercise yourself). This type is a binary tree whose labels are pairs, which we may think of as the domain and range values of a pair in some mapping. We may use a `mapTree` as a sort of binary search tree, if we use a $<$ ordering on the domain (first) component of each pair only.

* a) Write a function `lookup lt T a` that searches tree T for a pair (a, b) for some b and returns b. The comparison function `lt` compares domain elements of the pairs at the nodes of tree T and guides our search down the tree. If there is no such pair, then raise the exception `Missing`.

b) Write a function `assign lt T a b` that looks in tree T for a pair (a, c) and, if found, replaces c by b. If no such pair is found, `assign` inserts the pair (a, b) in the tree in a position that preserves the BST property. As in (a), comparison function `lt` applies to domain elements of the pairs and guides the search down the tree T.

Exercise 6.3.3: Partially instantiate the functions `lookup`, `insert`, and `delete` defined in this section to give two-argument functions that operate on a binary search tree and a value, where the less-than function is:

* a) $<$ on reals.

b) Lexicographic order on pairs of integers. That is, $(a, b) < (c, d)$ if $a < c$ or if $a = c$ and $b < d$).

c) Lexicographic order on lists of integers. That is, $L < M$ if either L is a proper prefix of M or in the first position where L and M differ, the element of L is smaller than the element of M.

*! **Exercise 6.3.4:** Suppose we have a set S of integers, and we want to write a program that will tell whether a given integer i is a member of S in time proportional to the logarithm of the number of members of S. Show how to create such a function by partially instantiating the function `lookup` of Fig. 6.9.

!! **Exercise 6.3.5:** There is a subtle problem with the function `preOrder` defined in Section 6.3.7. Since concatenation is implemented in ML by copying the first of the two lists involved, a call to `preOrder` on a given node N takes time proportional to the length of the preorder listing of the left subtree of N, plus the time to compute the preorder listings of all subtrees of N. Thus in the worst case (a tree with a long path extending to the left), this function can take time proportional to the square of the number of nodes in the tree. In conventional languages, a typical implementation of preorder traversal will take time that is linear in the number of nodes. Write a function `preOrder` that takes time proportional to the number of nodes. *Hint*: Use the "difference-list" trick discussed in Section 3.5. That is, write an auxiliary function `preOrder1(T,L)` that produces the preorder listing of a tree T followed by the arbitrary list L. We define `preOrder(T)` to call `preOrder1(T,nil)`, but `preOrder1` calls itself recursively and gradually builds up the preorder listing in the second component. By so doing, we can avoid using @ and can build our listing using only the cons operator ::.

6.4   Case Study: General Rooted Trees

In this section we shall examine a second notion of trees, different from binary trees, and see how to write some programs on these trees. There is a common notion of a (rooted) tree that is in a sense a generalization of a binary tree.

6.4.1   A Datatype for Trees

In the datatype `tree`, which we shall write, nodes are allowed to have any number of subtrees from 0 up. We can represent such trees with a single data constructor that we shall call `Node`. The datatype definition appears in Fig. 6.14, where we see that a node consists of a label and a list of trees of the same type. That is, type `'label tree list` is a list of elements, each of which is a tree with labels of type `'label`.

Example 6.10: In Fig. 6.15 is a tree with seven nodes and integer labels from 1 to 7 to identify the nodes. A node is drawn with lines downward to

```
datatype ('label) tree =
    Node of 'label * 'label tree list;
```
*datatype 'a tree = Node of 'a * 'a tree list*

Figure 6.14: Datatype for a general rooted tree

its *children*, which are the roots of its subtrees. Notice that node 3 has three children.

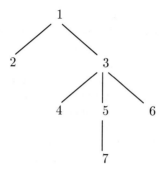

Figure 6.15: An example tree

Let us represent the tree of Fig. 6.15 as a value of datatype `tree`. First, note that any leaf with label *a* is represented by the expression `Node(a,nil)`. That is, the list of the subtrees of a leaf is empty. Thus the expression for the node labeled 2, for example, is `Node(2,nil)`.

Now we can work up the tree to build expressions for nodes that have children. First, node 5 has one subtree, the tree with only node 7, so the expression for the tree rooted at node 5 is `Node(5, [Node(7,nil)])`. Then, we can construct the expression for node 3. It has a list of three subtrees, so its expression has a second component that is a list of length three, as follows:

```
Node(3, [
    Node(4,nil),
    Node(5, [Node(7,nil)]),
    Node(6,nil)
])
```

Finally, we can construct the expression for the entire tree rooted at 1. The expression is shown in Fig. 6.16. □

There are several differences between binary trees and (general) trees, as we have defined them.

```
Node(1, [
    Node(2,nil),
    Node(3, [
        Node(4,nil),
        Node(5, [
            Node(7,nil)
        ]),
        Node(6,nil)
    ])
])
```

Figure 6.16: Expression for tree of Fig. 6.15

- Unlike nodes of a binary tree, a node with two children, like node 1 of Fig. 6.15, does not identify the first as a "left" child and the second as a "right" child. Rather, node 1 simply has two children and its list of children from the left is [2, 3].

- There is no way to represent the empty tree — that is, the tree with no nodes — in the datatype tree as we have defined it.

6.4.2 Summing the Labels of a General Tree

Let us write a function sum like that of Example 6.8, but for general trees. There are two interesting ways to approach this problem. Here, we shall exhibit an interesting form of recursion on general trees. Then, in Section 6.4.3 we show how to sum labels using higher-order functions that ML provides.

We shall design a recursive function that calls itself on new trees that are not subtrees of the original but are constructed from it by lopping off subtrees, one at a time. The function is shown in Fig. 6.17. Note that because there is no way to infer types for labels, the default interpretation — integer — is taken for the + operator on line (3), so sum works only on integer trees.

```
(1) fun sum(Node(a,nil)) = a
(2)   |   sum(Node(a,t::ts)) =
(3)            sum(t) + sum(Node(a,ts));
      val sum = fn : int tree → int
```

Figure 6.17: The function sum for general trees

Line (1) handles the case where the tree has only one node. We can identify such a tree by the fact that its second component, the list of subtrees, is empty. In this case, we return the label of the root node.

Lines (2) and (3) handle the case where there is at least one subtree. We break the list of subtrees into its head, the first subtree t, and the tail ts, consisting of the other subtrees, if any. In line (3) we see that we apply sum to the first subtree and then construct a new tree, represented by the expression Node(a,ts). This tree has the same root with its same label, a. It also has as its list of subtrees all the subtrees of the original, except for the first subtree.

When we apply sum to this new tree, we eventually get the sums of all the subtrees. Finally, after eliminating all the subtrees in recursive calls to sum, we are left with a tree that has root label a and no subtrees. At this point, the basis case of line (1) holds, and we add in the label at the root to the resulting sum.

Example 6.11: Consider applying sum to the tree of Fig. 6.15. The case of lines (2) and (3) applies. Here t represents only the node 2, so the new tree is that of Fig. 6.18. This tree is Fig. 6.15 with node 2 deleted. In general, all nodes descended from 2 would also be deleted.

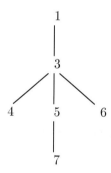

Figure 6.18: New tree for recursive application of function sum

The value of sum(t) in line (3) is clearly 2. We must now evaluate sum applied to the tree of Fig. 6.18; this sum is the second term in line (3). When we apply sum recursively to Fig. 6.18, we find that t, the head of the list of subtrees, is the 5-node tree rooted at 3, and the list of remaining subtrees is empty.

When we compute sum(t) this time, we get $3 + 4 + 5 + 6 + 7 = 25$ by a series of recursive calls that we do not show. To this sum we must add the result of sum applied to the tree of Fig. 6.18 with the first (and only) subtree of 1 deleted. This tree is the single node 1, and its sum is 1. Thus the call to sum on the tree of Fig. 6.18 returns $25 + 1 = 26$.

Finally, we return to the original call of sum. We noted that the call sum(t) returned 2, and we just deduced that the call sum(Node(a,ts)) returns 26. Thus the correct answer, 28, is returned.   □

6.4.3   Computing Sums Using Higher-Order Functions

Another approach is to use the power of the higher-order functions `map` and `foldr` that ML provides. The following function does the job:

```
fun sum (Node(a,L)) = a +
            foldr (op +) 0 (map sum L);
```

On the first line we take any tree, having a label a and a list of subtrees L. We start the sum by taking the label a and adding it to the complex expression on the second line.

Let us see what that second line does. At the end, we see an application of the built-in ML function `map`, which we described in Section 5.6.3, to a function and a list. The function is `sum` itself, and the list is the list of subtrees L. The effect of this application of `map` is to produce a list of the sums of the labels of the nodes in each subtree.

This list of sums is the third argument of an application of `foldr`, which we described in Section 5.6.4. The function used in the folding, `(op +)`, is addition, in prefix form. The second argument, which is the initial value for the sum, is 0. As a result, the second line of `sum` adds the elements on the list that `map` produced, giving us the sum of all the labels of all the subtrees of the root. Since we have added in the label of the root at the first line, the result of `sum` is the sum of all the labels of the tree.

6.4.4   Exercises for Section 6.4

* **Exercise 6.4.1:** Write a function that takes a general tree T and an element x and tells whether or not x appears as a label of T,

     a) Using the recursive style of Section 6.4.2.

     b) Using higher-order functions, as in Section 6.4.3.

Exercise 6.4.2: Write a function that takes a general tree T and an element x and returns the number of times that x appears as a label in T,

     a) Using the recursive style of Section 6.4.2.

     b) Using higher-order functions, as in Section 6.4.3.

! **Exercise 6.4.3:** Write a function that takes a general tree T and returns the *depth* of T, that is, the maximum length of a path from the root to a leaf in T,

     a) Using the recursive style of Section 6.4.2.

     b) Using higher-order functions, as in Section 6.4.3.

* **Exercise 6.4.4:** Write a function to list the labels of the nodes of a general tree in preorder,

a) Using the recursive style of Section 6.4.2.

b) Using higher-order functions, as in Section 6.4.3.

! **Exercise 6.4.5:** The published solution to Exercise 6.4.4(b) runs in time proportional to the number of nodes of the tree. Explain why? Would it be linear-time if `foldl` were used in place of `foldl`? *Hint*: Recall that the time to perform a concatenation of lists is proportional to the length of the left argument, but independent of the right argument.

*!! **Exercise 6.4.6:** The published solution to Exercise 6.4.4(a) does not run in time proportional to the number of nodes in the tree. Use the "difference-list" trick to write a function (plus auxiliaries) that does not use higher-order functions but is linear-time.

Chapter 7

More About ML Data Structures

In this chapter we shall take up some additional capabilities that ML offers us for the implementation of complex data structures. So far, we have learned about tuples and lists as ways to build data structures, and we saw that datatypes are a convenient tool for building tree-like data structures.

We begin our further study of data structures by discussing record structures, which are like records in Pascal or structs in C. We shall see that the tuple is really a shorthand for a special case of record structures.

We then examine two features of ML that violate the precept that a value binding for a variable may not change. In certain, carefully controlled circumstances it is indeed possible to change the binding. The constructs that allow such changes are references and arrays; we cover each in this chapter.

7.1 Record Structures

Section 2.4 introduced tuples, which are denoted by round parentheses surrounding a comma-separated list of components. The tuple is actually a simplification of, and a special notation for, a more basic concept: the *record structure*.

7.1.1 Records and Their Types

Records are denoted by curly brackets, { and }, around a comma-separated list of *fields* of the form

$$<\text{label}> = <\text{value}>$$

A label may be any identifier, or it may be a string of digits; the latter is a very important special case, as we shall see.

229

The *type* of a record is a comma-separated list of elements of the form

<label> : <type>

The list is surrounded by curly brackets. That is, the notation for record types is the same as for record values, except that instead of equal-signs followed by values, we find colons followed by types. We shall refer to the type of a record as its *record structure*.

Example 7.1: Let us design a record structure that can represent information about students. The fields will be

1. An integer ID, the "student ID number."

2. A string name, the student's name.

3. A string list that we call courses, indicating the courses in which the student is currently enrolled.

```
val Norm'sRecord = {
        ID=123,
        name="Norm dePlume",
        courses=["CS106X","E40","M43"]
};
```
val Norm'sRecord = {
   ID=123,
   courses=["CS106X","E40","M43"],
   name="Norm dePlume"
} : {ID:int, courses:string list, name:string}

Figure 7.1: Creating a record

In the val-declaration of Fig. 7.1, the identifier Norm'sRecord is assigned a value that is a record with three fields. The first field has label ID and value 123. The label of the second field is name, and the value of the second field is "Norm dePlume". The third field has label courses and a value that is a list of three strings. The response repeats the value of the record and indicates its type.[1] ML has discovered from the values of the fields that ID is an integer, name a string, and courses a list of strings. □

Here are a few important points about record structures to remember.

- ML reorders the fields in both the value and the type expressions. The SML/NJ compiler chooses lexicographic order for the fields.[2]

---

[1] The response from SML/NJ is *not* indented as shown.
[2] Remember that in the ASCII character code, all upper-case letters precede all lower-case letters, which explains why ID appears ahead of courses.

- In general, record structures are sets of fields, and the order doesn't matter. Thus, the record of Fig. 7.1 could have been expressed with any of the six possible orders of the three labels, as long as the value associated with each remained the same. For instance,

```
val Norm'sRecord = {name="Norm dePlume",
          courses=["CS106X","E40","M43"], ID = 123};
```

means exactly the same as the val-declaration of Fig. 7.1.

- Observe that the apostrophe in identifier `Norm'sRecord` has no special significance. The apostrophe is treated like an ordinary letter when it appears in the middle of an alphanumeric identifier.

7.1.2 Extracting Field Values

The operator `#` takes a label and a record and produces the value associated with that label in the given record. We usually write this operation as

$$\#<\text{label}>(<\text{record}>)$$

However, the parentheses around the record are not required, and space after the `#` is permissible.

Example 7.2: Assume the name `Norm'sRecord` is as defined in Fig. 7.1. The operation

```
#name(Norm'sRecord);
```
val it = "Norm dePlume" : string

illustrates the use of the field-accessing operator `#`. The result is the value of field `name` in the record `Norm'sRecord`. □

7.1.3 Tuples as a Special Case of Record Structures

In ML, the record structure is a primitive concept, and the tuple, which we have been using until now, is a special notation for certain record structures. That is, the tuple

$$(<\text{value 1}>, \ldots, <\text{value } n >)$$

is really a shorthand for the record

$$\{1=<\text{value 1}>, \ldots, n=<\text{value } n >\}$$

In this record, the labels are the integers from 1 to n, and they are the names of the n fields, in order. Thus, for example, the tuple (3, "four") is shorthand for the record {1=3, 2="four"}.

Recall that in Section 2.4.2 we introduced the # operator with an integer and a tuple as arguments, and we learned that #i extracts the ith component from a tuple. Now we see that this convention is an artifact of the definition of tuples as record structures; i is the label for the ith field of a tuple.

- Round and curly brackets are not interchangeable. Round parentheses only denote tuples with the "invisible" labels $1, 2, \ldots$. In contrast, curly brackets only denote records, and the labels are mandatory.

7.1.4   Patterns That Match Records

It is possible to use the record notation to define patterns for such uses as function definition. A pattern that matches a record will have the expected form. Between curly brackets we find a comma-separated list of fields of the form

<label> = <pattern>

The pattern can be any pattern expression, built along the lines suggested in Section 3.3. The pattern may also use the *wildcard for fields*, which is the symbol ... (*ellipsis*). Often, there will be many fields in a record structure, and we wish to use only one or a few of them. The ellipsis comes in handy to avoid our having to specify names for the values of all the irrelevant fields. When we match a particular record to a pattern, the ellipsis matches the set of fields that are not mentioned explicitly.

Example 7.3: In Fig. 7.2 we see a function getID that takes a string representing a student name and a list of records with the structure given in Example 7.1. Function getID finds the first record with that string as the student name and returns the ID for that student. If there is no such record in the list, the exception NotFound, defined in line (1), is raised.

In line (2) we treat the case where the list of available records is empty. Then the person searched for has not been found, so we raise the exception. In line (3) we consider the case where there is at least one more record, x. Using the keyword **as**, we express x in the alternative form {name=p,...}. This expression gives the value of the **name** field of the record x to the pattern variable p, and the wildcard ... is allowed to match the other two fields.

Line (4) checks whether the name p of the student in record x equals the person searched for, that is, **person**. If so, in line (5) we apply the operator #ID to x to return the value of the ID field of x. Note that at line (5) we also give the type for x, which is

```
{name:string, ID:int, courses:string list}
```

```
(1) exception NotFound;
```
    exception NotFound

```
(2) fun getID(person,nil) = raise NotFound
(3)  |   getID(person,(x as {name=p,...})::xs) =
(4)           if p = person then
(5)               #ID(x:{name:string,ID:int,courses:string list})
(6)           else getID(person,xs);
```
    val getID = fn
    *: string * {ID:int, courses:string list, name:string} list → int*

Figure 7.2: Finding the ID of a student with a given name

- Remember that order of fields is irrelevant, so this type will match records such as Norm'sRecord of Fig. 7.1.

Finally, line (6) handles the case where record x does not have a **name** field value that equals **person**. Then we must apply **getID** recursively on the tail of the list. □

Incidentally, in Example 7.3 we could have written line (3) in several other ways. For example, we could avoid the ellipsis and write

```
getID(person, {name=p, ID=i, courses=_}::xs) =
```

Then, we could use i in place of #ID(x) in line (5), and we would not have to specify the type of x or the type of the **courses** field. Another approach is to let the ellipsis stand for only the **courses** field, replacing line (3) by

```
getID(person, {name=p, ID=i,...}::xs) =
```

Again we could use i for #ID(x) in line (5), but we would still have to declare the record structure somewhere. Otherwise, ML could not deduce the set of field names represented by this use of the wildcard symbol ... , and an error would be indicated.

Example 7.4: Suppose we want to take student records as in Example 7.1 and compute the tuition charge. The rules we shall follow are:

1. A student registered for no courses pays a $1000 fee.

2. A student registered for only one course pays $2000.

3. A student registered for more than one course pays $4000 if an undergraduate and $5000 if a graduate student. Graduate students are given ID's of 100,000 or over, so we can identify which are the graduate students.

Establishing the Type of the Ellipsis

One might imagine that a use of the ellipsis in a record pattern would allow the pattern to match records with different types. For example, a pattern like {name=n,...} might be expected to match any record that has a name field, like {name="joe", addr="123 Maple St."} or {name="sue", phone="987-6543"}. However, as with all ML constructs, we can only use the ellipsis in such a way that the compiler can deduce a unique type for an occurrence of the ellipsis. That is, all records referred to by a pattern with an ellipsis *must* have the same type, which means that:

- Their field names must be exactly the same.

- The type for a field must be the same in each record, although as we see in Example 7.4, it is permissible in a function definition for the type to be a variable.

On the other hand, it is permissible for the order of fields and the values of those fields to vary among records.

The function `tuition` is shown in Fig. 7.3. Line (1) implements the first rule above; if the list of courses is empty, the tuition is $1000. Here, the patterns for the `name` and `ID` fields were chosen to be wildcard variables, because we do not need to use their values in the result of the function. The pattern for the `courses` field is the constant `nil`. Note that by specifying all the fields in the record, ML now has a sufficient idea of the record type. However, as we see from the response below line (5), `tuition` is partially polymorphic because ML never learns, nor needs to know, the type of student names or the names of courses.

Line (2) covers the second rule, where the student is taking a single course. The pattern for the list of courses is [_]. Here, the wildcard variable is used, but its position within square brackets creates a pattern that is matched by lists of length one, and only by those lists. We are able to use the ellipsis safely, since ML knows from line (1) what the other fields of the record must be named.

Lines (3) though (5) cover the case where there is more than one course in the course list, because the cases of zero and one course were already intercepted by lines (1) and (2). Now, we need to use the value of the `ID` field, so we give it a variable name i, while we elide the rest of the record-pattern.

- Note that it is permissible for *different* uses of the ellipses in one function to have different types.

```
(1) fun tuition({name=_, ID=_, courses=nil}) = 1000
(2)  |    tuition({courses=[ _ ],...}) = 2000
(3)  |    tuition({ID=i,...}) =
(4)          if i>=100000 then 5000
(5)          else 4000;
```
   val tuition = fn : {ID:int, courses='a list, name='b} → int

```
(6)  tuition(Norm'sRecord);
```
   val it = 4000

```
(7)  tuition({name="Mona Kerr",ID=54321,courses=["CS105"]});
```
   val it = 2000

```
(8)  tuition({name="Sue Dunham",ID=200000,
              courses=["CS105","CS022"]});
```
   val it = 5000

```
(9)  tuition({name="Alice O. Nunez",ID=6789,courses=nil});
```
   val it = 1000

Figure 7.3: Computing tuition by matching record patterns

In line (6) we apply `tuition` to the specific record `Norm'sRecord` defined in Fig. 7.1. It identifies the student as an undergraduate taking more than one course and determines the tuition to be $4000. Lines (7) through (9) test the other three possible outcomes. □

7.1.5 Shorthands in Record Patterns

Often a record pattern uses a single variable as the pattern for a field. ML provides a shorthand for this case if we are willing to use the field name itself as the variable. That is, instead of

$$<label> = <variable>$$

as a field, we just use <label>.

Example 7.5 : In line (3) of Fig. 7.3 we used `ID = i` as a field of the record-pattern, and we then used `i` as the value of the field in line (4). An equivalent way to write this code is

```
(3) |    tuition({ID,...}) =
(4)             if ID>=100000 then 5000
```

Here, just `ID` appears as the pattern for the field in line (3), and in line (4) we use `ID` itself as the value of that field, instead of variable `i`. In so doing, there is an increase in clarity. We can see that line (4) is asking if the student ID is at least 100,000. □

7.1.6   Exercises for Section 7.1

Exercise 7.1.1: Write expressions to do the following.

* a) Define the type `dino` to be an abbreviation for a record structure with fields `name` (a string), `weight` (a real), and `height` (a real).

  b) Create a record named `tyranno`, of type `dino`, that represents the facts that Tyrannosaurus weighed 7 tons and was 20 feet tall.

* c) Create a record named `brachio`, of type `dino`, that represents the facts that Brachiosaurus weighed 50 tons and was 40 feet tall.

  d) Write an expression that gets from the record `tyranno` the height of a Tyrannosaurus.

* e) Write an expression that gets from the record `brachio` the weight of a Brachiosaurus.

! **Exercise 7.1.2:** Write the following functions based on the `dino` record type of Exercise 7.1.1.

* a) Given a list of `dino` records, find the tallest dinosaur on the list.

  b) Find the heaviest dinosaur on a list of `dino` records.

  c) Find the average weight of dinosaurs on a list of `dino` records.

Exercise 7.1.3: Suppose we have a list L of items with the record structure introduced in Example 7.1. We can write several functions to search for records with given properties. Write the following functions:

* a) Given a list L and a name n, find all those records with n as the value of its `name` field.

  b) Given a list L and an ID i, find the list of courses in the first (and presumably only) record with ID field equal to i.

*! c) Given a list L and a course c, find the names of all the students who are taking course c.

7.2 Arrays

In this section we shall see the first ML construct that changes a value binding. Recall that normally, when we appear to be assigning a new value to a variable, in an "assignment" such as

```
val x = 1;
```

we are really creating a binding for a new variable named x. This binding goes above any other binding for x in the current environment, say a binding in which x was bound to the value 2. However, other function calls may still have access to the old binding and that binding still exists in the environment. If we were to change the binding for the "old" variable x, then functions that had access to the old x would see the value of x change from 2 to 1.

The guarantee that a value binding, once created, is available forever to functions that use it, is an important feature of ML. However, there are some situations where programs cannot be made adequately efficient unless we are allowed to change some value bindings. Thus, in this section we shall first motivate the need for arrays, with their attendant ability to change value bindings, and then show how ML allows us to create and use arrays.

7.2.1 Why Do We Need Arrays?

While we have seen that programming in a functional style is not hard when one gets used to it, there are certain situations where we need to have a "state" for the data used by a program, or where searching through long lists is too inefficient.

Example 7.6: Let us consider the problem of checking that each of the 26 lower-case letters appears in a string. In a language like Pascal we would use a strategy like:

1. Create a boolean array indexed by the letters. Initialize each element to `false`.

2. For each character of the string, set the corresponding array element to `true`.

3. After the entire string has been processed, check that each element of the array is `true`.

While the above strategy uses iteration in steps (2) and (3), it is possible to substitute a recursion for the iteration in ML. We can use a somewhat different strategy, seen in Fig. 7.4, to get the job done in ML.

The function `member` of lines (1) through (4) tests whether element x is on a list L. Since the ideas should be familiar, we omit a discussion of this function. Lines (5) through (7) are a function `memberAll(ch,L)` that checks

```
(* member(x,L) tests if x appears on list L *)
```

```
(1) fun member(x,nil) = false
(2)   |   member(x,y::ys) =
(3)             if x=y then true
(4)             else member(x,ys);
```
*val member = fn : "a * "a list → bool*

```
(* memberAll(ch,L) checks that character ch and all
     following characters up to "z" are on list L *)
```

```
(5) fun memberAll(ch,L) =
(6)             if ch > #"z" then true
(7)             else member(ch,L) andalso
                        memberAll(chr(ord(ch)+1),L);
```
*val memberAll = fn : char * char list → bool*

```
(8) memberAll(#"a",explode("qwertyuiopasdfghjklzxcvbnm"));
```
val it = true : bool

Figure 7.4: Checking that all letters appear: list-based solution

whether all the letters between *ch* and #"z" are on the list *L*. That is, line (6) checks if the letter that is the value of variable *ch* is beyond #"z", in which case there is nothing to check, and we return true. If there is still something to check, line (7) first checks that the letter represented by variable *ch* is on the list and then calls memberAll recursively on the next letter. Notice that the expression chr(ord(ch)+1) gives the character with the code one higher than that of *ch*. Finally, in line (8) we test the code with a call to memberAll. The first argument is #"a", so it checks all the letters, and the second argument is a list of characters formed by exploding the string of all the letters in keyboard order.   □

The solution of Fig. 7.4 works, but it is not a very efficient solution. To see the problem clearly, let us think of the generalization where there are n letters (instead of 26) and the strings to be checked have length at least n. Then member on the average must go distance $n/2$ down the list to find a given character, and memberAll calls member n times to get a positive answer. Thus, a call to memberAll that returns true takes average time proportional to n^2.

On the other hand, the array-based solution outlined at the beginning of Example 7.6 takes time proportional to n, provided the string is about n characters in length. Step (1) takes time proportional to the length of the array to initialize, and in our generalized scenario we need an array of length n. Step (2) takes time proportional to the length of the string, which we suppose is also about n. Step (3) again takes time proportional to the length of the array, or n. Thus, the whole algorithm takes time proportional to n.

This increase in efficiency is an important reason why ML provides arrays, even though the array violates the functional style of ML. In particular, arrays allow us to change the binding of an array element as a side-effect of a function called `update`. No other ML construct, except the reference to be discussed in Section 7.3, allows bindings to be changed.

7.2.2 Array Operations

There is a structure in the ML Standard Basis that gives us the ability to create and manipulate arrays. The array operations are not available in the top-level environment, so if we want to use arrays we may open the structure `Array` by:

```
open Array;
```

Alternatively, we can avoid opening structure `Array` if we prepend to each of the array operations the word `Array` and a dot; for example we may use `Array.update` for the `update` function on arrays, even if we have not opened structure `Array`.

Arrays have the limited form found in C, where the only permitted index sets are the integers from 0 up to some number. The variety of options for index sets found in languages such as Pascal is not available in ML. The most important operations on arrays are the following:

1. We can create an array A of n elements (numbered 0 through $n-1$), with each element initialized to value v, by the val-declaration:

   ```
   val A = array(n,v);
   ```

   We must specify the type of v if it is not obvious from the value (e.g., we must specify the type if v is `nil`). Further, there are limits on the type that v may have, for technical reasons we shall not discuss.

2. The value of the element numbered i of array A is produced by the expression `sub(A,i)`.

3. To store a value v in the element numbered i of array A, we use the expression `update(A,i,v)`. This function is one of the few in ML that has a side-effect. Notice that the value of an element of array A is permanently changed by this use of `update`.

- If `sub` or `update` are given a value of the subscript i that is out of the index set for the array, then the exception `Subscript` is raised.

Example 7.7 : In Fig. 7.5 we see a program to solve the same problem as that of Fig. 7.4, but it takes only linear time to do so. In line (1) we open the structure `Array`. The response, which is a listing of all the functions available in this structure, is not shown.

Lines (2) through (4) give a function `checkAll` that tells whether array A has only true elements with indices from 0 up to and including i. In line (3) we return `true` if $i < 0$, because there is nothing we need to check. Line (4) handles the case where something is left to check. We confirm that the element i of array A is true and, if so, we then check recursively that elements from 0 up to $i - 1$ are also true.

```
(1) open Array;

    (* checkAll(A,i) checks that array A has only true
        elements with indexes 0 through i *)

(2) fun checkAll(A,i) =
(3)          i<0 orelse
(4)              sub(A,i) andalso checkAll(A,i-1);
```
*val checkAll = fn : bool array * int → bool*

```
    (* fillAndCheck(A,L) sets the element of array A to true
        for each letter appearing on list L, then checks
        that all elements are true *)

(5) fun fillAndCheck(A,nil) = checkAll(A,25)
(6)  |   fillAndCheck(A,x::xs) = (
(7)          update(A,ord(x)-ord(#"a"),true);
(8)          fillAndCheck(A,xs)
        );
```
*val fillAndCheck = fn : bool array * char list → bool*

```
(9) fillAndCheck(array(26,false),
          explode("qwertyuiopasdfghjklzxcvbnm"));
```
val it = true : bool

Figure 7.5: Checking that all letters appear: array-based solution

Lines (5) through (8) are the function `fillAndCheck`, which takes an array A and a list L, and for each character on list L sets the appropriate element of A to `true`. After completing the examination of the list, `fillAndCheck` calls `checkAll` to verify that all elements of array A are true. In detail, line (5) handles the case where the list is exhausted, whereupon `checkAll` is called with second argument 25. The number 25 is the highest index for our array, so we are thereby checking that all elements are `true`.

Lines (6) through (8) handle the case where there are elements on the list L. After matching the pattern `x::xs` on line (6), we do a sequence of two steps. First, on line (7) we take the head element `x` and compute the corresponding array index by the expression `ord(x)-ord(#"a")`. Thus, the element indexed 0 corresponds to `#"a"`, 1 to `#"b"`, and so on, up to index 25, which corresponds to `#"z"`. Then, the `update` function, as a side-effect, sets the appropriate element of A to `true`. Second, line (8) calls `fillAndCheck` recursively on the tail of the list L.

Finally, line (9) is a use of function `fillAndCheck`. The first argument is the expression `array(26,false)` whose value is an array with 26 elements, indexed 0 to 25, each of which initially has the value `false`. The second argument is the list (exploded string) of the lower-case letters in keyboard order.   □

7.2.3   Exercises for Section 7.2

Exercise 7.2.1: Write expressions to perform the following operations.

* a) Create an array `A` of 20 elements, each of which is initially an empty list of reals.

  b) Create an array `A` of 100 reals, each of which is initially 0.

* c) Find the 30th element in an array `A` of 100 reals.

  d) Find the 10th element in an array `A` of 20 integers.

* e) Change the element with index 10 in array `A` to 43.

  f) Change the element with index 0 in array `A` to [1,2,3].

Exercise 7.2.2: Write programs to sort an array A of length n, using:

* a) A simple n^2-time sort such as bubblesort or insertion sort.

! b) Mergesort. *Hint*: Create temporary arrays and merge from two small arrays into one of twice the size.

Exercise 7.2.3: Write functions to perform the following tasks:

* a) Cycle an array A of length n by one position.

! b) Create a list of the elements of an array A of length n, in order, starting at position 0.

*! c) Reverse an array A of length n.

! d) Given a function f and an integer n, create a function g that applies f to each element of an array of length n. Function g returns an array of the n results.

7.3   References

Standard ML has a mechanism for associating new values with names of any type, not just with array elements. This feature, called the *reference*, is the second way to violate the functional, side-effect-free style. We advocate its use only in situations where it simplifies the programming.

7.3.1   The `ref` Type Constructor

It is possible to associate with some identifier x a value that is a "reference," which we may think of as a box capable of holding any value of a particular type. We add the binding between x and this "box" to the environment by:

```
val x = ref v;
```

Here, v can be a value of any type, say type T, whereupon ML will respond with

val x = ref v : T ref

However, we should be aware that expressions that involve a reference are always expansive (recall Section 5.3.1). A consequence is that, at the top level (i.e., if the expression is not part of a definition of a function or other element), it is not permissible for the type T to involve type variables. For example,

```
val x = ref(fn x=>x);
```

Gives us a "nongeneralizable type variable" error message, because the type of the value v (i.e., the identity function) is `fn : 'a -> 'a`, which involves a type variable.

The value in the "box" associated with x can later be changed to another value of type T by using the `:=` operator. In contrast, binding identifier x to value v rather than to value `ref` v would not allow the binding to be modified in any way.

Example 7.8 : The statement

```
val i = ref 0;
```
val i = ref 0 : int ref

binds identifier i to a "box" whose initial value is `ref` 0. Figure 7.6 suggests what the box i might look like, with the type constructor `ref` wrapping the current value in the box. Note that it will be possible to change the value in the "box" of Fig. 7.6 without having to create a new binding.   □

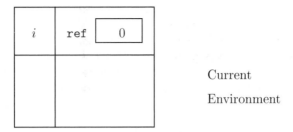

Figure 7.6: A variable i of type `ref int`

7.3.2 Obtaining the Value of a Ref-Variable

The operator !, applied to a reference, produces the value to which the reference refers. For instance, if i is the ref-variable of Example 7.8, which was made to refer to the integer 0, then the value of !i is 0. In contrast, the value of the expression i is *not* 0 but rather `ref` 0. Function ! is not defined for expressions that are not references. ML will detect and indicate an error if we write a program that could apply ! to a non-reference.

One way to understand the distinction between the value of a ref variable and the value to which it refers is to imagine there is a datatype `ref` with one data constructor, also called `ref`. This datatype has one type variable and is defined by

```
datatype 'a ref = ref of 'a;
```

That view is consistent with the picture in Fig. 7.6, where the variable i has the value `ref` 0 and is of type `int ref`.[3]

In this view, the function ! is defined by

```
fun !(ref v) = v;
```

Note ! is not defined for non-reference arguments.

However, there is more to references than a datatype. Only ref-variables can change the value to which they are bound. Other identifier bindings remain the same and can only be overwritten by new additions to the environment that bind the same identifier, as we discussed in Section 2.3.4.

7.3.3 Modifying Ref-Variables

The function denoted by the infix operator := changes the value inside the box that is bound to a ref-variable. For instance, if i is the ref-variable from Example 7.8, the assignment

---

[3]We use `ref` 0 rather than `ref(0)` to represent references, although either is correct. Recall that parentheses are optional in function applications and data constructor applications as well.

```
i := 1;
```

replaces by 1 the value in the box that is bound to identifier i. The value to which i is bound has not changed; it is still **ref** applied to the same "box" suggested in Fig. 7.6. In ML terms, the current *store* (association of locations or "boxes" with values) has changed. In contrast, other ML operations that change things, such as var-declarations, act directly on the environment, creating new bindings for variables and thereby obscuring previously made bindings for variables with the same identifiers.

- Note that `:=` can only be used on a ref-variable that has already been defined. It cannot be used to initialize a ref-variable.

7.3.4   The While-Do Statement

The expression

$$\text{while } <\text{expression}> \text{ do } <\text{expression}>$$

has the expected meaning in ML:

1. Evaluate the first expression.

2. If the first expression is false, end. If the first expression is true, evaluate the second expression and go to step (1).

Of course, we shall loop indefinitely if the second expression does not change something that affects the value of the first expression. Ref-variables make it easy to have the evaluation of the second expression change the value of the first expression. They thus let us create loops that perform some useful computation and then terminate.

- The value produced by a while-do expression is always the unit, even if the expression after the **do** has a type other than unit.

Example 7.9: A simple example of a while-loop is shown in Fig. 7.7. The effect is that the integers from 1 to 10 will be printed on a line. Each time we execute the "body" of the loop (the three statements after the **do**), we increment i by 1 until it exceeds 10.   □

Here are a few useful points to remember about the code in Fig. 7.7:

- We must print the value `!i`, not `i`. The value of `i` is something like **ref 3**, and there is no way to print a ref value without first extracting the value inside and printing that value.

- Notice that after we do extract the value to be printed by `!i`, we use the appropriate conversion function, **Int.toString**, which converts an integer to a string.

```
val i = ref 1;
```
val i = ref 1 : int ref


```
while !i<=10 do (
    print(Int.toString(!i));
    print(" ");
    i := !i + 1
);
```
1 2 3 4 5 6 7 8 9 10 val it = () : unit

Figure 7.7: A while-do loop

- The termination test is `!i<=10`, not `i<=10`. The latter expression would try to compare a value of type `int ref` with the value 10 of type `int` and cause a type mismatch.

7.3.5 Exercises for Section 7.3

Exercise 7.3.1: Write expressions that do the following:

* a) Create a ref-variable i whose initial value is a reference to 10.

  b) Create a ref-variable `word` whose initial value refers to `"foo"`.

* c) Change existing ref-variable i to refer to 20.

  d) Change existing ref-variable `word` to refer to `"bar"`.

Exercise 7.3.2: Write expressions to compute the following functions of the values referred to by ref-variables x and y, which we shall assume refer to reals.

* a) The square of the sum of the values referred to by x and y.

  b) The average of the values referred to by x and y.

*! **Exercise 7.3.3:** What happens in response to the ML code

```
val i = 1;
while i<10 do val i = i+1;
```

! **Exercise 7.3.4:** Early versions of ML had operators inc i and dec i that would increment and decrement by 1 the value referred to by a variable i of type `int ref`. Write functions inc and dec that have the desired effect.

! **Exercise 7.3.5 :** In Pascal, C, and many other languages, there is a linked-list data structure that we assume is familiar to the reader. There is generally no need to implement this sort of data structure in ML because we have such lists as a primitive, and the implementation of lists in ML is, "behind the scenes," very much like the standard linked list. However, it is an interesting exercise to mimic the linked list using records and references in ML. That is, each cell of a linked list is a record with an `element` field carrying the data and a `next` field that is a reference to the next cell.

Hint: In other languages, a "nil pointer" is a legitimate value of any pointer type, but we do not have the luxury in ML of such a versatile value (although `nil` essentially has that versatility for normal ML lists). Thus, we need to create a datatype with two constructors, `Nil` and `Cell`, to indicate whether a `next` field "points" to another cell or is "nil."

* a) Devise the datatype for cells of "conventional" linked lists.

 b) Write a function `pop` that takes a linked list as argument and produces the tail of that linked list. Raise the exception `Empty` (a built-in exception of ML) if the linked list is empty.

* c) Write a function `skip` that takes a cell C as argument and changes the `next` field of C to point to the cell pointed to by the cell that C originally pointed to. Raise the exception `BadCell` if this operation is impossible.

 d) Write a function that takes a linked list and produces an ML list of all the elements in all its cells.

7.4   Case Study: Hash Tables

The hash table is an important data structure that makes it possible to maintain sets by inserting and deleting elements in average time per action that does not grow with the size of the set. Hash tables also allow average-constant-time lookup on the set, to test whether a given element is currently a member of the set. Arrays are essential if we are to make hash tables work efficiently.

7.4.1   The Dictionary Operations

A set with the operations insert, delete, and lookup is sometimes called a *dictionary*. We can implement a dictionary as a list. However, if the list grows to length n, then operations will take about $n/2$ steps on the average, since we must go about half way down the list. We also saw in Section 6.3 that the dictionary operations can be implemented on a binary search tree in time proportional to the logarithm of n. However, the hash table is better than either of these methods of supporting the dictionary operations; it does the same operations using an average of a small constant number of steps per operation, independent of the size of the set.

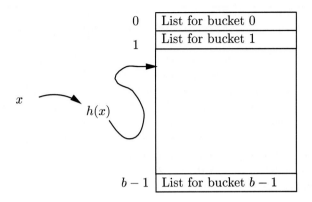

Bucket Headers

Figure 7.8: A hash table

7.4.2 How a Hash Table Works

The idea of the hash table is sketched in Fig. 7.8. At the heart is an array called the *bucket headers*. The set being represented is divided into some number b of *buckets*, numbered 0 through $b - 1$. Each bucket is represented by a list of the elements in that bucket. If we pick b approximately equal to n, which is the size of the set, then there will be an average of about one element per bucket. However, in rare cases there could be a large number of elements, or even all the elements, in one of the buckets.

Which bucket an element x belongs to is determined by a *hash function* $h(x)$ that produces an integer in the range 0 to $b - 1$. The hash function can be anything we like, although it is desirable that it "randomize" the buckets so that in any typical set of elements, about an equal number of elements will belong in each bucket.

7.4.3 An Example of Hash Table Implementation

We shall build a simple hash table that stores strings in ten buckets (i.e., $b = 10$). Elements are strings, and the buckets will be represented by lists of strings. Figure 7.9 shows how we first open the structure `Array`, define the constant b to be 10, and then define a simple hash function for strings, which we call `h`.

Function `h` uses an auxiliary function `h1` that takes a list of characters, applies `ord` to each, and sums these integers modulo b. The result is always an integer between 0 and $b - 1$, so it may be used as a bucket number. The function `h` takes its string argument `x`, explodes it into a list of characters, and applies `h1` to this list in order to get the bucket number for string `x`.

Following the definition of the hash function is a function `insert`, which

---

Arrays and References

The elements of an array may be thought of as references, although in practice there is a more efficient implementation of arrays in ML as a block of storage, much like the implementations of arrays in other languages. That is, the picture of an array in Fig. 7.8 is not precisely correct. Strictly speaking, the element for index value 0 should be "**ref**(list for bucket 0)," and similarly for the other elements. Then, the function `sub(A,i)` can be thought of as finding the element with index i and applying the ! operator to it. We can think of `update(A,i,v)` as performing `e := v`, where e is the element of the array A having index i.

---

inserts a string into the hash table. It uses an auxiliary `insertList`, which inserts a string into a list of strings. The working of `insertList` should be obvious. If the list is empty, it creates a list consisting of only the inserted string. If the list is nonempty, we ask if the element to be inserted is at the head. If so, we are done, and if not we insert the element into the tail.

The function `insert(x,A)` then works as follows, where x is the element to be inserted, and A is the array of bucket headers. We calculate the appropriate bucket for element x by applying the hash function $h(x)$. We get the list L that is the list in the appropriate bucket, insert x into L, and then update A by replacing the bucket for x by the new list.

Function `delete` similarly uses an auxiliary `deleteList` that deletes an element from a list. It assumes that no element appears more than once on the list, which is guaranteed if all insertions are made by `insertList`. The function `delete(x,A)` works in a manner similar to `insert`. Given an element x to delete, we compute the bucket $h(x)$, delete from the list of that bucket, and then update the array by replacing the old list by the new one.

Similarly, `lookup` uses an auxiliary `lookupList` that tests whether an element x is on a list L. First, `lookup(x,A)` computes the bucket $h(x)$ for element x. Then, `lookup` uses `lookupList` to search for x in the list of bucket $h(x)$.

The final line of Fig. 7.9 creates an array called `headers` of the appropriate size, using the parameter b that we defined prior to the hash function `h`. Notice that by using the parameter b twice, we are sure that the hash function is suitable for the header array.

Now we can execute operations on the dictionary represented by array `headers`. Here are three examples of these operations.

```
insert("foo", headers);
```
val it = () : unit

```
open Array;

val b = 10;

fun h1(nil) = 0
|   h1(x::xs) = (ord(x)+h1(xs)) mod b;

fun h(x) = h1(explode(x));

fun insertList(x,nil) = [x]
|   insertList(x,y::ys) =
        if x=y then y::ys
        else y::insertList(x,ys);

fun insert(x,A) =
    let
        val bucket = h(x);
        val L = sub(A,bucket)
    in
        update(A,bucket,insertList(x,L))
    end;

fun deleteList(x,nil) = nil
|   deleteList(x,y::ys) =
        if x=y then ys
        else y::deleteList(x,ys);

fun delete(x,A) =
    let
        val bucket = h(x);
        val L = sub(A,bucket)
    in
        update(A,bucket,deleteList(x,L))
    end;

fun lookupList(x,nil) = false
|   lookupList(x,y::ys) =
        if x=y then true
        else lookupList(x,ys);

fun lookup(x,A) = lookupList(x,sub(A,h(x)));

val headers = array(b, nil: string list);
```

Figure 7.9: Implementing a hash table

```
lookup("bar", headers);
```
val false : bool


```
delete("baz", headers);
```
val it = () : unit

Note that the operations `insert` and `delete` produce a unit as value, since they do their work by a side-effect and do not return a value.

7.4.4   Exercises for Section 7.4

*! Exercise 7.4.1: Another approach to hashing, called *closed hashing*, is to store only one element in each bucket, rather than a list of elements. If we want to store an element x in bucket $h(x)$, but that bucket is filled, then we instead try buckets $h(x) + 1$, $h(x) + 2$, and so on. If we reach the last bucket, we go around to bucket 0 and continue searching for an empty bucket. If we come back to where we started, then the table is full, and the insertion fails.

To lookup element x, we must search not only bucket $h(x)$, but the following buckets (continuing to bucket 0 if we reach the last bucket), until we find an empty bucket. Moreover, when we delete, we cannot simply mark the bucket as empty. If we did, then lookups might stop too soon. Instead, we need another value that says "this bucket may be filled, but in lookups it should not be considered empty."

Write functions `insert`, `delete`, and `lookup` that use the strategy outlined above. *Hint*: A useful datatype to define for the cells of the array is a generalization of the `option`. This datatype has two parameterless data constructors, `Empty` for a bucket that has never been filled, and `Deleted` for a bucket that was once filled but whose element was deleted. In addition, there is a third data constructor, say `Filled`, that takes a parameter: a value of the type of hash-table elements.

! Exercise 7.4.2: The function `insertList` of Fig. 7.9 can be made more efficient if we just insert the element onto the front of the list without checking whether or not it is already on the list. However, if we do so, then the `deleteList` function must be modified as well. Why? (*Hint*: consider what happens if x is inserted, inserted again, and then deleted.) Write revised functions to support duplicate elements on a bucket list.

7.5   Case Study: Triangularization of a Matrix

The next extended example is intended to give an appreciation of the way references, arrays, and while-loops can be used productively. We consider the problem of turning an n-by-n matrix of reals into an *upper-triangular matrix* (a matrix in which all elements below the main diagonal are 0, as suggested by Fig. 7.10). The solution uses row operations in which a multiple of one row is subtracted from another. Upper-triangularization is the key step in the algorithm for solving simultaneous linear equations known as "Gaussian elimination."

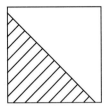

Figure 7.10: An upper-triangular matrix; shaded area is all 0's

7.5.1 Creating and Initializing the Matrix

The creation of a matrix M begins in Fig. 7.11. Line (1) opens the `Array` structure, which we need for our program. As always, opening `Array` is optional, and may be inadvisable for several reasons. Instead of opening `Array`, we could prepend `Array` and a dot to all uses of `array`, `sub`, and `update` in our code.

Line (2) sets n, the dimension of the matrix, to 10. The rest of the code is written with n as the side of the matrix. The matrix M will be represented by an array of length n, each element of which is a row. Each row is itself an array of length n, and its elements are reals. The matrix element M_{ij}, the element in row i and column j, is obtained by the expression `sub(sub(M,!i), !j)`, assuming `i` and `j` are variables of type `int ref`. Note that we must use the `!` operator to get the integer value of such a variable.

Line (3) creates the array M with n elements numbered 0 to $n-1$. Initially, each element has an array of n reals as value; those reals are all initially 0.

- We might think we are done with the creation of the matrix, but there is a subtle error. The subexpression `array(n,0.0)` has created a single array of n reals, and this one array has become the value of each element of M. Should we leave M as it is, changing one element of M would change every element in its column. Figure 7.12 shows the difference between what we have after line (3) and what we want and achieve after line (7).

Thus, in lines (4) through (7) we create a new array for each element of M except that with index 0.

Line (4) creates a ref-variable `i` to serve as the iterator. Line (5) begins a while-loop, in which the condition is that the value referred to by `i` must be less than n. The body of this while-loop does two things. First, line (6) puts a new row-array in the element of M with index i. Note that we do not need to replace the array of row 0; the original row-array will serve for this one

```
(1) open Array;

(2) val n = 10;

(3) val M = array(n,array(n,0.0));

(4) val i = ref 1;

(5) while !i<n do (
(6)      update(M,!i,array(n,0.0));
(7)      i := !i + 1
     );

(8) i := 0;

(9) val j = ref 0;

    (* initialize M to be a particular matrix *)

(10) while !i<n do (
(11)     while !j<n do (
(12)         update(sub(M,!i),!j,1.0/real(!i + !j + 1));
(13)         j := !j + 1
         );
(14)     j := 0;
(15)     i := !i + 1
     );
```

Figure 7.11: Creating and initializing a matrix

row. Then, line (7) increments i. As a result of this incrementation, the loop terminates after putting a new row-array in the element of M with index $n-1$, which is the last row.

Lines (8) through (15) of Fig. 7.11 are a doubly nested loop to initialize the matrix M in a particular way: $M_{ij} = 1/(i + j + 1)$. This particular matrix serves as a good test of the precision of the algorithm, because the rows are almost, but not quite, multiples of one another. However, in reality, a program for upper-triangularization would at this point read in the data rather than creating it.

Lines (8) and (9) initialize i and j, the row and column indices respectively. Notice that i can be initialized with a use of :=, while j, which has not been used before, must be initialized by a val-declaration. Line (10) begins the outer loop.

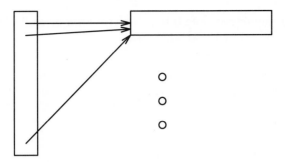

(a) Initialization after line (3)

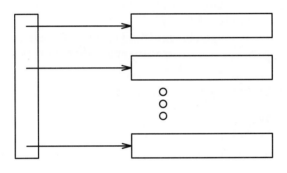

(b) Initialization after line (7)

Figure 7.12: Function `array` creates only one array, which is erroneously used as the value of each row

The inner loop, on j, is lines (11) through (13). The matrix element M_{ij} is given the desired value at line (12), and j is incremented at line (13).

- Note that in line (12) a space is needed between the + and the !. Without it, the substring `+!` would be interpreted as a symbolic identifier and an error would result.

Lines (14) and (15) complete the outer loop; we reset j to 0 at line (14) and increment i at line (15).

7.5.2 Triangularization by Row Operations

The actual algorithm is shown in Fig. 7.13. In explanation, we use each row i, except the last row (numbered $n - 1$), to put 0's in the column numbered i, below the *main diagonal* (the line running from upper left to lower right). Figure 7.14 shows what the matrix looks like when we begin working on row i.

All the columns numbered from 0 to $i - 1$ have been given 0's below the main diagonal, as suggested by the shaded area.

```
(16) i := 0;
(17) while !i<n-1 do (
(18)     j := !i+1;
(19)     while !j<n do
             let
(20)             val ratio = sub(sub(M,!j),!i)/sub(sub(M,!i),!i);
(21)             val k = ref (!i+1)
             in
(22)             update(sub(M,!j),!i,0.0);
(23)             while !k<n do (
(24)                 update(sub(M,!j), !k, sub(sub(M,!j),!k) -
                         ratio*sub(sub(M,!i),!k));
(25)                 k := !k + 1
                 );
(26)             j := !j + 1
             end;
(27)     i := !i + 1
     );
```

Figure 7.13: Upper-triangularization of a matrix (continues Fig. 7.11)

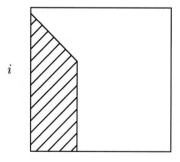

Figure 7.14: Situation when we begin working on row i

The strategy for a given value of i is as follows. We need to subtract a multiple of row i from each row $j = i + 1, i + 2, \ldots, n - 1$. This multiple must be chosen so that M_{ji} becomes 0; thus the appropriate multiplier for i and j is M_{ji}/M_{ii}. We call this multiplier `ratio` in the code of Fig. 7.13. To subtract a multiple of row i from row j under these conditions, we can set M_{ji} to 0, but

---

A Comment About Style

There are cleaner ways to write the code of Section 7.5 than the reference-based approach we use. For example, Exercise 5.2.4 discusses a similar problem and solves it using lists of lists. Exercise 7.5.6 suggests how we could redo this code using arrays but not references. However, the present example illustrates the use of references and also suggests that, when it is really needed, we could write pieces of ML code in a "conventional" style.

---

then must replace each M_{jk} by $M_{jk} - ratio * M_{ik}$, for $k = i+1, i+2, \ldots, n-1$.[4]

Let us now look at the code in Fig. 7.13. Lines (16) and (17) begin the outer loop. Index i will run from 0 to $n-2$, thus letting us consider each row in turn except the last. Lines (18) and (19) similarly begin the second loop, and index j runs from $i+1$ to the last row, $n-1$, to let us zero column i below the main diagonal.

At line (20) we compute the value of `ratio`, which is M_{ji}/M_{ii}. Then line (21) initializes the third index, k, which will range from $i+1$ to $n-1$ and allow us to subtract a multiple of row i from row j. Line (22) sets M_{ji} to 0, and lines (23) through (25) are an inner loop in which we subtract $ratio * M_{ik}$ from M_{jk}, for $k = i+1, i+2, \ldots, n-1$. Finally, lines (26) and (27) complete the middle and outer loop, respectively.

- Note the need for a let-expression in lines (20) through (25). We cannot use a val-declaration inside the while-loop. The `let` allows us to make an addition to the current environment, where we can put the local variables `ratio` and `k`. Without the `let`, there is no place to put additional variables.

7.5.3   Exercises for Section 7.5

*! **Exercise 7.5.1:** In Exercise 5.2.4 we discussed the pivotal condensation method of taking the determinant of a matrix, and we asked for a list-based solution. We can use references and arrays to give a solution that follows more closely the description of the algorithm given informally in Exercise 5.2.4. Write this function.

*! **Exercise 7.5.2:** Is your solution to Exercise 7.5.1 more efficient than the list-based solution requested in Exercise 5.2.4? Why or why not?

---

[4]This algorithm is not the best way to put a matrix in upper-triangular form. It risks a division by 0 even if the matrix is nonsingular, and it can lead to loss of precision where other approaches could achieve more accuracy. However, it will do as a programming example.

! **Exercise 7.5.3:** Add to the triangularization code of Figs. 7.11 and 7.13 to make a complete Gaussian elimination algorithm.

Exercise 7.5.4: Write the following functions that implement $n \times m$ matrices of reals:

* a) `matrix(n,m,v)` returns an $n \times m$ matrix with each element initially v.

  b) `matrixSub(M,i,j)` returns the element in row i and column j of the matrix M.

  c) `matrixUpdate(M,i,j,v)` changes the element in row i and column j of matrix M to be v.

! **Exercise 7.5.5:** An improved version of the upper-triangularization algorithm given in this chapter allows rows to be interchanged in order to avoid division by 0 and to minimize roundoff errors. In particular, when it is time to zero column i below the main diagonal, we pick that row among rows i and greater such that the element in the ith column has as large a magnitude as possible. Thus, if any row is nonzero in column i we shall avoid a division by 0 when we compute `ratio` as in line (20) of Fig. 7.13. Also, since `ratio` is as small as possible, we tend to subtract small numbers from the elements of the matrix, often avoiding large roundoff errors. As an exercise, write this improved version of the triangularization algorithm.

Exercise 7.5.6: Code like that of Fig. 7.11 and 7.13 uses integer references to simulate for-loops in languages like Pascal. We can replace these uses of references if we define a higher-order function

```
fun for(a,b,F) =
        if a>b then ()
        else (F(a); for(a+1,b,F));
```

That is, the function `for` applies function F to each of the integers between a and b. The type of `for` is `int * int * (int -> 'a) -> unit`. Intuitively, F is the body of the for-loop, with the current loop index as an argument.

*! a) Rewrite the while-loop of Example 7.7 that prints the integers from 1 to 10, using `for`.

!! b) Rewrite the code of Figs. 7.11 and 7.13 using `for` to avoid all use of references.

Chapter 8

Encapsulation and the ML Module System

One of the great themes of modern programming language design is facilitating the *encapsulation* of information, that is, the grouping of concepts such as types and functions on those types in a cluster that can be used only in limited ways. The limitation on use is not intended to make programming difficult, but rather:

- To prevent data from being used in unexpected ways that result in hard-to-discover bugs.

- To encourage reuse of code by allowing the definitions supporting a common idea to be packaged with a simple and precisely defined interface.

In this chapter, we shall learn about the features of ML that support encapsulation: structures, signatures, and functors. Together, these concepts are called the *ML module system*.

There are a number of other features of ML that support encapsulation, some involving the module system and some not. We shall also cover these ideas — local definitions, abstract types, and structure sharing — in this chapter.

8.1 Why Modules?

The ML *module system* has three major building blocks:

1. *Structures* are collections of types, datatypes, functions, exceptions, and other elements that we wish to encapsulate. The definitions of these elements appear in the structure. We have actually met certain structures that appear in the ML standard basis, such as `Int` or `TextIO`. In Section 8.2 we shall learn how to create and use structures of our own.

257

2. *Signatures* are collections of information describing the types and other specifications for some of the elements of a structure.

3. *Functors* are operations that take as arguments one or more elements such as structures and produce a structure that combines the functor's arguments in some way.

In effect, a signature is a "type" for a structure, and the syntax of ML reflects this view. That is, we can attach a signature to a structure with a colon, just as we attach a type to an expression with a colon. An alternative, and similar view is that the signature is a declaration, while the structure is a definition.

8.1.1   Information Hiding

One important capability of the module system in ML and other languages is *information hiding.* We hide information by arranging that certain definitions within a package are not usable outside the package. Those terms that are not hidden, and thus are available outside the package, are said to be *exported* by the module. The structure is one important kind of package we may use to hide information. A number of other mechanisms for information hiding will be taken up in Section 8.5.

Example 8.1: In Section 6.3 we discussed a datatype `btree` and gave three useful functions for implementing binary search trees: `lookup`, `insert`, and `delete`. We also defined an exception `EmptyTree` and an auxiliary function `deletemin` that helps with the implementation of `delete` in Fig. 6.12. The binary search tree is a common concept that might be packaged and used in many programs.

In a binary-search-tree package, we might want to hide `deletemin` because it is not an operation we typically need with binary search trees. Hiding this function has the advantage that we can be sure no one will use it other than through a call to `delete`. Recall that `deletemin` fails when given the empty tree as an argument, but in `delete`, we were very careful to call `deletemin` only on nonempty trees. A user of `deletemin` might not know of this problem and might not be so careful. Moreover, if we hide `deletemin` we can also hide the exception `EmptyTree`, since there is no way for the user to cause the corresponding error.

We might even want to hide the data constructors `Empty` and `Node` for binary search trees. The motivation is similar. If we make the constructors available outside the package, an unknowing programmer might use them to build binary trees that did not obey the BST property. On the other hand, if we limit the construction of binary search trees to the `insert` and `delete` functions, we can be sure that the BST property will be preserved. We do, however, need to add another function `create` that takes no argument and returns the empty tree, or else we would never be able to get started building binary search trees outside the package. Figure 8.1 suggests what the binary-search-tree package would look like from the outside if we hid the constructors, the exception, and the function `deletemin`. We shall return to this example and to the subject of information hiding in Section 8.5. □

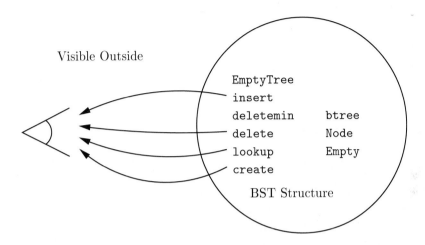

Figure 8.1: Exporting only the essentials of the binary-search-tree

8.1.2 Clustering Connected Elements

In addition to hiding capabilities that we do not want to offer the user, ML offers us capabilities to group related elements properly. To see the problem, let us again consider the matter of functions on binary search trees. In Section 6.3 we wrote each of the functions `lookup`, `insert`, and `delete` to take a function parameter `lt` that implements the particular less-than needed for a particular binary search tree. However, how do we know that these three functions will be called with the same `lt`?

A slightly safer approach is to remove the parameter `lt` from `lookup`, `insert`, and `delete`. First define a function `lt`, and then define `lookup`, `insert`, or `delete` to refer to this function `lt`. In the future, all comparisons within the three functions will all use this `lt`, even if `lt` is subsequently redefined.

Example 8.2 : Figure 8.2 shows versions of the functions `insert`, `delete`, and `lookup`. We have removed the parameter `lt` from each of the three functions that used in it Section 6.3, although the three functions still refer to `lt` when they need to compare elements. We have also written them in non-Curried form, since Currying without the parameter `lt` is less compelling than if we have the opportunity to partially instantiate the functions by binding `lt`. Finally, we have reversed the order of the tree and label arguments, because clarity is

```
datatype 'label btree =
    Empty |
    Node of 'label * 'label btree * 'label btree;

fun lower(nil) = nil
|   lower(c::cs) = (Char.toLower c)::lower(cs);

fun lt(x,y) =
        implode(lower(explode(x))) <
            implode(lower(explode(y)));

fun lookup(x, Empty) = false
|   lookup(x, Node(y,left,right)) =
        if lt(x,y) then lookup(x, left)
        else if lt(y,x) then lookup(x, right)
        else (* x=y *) true;

fun insert(x,Empty) = Node(x,Empty,Empty)
|   insert(x, T as Node(y,left,right)) =
        if lt(x,y) then Node(y,insert(x,left),right)
        else if lt(y,x) then Node(y,left,insert(x,right))
        else (* x=y *) T; (* do nothing; x was
                                already there *)

(* exception EmptyTree and function deletemin are defined
   exactly as before *)

fun delete(x, Empty) = Empty
|   delete(x, Node(y,left,right)) =
        if lt(x,y) then Node(y,delete(x,left),right)
        else if lt(y,x) then Node(y,left,delete(x,right))
        else (* x=y *)
            case (left,right) of
                (Empty,r) => r |
                (l,Empty) => l |
                (l,r) =>
                    let
                        val (z,r1) = deletemin(r)
                    in
                        Node(z,l,r1)
                    end;
```

Figure 8.2: Removing lt from the functions that access binary search trees

enhanced when we put the label being searched for in front of the often complex tree that is the second argument.

Instead of defining a function `strLT` to use as a parameter to `lookup` and the other functions, we use the identical definition of a comparison function, but we call it `lt`. □

ML provides a way to generate versions of `lookup`, `insert`, and `delete` using a template called a functor that we shall take up in Section 8.3. With the proper functor, we can turn a particular `lt` function into a structure that contains the functions of Fig. 8.2 but restricted to use this function `lt`.

8.2 Structures

We have actually met structures in one guise: the built-in structures of the ML standard basis that provide collections of related functions, exceptions, and constants. These structures are generally associated with a particular type, and they are not intended to be changed by the user. The same grouping and organization that the designers of ML used for the ML standard basis is available to the application programmer who uses the structure-defining statement of ML.

A structure definition has the following form:

```
structure <identifier> =
    struct <elements of the structure> end
```

There are a number of different kinds of elements that may appear in a structure. The ones we shall use principally are:

1. Function definitions,

2. Exceptions,

3. Constants, and

4. Types.

However, there are several others. Section 9.6.8 has a complete listing of the elements that may appear in structures.

The elements of the structure optionally may be ended by semicolons. We shall adopt the same "Pascal-style" convention that we use for elements of a let-expression and follow each but the last by a semicolon.

Example 8.3 : Let us reconsider the mapping type introduced in Example 6.2. The mapping is a list of pairs of the type (`'d`,`'r`), where `'d` is the domain type and `'r` the range type. We make the tacit assumption that for any domain value, there is at most one pair on a list with that value as the first component of a pair. There are three functions we need to use a mapping:

1. `create` to produce the empty list and get us started.

2. `lookup` to find the range value associated with a given domain value.

3. `insert` to take a domain and range element, d and r, and make r the unique range value associated with d.

Figure 8.3 shows the definition of a suitable structure for a mapping, along with the ML response. Line (1) begins the structure declaration for a structure named `Mapping`. The first element of the structure is an exception, declared on line (2). Then, line (3) introduces the identifier `create`. The name `create` is provided by the structure to produce the empty mapping (represented by the empty list). We may view `create` as a function with zero parameters that returns the empty mapping when you "call" it, but it is, in fact, an ordinary variable.

- Recall that there is no such thing as a zero-parameter function in ML. However, sometimes, we see a function such as `foo()`, which is really a function named `foo` whose argument type is `unit`.

Lines (4) through (7) define the function `lookup(d,M)`, which finds the value r paired with d in the mapping M. We shall not go into the details of how it works. Similarly, lines (8) through (11) define a function `insert(d,r,M)`, which makes r the unique value paired with d in the mapping M.

After the `end` keyword comes the ML response, which gives the "signature" of this structure. A signature names the elements of the structure and their types. We shall have more to say about signatures shortly, but let us notice what ML has deduced about the types of the structure elements. It sees that `create` is a list of some type, expressed by the type `'a list`. For `insert` and `lookup`, ML notes that the domain type in each case must be an equality type, which it represents as `''a`. Recall that type variables starting with two quote marks can only be instantiated to equality types. The reason an equality type is needed is that in lines (6) and (10), the equality operator `=` is applied to values of the domain type of each function. □

8.2.1 Signatures

An identifier denoting a structure, such as identifier `Mapping` of Example 8.3, has a *signature* that serves as the "type" of the structure. As we saw in Example 8.3, the signature gives the types of the structure elements.

A signature has the form

$$\text{sig <specifications> end}$$

Some important kinds of specifications are listed below. We shall discuss others later, and the complete syntax for specifications is in Fig. 9.21.

```
(1) structure Mapping = struct

(2)      exception NotFound;

         (* create the empty mapping *)

(3)      val create = nil;

         (* lookup(d,M) finds the range value r such that
            (d,r) is a pair in mapping M *)

(4)      fun lookup(d,nil) = raise NotFound
(5)        |   lookup(d,(e,r)::es) =
(6)               if d=e then r
(7)               else lookup(d,es);

         (* insert(d,r,M) puts (d,r) in mapping M and removes
            any other pair (d,s) that was present in M *)

(8)      fun insert(d,r,nil) = [(d,r)]
(9)        |   insert(d,r,(e,s)::es) =
(10)              if d=e then (d,r)::es
(11)              else (e,s)::insert(d,r,es)
     end;
```

structure Mapping :
  sig
    exception NotFound
    val create : 'a list
    *val insert : "a * 'b * ("a * 'b) list → ("a * 'b) list*
    *val lookup : "a * ("a * 'b) list → 'b*
  end

Figure 8.3: The Mapping structure and its signature

---

structure Versus struct

Note the difference between keywords `structure` and `struct`. The first is a declaration word like `fun`; `structure` precedes an identifier being declared to be a structure. On the other hand, `struct` is paired with `end` to bracket the elements of a structure.

---

1. `type`, followed by an identifier, possibly parametrized by type variables. Two examples are `type foo` and `type ('a,'b) bar`.

2. `eqtype`, followed as in (1). This keyword declares that the named type must be an equality type. A datatype in a structure can correspond to a type or (if the datatype definition does not involve function types) an eqtype in the signature.

3. `exception`, followed by an exception name.

4. `val`, followed by an identifier, a colon, and a type expression. Examples were seen in the response of Fig. 8.3. The type may be arbitrary, including function types. There is no special keyword to introduce declarations of functions in signatures the way `fun` or `fn` do in other contexts.

We can bind an identifier to a value that is a signature by

    signature <identifier> =
        sig <specifications> end

Here are a few important points to remember about signatures:

- Keywords `signature` and `sig` are related like `structure` and `struct`. Word `signature` introduces a signature definition, while `sig`, along with `end`, brackets the specifications in the signature.

- Note in (1) and (2) above that type names do not begin with a quote mark; they are the type constructors. However, any type-valued parameters, such as the parameters `'a` and `'b` in the hypothetical type `bar` of (1) above, *are* represented by type variables and *do* begin with a quote mark.

- As for structures, specifications of a signature may optionally be ended with a semicolon. We shall adopt the Pascal style for semicolon use.

8.2.2   Restricting Structures Through Their Signatures

In analogy with types and ordinary identifiers, the signature can be used to restrict a structure. To begin, here is a simple example of how types restrict the value of an identifier; no structures are involved in this example.

Example 8.4: We might define a polymorphic function `foo(x)` to be of type
`'a -> 'b`, that is, a function from some type to another type. When we use it,
we may wish to or need to restrict the parameter `x` to a particular type, say by
using it as `foo(x:int)`. Or, we might wish to restrict it partially by a use such
as `foo(x:'c list)`, which restricts the argument to be some kind of list.   □

   Now, let us extend the type-restriction idea to structures and their signatures. There are two principal ways that a signature can restrict the structure
to which it is attached.

  1. The signature can specify a more restrictive type for an identifier than is
     implicit in the structure definition.

  2. The signature can omit certain identifiers, thus hiding them in any struc-
     ture defined to have this signature.

Example 8.5: If we did not want a user to be able to modify a mapping, we
might eliminate all mention of **create** and **insert** in the `Mapping` structure.
An appropriate signature is:

```
sig
    exception NotFound;
    val lookup : ''a * (''a * 'b) list -> 'b
end
```

□

Example 8.6: Suppose we want to have a structure that is a mapping, specialized to the case of Example 6.2, where the domain is strings and the range
is integers. We shall call this kind of mapping a "string-int mapping." We can
define a structure based on the `Mapping` structure from Fig. 8.3 by defining a
signature in which the types of the functions are restricted to have string do-
mains and integer ranges. Figure 8.4 shows the definition of a suitable signature
`SIMAPPING`.

```
signature SIMAPPING = sig
    exception NotFound;
    val create : (string * int) list;
    val insert : string * int * (string * int) list ->
            (string * int) list;
    val lookup : string * (string * int) list -> int
end;
```

Figure 8.4: A signature for string-int mappings

   We can now use the signature `SIMAPPING` of Fig. 8.4 to restrict the structure
`Mapping` of Fig. 8.3. We do so by defining another structure, which we shall

call `SiMapping`, to be equal to `Mapping`, but with the signature `SIMAPPING`. The declaration

```
structure SiMapping: SIMAPPING = Mapping
```

defines the new structure. The functions `create`, `insert`, and `lookup` from the `SiMapping` structure can only be applied to string-int mappings. □

The definition of structure `SiMapping` above illustrates another useful form of structure definition, where instead of defining a structure explicitly, with `struct ··· end`, we define one structure equal to another structure. We then attach a signature to the first structure with a colon, to restrict the newly defined structure. Another option is to define a signature in advance and attach it with a colon to the name of the structure as it is being defined.

Example 8.7: We could also have defined structure `SiMapping` directly by:

```
structure SiMapping: SIMAPPING = struct
    (* same as lines (2)-(11) of Mapping definition *)
end;
```

Here, we append a colon and a signature to the structure `SiMapping` being defined. We have chosen to use the signature `SIMAPPING` from Fig. 8.4, referring to it by name. However, we could also have used a signature defined explicitly by `sig...end` in place of `SIMAPPING`. The material appearing between `struct...end` is exactly what appeared in lines (2) through (11) of Fig. 8.3. □

8.2.3 Accessing Names Defined Within Structures

Executing a structure-statement causes the names defined within the structure to become part of the environment. However, in the environment, these names are qualified by being prefixed by the structure name and a dot.

Example 8.8: Suppose we have defined the structure `SiMapping` as in Example 8.6. Having executed the statement

```
structure SiMapping: SIMAPPING = Mapping
```

preceded by the definitions of structure `Mapping` and signature `SIMAPPING`, we can then use string-int mappings. We might, for example, initialize an empty string-int mapping `m` by

```
val m = SiMapping.create;
```
*val m = nil : (string * int) list*

Long Identifiers

A structure name followed by a dot and a variable is called a *long* identifier. Formally, the long identifiers in ML are sequences of alternating structure names and dots, followed by a variable name. Since structures may be components of other structures, these sequences can make sense. For example, `A.B.foo` is the variable `foo` belonging to the structure B, which is a substructure of structure A.

Then, we can insert pairs into mapping m. For example:

```
val m = SiMapping.insert("in",6,m);
```
*val m = [("in", 6)] : (string * int) list*

```
val m = SiMapping.insert("a",1,m);
```
*val m = [("in", 6), ("a", 1)] : (string * int) list*

Last, a lookup operation like

```
SiMapping.lookup("in",m);
```
val it = 6

allows us to obtain information from the mapping.   □

8.2.4   Opening Structures

Using long identifiers — that is, attaching the structure name to the functions and other elements of a structure — helps us avoid some mistakes. For example:

- Function names like `insert` and `lookup` were used above as operations on mappings, but in Section 6.3 they were used for different operations on binary search trees. It is possible that structures based on both the mapping and the binary search tree would be useful in one program. To which would names `insert` and `lookup` refer?

- The built-in structures of the standard basis sometimes have different functions of the same name. For example, `toString` appears in the structures `Int` and `Real`, among others. The structures `List` and `Array` both have a function `length`.

By specifying both the operation and the structure, we avoid having one member of a programming team refer to the wrong function, perhaps unaware of the existence of the other.

However, it is cumbersome to repeat the structure name every time we refer to one of its elements. So, ML allows a structure to be *opened* by the declaration

---

An Alternative to Opening Structures

There is a risk in using **open**, because a structure written by someone else may contain declarations you are not aware of, and thereby some variable you use may have its meaning changed accidentally. With a little more effort, we can protect ourselves against such an error by defining only the identifiers we know about and need from the structure, for example

```
val create = Simapping.create;
val insert = SiMapping.insert;
```

and so on. Now, **create** and **insert** will refer to elements of structure **SiMapping**, although other elements of that structure must be referred to by their long name.

```
open <structure name>;
```

This statement causes all the names exported by the structure to be added to the current environment, where they shield from view any other name with the same identifier. However, identifiers appearing in another structure can still be referenced by prepending the structure name and a dot.

Example 8.9 : If we execute

```
open SiMapping;
```

then the identifiers **NotFound**, **create**, **insert**, and **lookup** will refer, respectively, to the exception, variable, and functions with those names belonging to the structure **SiMapping**. We can then replace the statements of Example 8.8 by removing "SiMapping." everywhere it appears. □

8.2.5   Exercises for Section 8.2

* **Exercise 8.2.1 :** Define a structure **Tree** with a datatype **tree** representing general trees as in Section 6.4 and the following operations:

1. **create(a)** returns a one-node tree with label a.

2. **build(a,L)** returns a tree with a root labeled a and list of subtrees L for the root.

3. **find(i,T)** finds the ith subtree of the root of tree T and raises the exception **Missing** if there is no such subtree.

* **Exercise 8.2.2:** Note that in Exercise 8.2.1 `create(a)` means the same as `build(a,nil)`. We may thus wish to define a new structure `SimpleTree` that has all the elements of structure `Tree` except `create`. Also, we may choose to restrict simple trees to have integer labels. Write a signature `SIMPLE` that makes these restrictions. Then use `SIMPLE` and `Tree` to define structure `SimpleTree`.

* **Exercise 8.2.3:** Use your structure `SimpleTree` from Exercise 8.2.2 to construct a tree with a root labeled 1 and three children labeled 2, 3, and 4. Apply function `subtree` to obtain the second subtree of the root of your tree.

Exercise 8.2.4: Design a structure `Stack` that represents a stack of elements of some arbitrary type. Include the functions: `create` (return an empty stack), `push` (add an element to the top of the stack and return the resulting stack), `pop` (delete the top element and return the resulting stack), `isEmpty` (test whether a given stack is empty), and `top` (return the top element). Also include an exception `EmptyStack` to catch attempts to read or pop the top element of an empty stack.

Exercise 8.2.5: Design a suitable signature that will allow us to create from `Stack` of Exercise 8.2.4 a structure `StringStack` whose stacks have elements that are strings, and that omits the operation `top`.

* **Exercise 8.2.6:** Design a structure `Queue` that represents a queue of elements of some arbitrary type. Include operations: `create` (return an empty queue), `enqueue` (add an element to the end of the queue and return the result), `dequeue` (return a pair consisting of the first element on the queue and the rest of the queue), and `isEmpty` (tell whether the queue is empty). Also include the exception `EmptyQueue` to catch attempts at dequeueing from the empty queue.

Exercise 8.2.7: Design a suitable signature that will allow us to create from `Queue` of Exercise 8.2.6 a structure `PairQueue` whose queues have elements that are pairs consisting of a string and an integer. Do not omit any of the functions.

! **Exercise 8.2.8:** Write a structure that can serve as a simple matrix package, modeled on the operations used in Section 7.5. For example, you will want to include functions such as:

1. `create(n)` returns an $n \times n$ matrix of 0.0's.
2. `assign(M,i,j,x)` sets element M_{ij} to x.
3. `assignRow(M,i,L)` sets the ith row of matrix M to the list of elements L.
4. `rowOp(M,c,i,j)` subtracts c times the ith row from the jth row of matrix M.
5. `columnOp(M,c,i,j)` subtracts c times the ith column from the jth column.

What other functions would be useful to have?

For C++ Fans Only

One can see an ML structure as a generalization of the idea of a class. Typically, a structure involves a single type, like the class, and the structure offers some functions (methods) applicable to that class. However, structures may define many different types or datatypes, and may provide functions that apply to any of these types or to different types altogether (analogous to "friend" classes in C++).

Similarly, an ML functor generalizes the idea of a template in C++. *Templates* are parametrized classes that can be instantiated by designating particular types for the parameters of the template. Functors can do the same, but also can transform or combine the types or structures that are its arguments in ways that are limited only by the programmer's imagination.

8.3 Functors

In this section we shall introduce a powerful ML tool called the "functor." This idea is probably unfamiliar to users of other languages. Having written a structure, we might wonder whether it is possible to create a large number of similar structures, perhaps each providing the same operations on a different type, in a manner that is easier than rewriting the structure many times. The functor provides this capability in a surprising way. A functor is actually a higher-level function[1] that takes structures or certain other kinds of elements as arguments and returns a structure as a result.

8.3.1 Motivation for Functors

Often we want a structure to take some "input," which helps determine some features of the structure. For example, in Fig. 8.2 we wrote functions to operate on a binary search tree, using an externally specified function lt to compare elements of the label type of the trees. If we simply define a structure that refers to lt, without there being any object in the current environment with that identifier, we shall cause an error. However, if we first write a suitable definition for lt and then define a structure using lt, this structure will always use that definition of lt, even if the identifier lt is redefined later. While we shall see better ways to handle the problem, this approach does allow us to write one structure definition that, if retyped in different environments with different structure names, results in structures with different meanings for the name lt. When we use externally defined names in a structure, those names are said to be *imported*.

---

[1] Not to be confused with the higher-order functions discussed in Section 5.4.

- Note that, as with other sorts of definitions, all names in the current environment may be used when a structure or signature is defined. Imported names like lt have their values incorporated into the definition of the structure so that, even if an imported name is redefined after the definition, it is still the original value that is used when elements of the structure are invoked.

Example 8.10 : Let us define a structure StringBST that incorporates the definitions and functions of Fig. 8.2. This definition is sketched in Fig. 8.5. We have completely omitted the definitions of the various functions and the auxiliary functions for lt, which are all the same as Fig. 8.2.

```
fun lt(x:string,y) = ... ;
```
*val lt = fn : string * string → bool*

```
structure StringBST = struct
    datatype 'label btree = Empty |
        Node of 'label * 'label btree * 'label btree;
    fun lookup(x,T) = ... ;
    fun insert(x,T) = ... ;
    exception EmptyTree;
    fun deletemin(T) = ... ;
    fun delete(x,T) = ... ;
end;
```
structure StringBST :
  sig
    datatype 'a btree = Empty | Node
    exception EmptyTree
    *val delete : string * string btree → string btree*
    *val deletemin : 'a btree → 'a * 'a btree*
    *val insert : string * string btree → string btree*
    *val lookup : string * string btree → bool*
  end

Figure 8.5: Defining a structure that imports a value for lt

The definitions of insert, delete, and lookup use the definition of lt that appears at the top of Fig. 8.5. Notice that in the response to this structure definition, ML gives it a signature that is as general as possible. It has determined from the use of this lt that insert, delete, and lookup involve strings and string btree's, but it has not determined that deletemin requires any special type for the labels of its btree's, and in fact it does not because deletemin only navigates in the tree and does not examine labels.

Figure 8.6 is an example of how we might create an empty binary search tree, populate it with two strings, and perform some operations. Notice that at the second line, we must give the empty tree `t1` the appropriate type, `string btree`, since ML cannot tell the type of the labels from the data constructor `Empty`. □

```
open StringBST;

val t1 = Empty: string btree;
val t1 = Empty : string btree


val t2 = insert("foo", t1);
val t2 = Node("foo",Empty,Empty) : string btree


val t3 = insert("bar", t2);
val t3 = Node("foo",Node("bar",Empty,Empty),Empty) :   string
    btree


lookup("bar",t3);
val it = true : bool


val t4 = delete("baz",t3);
val t4 = Node("foo",Node("bar",Empty,Empty),Empty) :   string
    btree
```

Figure 8.6: Examples of binary search tree operations

8.3.2   Using Functors to Import Information

There are certain undesirable features of the approach to importation suggested by Example 8.10.

1. The typing of elements in the structure is rather haphazard, being whatever ML can deduce from the clues given. Compare, for example, the types of `delete` and `deletemin`.

2. We never really created an object that is "a binary search tree that works on any type with a less-than function." Rather, we created a structure that in effect is a binary search tree with string labels (although we could

retype the same structure definition in another environment to create binary search trees with another label type). It is dangerous to have the meaning of a structure definition change, depending on what code precedes it.

ML provides a way to handle both of these problems through a mechanism called the *functor*. A functor typically operates on structures to produce other structures. We can define a functor that takes as its argument a structure defining a type T and a less-than operation lt on type T. The result of this functor is a binary-search-tree structure that incorporates the given lt and T to provide versions of insert, delete, and lookup, that expect node labels of the given type T and compare labels using the function lt. The idea of "a binary search tree working on any type with a less-than function" is embodied by the functor. This functor may be applied to any number of structures, each of which specifies a type and a suitable lt function.

The steps we must take to create the functor and the example of binary search trees with string labels is outlined below.

1. Define a signature, which we shall call TOTALORDER, that is satisfied only by structures that are suitable as functor inputs. That is, the structure must have a type and a function that takes pairs of elements of this type and returns a boolean.[2]

2. Define a functor, called MakeBST, that takes a structure S with signature TOTALORDER as its argument and produces a structure as a result. The resulting structure defines binary search trees whose labels are of the type described by the structure S.

3. Define a structure String that describes character strings with a function lt to compare strings. The signature of String is TOTALORDER.

4. Apply the functor MakeBST to the structure String, to produce the desired structure: StringBST.

We shall show how to perform these steps in a sequence of examples.

Defining a Signature for the Functor's Parameter

Example 8.11: Here is a suitable definition for the signature TOTALORDER.

```
signature TOTALORDER = sig
    type element;
    val lt : element * element -> bool
end;
```

---

[2]Technically, we expect more than a type T and a function of type $T * T \to$ bool. We also expect that the function will define a total order on values of type T. However, the signature cannot specify arbitrary properties of functions, so we may wind up applying our functor to structures that do not represent total orders.

We first name a type `element`, which is intended to be the type of labels in binary search trees. This is the type we referred to as T in our introductory remarks. We expect in later examples that the type `element` will be `string`.

The only operation we require for the type `element` is the function `lt`, which takes two elements and produces true or false as a value. That is all we need to know about `lt` at this point; we do not need to know how it computes its boolean-valued result.   □

- Note that the name `element` of the type in signature `TOTALORDER` is an ordinary identifier, not a type variable beginning with a quotation mark.

Defining a Functor

To define a functor that transforms one structure into another, we use a definition of the form

> `functor` <identifier> (<structure name> : <signature>)
> = <structure definition>

An optional colon and signature describing the result of the functor may appear immediately before the equal-sign. The following example illustrates this form as it applies to the problem of defining binary search trees.

Example 8.12: In Fig. 8.7 is a sketch of the definition of the functor `MakeBST`. In line (1) we see the beginning of the functor definition. The parameter name is `Lt`, and the signature for this parameter is `TOTALORDER`, the signature from Example 8.11.

In lines (2) through (8) we see the definition of a signature for the structure that is to be produced by the functor `MakeBST`. Specifying the signature here is optional, but we include it for instructional value.

Notice that in the signature, line (2) refers to the datatype `btree` as a "type," not a datatype. The fact that it takes a type parameter, which we call `'label` as usual, is indicated. However, the existence of constructors `Node` and `Empty` is not mentioned. The usual definition of this datatype appears in the structure definition at line (10).

Following the signature describing the functor's result is the required = sign and the structure definition itself. We open `Lt` in line (9), so uses of the function `lt` in the unseen code for `insert` and other functions will refer to `lt` in the structure `Lt` (otherwise, these functions would have to refer to `Lt.lt`).

At line (11) we have added a new variable `create`, whose value is an empty tree. Recall that there is a problem if we try to assign to a variable the value `Empty` of type `'label btree`, because the ML compiler cannot know the type of `'label`. The problem is similar to using `nil` as a value of a list, without specifying the type of the list.

However, by putting `create` in the structure that is the output of functor `MakeBST`, we are actually defining a value for `create` after a concrete structure is substituted for the structure-parameter `Lt` and therefore a concrete type has

```
(1)  functor MakeBST(Lt: TOTALORDER):
          sig
(2)           type 'label btree;
(3)           exception EmptyTree;
(4)           val create : Lt.element btree;
(5)           val lookup : Lt.element * Lt.element btree -> bool;
(6)           val insert : Lt.element *  Lt.element btree ->
                      Lt.element btree;
(7)           val deletemin : Lt.element btree ->
                      Lt.element * Lt.element btree;
(8)           val delete : Lt.element *  Lt.element btree ->
                      Lt.element btree
          end

     =

          struct
(9)           open Lt;

(10)          datatype 'label btree =
                  Empty |
                  Node of 'label * 'label btree * 'label btree;

(11)          val create = Empty;
(12)          fun lookup(x, Empty) = ... ;
(13)          fun insert(x,Empty) = ... ;
(14)          exception EmptyTree;
(15)          fun deletemin(Empty) = ... ;
(16)          fun delete(x, Empty) = ... ;
          end;
      functor MakeBST : <sig>
```

Figure 8.7: Definition (sketch) of the functor `MakeBST`

been substituted for the type `element`. For instance, we shall soon see an example where `element` becomes `string`, and therefore, the type of `create` in the resulting structure is `string btree`. Since the type of `create` is declared in line (4) of the signature to be `Lt.element btree`, ML will deduce that the type of `Empty` is `string btree` in the resulting structure.

- If we had not included the signature of lines (2) through (8) in Fig. 8.7, then in the structure that is output from the functor `MakeBST` the type of `create` would involve a type variable, and we could not use `create` without specifying the correct type.

The definitions of the other functions are as in Fig. 8.2 and are again omitted. Notice the succinct response of ML to this functor definition at the end. □

Defining a Functor Argument

Next, we need to define a particular structure that can be the argument corresponding to the parameter `Lt` in the functor `MakeBST`.

Example 8.13 : An appropriate definition is shown in Fig. 8.8 The first line in Fig. 8.8 says that `String` is a structure, and its signature is `TOTALORDER`. The structure specification begins by defining the type `element`. That is, in structure `String`, the type `element` mentioned in the signature `TOTALORDER` is defined to be the type `string`. Here the type definition is an ordinary type abbreviation introduced by the keyword `type`. It would also have been possible to replace the line

```
type element = string;
```

by a datatype definition. However the number of type parameters in the signature and structure must agree. So in this case, since `element` was defined in the structure to be a parameterless type, the datatype would likewise have to be parameterless like the datatype `fruit` of Example 6.3.

The remainder of Fig. 8.8 gives a definition for function `lt`; this definition is the one we have used several times previously. Notice that we have defined the auxiliary function `lower` to be local to `lt` by using a let-expression. Since the signature `TOTALORDER` defines the type of `lt` to be

```
element * element -> bool
```

and `element` has been defined to be `string`, the function `lt` is properly written so its type is `string * string -> bool`. □

Applying the Functor

The last step in our process is to apply the functor `MakeBST` to the structure `String` to produce the structure `StringBST`, which is an appropriate structure representing binary search trees with string labels. The form of this functor application is

```
structure String: TOTALORDER =
    struct
        type element = string;
        fun lt(x,y) =
            let
                fun lower(nil) = nil
                |   lower(c::cs) =
                        (Char.toLower c)::lower(cs);
            in
                implode(lower(explode(x))) <
                        implode(lower(explode(y)))
            end;
    end;
```

Figure 8.8: The structure `String`

```
structure <new structure name> =
    <functor name>(<structure argument>)
```

An optional colon and signature may appear before the equal sign to describe the new structure.

Example 8.14 : The following functor application:

```
structure StringBST = MakeBST(String);
```

produces the desired structure `StringBST`. □

If we open `StringBST`, operations like `insert` have their desired meaning; they apply only to binary search trees with string labels. Even if we do not open `StringBST`, we can get these operations by names like `StringBST.insert`.

8.3.3 More General Forms for Functor Parameters and Arguments

In Section 8.3.2, we used a simple form for defining one-parameter functors. The parameter is an identifier standing for a structure, followed only by a colon and a signature describing the structure. An example was given in line (1) of Fig. 8.7. When we apply the functor, we have only to provide an actual structure as argument. For instance, we provided the structure `String` as argument in Example 8.14.

One extension is that we may provide the argument structure explicitly, instead of by name. For example, we could have skipped the definition of `String` in Fig. 8.8 and instead have written the declaration of structure `StringBST` in

```
structure StringBST = MakeBST(
    struct
        type element = string;
        fun lt(x,y) =
            let
                fun lower(nil) = nil
                |   lower(c::cs) =
                        (Char.toLower c)::lower(cs);
            in
                implode(lower(explode(x))) <
                        implode(lower(explode(y)))
            end;
    end
);
```

Figure 8.9: Applying a functor to an explicit structure

Example 8.14 as in Fig. 8.9. That is, the entire structure definition appears as the argument of the functor.

There are more flexible ways to write the parameters and arguments of functors. We may have more than one parameter, and parameters may be any declarable element such as a value, function, or exception. The entire syntax of functor declarations is in Fig. 9.25, and the syntax of functor use is in Fig. 9.24.

To begin, we can declare structure parameters of a functor using the keyword `structure`. The form is

```
functor <identifier>(structure <structure name> : <signature>)
    = <structure definition>
```

As always, an optional colon and signature may appear before the equal sign to describe the result of the functor.

When we use the word `structure` in the definition of the parameter of a functor, then when we apply this functor we need to provide its argument in a somewhat different form:

```
<functor name>(
    structure <functor parameter> = <argument>
)
```

The argument may be a structure name or the explicit definition of a structure, using `struct...end`.

Example 8.15: We may begin the definition of functor `MakeBST` by replacing line (1) of Fig. 8.7 by:

```
functor MakeBST(structure Lt: TOTALORDER):
```

If we do so, then we must change the application of functor `MakeBST` in Example 8.14 to:

```
structure StringBST = MakeBST(structure Lt = String);
```

□

More generally, a functor can have several structure parameters, each paired with its signature using the syntax

functor <identifier>(structure S_1:$\mathcal{S}_1$ and ... and S_n:$\mathcal{S}_n$)
      = <structure definition>

where the S's are structures and the $\mathcal{S}$'s are signatures.

We may also have, as parameters for the functor, several specifications separated by optional semicolons. A specification may involve one or more structures in the form above. A specification may also tell about a value, function, or in fact be of any of the forms for specifications that may appear in signatures. The complete syntax for specifications is in Fig. 9.21.

Example 8.16: To illustrate some of the possible forms, let us define two simple signatures by:

```
signature INT = sig val i: int end;
signature REAL = sig val r: real end;
```

Signature `INT` describes a structure consisting of one integer called i, and signature `REAL` describes a structure with a real number r. Here are some possible beginnings of functor definitions. In each case we have not continued past the equal sign and thus omit defining the result of the functor.

```
(1) functor Foo(structure I: INT and R: REAL) =
(2) functor Foo(structure I: INT; structure R: REAL) =
(3) functor Foo(structure I: INT and R: REAL; val x : int) =
```

Definition (1) says that functor `Foo` has two arguments, which are structures I and R, with signatures `INT` and `REAL` respectively. Definition (2) says exactly the same thing but uses separate structure specifications for the two structure parameters. Definition (3) says that functor `Foo` has these two structure parameters but also has a third parameter, which is an integer x.   □

The rule regarding parameter and argument forms, illustrated in Example 8.15, generalizes to functors whose parameters are defined using **structure** and/or other specifications. When we apply such a functor, we use the same specification keyword, such as **structure** or **val**, and follow it by

= <argument>

More generally, several parameters may be bound to their corresponding arguments following one use of a keyword such as `structure`, if we separate the parameter-argument pairs with `and`. Several groups of bindings may be separated by optional semicolons.

Example 8.17: Let us define two structures

```
structure Int = struct val i = 0 end;
structure Real = struct val r = 0.0 end;
```

to match the signatures `INT` and `REAL` of Example 8.16 Here are several ways a structure `Bar` could be defined by applying one of the functors of Example 8.16. Either of the definitions

```
structure Bar = Foo(structure I = Int; structure R = Real);
structure Bar = Foo(structure I = Int and R = Real);
```

can be used with either of the functor declaration forms (1) or (2) of Example 8.16. The following definitions

```
structure Bar =
    Foo(structure I = Int; structure R = Real; val x = 2);
structure Bar =
    Foo(structure I = Int and R = Real; val x = 2);
```

are appropriate with definition (3) of Example 8.16. □

8.3.4 Exercises for Section 8.3

Exercise 8.3.1: In place of the structure `String` of Fig. 8.8, write a structure that defines elements to be tuples of three real numbers. For the `lt` ordering on triples, say that $(a, b, c) < (x, y, z)$ if either

1. $a < x$, or

2. $a = x$ and $b < y$, or

3. $a = x$, $b = y$, and $c < z$.

Then show how to apply the functor `MakeBST` of Fig. 8.7 to your new structure and get a structure that stores triples of reals in binary trees.

*! Exercise 8.3.2: A useful class of structures implements a set of elements of some type with a "similarity" relation that is defined by a function that tells whether two elements are "similar." For instance, the set could have strings as elements. Strings could be deemed similar if they where the same after converting upper-case letters to lower case. Alternatively, strings could be considered similar if they differed in only one position. For another example, elements could be lists of bits indicating whether a document discussed various topics of interest, and "similar" could mean that two documents covered at least two topics in common.

a) Write a signature `SIM` that describes structures that are an element type with a similarity relation on that type.

b) Write a functor `MakeSimSet` that takes as argument a structure `Sim` that includes an element type and a function that decides similarity. The result of your functor should be a structure that implements sets with the given type and notion of similarity. The operations in the result structure should include:

    1. A function `findSim` that takes an element x and a set S and returns the set of elements in S that are similar to x,

    2. A value `create` to be an empty set, and

    3. A function `insert` to return a set with a new element inserted.

c) Write a structure `Misspell` that defines elements to be strings and defines two strings to be similar if they are identical or differ in exactly one character. Apply your functor from (a) to produce the structure `MisspellSet` that implements sets of strings and allows searches for slightly misspelled words.

Exercise 8.3.3: Specify a functor `MakeHashTable` that takes a structure consisting of

1. A type `eltype` for the elements of the hash table,

2. A number of buckets, b, and

3. A hash function h that takes an element of type `eltype` and returns an integer from 0 to $b - 1$

and produces a structure with functions `insert`, `delete`, and `lookup` that operate upon the hash table. Also included in the result structure must be a function `create()` that returns an empty hash table.

Exercise 8.3.4: Write a functor `MakeHashFn` that produces structures that are suitable as input to the functor `MakeHashTable` of Exercise 8.3.3. In particular, `MakeHashFn` takes only an integer b as input. Its output is a structure in which the type `eltype` is defined to be `string`, the integer b is the same as the input b, and the hash function h is the function h from Fig. 7.9. Use your functor `makeHashFn` to create a structure `HashFn100` for $b = 100$ and then apply your functor `MakeHashTable` from Exercise 8.3.3 to structure `HashFn100` to create a structure `Hash100` that is a 100-bucket hash table for strings.

8.4 Sharings

A "sharing" is another kind of specification that can appear in signatures. Sharings play a unique role, connecting parts of the signature by forcing them to be equal. The problem comes up when a signature includes several types and/or substructures among its specifications. We may want to require that the types contained in two different substructures are arbitrary, but equal. In this section we shall first look at the syntax of sharings and then see the effect they have on structures that satisfy a signature with one or more sharings.

8.4.1 Sharing Specifications

A *sharing specification* is an element that may appear within a signature. This specification can be of the form

$$\text{\bf sharing type } <\text{type}> = <\text{type}> = \cdots = <\text{type}>$$

or of the form

$$\text{\bf sharing } <\text{structure}> = <\text{structure}> = \cdots = <\text{structure}>$$

The first form, *type sharing*, allows us to assert that two or more types mentioned in the signature must actually be the same type. The second form, *structure sharing*, allows us to assert that two or more substructures mentioned in the signature are "the same."

- Remember that the keyword `type` appears after the keyword `sharing` for type sharing, but there is no keyword analogous to `type` for substructure sharing.

- In earlier versions of ML, both structure and type sharings were defined independently. In ML97, however, only the type sharing is a basic construct, and the form of structure sharing described above is permitted as a shorthand for the sharing of identically named types within the equated structures. Structure sharing does *not* imply that the structures are identical.

- As a consequence, although sharing of types is transitive, the sharing of structures is not. For example, one structure-sharing statement might assert $S_1 = S_2$, and a second might assert $S_2 = S_3$, and yet there is a type found in structures S_1 and S_3 (but not in S_2) that are not thereby equated. Thus, $S_1 = S_2$ and $S_2 = S_3$ does not necessarily imply $S_1 = S_3$, when S_1, S_2, and S_3 are structures.

8.4.2 Substructures

In order to use sharings, we need another kind of specification, in which we declare a structure to have a substructure. The basic form of this specification within a signature is

structure <identifier> : <signature>

which asserts that the identifier is a structure with the given signature. Optionally, we can assert the existence of several structures, each with a specified signature, if we connect groups of the form <identifier> : <signature> by the keyword **and**.

In addition, structures can define substructures within themselves. The form of a substructure declaration within a structure (as opposed to within a signature) is

```
structure <identifier> : <signature> = struct
     <definition of the structure>
end
```

- The **struct**, the signature definition, and the **end** can be replaced by the name of a previously defined structure.

- The colon and signature are optional in structure definitions, but not in structure specifications that occur in signatures. There is a sound reason for this difference. In a structure definition, a suitable signature can be deduced from the definition of the substructure itself, but in a signature we have no way of deducing the signature for a substructure if we do not declare that signature.

8.4.3 Sharing of Types

Let us now see how the first kind of sharing, the specification that two types are the same, is accomplished.

Example 8.18: Consider the top two signatures in Fig. 8.10. First, signature ELEMENT in lines (1) and (2) describes a structure that has a type called element and a function similar on that type. As two examples from among an unlimited number of possibilities, function similar could be equality, or it could be equality of the first components if the type element were a pair. In realistic examples, we would expect there to be more functions than one within the signature.

Then in lines (3) through (9) we have another signature BTREE that describes a structure for binary trees. In line (3) we see there is a substructure Element whose signature is ELEMENT; that signature is the one we just saw in lines (1) and (2). Then in line (4) we specify a type elt that is local to the signature BTREE. We have decided to require that this local type be an equality type,

```
      signature ELEMENT = sig
(1)       type element;
(2)       val similar : element * element -> bool;
      end;

      signature BTREE = sig
(3)       structure Element: ELEMENT;
(4)       eqtype elt;
(5)       sharing type elt = Element.element;
(6)       datatype btree = Empty | Node of elt * btree * btree;
(7)       val leaf : elt -> btree;
(8)       val build : elt * btree * btree -> btree;
(9)       val lookup : elt * btree -> bool
      end;

      signature TREE = sig
(10)      structure Element: ELEMENT;
(11)      eqtype elt;
(12)      sharing type elt = Element.element;
(13)      datatype tree = Tree of elt * tree list;
(14)      val build : elt * tree list -> tree;
(15)      val lookup : elt * tree -> bool
      end;

      signature ALLTREES = sig
(16)      structure Btree: BTREE;
(17)      structure Tree: TREE;
(18)      sharing Btree.Element = Tree.Element;
(19)      sharing type Btree.elt = Tree.elt
      end;
```

Figure 8.10: Signatures that equate types and substructures

and we so indicate by using the keyword `eqtype` rather than `type`. A possible reason is that we believe the function `lookup` requires an equality test.

However, we also wish to require that the type `element` mentioned in the signature `ELEMENT` be the same as the local type `elt`. Hence, at line (5) there is a sharing specification that requires these two types to be the same. Should the functions in lines (7) through (9) refer to both the types `Element.element` and `elt`, we can be sure these are the same type in any structure that matches the signature `BTREE`. An additional effect of the sharing on line (5) is that `Element.element` is forced to be an equality type wherever it is used in lines (7) through (9) because it has been equated to the equality type `elt`. □

8.4.4 Sharing of Substructures

The other kind of sharing specification allows us to require that types of the same name within two substructures be the same.

Example 8.19: Continuing with our discussion of Fig. 8.10, we see in lines (10) through (15) another signature `TREE`. Like `BTREE`, it uses a substructure with signature `ELEMENT`, specifies a local equality type called `elt`, equates the local type and the type `element` of the substructure by a type sharing specification, and then specifies a datatype and some functions.

Then in lines (16) through (19) we see a final signature `ALLTREES`. This signature describes a structure that has two substructures. The first, on line (16), is called `Btree` and has `BTREE` for its signature. Line (17) adds a structure `Tree` with signature `TREE`.

We must find a substructure `Element` within structure `Btree` and within structure `Tree`, because their respective signatures require that substructure. However, there is no reason to believe that these two substructures are the same. In principle, `element` could refer to different types in each, and/or the function `similar` could be differently defined in each. The purpose of the structure-sharing statement on line (18) is to say that at least the types `element` within each of the two substructures called `Element` must be the same. The two substructures called `Element` could have different functions `similar`, however.

Finally, we note on line (19) an additional type sharing that equates the types `elt` belonging to the two substructures `Tree` and `Btree`. This sharing specification is legal, although it happens to be redundant. The fact that these types are equated to `Btree.Element.element` and `Tree.Element.element` at lines (5) and (12), respectively, forces them to be equal because the latter two types were equated by line (18). □

8.4.5 Exercises for Section 8.4

* **Exercise 8.4.1:** Give an example of a structure S that can be `Element` in line (3) of Fig. 8.10 and a structure with signature `BTREE` (as defined in lines (3) through (9) of that figure) that uses structure S at line (3) and satisfies the type-sharing constraint of line (5). Then, give another example of a structure with signature BTREE that uses the structure S but does *not* satisfy the sharing constraint.

Exercise 8.4.2: Give examples of:

  a) Structures with signatures BTREE and TREE, as defined in Fig. 8.10, that satisfy the type-sharing constraints of lines (5) and (12) in that figure.

  b) Structures that do *not* satisfy these type-sharing constraints.

8.5   ML Techniques for Hiding Information

The ML module system — structures, signatures, and functors — facilitates the design and reuse of software. We can implement a package of definitions, such as datatypes, functions, and exceptions, as a structure and reuse it many times in many different programs. Several programmers can work on structures independently and agree on a shared interface.

ML helps these processes is several ways. Signatures allow us to enforce certain requirements on a structure or functor. For example, signatures may require that functions and other elements be present and that these elements have specified types. Functors make it easy for us to abstract common parts of related structures and produce any of a family of structures without repeating common code. Using substructures and type sharing, as described in Section 8.4, we can control this interface quite flexibly and accurately.

However, there are several other features of ML that also assist in the structuring and validation of large, complex bodies of code. In this chapter we shall discuss techniques for *information hiding*, that is, making all, or certain parts of, a package of definitions inaccessible to the user. Information hiding improves the effectiveness of encapsulation, since it limits the ways in which the elements of the package can be used. Other auxiliary functions or definitions may exist within a package. However, they are not usable from outside the package, and the user is therefore prevented from applying these auxiliary elements in ways unanticipated by the designer of the package. As a result, we minimize the chance of an error due to misunderstanding between the implementor and user of the encapsulated facilities. There are many ways to hide information. We shall discuss:

  1. Defining a signature that fails to mention the hidden elements.

  2. Using an "opaque" signature to hide certain structure elements.

  3. Using an "abstract type" in place of a datatype to make its data constructors invisible.

  4. Using "local" definitions within an abstract type or structure to hide certain elements.

8.5.1 An Information-Hiding Problem

Let us begin by describing a particular problem we would like to solve. We shall focus on our running example of binary search trees. We want to offer the user a binary-search-tree package that allows for creation of empty trees, insertion, deletion, and lookup in binary search trees, but nothing else. The picture was suggested in Fig. 8.1. If we use our standard representation of the `btree` datatype, then the user should not be able to use the function `deletemin`, the exception `EmptyTree`, or the data constructors `Empty` and `Node`. In fact, it should appear to the user only that *some* implementation of a dictionary (set with insert, delete, and lookup) is being used, perhaps a binary search tree; perhaps not.

No scheme for information hiding is foolproof. Someone could always get control of the relevant code and use it in unintended or improper ways. However, the mechanisms described in this section each prevent a specific set of common actions that could lead to misuse of code.

8.5.2 Using Signatures to Hide Information

We may define one structure S_2 to be equal to another structure S_1, but with a specific signature $\mathcal{S}$. As was discussed in Section 8.2.2, the form of the definition is

> structure S_2: $\mathcal{S}$ = S_1

For instance, we saw in Example 8.5 that signature $\mathcal{S}$ can omit some elements that appear in the structure S_1. These elements will not be available to users of the structure S_2. However, should a function that is exported by S_2 use in its body a function of S_1 that is not exported by S_2, the needed function is available and no error is caused.

Example 8.20: Let us see how to write a variant of the structure `StringBST` that we generated in Section 8.3.2 by applying the functor MakeBST of Fig. 8.7 to the structure `String` of Fig. 8.8. The structure `StringBST` makes available all the elements in lines (10) through (16) of Fig. 8.7: the datatype `btree` with its data constructors `Empty` and `Node`, the value `create`, the exception `EmptyTree`, and the functions `create`, `lookup`, `insert`, `delete`, and `deletemin`.

We want our new structure to hide the function `deletemin` and the exception `EmptyTree`. Recall that the motivation for doing so is that `deletemin` is a function that is only needed by `delete`. Because `deletemin` does not work on an empty tree, it is best not made available to the user. When we make `deletemin` unavailable, we can also hide the exception, since its sole purpose is to catch erroneous uses of `deletemin`, which now cannot occur.

Figure 8.11 shows the signature that we need for our new structure. It makes visible the functions we want, while not exporting the function `deletemin` or the exception `EmptyTree`.

```
signature NEW_STRING_BST = sig
    type 'label btree;
    val create : string btree;
    val insert : string * string btree -> string btree;
    val delete : string * string btree -> string btree;
    val lookup : string * string btree -> bool
end;
```

Figure 8.11: Signature to hide `deletemin` and `EmptyTree`

Binding Type Variables in Datatype Definitions

Note that in the signature of Fig. 8.11 it is sufficient to refer to `btree` as a "type" rather than a "datatype." We might be tempted to describe the type `btree` as

```
type string btree
```

However, a concrete type like `string` may never be used as a type parameter in a type or datatype declaration. We must use a type variable, such as the variable `'label` that was used in Fig. 8.11. On the other hand, it would make sense first to define a new alias `stringBtree`, with no parameter, to stand for the type `string btree` and define types of elements in signature NEW_STRING_BST as

```
val create :  stringBtree;
```

and so on.

Now let us create a new structure that has the signature of Fig. 8.11 by the structure definition:

```
structure NewStringBST: NEW_STRING_BST = MakeBST(String);
```

This statement is almost identical to that of Example 8.14. The only difference is that we have specified a signature for the resulting structure.

The effect of the signature NEW_STRING_BST on the structure NewStringBST is that elements we want hidden are hidden, and those we want accessible are accessible. If we then open the new structure with

```
open NewStringBST;
```

we can use the elements mentioned in the signature NEW_STRING_BST of Fig. 8.11, as in

```
insert("foo", create);
```
val it = Node("foo",Empty,Empty) : string btree

which creates an empty tree and then inserts the string `"foo"`.

Similarly, a call to `delete` is permitted. This call results in a call to `deletemin`, even though the user is not permitted to call `deletemin` directly. That is, if we try to use `deletemin`, as in

```
deletemin(create);
```
Error: unbound variable or constructor: deletemin

we are told that there is no meaning for the identifier `deletemin`.

Further, since the data constructors `Empty` and `Node` are not mentioned in the signature `NEW_STRING_BST`, we cannot use them outside the structure `NewStringBST`. The following responses may seem surprising:

```
val t = Empty;
```
val t = Empty : exn

```
val t = Node("foo", Empty, Empty);
```
Error: unbound variable or constructor: Node

What has happened is that `Empty` is interpreted as the exception in the top-level environment that is ML's response to erroneous uses of `hd` or `tl`, like `hd(nil: int list)`. However, `Node` has no meaning in the top-level environment, so ML complains about its use.

On the other hand, the type constructor `btree` is exported by the structure `NewStringBST`. We can use it in limited ways, such as

```
type foo = int btree;
```
type foo = int btree

However, there is no way to use the type `foo`, since its data constructors `Empty` and `Node` are not available. □

8.5.3 Abstract Types

An *abstract type* is essentially a datatype that hides its data constructors. We use the keyword `abstype` to define an abstract type with almost the same syntax as we use to define a datatype. However, for the abstract type we must follow it by the keyword `with` to introduce the only functions, variables, exceptions, and types that have access to the data constructors. The form of an abstract type definition is

```
abstype <datatype definition>
     with
              <declarations using the constructors>
     end
```

Example 8.21 : Figure 8.12 shows an abstract type similar to the structure `StringBST` of Fig. 8.5. As in Fig. 8.5, we have used a previously defined function `lt` to compare strings. We have also restricted the datatype to have string labels by not using a type parameter `'label`. Instead, we have embedded the type string into the definition of the abstract type `sbtree`.

```
fun lt(x,y) = ... ;
```
*val lt = fn : string * string → bool*

```
abstype sbtree = Empty |
        Node of string * sbtree * sbtree
    with
        val create = Empty;
        fun lookup(x,T) = ... ;
        fun insert(x,T) = ... ;
        exception EmptyTree;
        fun deletemin(T) = ... ;
        fun delete(x,T) = ... ;
    end;
```
type sbtree
val create = - : sbtree
*val lookup = fn : string * sbtree → bool*
*val insert = fn : string * sbtree → sbtree*
exception EmptyTree
*val deletemin = fn : sbtree → string * sbtree*
*val delete = fn : string * sbtree → sbtree*

Figure 8.12: String binary search trees defined as an abstract type

There is one other difference between Figs. 8.12 and 8.5. We have defined a variable called create, whose value is the empty tree. The reason for doing so is that the data constructors of the abstract type `sbtree` will not be visible to users of `sbtree`. They are only visible between the keywords `with` and `end`. As a result, we shall not be able to start a new binary search tree by setting it to `Empty`. On the other hand, the variables and functions defined between `with` and `end`, such as create and lookup, *are* available to the users of the abstract type `sbtree`. Thus, we can get an empty binary search tree by referring to the variable create.

`local` Versus `let`

Do not confuse the local-in-end form with the let-in-end form. The former has a list of definitions between the **in** and **end**, while the latter has a list of expressions there. For example, a val-declaration may not follow the keyword **in** in a let-expression, while it may in a local-declaration.

For instance, we can write

```
insert("foo",create);
```
val it = – : string btree

to obtain a binary search tree containing the one string `"foo"`. Notice ML does not print the value of tree `Node("foo",Empty,Empty)`, because it would reveal the constructors by so doing. In contrast, when we concealed the data constructors by signature, as in Example 8.20, we could see what those constructors were but not have access to them.

However, should we try to use the data constructors of an abstract type, as in

```
Node("foo",Empty,Empty);
```
Error: unbound variable or constructor: Node

we get the error message as in Example 8.20. □

8.5.4   Local Definitions

We can hide some elements in an abstract type definition or a structure definition by using the construct

```
local
    <definitions>
in
    <definitions>
end
```

The second group of definitions can use the definitions in the first group, but only the second group of definitions is exported; the first group is hidden.

Example 8.22: In Fig. 8.13 we see a revision of Fig. 8.12, in which the definitions of `EmptyTree` and `deletemin` are made local to the definition of `delete`. Notice that `EmptyTree` and `deletemin` do not appear in the ML response to this abstract type definition.

We could also make a similar change to the structure definition for the structure `StringBST` in Fig. 8.5. That is, the definitions of `EmptyTree` and

```
fun lt(x,y) = ... ;
```
*val lt = fn : string * string → bool*

```
abstype sbtree = Empty |
       Node of string * sbtree * sbtree
    with
       val create = Empty;
       fun lookup(x,T) = ... ;
       fun insert(x,T) = ... ;
       local
           exception EmptyTree;
           fun deletemin(T) = ... ;
       in
           fun delete(x,T) = ... ;
       end
    end;
```
type sbtree
val create = - : sbtree
*val lookup = fn : string * sbtree → bool*
*val insert = fn : string * sbtree → sbtree*
*val delete = fn : string * sbtree → sbtree*

Figure 8.13: Hiding the exception `EmptyTree` and the definition of `deletemin`

`deletemin` could be placed in a local-declaration for the function `delete`. If we did, then the signature in the ML response would omit `EmptyTree` and `deletemin`. □

8.5.5 Opaque Signatures

ML97 introduces a way to hide certain components of a structure, even if they are mentioned in its signature. An *opaque* signature is attached to a structure by using the symbol `:>` rather than a single colon. The significance of using `:>` is that types defined abstractly in the signature — that is, by a type name such as `element` in Example 8.11, rather than by a concrete type such as `int` — are not available outside the structure in which those types are used.

To be more precise, when we have an abstract type T in the signature, all variables of type T that belong to the structure, and all functions in the structure that take a value of type T as an argument, may be used outside the structure. However, these are the only variables and functions that may involve type T. Any attempt to use a variable or function with another type S in place of T will fail, even if T was defined in the structure to be the same as type S.

```
open Struct2;
```
open Struct2
val i = 3 : int
val x = 4 : t
val y = 5 : t
*val f = fn : t * t → bool*

```
f(x,y);
```
val it = false : bool

```
f(i,y);
```
val it = false : bool

Figure 8.15: A structure without an opaque signature

```
open Struct3;
```
open Struct3
val i = 3 : int
val x = - : t
val y = - : t
*val f = fn : t * t → bool*

```
f(x,y);
```
val it = false : bool

```
f(i,y);
```
Error: operator and operand don't agree [tycon mismatch]
  *operator domain: t * t*
  *operand: int * t*
  in expression:
   f (i,y)

Figure 8.16: The same structure with an opaque signature

An Application of Opaque Signatures

One way that opaque signatures are important is in creating tokens that cannot be accidentally or intentionally "forged." Following on Example 8.23, suppose that the type t was intended to be a token that is granted by some mechanism to authorized users. The token is later presented and compared with the correct value using the equality-testing function f.

Suppose we are using `Struct3`, which we recall was created from `Struct1` using `SIG1` as an opaque signature, in such a token-managing mechanism. Then suppose a "hacker" gets a copy of the text of `Struct1` and signature `SIG1`, and uses them illicitly to create `Struct2`. The hacker then creates `Struct2.x` and tries to present this x as the x from `Struct3`. That is, the hacker executes

```
Struct3.f(Struct3.x, Struct2.x)
```

The hacker is thwarted, because although both x's are ostensibly of type t and have the value 4, the ML system regards the type t belonging to `Struct3` as distinct from any other type whatsoever, even from another type called t, standing for `int`, and created from the same underlying structure and signature.

---

to be integers, appear only at the leaves. The subtrees of a node preserve order; that is, the labels in the first subtree are less than those of the second subtree, which are less than the labels of the third subtree if it exists. A node with two subtrees has one *separator*, an integer equal to the lowest of the labels of the second subtree. A node with three subtrees has two separators, one giving the lowest label of the second subtree and the other giving the lowest label of the third subtree. Thus, as we search down the tree for a given integer x, the separators tell us which way to go, just as the labels at interior nodes do for a binary search tree. Figure 8.17 suggests the structure of a 2-subtree and a 3-subtree node.

2-3 trees allow fast insertion, deletion, and lookup, just like binary search trees. However, 2-3 trees remain balanced; that is, all leaves remain the same distance from the root if insertion and deletion are performed properly. That balance guarantees time per operation that is proportional to the logarithm of the number of nodes in the tree, while in the worst case, binary-search-tree operations can be linear per operation. In this exercise, we shall deal only with lookup and insertion.

The insertion algorithm is complex. The idea is that if we are to insert x into the tree T rooted at some node N, there are three cases.

1. If N is a leaf, we return a pair of 2-3 trees; one consists of the leaf N and

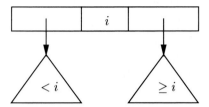

(a) Node with two subtrees.

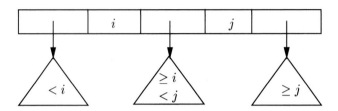

(b) Node with three subtrees.

Figure 8.17: Nodes of a 2-3 tree

the other consists of a leaf with label x. We shall call this form of return value a *pair*.

2. If N has two subtrees, use the separator to tell where x should be inserted and recursively insert x into that subtree. The value returned is either a pair of trees or a single tree. If it is a single tree, that tree replaces the subtree into which the insertion was made. If the result is a pair, those trees become subtrees of N, which now is a 3-subtree node. Adjust the separators appropriately. Note that in order to have the proper separators, when a pair of trees is returned a third component must be returned as well to separate the two trees.

3. If N has three subtrees, use the separators to tell into which subtree x must go, and recursively insert x there. If a single tree is returned, substitute it as in case (2). However, if a pair is returned, N now has four subtrees. Split them into two groups of two subtrees, and split N into two nodes that become the roots of two new trees. Then return the resulting pair of trees. The situation is suggested by Fig. 8.18, where we assume the insertion has been in the middle subtree.

If at the root a pair is returned, create a new root with these trees as subtrees. For a more detailed explanation of how 2-3 trees work, see A. V. Aho,

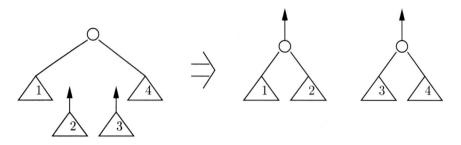

Figure 8.18: Splitting a 3-subtree node into two 2-subtree nodes

J. E. Hopcroft, and J. D. Ullman, *Data Structures and Algorithms*, Addison-Wesley, Reading MA, 1983.

In this exercise, you are asked to write a structure that supports the operations of `create` (create a tree consisting of one leaf with a given integer label), `lookup`, and `insert` on 2-3 trees. We shall not deal with deletion here. Start with a datatype having no parameters and three data constructors, for leaves, 2-subtree nodes, and 3-subtree nodes. Note the labels of leaves are integers, so there is no need for type parameters in this datatype. Next, create a datatype that wraps either a single tree in data constructor `S` or wraps a pair of trees and an integer separator in the data constructor `P`. You will need a number of auxiliary functions including, but not limited to, a function we shall call `insert1`. This function takes an integer x to be inserted and a tree T into which the insertion occurs and returns a wrapped tree (in `S`) or a wrapped pair of trees (in `P`). Consult the solutions if you cannot write this code, since it is necessary for the exercises that follow.

Exercise 8.5.2: Write a signature that will not allow the functions other than `create`, `lookup`, and `insert` to be available through your 2-3-tree structure of Exercise 8.5.1. Then, create a new structure that will offer the user 2-3 trees with only these three functions available.

Exercise 8.5.3: Accomplish the same goal as Exercise 8.5.2 without a new signature by making auxiliary functions local.

Exercise 8.5.4: Show how to make the data constructors of the datatypes used in your solution to Exercise 8.5.1 unavailable by using an abstract type.

! **Exercise 8.5.5:** Specify a structure `Hash` similar to the result structure for the functor `MakeHash` of Exercise 8.3.3. However, your structure should incorporate the elements of the hash table designed in Fig. 7.9 and work for elements that are strings. Your structure will need:

1. The number of buckets, b,

2. The hash function h defined as in Fig. 7.9,

3. The functions `lookupBucket`, `lookup`, `insertBucket`, `insert`, `delete-Bucket`, and `delete`, as in Fig. 7.9,

4. A function `create()` that returns an empty hash table.

* a) Which of the above elements is it appropriate to make available to users of the structure `Hash`?

* b) Show how to hide the inappropriate elements [as determined in part (a)] by using a signature.

c) Show how to hide the inappropriate elements by using local definitions.

8.6   Case Study: Feedback Shift Registers

A simple way to generate a sequence of random bits is to use a *feedback shift register* with a well selected feedback function. We may think of a feedback shift register as in Fig. 8.19. There is a sequence of n "cells," wherein bits are kept. In Fig. 8.19, $n = 4$, and the current sequence of bits is 1000.

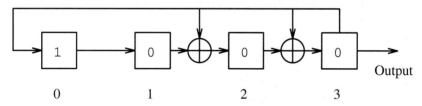

Figure 8.19: A small feedback shift register

8.6.1   Operation of a Feedback Shift Register

In one step of operation, we do the following:

1. Output the bit in the rightmost $(n-1\text{st})$ cell. Let us call this bit f; it is both the output bit and the *feedback bit*.

2. Shift all the bits right one position, so what was in cell i moves to cell $i+1$ for $i = 0, 1, \ldots, n-2$.

3. Put the bit 0 in cell 0.

4. If $f = 0$, do nothing else. However, if $f = 1$, then complement those cells to which the output is "fed back." In Fig. 8.19 we indicate feedback to cell 0 by the line running from the output to cell 0. We also indicate feedback to cells 2 and 3 with the lines running to a "sum-mod-2 gate" (the circle and plus) from the output. A sum-mod-2 gate has the effect of complementing the bit being shifted right from the previous cell if $f = 1$ and it has no effect if $f = 0$. There is no feedback to cell 1 in Fig. 8.19.

Example 8.24: Let us trace the contents of the four cells of Fig. 8.19 for several cycles of operation. The contents of the four cells for the first seven cycles is shown in Fig. 8.20. When the contents are 1000, the output and feedback bit f is 0. Thus, we just shift everything right and bring in a 0 at the left end. That gives us the second line 0100. The same argument explains the next two lines 0010 and 0001.

Round	Cell 0	Cell 1	Cell 2	Cell 3
1)	1	0	0	0
2)	0	1	0	0
3)	0	0	1	0
4)	0	0	0	1
5)	1	0	1	1
6)	1	1	1	0
7)	0	1	1	1

Figure 8.20: Operating the feedback shift register of Fig. 8.19

At line (4), the output bit is 1, and we must apply the feedback function. We shift right to get 0000, and then complement the first, third, and fourth bits. That gives us 1011 as in line (5) of Fig. 8.20. To get line (6), we observe that the feedback bit is again 1. We shift line (5) right and bring in a 0, giving us 0101. We must again complement the first, third, and fourth positions, giving us 1110, as in line (6).

Line (7) is obtained by shifting line (6) right, as the feedback bit in line (6) is 0. When we work on line (7), we first shift to get 0011 and then complement positions one, three, and four to get 1000. Since this is the same as line (1), the feedback shift register has cycled. It will repeat the cell contents of Fig. 8.20 forever, and it will output the rightmost column of that figure, 0001101 repeatedly.

This sequence of bits is not very "random," but it is close to the best we can expect with a tiny shift register of four cells. In principle, we might hope that an n-cell shift register would run through $2^n - 1$ different contents before looping back on itself.[3] In this example, we find that in addition to the loop of length seven shown in Fig. 8.20, there are two loops of length one — 0000 and 1101 — and another loop of length seven. Unless we start with one of the two self-looping bit vectors, we get almost as long a sequence as we could possibly expect. More to the point, if we pick a larger shift register, say of size 32, we are likely to get loops whose length is in the millions or billions before repetition, and the sequence of output bits will look very "random." □

---

[3] It cannot run through all 2^n possible contents, because all-0's always loops back to itself.

8.6.2   A Functor to Create Random Number Generators

We shall write a functor that takes a description of a feedback shift register and produces from it a structure that implements this feedback shift register. The structure will actually offer only two functions:

1. `init`, which initializes the feedback shift register to have all 0's except for a 1 in the rightmost bit.

2. `genBit`, which produces the next random bit, performing one cycle of the shift register as it does so.

In Fig. 8.21 we see a signature that describes what we need to specify a feedback shift register. We need:

1. An integer `n`, the number of cells in the shift register.

2. A list of integers called `feed`. This list indicates the positions that get complemented when the feedback bit is `1`. It is desirable that this list include position 0, the leftmost position, because otherwise we shall always have 0 in that position after the first cycle.

For instance, the feedback shift register of Fig. 8.19 would be described by $n = 4$ and the list `feed = [0,2,3]`.

```
signature RANDOM_DATA = sig
    val n : int;
    val feed : int list;
end;
```

Figure 8.21: The signature for structures that describe feedback shift registers

Figure 8.22 begins the definition of the functor `MakeRandom`. It takes a structure parameter `Data`, whose signature is `RANDOM_DATA` of Fig. 8.21. That is, `Data` will provide n and the feedback positions.

We have attached to the functor a signature, lines (2) and (3), that specifies the two functions `init` and `getBit` that are exported by any structure generated by the functor. Note that this strategy follows the idea outlined in Section 8.5.2: using a signature to hide elements that we do not want exported. However, here we have attached the restricting signature to the functor, so *every* structure it generates will have the restriction. In contrast, in Example 8.20 we restricted only one structure by applying a restrictive signature when we generated structure `NewStringBST`.

In line (4) we open the input structure `Data`, and in line (5) we open the structure `Array`, which we'll need for the functions in the output structure.

```
(1) functor MakeRandom(Data: RANDOM_DATA):
        sig
(2)         val init: unit -> unit;
(3)         val getBit: unit -> int;
        end
    =
    struct
(4)     open Data;
(5)     open Array;

(6)     val register = array(n,0);

(7)     fun feedback1(nil) = ()
(8)       | feedback1(x::xs) =
            (
(9)             update(register,x,1-sub(register,x));
(10)            feedback1(xs)
            );

(11)    fun feedback() = feedback1(feed);

(12)    fun shift1(0) = update(register,0,0)
(13)      | shift1(i) =
            (
(14)            update(register,i,sub(register,i-1));
(15)            shift1(i-1)
            );

(16)    fun shift() = shift1(n-1);
```

Figure 8.22: The functor MakeRandom (beginning)

Line (6) defines an array called `register` that represents the n cells of the feedback shift register in its own n cells.

Lines (7) through (11) define the function `feedback`, which complements certain cells of the array `register` according to the list of positions given by the list `feed`. Recall `feed` is an element of the input structure `Data`. The work is actually done by the function `feedback1` of lines (7) through (10). This function takes an arbitrary list of integers and complements each position on the list. Observe especially line (9), where we take the head element x on the list, find the bit in cell x of `register` with `sub(register,x)`, compute the complement of that bit by subtracting it from 1, and then update cell x of `register` with the complemented bit as value.

- Notice that the type of `feedback` is `unit -> unit`. The `()` as argument to `feedback` in its definition on line (11) is the unit, not an absence of parameters. Function `feedback` returns a unit because `feedback1` does so.

Lines (12) through (16) define function `shift`, whose job is to shift the array `register` one position right. The work is done by the recursive function `shift1`, which not only shifts the bits but sets `register[0]` to 0 as the basis case on line (12).

The functor definition continues in Fig. 8.23. Lines (17) through (23) give us the function `init`, whose work is done primarily by function `init1`. The latter function counts down, and in the recursive part of lines (20) through (22) puts 0 in one cell and then calls itself recursively on the cell with the next lower number. In the basis of lines (18) and (19), `init1` puts 1 in the highest-numbered cell $(n-1)$ and 0 in the lowest-numbered cell (0), to end the initialization. The call of `init1` by `init` at line (23) puts 0's in all cells from $n-2$ down and 1 in cell $n-1$. Thus, the initial contents of the shift register is always $00\ldots01$.

Function `getBit` of lines (24) through (28) implements the basic cycle of the shift register. It stores the feedback bit in variable `bit` at line (25). Then, `shift` is called at line (26) to shift the register one position right. Line (27) tests whether the feedback bit is 1. If so, a call to `feedback` complements all the positions on the list `feed`, and if not, then nothing is done. Finally, line (28) makes the return value for `getBit` be the feedback bit, which is also the output bit.

8.6.3 Generating a Feedback Shift Register

Figure 8.24 gives an example of how functor `MakeRandom` could be used. In lines (1) through (3) appears the definition of a structure `MyData` that can be input to the functor, since it conforms to the signature `RANDOM_DATA`. Line (2) says that the shift register has length 20, and line (3) gives the positions for feedback.

```
(17)      fun init1(0) =
             (
(18)               update(register,n-1,1);
(19)               update(register,0,0)
             )
(20)      |   init1(i) =
             (
(21)               update(register,i,0);
(22)               init1(i-1)
             );


(23)      fun init() = init1(n-2);


(24)      fun getBit() =
             let
(25)               val bit = sub(register,n-1);
             in
                (
(26)                  shift();
(27)                  if bit=1 then feedback() else ();
(28)                  bit
                )
             end;
      end;
```

Figure 8.23: The functor `MakeRandom` (continues Fig. 8.22)

Line (4) applies the functor to the structure `MyData`. The result is a structure `Random` that implements this particular feedback shift register. Because all structures generated by `MakeRandom` have the limited signature of lines (2) and (3) of Fig. 8.22, the only functions we get when we open `Random` on line (5) of Fig. 8.24 are `init` and `getBit`. Those are all we need, however, to write the functions we want.

In lines (6) through (10) we see function `random1(i)`, which generates i random bits. The basis, line (6) says that if $i = 0$, just print a newline character. In the inductive part, we check at line (8) if i is a multiple of 72, and if so, print a newline. This step is not necessary, but it is convenient if we want to view the output, which otherwise would come out as a single enormous line. Line (9) calls `getBit`, which executes one round of the feedback shift register's operation and also returns the output bit. This bit is printed, and the recursion occurs at line (10), where $i - 1$ more bits are generated and printed.

Lines (11) through (13) define the "real" function `random(i)`, which calls `init` to initialize the shift register and then calls `random1(i)` to generate i

```
(1)  structure MyData: RANDOM_DATA = struct
(2)      val n = 20;
(3)      val feed = [0,2,4,6,7,14,17,19];
     end;

(4)  structure Random = MakeRandom(MyData);

(5)  open Random;

(6)  fun random1(0) = print("\n")
(7)  |   random1(i) =
         (
(8)          if i mod 72 = 0 then print("\n") else ();
(9)          print(Int.toString(getBit()));
(10)         random1(i-1)
         );

(11) fun random(i) =
         (
(12)         init();
(13)         random1(i)
         );

(14) random(1000);
```

Figure 8.24: Generating and using a random bit generator

random bits. In line (14) we see a call to `random(1000)`, which will cause 1000 random bits to be generated.

8.6.4   Exercises for Section 8.6

Exercise 8.6.1: Find all the cycles of contents of the four cells that a feedback shift register with four cells ($n = 4$) can enter, if the list `feed` of feedback positions is:

* a) [0,1,3].

   b) [0,1].

   c) [0,1,2].

   d) [0,1,2,3].

Exercise 8.6.2: Rewrite the functor `MakeRandom` so it only exports the function `random(i)`, as described in Fig. 8.24.

Exercise 8.6.3: Rewrite the functor `MakeRandom` so that it may be initialized to any desired contents of the cells, instead of only to $00\ldots01$.

Chapter 9

Summary of the ML Standard Basis

As we illustrated in Fig. 4.3, all the features of ML are grouped into structures, and these structures form the *standard basis*. Some of these features are present in the *top-level environment* and some need to be accessed through their structure, either by giving their long name (including the structure) or by opening the structure. We have seen almost all of the types, datatypes, exceptions, operators, and functions in the top-level environment. In this section, we shall review them, fill in the few that have not been covered elsewhere, and discuss a few unifying issues such as the way precedence and associativity of operators are controlled.

We then look at the entire standard basis. A description of the contents of each of the required structures and the optional ones (structures that may or may not be included in a given ML implementation) could fill a book by itself. Fortunately, book-sized, on-line documentation for the standard basis exists and is available on the web or by anonymous ftp (see Section 1.4 for directions on how to get this material). Therefore, in this chapter we shall only give highlights and an overview of what is available should you need these features.

We then close with a summary of the syntax of the ML97 language. The principal syntactic categories are represented graphically by a collection of syntax diagrams.

9.1   The Infix Operators

Functions like + that are used as *binary* (two-argument) *infix* (between-the-operands) operators in arithmetic expressions are a staple of almost every programming language, and ML is not an exception. The binary-infix style of expressions is useful because there are familiar conventions, embodied in associativity and precedence rules, that allow us to group operands to their operators, with relatively few parentheses needed to force grouping.

In this section, we review the infix operators of the top-level environment. ML also allows us to extend the power of infix notation to operators that we define as functions and to data constructors of a datatype. Likewise, built-in two-argument functions of the standard basis may be made infix if we like. Additionally, we can change the grouping strategy for existing operators, and we can turn infix operators back into ordinary functions. This section discusses the mechanisms for doing so.

9.1.1   Precedence

It is conventional to give infix operators a *precedence*, which is an integer associated with that operator. When we group operands to operators, we group the higher-precedence operators first. To *group* an occurrence of an operator to its operands, we look to the immediate right of the operator. We then find the shortest sequence of operators, operands, and parentheses that form an expression with balanced parentheses; this sequence is the *right operand*. Looking to the immediate left of the operator we find the *left operand*, which is the shortest sequence of symbols on the left that constitutes a well-formed expression. These left and right operands are grouped with the operator occurrence by placing a left parenthesis just before the left operand begins and placing a right parenthesis just after the right operand ends.

Example 9.1 : Consider the expression $a + b - c$. If we choose to group the $+$ first, we look to the right and find the symbol b, which is an expression by itself. Thus we need go no further; b is the right operand. Similarly, looking to the left of the $+$ we find that a is the shortest well-formed expression and thus constitutes the left operand. We group the operands of the $+$ by rewriting the expression as $(a + b) - c$.

Now, let us group the operands of the $-$ operator. The right operand is c. Looking left, we first find a right parenthesis. We must go as far left as the matching left parenthesis, and we therefore identify $(a + b)$ as the left operand. The grouping for $-$ thus gives us the fully parenthesized expression $\big((a+b)-c\big)$. □

The order in which we choose to group an operator occurrence to its operands usually affects the value of the expression, so we must know the proper order to do the grouping. One important convention is that of operator precedence. We assign to each binary infix operator a precedence, and we group the operator occurrences in order of their precedence, highest first. Each language has its own policy regarding precedence of operators, but they tend to be fairly similar. Multiplicative operators such as `*` and `/` have higher precedence than the additive operators `+` and `-`. These arithmetic operators have higher precedence than the comparison operators like `<=`, and the comparison operators have higher precedence than the logical connectives like `andalso`.

9.1.2 Precedence Levels in ML

Figure 9.1 gives the precedence levels of the infix operators. Precedence levels are represented by nonnegative integers. The operators are positioned as shown, with nothing at levels 1 and 2. Since it is possible for the user to define new operators, levels 1 and 2 can be populated, as can levels above 7. We may also add new operators at the levels 0 or 3 through 7.

PRECEDENCE	OPERATOR	SECTION	COMMENTS
0	`before`		Second argument executed only for side-effects
3	`o`	5.6.2	Function composition
	`:=`	7.3.3	Assignment for `ref` values
4	`=, <>, <,` `>, <=, >=`	2.1.4	Comparison operators
5	`::, @`	2.4.4	Concatenation and cons for lists
6	`+, -`	2.1.2	Additive operators
	`^`	2.1.3	String concatenation
7	`*, /,` `div, mod`	2.1.2	Multiplicative operators

Figure 9.1: Precedence of binary infix operators

We have seen all of the operators in Fig. 9.1 except for the `before` operator. This operator evaluates its left argument, then its right argument, but it returns the value of its *left* argument. Thus, the right argument is executed only for side effects.

Example 9.2 :

```
fun f(x) = x before print("hello world\n");
```
val f = fn : 'a → 'a

```
f(1);
```
hello world
val it = 1 : int

Notice that while the second argument of `before` is executed during evaluation of expression `f(1)`, resulting in the printing of "hello world," the value returned by `f(1)` is not the unit, as it would be if f just printed the message. Rather, the value returned by `f(1)` is the left argument of `before`, which is x, or 1 in this case. □

Complicating matters is the fact that not all the symbols we think of as binary infix operators are represented by the "main sequence" of precedences represented by Fig. 9.1. The complete story appears in Fig. 9.13. If we look ahead to Section 9.6.3, we find that the keywords `andalso` and `orelse`[1] are deemed to have precedence below that of any operator on the main sequence, with `andalso` having higher precedence than `orelse`. In effect, we can think of `andalso` as having precedence -1 and `orelse` as having precedence -2.

In addition, we see in Fig. 9.13 that the operation of applying a function to its argument, which is represented by juxtaposition of expressions, has higher precedence than any on the main sequence. It is as if function application had infinite precedence.

9.1.3   Associativity of Operators

Precedence is only one of the two ways that order of evaluation is controlled. We normally group operators of equal precedence from the left; such operators are said to be *left-associative*. It is also possible to have operators group from the right; these operators are *right-associative*.

Example 9.3 : In Fig. 9.1 all the operators are left-associative except for `::` and `@`, which are right-associative. Thus $3 - 4 - 5$ is grouped from the left as $(3-4)-5$. Its value is -6 rather than 4, as would be the case if we incorrectly grouped from the right as $3 - (4 - 5)$.

On the other hand, `a::b::cs` groups from the right as `a::(b::cs)`. Thus this expression makes sense if `a` and `b` are elements of some type T and `cs` is a list of elements of type T, as we have conventionally assumed. If we were to group from the left as `(a::b)::cs`, we would have to interpret `a` as an element of some type T, `b` as a list of elements of type T, and `cs` as a list of lists of elements of type T.

There is another example of a right-associative operator from the type expressions of ML. The operator `->`, which constructs function types, is right-associative. Thus $T \rightarrow S \rightarrow R$ is interpreted as $T \rightarrow (S \rightarrow R)$, that is, a function whose domain type is T and whose range type is the set of functions from type S to type R.   □

9.1.4   Creating New Infix Operators

We can define any function, data constructor, or exception constructor to be an infix operator by using the statement

`infix` <level> <identifier list>

Here <level> is the precedence level, a nonnegative integer. The operator or operators being defined to have this precedence form the <identifier list>.

---

[1]Which technically are not "operators," because they may not evaluate both of their operands.

These operators will be left-associative. Of course, each function or constructor
so declared must be binary; that is, it must have two arguments. Some useful
points about infix declarations are:

- If we wish an operator or operators to be right-associative, we use the
  keyword `infixr` in place of `infix`.

- We may omit the <level> from the declaration, in which case the precedence level is taken to be 0.

- To remove the infix property from an identifier or identifiers, use the
  keyword `nonfix` followed by the list of identifiers we wish to turn back
  into ordinary identifiers.

- It is also possible to turn an identifier *temporarily* into a nonfix function
  name by preceding it by the keyword `op`, as discussed in Section 5.4.4.

Example 9.4: Suppose we define the function `comb` in our conventional way
as in Fig. 3.6. We can then declare it to be a left-associative infix operator by

```
infix 2 comb;
```
infix 2 comb

We have given `comb` precedence level 2, so its arguments are grouped after any
of the usual arithmetic operators. For instance:

```
5 comb 2 comb 4;
```
val it = 210 : int

This expression is grouped as (`5 comb 2`) `comb 4`, or

$$\binom{\binom{5}{2}}{4}$$

Since $\binom{5}{2} = 10$ and $\binom{10}{4} = 210$, we see that the correct result is computed.

The identifier `comb` no longer has its normal syntax as a function. If we try
to use it that way, we get an error message:

```
comb(5,2);
```
Error: expression or pattern begins with infix identifier "comb"

If we wish to turn `comb` back into such an identifier, we may declare

```
nonfix comb;
```
nonfix comb

Alternatively, we could leave `comb` as an infix operator, but use it once as a function by writing `op comb(5,2)`.

The infix operator `comb` can also be used with other infix operators. For instance

```
5 comb 2 comb 2 + 2;
```
val it = 210 : int

Notice that `+`, with precedence 6, takes precedence over `comb`, with precedence 2, so the subexpression $2 + 2$ is grouped first.

However, functions that are not defined to be infix apply to their operators before binary infix operators are applied. For example, suppose we define the function `square` to apply to integers:

```
fun square(x) = x*x;
```
val square = fn : int → int

Then we could write an expression like

```
square 2 comb 2 comb 4;
```
val it = 15 : int

The use of `square` is grouped with its operand first, so this expression is interpreted as

$$\left(\binom{\binom{2^2}{2}}{4} \right) = \left(\binom{\binom{4}{2}}{4} \right) = \binom{6}{4}$$

or 15.   □

Example 9.5 : We can also make built-in functions become infix operators if they take two arguments. For example, if we have opened the structure `Array`, then

```
infix 3 sub;
```
infix 3 sub

declares the `sub(A,i)` function from the structure `Array` to be a left-associative, infix operator. Then we can write the more natural `A sub i` in place of `sub(A,i)`. As another example, line (20) of Fig. 7.13, which is the program to upper-triangulate a matrix, could then be written

```
val ratio = (M sub !j sub !i)/(M sub !i sub !i);
```

instead of the original

```
val ratio = sub(sub(M,!j),!i)/sub(sub(M,!i),!i);
```

The left-associativity of `sub` gives this expression the correct interpretation.

Because we have defined the precedence level of `sub` to be 3, which is lower than that of the arithmetic operators, we get a specific behavior of expressions that involve `sub`. For example, `A sub i+1` is grouped as `A sub (i+1)`. If we would prefer to have such an expression grouped as `(A sub i)+1`, then we need to give `sub` a high precedence, such as 8 or 9. □

9.1.5 Infix Data Constructors

If in the definition of a datatype we use a data constructor that takes two arguments, we may declare this constructor to be an infix operator and write instances of the datatype in a form similar to arithmetic expressions.

Example 9.6: In Fig. 9.2 we see a variant of the binary tree that we discussed in Section 6.3. Here, only leaves have labels. The definition of datatype `btree` is in lines (1) and (2). In line (1) the data constructor `T` is defined; it has two arguments, both of which are binary trees. This data constructor is used for interior nodes. Line (2) has the data constructor `Leaf`, which takes a label of the arbitrary type `'a`.

In line (3), we define data constructor `T` to be a binary infix operator of low precedence. Thus, although `Leaf` will still precede its argument, the constructor `T` will be placed between the left and right subtrees that form the tree it constructs.

Lines (4) through (10) describe a function `printTree` that prints the leaves of a binary tree, from left to right. This function requires that the labels be of type integer. Line (4) handles the basis case where the tree is a leaf; we simply print the label. Line (5) covers the case of a tree constructed by `T`. Note that the pattern on line (5) shows `T` between its operands, as it must be. In lines (6) through (10) we call `printTree` recursively on the left and right subtrees. A comma is placed between the results at line (8) and the entire output is surrounded by parentheses on lines (6) and (10).

Line (11) creates a value of type `int btree`. Since constructor `T` associates from the left, the value of identifier `t` represents the tree shown in Fig. 9.3 On line (12) we print the leaves of this tree from the left. They appear with the proper parentheses to suggest the structure of the tree. Since for simplicity we have not printed a newline after the complete tree, the response of ML giving the value of `it` appears on the same line.

A more complicated example of a tree is shown in lines (13) and (14). Here parentheses are used to guide the order of grouping for the various occurrences of constructor `T`. This grouping is reflected in the output on line (14). The grouping of leaves 2 and 3 is implicit in the left-associativity of `T`. □

```
(1) datatype 'a btree = T of 'a btree * 'a btree |
(2)      Leaf of 'a;
```
   *datatype 'a btree = Leaf of 'a | T of 'a btree * 'a btree*


```
(3) infix 2 T;
```
   infix 2 T


```
(4) fun printTree(Leaf(x)) = print(Int.toString(x))
(5)  |   printTree(t1 T t2) =
             (
(6)              print("(");
(7)              printTree(t1);
(8)              print(",");
(9)              printTree(t2);
(10)             print(")")
             );
```
   val printTree = fn : int btree → unit


```
(11) val t = Leaf(1) T Leaf(2) T Leaf(3);
```
   val t = Leaf 1 T Leaf 2 T Leaf 3 : int btree


```
(12) printTree(t);
```
   ((1,2),3)val it = () : unit


```
(13) val t =
         Leaf(1) T (Leaf(2) T Leaf(3) T (Leaf(4) T Leaf(5)));
```
   val t = Leaf 1 T (Leaf 2 T Leaf 3 T (Leaf 4 T Leaf 5)) : int btree


```
(14) printTree(t);
```
   (1,((2,3),(4,5)))val it = () : unit

Figure 9.2: An infix tree-construction operator

Figure 9.3: The binary tree defined on line (11) of Fig. 9.2

9.1.6 Exercises for Section 9.1

Exercise 9.1.1: If we instead define `infixr 3 T` at line (3) of Fig. 9.2, would the interpretation change for

* a) Line (11)?

 b) Line (13)?

! **Exercise 9.1.2:** Suggest a way to redefine the precedence and/or associativity of + and * so that

* a) $a+b*c$ is interpreted as $(a+b)*c$, and $a*b+c$ is interpreted as $(a*b)+c$.

 b) $a+b*c+d$ is interpreted as $a + \big((b*c)+d\big)$.

* **Exercise 9.1.3:** Figure 3.27 gave three functions that operated on polynomials: `padd` (polynomial addition), `smult` (multiplication of a scalar by a polynomial), and `pmult` (multiplications of polynomials). Each is a function of two parameters, so we can make them be infix operators.

 a) Suggest a way to define these operators so that

 1. `pmult` takes precedence over `padd`.
 2. `smult` takes precedence over `pmult`.
 3. All three are left-associative.
 4. The arithmetic operators on reals take precedence over the polynomial operators. For example, `2.0 + 3.0 smult P` is interpreted as $(2+3)P$ rather than an erroneous attempt to add 2 to the polynomial $3P$.

 b) Show how to write the expression $(P+2Q) \times R$, where P is the polynomial $3x^4 + 5x^2 - 6$, $Q = x^3 + 2x^2 - 3x + 4$, and $R = x + 1$, using the infix operators and using parentheses only when necessary.

Exercise 9.1.4: Repeat Exercise 9.1.3 but require that all operators be right-associative and that polynomial operators take precedence over arithmetic operators.

Exercise 9.1.5: For the binary tree datatype of Fig. 9.2, write a function that

* a) Sums the labels of the leaves of a tree, assuming labels are reals.

! b) Sums the labels of those leaves that have a leaf for a *sibling*. Siblings are
     nodes that have the same parent.

Exercise 9.1.6: Let E_1 and E_2 be ML expressions. Explain the difference
between E_1 `before` E_2 and $(E_1;\ E_2)$.

9.2   Functions in the Top-Level Environment

In this section we shall review the functions available in the top-level environment. Most of these functions have been seen before, and those that were
not will be introduced briefly here. Note that the infix operators discussed in
Section 9.1.2 are also functions available at the top level.

9.2.1   Functions on Integers

In addition to the infix comparison and arithmetic operators on integers discussed in Section 9.1.2, the top level provides the following unary operators:

1. The negation operator ˜.

2. The absolute-value operator `abs`. For instance, `abs` ˜3 equals 3.

3. The operator `real`, which converts an integer to an equivalent real; see
   Section 2.2.2.

4. The operator `chr`, which converts an integer to the character with that
   integer as its ASCII code; see Section 2.2.3.

9.2.2   Functions on Reals

In addition to the infix comparison and arithmetic operators, which work for
reals as well as integers, there are the following top-level functions that we may
apply to reals:

1. The functions ˜ and `abs`, which we mentioned in Section 9.2.1 for integers,
   apply to reals as well.

2. The functions `floor`, `ceil`, `trunc`, and `round`, which we discussed in
   Section 2.2.2, convert real numbers to approximately equivalent integers
   in various ways.

9.2.3 Functions on Booleans

In addition to the connectives `andalso` and `orelse`, which we discussed in Section 9.1.2, the ML top-level environment provides the unary operator `not`. Recall that `andalso` and `orelse` are really shorthands for case expressions, as discussed in Exercise 5.1.4. Thus, these keywords are essentially the equivalent of functions on booleans. All three functions were covered in Section 2.1.5.

9.2.4 Functions on Characters

The top level of ML's environment offers the following operators on characters:

1. The function `ord` converts a character to its integer, ASCII code; see Section 2.2.3.

2. The function `str` converts a character to a string of length 1 consisting of that one character; see Section 2.2.4.

3. The function `implode` converts a list of characters to a string containing those characters, in order; see Section 2.4.5.

9.2.5 Functions on Strings

In addition to the operator `^` for concatenating strings, which we covered in Section 9.1.2, the top-level environment has the following functions on strings:

1. Function `print` prints the value of a string; see Section 4.1.1.

2. The function `explode` takes a string and returns a list of the characters in the positions of that string; see Section 2.4.5.

3. The function `concat` takes a list of strings and produces the one string that is the concatenation of all these strings; see Section 2.4.5.

4. The function `size(s)` returns the integer that is the length of string s. For instance:

   ```
   size "abc";
   val it = 3 : int
   ```

5. If s is a string, and i and j are integers, then `substring(s,i,j)` is the string of length j formed by taking the j positions of s starting at position i. Note that positions of a string are numbered beginning at 0, not 1. Thus:

   ```
   substring("abcdefg", 2, 3);
   val it = "cde" ; string
   ```

This use of `substring` asks for the 3 positions starting at position 2. Notice that `a` is in position 0, `b` in position 1, and `c` in position 2.

9.2.6   Functions on Options

We introduced in Section 4.2.5 the type constructor `option`. Recall that if T is a type, then the type T `option` has values `NONE` and `SOME` v, where v is a value of type T. The top-level environment has the following three operators on options, the first two of which we illustrated in Section 4.2.5.

1. Function `isSome` returns `true` if its argument is of the form `SOME` v and returns `false` otherwise.

2. Function `valOf` returns v if applied to `SOME` v. When applied to `NONE`, it raises the exception `Option`.

3. Function `getOpt` takes a pair of arguments. The first argument is of type T `option` for some type T, and the second is of that type T. If the first argument is of the form `SOME` v, then v is returned. If the first argument is `NONE`, then the second argument is returned. For instance:

   > ```
   > getOpt(SOME 3, 4);
   > ```
   > *val it = 3 : int*

   > ```
   > getOpt(NONE, 4);
   > ```
   > *vat it = 4 : int*

   In each case, the arguments are an integer-option and an integer. In the first use of `getOpt`, the presence of `SOME` in the first argument causes the integer inside the option to be used as the result. In the second case, the presence of `NONE` makes the second argument be the result.

9.2.7   Functions on References

There are also three operators involving references in the top-level environment. We met each of them in Section 7.3. One is the assignment operator `:=`, from Section 7.3.3. Since it is an infix operator, we also mentioned it in Section 9.1.2. The other two are:

1. Function `ref` takes a value v and produces a reference to v; see Section 7.3.1.

2. Function `!` takes a reference to a value v and returns v; see Section 7.3.2.

9.2.8   Functions on Lists

The infix operators `::` and `@` on lists were mentioned in Section 9.1.2. The functions `concat`, `implode`, and `explode`, mentioned in Sections 9.2.4 and 9.2.5 are also functions that involve lists. The additional functions on lists found in the top-level environment are:

1. Functions `hd` and `tl` return the head and tail of a list; see Section 2.4.4.

2. Function `null` returns `true` when applied to an empty list and returns false if applied to any other list.

3. Function `length` returns the length of a list. For instance:

    ```
    length ["a", "b"];
    ```
    val it = 2 : int

4. Function `rev` returns the reverse of a list. For instance:

    ```
    rev [1,2,3];
    ```
    val it = [3,2,1] : int list

5. Function `map` takes a function as argument and returns a function that applies the same function to every element of a list. We discussed `map` in Section 5.6.3.

6. Functions `foldr` and `foldl` "fold" the elements of a list in the sense discussed in Section 5.6.4.

7. Function `app` takes a function f whose range type is `unit` and produces a function that applies f to every element of a list. Thus, `app` is similar to `map`, but specialized to a function that returns a unit. Also, the function on lists produced by `app` itself produces a `unit` rather than a list of some type. For instance,

    ```
    val printList = app print;
    ```

    makes `printList` a function that takes a list of strings and prints each one.

8. Function `vector` takes a list and produces a "vector" of the elements. We shall discuss vectors in Section 9.4.9. Roughly, vectors are arrays that cannot be updated (often called *immutable* arrays). Vectors are represented like lists, but with a `#` prefix. For instance:

    ```
    vector [1,2,3];
    ```
    val it = #[1,2,3] : int vector

9.2.9   Functions on Exceptions

There are two functions in the top-level environment that take exceptions as arguments. Neither has been discussed previously.

1. Function `exnName` applies to an exception and returns a string that is the name of that exception. Usually, the name returned is the exception constructor itself. However, since one exception can become the value of another, the name returned could be different.

2. Function `exnMessage` applies to an exception and returns, as a string, the message that the system will produce if that exception is not handled by the program. This message is implementation dependent.

```
(1)  exception Foo of string;
```
exception Foo of string

```
(2)  exnName(Foo "bar");
```
val it = "Foo" : string

```
(3)  exnMessage(Foo "bar");
```
val it = "Foo" : string

```
(4)  val Foo1 = Foo;
```
val Foo1 = fn : string → exn

```
(5)  exnName(Foo1 "bar");
```
val it = "Foo" : string

Figure 9.4: Exception names and messages

Example 9.7 : In Fig. 9.4 are some exception declarations and uses of the functions `exnName` and `exnMessage`. Line (1) shows the declaration of an exception Foo that takes a string argument. At line (2) we apply `exnName` to this exception with a string argument `"bar"`. The name of the exception is identified as `"Foo"`; the string argument `"bar"` is not part of the name.

Line (3) shows that the message associated with the user-defined exception Foo in the SML/NJ implementation is also `"Foo"`. The string argument `"bar"` is not considered part of the message in this implementation. Then, at line (4) we define Foo1 to be equal to the exception Foo. The response characterizes

Foo1 as a function from strings to exceptions, which incidentally is exactly the type assigned to Foo. When we ask for the name of Foo1("bar") at line (5), SML/NJ gives us the original name Foo. □

9.2.10 Functions Affecting Return Values

There are two operators whose job is to change the expected type of the return value. We mentioned one of them in Section 9.1.2, the infix operator before. Recall that before causes both arguments to be evaluated, but the value of the entire expression is the value of the left argument rather than the right.

The second operator is ignore. Applied to any expression, the result is the unit. Of course, side effects in the expression still have their effect.

```
(1) fun inc(x) = (
(2)          x := !x + 1;
(3)          !x
        );
    val inc = fn : int ref → int


(4) val i = ref 1;
    val i = ref 1 : int ref


(5) ignore(inc(i));
    val it = () : unit


(6) inc(i);
    val it = 3 : int
```

Figure 9.5: Ignoring a function changes its return value to ()

Example 9.8: Figure 9.5 shows a function inc in lines (1) through (3) that increments an integer reference and returns the incremented value. Line (4) initializes i, an integer reference to refer to 1. At line (5) we apply inc to i, but we ignore its return value so the value of the expression is () rather than 2, which is the value of inc(i) at that point. At line (6) we see that i was correctly incremented, since a second use of inc, this time without ignore, returns value 3. □

9.2.11 Exercises for Section 9.2

* **Exercise 9.2.1:** Without using the if-then-else operator, write an expression

equivalent to if x>0.0 then x else 0.0.

*!! Exercise 9.2.2: Is it possible to implement if x>3.0 then x else 0.0 using only the abs operator and arithmetic?

Exercise 9.2.3: Give the values of the following:

* a) substring("123456",1,2).

  b) substring("123456",0,4).

  c) substring("123456",3,0).

 * d valOf(SOME "abc").

 * e) getOpt(SOME "abc", "123").

  f) getOpt(NONE, "123").

! Exercise 9.2.4: Write a function that constructs a list of the prefixes of a given string using the substring and size operators.

! Exercise 9.2.5: Use app to write a function that prints a list of lists.

Exercise 9.2.6: Write a function addToRef(r,x) that adds *x* to ref *r*, returning the unit

* a) Using ignore.

  b) Using before.

  c) Using neither ignore nor before.

! Exercise 9.2.7: What is the difference between the functions app print and map print?

Exercise 9.2.8: Several of the functions of the top-level environment can be defined by using other functions of the top-level environment. Write the following in terms of other top-level functions:

* a) isSome.

  b) valOf.

* c) getOpt.

  d) null.

*! e) ignore.

  f) before.

*! g) `app`.

    h) `not`.

    i) The dereferencing function `!`.

 ! j) `substring`.

9.3   Top-Level Types and Exceptions

In this section we review the built-in types that are provided by the ML top-level environment. There are a few that we haven't seen before, and we study those in detail. We shall also enumerate the built-in exceptions and explain when they get raised by the system.

9.3.1 Primitive Types

The following are the primitive types available in the top-level basis. There are certain other types that are actually datatypes or type constructors, rather than primitive types.

1. `unit`, the type with the single value `()`. This type is used when no other type is appropriate, such as when a function like `print`, which does its work by side-effect, needs to return some value. The unit is also used as the "argument" to a zero-argument function.

2. `int`, the integers.

3. `real`, the real, or floating-point, numbers.

4. `char`, the characters.

5. `string`, the strings of characters.

6. `exn`, the exceptions.

7. `substring`. This type, which we have not seen before, is an abstract representation of the triples (base string, beginning position, length) that we discussed in connection with the function `substring` in Section 9.2.5. Note, however, that the function `substring` in the top-level environment that we discussed in Section 9.2.5 returns a value of type `string`, not a value of type `substring`. The substring type will be covered in Section 9.4.6.

8. `word`. We have not seen this type before. It consists of unsigned integers, and we shall introduce the type briefly in Section 9.4.2.

There may be some surprising omissions on the list above. For example, we mentioned `instream` and `outstream` as primitive types in Chapter 4. However, these are only available through the structure `TextIO`; they are not part of the top-level basis. Also missing is the type `bool`. Technically, `bool` is a datatype, as we shall see in Section 9.3.3.

9.3.2   Primitive Type Constructors

There are also three type constructors in the top-level environment:

1. `ref` constructs a reference type from any concrete type. For instance, `int ref` is the type whose values are references to integers.

2. `array` constructs an array type whose elements are of any concrete type. For instance, `(int * real) array` is the type of an array whose elements are pairs consisting of an integer and a real. Note that although the type constructor `array` is available in the top-level environment, the function `array` that creates an array, along with the other functions, such as `update`, that operate on arrays, are only available through the structure `Array`.

3. `vector` constructs a vector type whose elements are vectors (immutable arrays) of any concrete type. We mentioned the vector type in Section 9.2.8. We shall cover the concept and its structure `Vector` in more detail in Section 9.4.9.

9.3.3   Primitive Datatypes

There are four datatypes built into the top-level environment. Three of them we have met before.

1. The datatype `bool` has the definition:

   ```
   datatype bool = true | false;
   ```

   That is, `true` and `false` are the data constructors, and there are no type parameters.

2. The datatype `list` is defined by:

   ```
   datatype 'element list = nil |
       :: of 'element * 'element list;
   ```

   That is, `nil` and `::` (cons) are the data constructors, and there is one type parameter, the type of list elements. Notice that `::` constructs a list from a pair consisting of an element (the head) and a list of elements (the tail).

3. The datatype `option` has definition:

   ```
   datatype 'a option = NONE | SOME of 'a;
   ```

   Here, `NONE` and `SOME` are the data constructors.

4. The datatype `order` is a parameterless datatype that we have not seen previously. Its definition is:

   ```
   datatype order = LESS | EQUAL | GREATER;
   ```

   This datatype is present in the top-level environment for the convenience of those who need to write a comparison function that returns one of these three outcomes. We shall see an example below. Values from this datatype are returned by certain functions in the standard basis. However, application programmers are free to use this datatype or not in their own programs. In a sense, datatype `order` is no different from any other datatype, like `fruit` of Example 6.3, that has three values.

```
fun f((a,b),(c,d)) =
        if a<c then LESS
        else if a>c then GREATER
           (* here a=c *)
        else if b<d then LESS
        else if b>d then GREATER
        else EQUAL;
```
val f = fn : (int * int) * (int * int) → order

```
f((1,2),(3,4));
```
val it = LESS : order

```
f((1,3),(1,2));
```
val it = GREATER : order

```
f((4,5),(4,5));
```
val it = EQUAL : order

Figure 9.6: A function that returns a value of datatype `order`

The Equality Types

Each of the primitive types mentioned in Section 9.3.1 is an equality type, with the exception of `substring`, `real`, and `exn`. Also, the type constructors and datatypes of Sections 9.3.2 and 9.3.3 construct equality types if they are applied to equality types.

Example 9.9: In Fig. 9.6 we see a function f that takes as argument two pairs of integers and orders them lexicographically. That is, f first sees if the corresponding first components a and c are different, and if so orders the pairs according to the order of the first components. If the first components are equal, then f compares the second components, ordering the pairs according to their second-component values.

Following the definition of f are three uses of this function. The first is resolved by first components; the second requires that the second components be compared, and the third is an example of the comparison of equal pairs. □

9.3.4 Top-Level Exceptions

There are several exceptions that are part of the top-level environment. Depending on the implementation, we may or may not see these raised, since the system may instead print the associated message (which we can discover by applying function `exnMessage` to the built-in exception name. We shall list below the exceptions of the top-level environment and give some examples of responses in SML/NJ.

1. The exception `Bind` means that an attempt to bind a value to a pattern in a val-declaration has failed. For instance:

   ```
   val x::xs = nil;
   ```

   raises this exception.

2. Exception `Match` is raised during a match if there is no pattern that matches the given value. Recall that when writing such a match we get the message

   Warning: match nonexhaustive

   However, raising `Match` is more serious. It means that at run time we have actually tried to use the match in a way that we had not expected possible (or else we would have written a pattern to cover that case). For instance, if we write the function definition

```
fun f(0) = 1;
```

we get the warning of a nonexhaustive match, since we cover only the argument 0 in our trivial match. If we then say

```
f(2);
```

we get from SML/NJ the message

uncaught exception Match [nonexhaustive match failure]

Note, incidentally, that the message "nonexhaustive match failure" is the message SML/NJ associates with exception `Match`, as the following response shows:

```
exnMessage(Match);
```
val it = "nonexhaustive match failure" : string

3. Exception `Div` indicates a division by 0.

4. Exception `Chr` is the response to an attempt to create a character whose code is outside the range of legal codes. For instance, `chr(500)` will raise this exception if the ASCII code, with values between 0 and 127 only, is in use.

5. In cases other than these, exception `Domain` is raised if a built-in function is applied to a value for which it does not make sense, such as the square root of a negative number.

6. Functions that create a value outside the range representable by the machine will raise the exception `Overflow`.

7. Exception `Size` is raised by attempts to create a data structure whose size is either impossible (e.g., negative) or so large that it violates some machine constraint. For instance `array(A, ~1, 0)` will raise this exception.

8. Similarly, exception `Subscript` is raised if we try at run time to access an element outside the bounds of a structure. For example, if array A is declared by `array(A, 10, 0)`, then `sub(A, 10)` raises `Subscript`. Recall that an array of length 10 has elements numbered 0 through 9.

9. The exception

```
Fail of string
```

is an exception that is provided for the user who does not wish to define his or her own exceptions. For instance, the following function doesn't like the argument 0:

```
fun f(x) = if x<>0 then x else raise Fail("yucch");
```

It provokes the response:

```
f(0);
```

uncaught exception Fail [Fail: yucch]

9.3.5   Exercises for Section 9.3

* Exercise 9.3.1: Write a function that takes two lists of integers, compares them lexicographically, returning a value of type `order`.

! Exercise 9.3.2: Write a function $f(s, t, i)$ that tells if the last i positions of string s are lexicographically less than the last i positions of string t, returning a value of type `order`. If either or both of s and t are shorter than i, use the entire string as the "last i positions."

! Exercise 9.3.3: Write a function that takes as arguments a function f and a value v. The output of your function should be a function g that acts just like f, but if there are any binding errors in f, function g should produce the value v.

9.4   Structures of the Standard Basis

The standard basis for ML includes a large number of structures; there are 38 structures required in any implementation of ML97 and another 44 optional structures defined. Some of these we have seen partially, either because like `Int` they have some of their functions in the top-level environment, or because, like `Array` or `TextIO`, we have already discussed some of the important capabilities one gets from these structures. Since there are so many structures, and some of them contain many functions, types, constants, and exceptions, we are not going to enumerate the entire standard basis. Fortunately, there exists complete on-line documentation for the standard basis, enumerating each element of each structure; see the references in Chapter 1 (Section 1.4) for guidance on obtaining this documentation. Thus, in this section we "hit the highlights," discussing only the most important or representative structures, and covering only some of the elements of these structures.

Accessing Structure Elements

Recall the rules for accessing the components of a structure. We may either:

1. Open the structure, in which case all its elements may be referred to by their (short) name. This choice makes use of these elements easier, but it obscures other elements of the same name, including those of the top-level environment.

2. Not open the structure, in which case structure elements must be referred to by their long name, which is the name of the structure, a dot, and the name of the element, e.g., `Array.update`.

In this section, we shall refer to elements by their short name when the structure to which they belong is clear. However, in code examples, we shall use the long name of the element.

9.4.1 The Structure `Int`

In addition to the type `int`, the arithmetic and comparison operators, and the operator `abs` discussed in Section 9.2.1, here are some of the functions that are available in the structure `Int`.

1. `quot` is a variant of `div` that behaves differently when the result is negative. That is, while `div` always produces the next lower integer when the result is nonintegral, `quot` produces the integer that is closer to 0. For instance, 8 `div` ~3 has value ~3, while 8 `quot` ~3 has value ~2.

2. `rem` is a variant of `mod` that behaves differently when the result is negative. To be precise, a `mod` b is the integer we must add to $b \times (a$ `div` $b)$ to get a, for any positive or negative integers a and b. In contrast, a `rem` b is the integer we must add to $b \times (a$ `quot` $b)$ to get a. The following table illustrates the difference:

   8 mod 3 = 2   ~8 mod 3 = 1   8 mod ~3 = ~1   ~8 mod ~3 = ~2
   8 rem 3 = 2   ~8 rem 3 = ~2   8 rem ~3 = 2   ~8 rem ~3 = ~2

3. Functions `min` and `max` return the smaller and larger, respectively, of two integers. For instance:

   ```
   Int.max(3,4);
   ```
   val it = 4 : int

4. Function `sign(i)` returns the integer ~1, 0, or 1, depending on whether integer i is negative, 0, or positive, respectively.

5. Constants `minInt` and `maxInt` are the most negative and most positive integers representable. However, the value is returned as an integer-option, since it is possible that there is no limit (see the discussion of the optional structure `IntInf` below), in which case `NONE` is returned. The values of these constants are dependent on the ML implementation and perhaps the machine. For instance, SML/NJ running on a SUN workstation produces:

> ```
> Int.maxInt;
> ```
> *SOME 1073741823*

That is, 30-bit integers plus a sign bit are supported in this implementation.

There are also several structures related to integers that are included or optional in the standard basis. The structure `LargeInt` is required. It has the same signature as `Int`, but there may be a larger range of values allowed. For instance, SML/NJ on a SUN has twice as many values available for large integers, as witnessed by the following response:

> ```
> LargeInt.maxInt;
> ```
> *SOME 2147483647*

which should be compared with the response to `Int.maxInt` in item (5) above.

Another optional structure is `IntInf`. This structure has values that behave like integers, but also includes the value `inf` representing the infinite integer. This value is used in places where an exception would be raised in the structure `Int`, such as `1 div 0`. SML/NJ version 109.30 does not provide structure `IntInf`.

9.4.2   The Structure `Word`

The type `word` in ML designates unsigned integers. Values of this type are represented by the characters `0w` followed by either a decimal integer, or the character `x` and a hexadecimal integer. Recall our discussion in Section 2.1.1 of the hexadecimal representation.

Example 9.10: Here is an assignment of a word constant to variable w:

> ```
> val w = 0w123;
> ```
> *val w = 0wx7b : word*

Notice that unlike integers, where ML prefers the decimal representation, the hexadecimal representation is preferred for words. The response gives the hexadecimal equivalent of the decimal constant 123 in its response, and indicates that the type of the value is `word`.   □

2's Complement Notation

The most common way to represent positive and negative integers in an n-bit computer word is to represent nonnegative integers in the range 0 to $2^{n-1} - 1$ by their n-bit binary representation. Note that all these numbers have a leading 0. A negative number i in the range -1 to -2^{n-1} is represented by writing the n-bit binary representation of $2^n - i$. Note that all these numbers have a leading 1. Thus, the first bit functions as the "sign bit."

For example, if $n = 6$, then we can represent numbers between -32 and $+31$. The number 6 is represented by 000110, while -6 is represented by writing the integer $2^6 - 6 = 58$ in binary. This number is 111010.

Note that it is not necessary to open the structure `Word` in order to use constants of type `word`. Also, the operations of the top-level environment that make sense on words, such as `+` or `<`, will work on words without opening the structure. However, there are a number of specialized operators that apply to words but not integers. These are found in the structure `Word`. Here are some of the most important operators on words:

1. Function `toInt` converts a word to the equivalent positive integer. Since words often have more bits than (signed) integers, exception `Overflow` is raised if the word cannot be represented as an integer. For instance:

   Word.toInt 0w1234;
   val it = 1234 : int

   Word.toInt 0wx7FFFFFFF;
   uncaught exception Overflow [overflow]

   In the first example, a word of modest size is converted to an integer. In the second example, the word, which is 31 1's, is legitimate, but its value, $2^{31} - 1$, is too big to be an integer.[2]

2. The function `toIntX` converts a word to a positive or negative integer, assuming that the word represents an integer in 2's-complement notation (see the box "2's Complement Notation" for a definition of this notation). For instance,

   Word.toIntX 0wx7FFFFFFF;
   val it = ˜1 : int

---

[2]More precisely, SML/NJ uses 31 bits for words and 30 bits plus a sign for integers, so this example is valid for SML/NJ. Other ML implementations could give another response, but there will normally be some words that cannot be converted to integers.

3. Function `fromInt` turns an integer into the corresponding word. A negative integer is assumed represented in 2's complement. For example,

    ```
    Word.fromInt 1234;
    ```
    val it = 0wx4d2 : word

    ```
    Word.fromInt ~1234;
    ```
    val it = 0wx7ffffb2e : word

4. Functions `andb`, `orb`, and `xorb` perform the logical AND, OR, and exclusive-OR, respectively, bitwise on words. For example, Fig. 9.7 shows the declaration of two words a and b whose last twelve bits are respectively 010101010101 and 000000110011. Then, we apply the bitwise logical AND to these words and get the result 000000010001 in the last twelve bits. These bits are represented by 11 in hexadecimal. Similarly, the bitwise logical OR of a and b is 010101110111, or 577 in hexadecimal, and the bitwise exclusive-OR is 010101100110, or 566 in hexadecimal.

```
val a = 0wx555;
```
val a = 0wx555 : word

```
val b = 0wx33;
```
val b = 0wx33 : word

```
Word.andb(a,b);
```
val it = 0wx11 : word

```
Word.orb(a,b);
```
val it = 0wx577 : word

```
Word.xorb(a,b);
```
val it = 0wx566 : word

Figure 9.7: Logical operations on words

5. The function `<<(w,k)` shifts word w left by k bits. However, k must be represented by a word, not an integer. 0's are brought in from the right, and bits shifted left past the left end of the fixed length word are lost. For instance, suppose that words are 31 bits long as in SML/NJ, and let

    ```
    val a = 0wx2AAAAAAA;
    ```

That is, a is alternating 0's and 1's, starting with a 0. Then `<<(a,0w5)` shifts a five bits left, yielding `0wx55555540`.

6. The function >>(w,k) shifts word w right by k bits. Bits shifted past the right end are lost, and 0's are brought in from the left. Thus, if word a is as above, then the result of >>(a,0w5) is 0wx1555555.

7. Similarly, function ~>> is like >>, except that instead of bringing in 0's from the left, the leftmost bit is duplicated. There is no difference if the leading bit is 0, but if the leading bit is 1, then the effect of ~>> is to bring leading 1's in from the left. For example, suppose

    ```
    val b = 0wx55555555;
    ```

    This word is 31 alternating bits starting with a 1. Then the result of ~>>(b,0w5) is 0wx7eaaaaaa.

9.4.3 The Structures `Real` and `Math`

The structure `Real` contains familiar operations on real numbers such as arithmetic operators, comparison operators, and the operators for converting from reals to integers, such as `floor`, that we learned in Section 2.2.2. The operators `min`, `max`, and `sign` that we learned in Section 9.4.1 for integers apply as well to reals.

There are many other functions in the structure `Real` that we shall not cover in this book. However, within the structure `Real` is a substructure called `Math` that is a library of important mathematical functions. We shall survey this substructure here.

1. Function `sqrt` takes the square root of a real number. For example:

    ```
    Real.Math.sqrt(4.0);
    ```
    val it = 2.0 : real

    ```
    Real.Math.sqrt(~4.0);
    ```
    val it = nan : real

    The second response reminds us that there is no number that is the square root of a negative number.

2. Functions `sin` and `cos` take the sine and cosine of angles measured in radians.

3. Function `atan` computes the arctangent of a number; the result is returned in radians.

4. Function `exp(x)` returns e^x.

5. Function `ln(x)` returns the natural logarithm of x.

9.4.4   The Structure `Char`

In the structure `Char` are a number of useful functions on characters that we have not seen before. Here are some of them:

1. Function `toLower` converts any character that is an upper-case letter to the corresponding lower-case letter. Other characters are unchanged. Similarly, `toUpper` converts a lower-case letter to its upper-case version and leaves any other character unchanged.

2. There are a number of predicates (functions from characters to booleans) that tell whether a given character is in a certain class of characters. Some of these are:

    (a) `isAlpha`: an upper- or lower-case letter.

    (b) `isDigit`: a digit.

    (c) `isSpace`: a *whitespace* character. The whitespace characters are the space, tab, newline, carriage return, vertical tab, and formfeed.

    (d) `isPrint`: a printable character.

3. The function `contains` takes a string and a character and returns `true` if and only if the character appears at least once in the string. This function is defined in Curried form, so it can be applied to the string. The result will be another function that takes a character as argument and tells whether the character appears in the given string.

Example 9.11 : Line (1) of Fig. 9.8 shows a use of function `contains`. We have asked if the character `a` appears in `"hello world"`; it does not, so the response is `false`. Note that because `contains` is Curried, we must pass the two arguments without punctuation. Line (2) shows a partial instantiation of `contains` using the string `"abc"`. The resulting function f will tell us whether any character is either `a`, `b`, or `c`. We see in line (3) an application of the function f.   □

An optional structure called `WideChar` has the same signature as `Char`. However, "wide characters," if supported by a given ML implementation, may extend the ASCII set, perhaps to 8 bits or more. Examples of possible wide character sets are the 256-character HTML set and the 16-bit Java set.

9.4.5   The Structure `String`

In addition to the comparison operations on strings, the concatenation operators `^` and `concat`, the conversion operators `implode` and `explode`, and the function `substring` introduced in Section 9.2.5, the structure `String` contains these constants and functions:

(1) `Char.contains "hello world" #"a";`
    val it = false : bool

(2) `val f = Char.contains "abc";`
    val f = fn char → bool

(3) `f(#"b");`
    val it = true : bool

Figure 9.8: The function `contains`

1. The constant `maxLen` is the longest allowable length of a string in the ML implementation. For example, SML/NJ gives the following response:

   `String.maxLen;`
   val it = 33554431 : int

   That number is $2^{25} - 1$, incidentally.

2. The function `sub(s,i)` produces the character in position i of string s. As always, we count positions starting at 0. For instance:

   `String.sub("abcdefg", 2);`
   val it = #"c" ; char

   Notice that `sub` on strings has a meaning analogous to that for `sub` on arrays. We shall see in Section 9.4.9 that strings are really vectors of characters, and vectors in turn are arrays that cannot change their values. Thus, the connection is more than coincidence.

3. The function `tokens` takes a predicate on characters and a string. The string is broken into *tokens*, which are maximal sequences of characters that *do not* satisfy the predicate. Thus, the predicate describes "punctuation" characters that separate tokens, and the function `tokens` produces a list of the tokens themselves. Since `tokens` is written in Curried form, with the predicate first, it is convenient to apply `tokens` to a predicate alone and return a function that breaks a string into a list of tokens according to that predicate.

Example 9.12 : Let us consider an example in which we want tokens to consist of letters only. We can define a predicate that is the negation of the predicate `isAlpha` that we discussed in Section 9.4.4. This predicate, defined as an anonymous function, is applied thusly:

```
val f = String.tokens (fn x => not (Char.isAlpha x));
```
val f = fn : string → string list

to produce function f. The function f takes a string and produces from it a list of the maximal substrings of letters. For instance,

```
f("if x <= y then x else y");
```
val it = ["if","x","y","then","x","else","y"] : string list

In this example string, each token is separated from the next by a single blank, except for the first x and the first y, which are separated by the sequence of four characters " <= ", each of which satisfies the predicate.   □

   Incidentally, there is also in structure `String` a function `fields` related to `tokens`. The difference is that "fields" can only be separated by one punctuation character, not any sequence of punctuation characters. As a result, some fields may be empty strings, while tokens are always nonempty strings. For example, had we defined f using `fields` instead of `tokens` in Example 9.12, the result would have changed by the addition of three empty strings between the first "x" and "y" in the output list.

9.4.6   The Structure `Substring`

A substring is an abstraction whose values are not visible to the programmer. However, we may think of a value of type `substring` as representing the following triple of type `string * int * int`:

a) A *base* string,

b) A position in the base string where the substring begins, and

c) The length of the substring.

The type `substring` and a number of useful functions on substrings are contained in the structure `Substring`. Here are some important elements in `Substring`.

1. Function `substring` takes as argument a triple consisting of a string s and two integers i and j. It returns an abstract representation of the substring consisting of the j positions of string s beginning at position i. For example:

    ```
    val ss = Substring.substring("abcdefg", 2, 3);
    ```
    val ss = − : substring

String.substring Versus Substring.substring

The reader should remember from Section 9.2.5 that the top-level environment contains a function called `substring`. This function is from the structure `String`, not substring. Both functions named `substring` take the same arguments, but `String.substring` returns the substring itself, as a string, while `Substring.substring` returns some abstract representation of the substring.

Since `String.substring` is in the top-level environment, we must be especially careful that when we need `Substring.substring` we have either opened `Substring` or use its long name. Otherwise, there will appear to be a function of that name, but it will be the wrong function, returning a string instead of an abstract substring.

Notice that no value for this substring is visible; only a dash appears where there should be some representation of a value. The true representation is some internal, implementation-dependent data structure. In some sense, the value of `ss` is the substring `"cde"` of `"abcdefg"`, because that is the substring of length 3 beginning at position 2 (recall positions begin at 0).

2. Function `base` takes a substring and returns the triple it represents. For instance, if we have defined `ss` as we did in connection with the function `substring` above, then we can apply `base` to it as:

```
Substring.base ss;
```
*val it = ("abcdefg",2,3) : string * int * int*

3. The function `getc` takes a substring and separates it into its first character and the substring that is the remaining characters. In a sense, `getc` splits a string the way `hd` and `tl` split lists. More precisely, `getc` applied to a substring `ss` returns a value of type `(char * substring) option`. The value is `NONE` if `ss` is the empty string. Otherwise, the value is `SOME(c, ss1)`, where c is the first character of `ss` and `ss1` is the substring that represents all but the first character of `ss`.

Example 9.13: The function `printChars` of Fig. 9.9 prints each of the characters of a string, one to a line. It takes a substring `ss` and applies `getc` to it in a case-statement at line (2). The first case, line (3), is where the substring `ss` is empty. Then, we are done printing characters and return the unit.

In the case where `ss` is not empty, starting at line (4), we print the first character c at line (5), print a newline at line (6), and recursively print the remainder of the substring at line (7).

```
(1) fun printChars(ss) =
(2)           case Substring.getc(ss) of
(3)               NONE => () |
(4)               SOME (c, ssTail) =>
                      (
(5)                       print(str(c));
(6)                       print("\n");
(7)                       printChars(ssTail)
                      );
```
val printChars = fn : substring → unit

```
(8) printChars(Substring.substring("abcdefg", 2, 3));
    c
    d
    e
```
val it = () : unit

Figure 9.9: Printing a string of characters vertically

Finally, at line (8) we use **printChars** by applying it to the abstract substring formed by taking positions 2 through 4 of the base string **"abcdefg"**. We see those characters printed vertically as a response. □

9.4.7 The Structure List

We have already seen many of the important functions in the structure **List**. These include the basic operations to take the head and tail, concatenate or "cons" lists, reverse lists, and compute the length of the list. We have also seen some of the higher-order functions that are available for lists, such as **map** and the two versions of folding: **foldr** and **foldl**. There are a number of other functions worth mentioning.

1. Function **take(L,i)** returns the first i elements of the list L. For instance:

    ```
    List.take([1,2,3,4,5], 3);
    ```
    val it = [1,2,3] : int list

2. Symmetrically, function **drop(L,i)** returns what is left when the first i elements are removed from list L. Thus:

    ```
    List.drop([1,2,3,4,5], 3);
    ```
    val it = [4,5] : int list

3. Function `nth(L,n)` returns the *n*th element of list *L*, counting from 0 as the first element. For example:

   ```
   List.nth([1,2,3,4,5], 3);
   ```
   val it = 4 ; int

4. Function `tabulate` takes a pair consisting of an integer *n* and a function *f* that has an integer domain, and returns the list $[f(0), f(1), \ldots, f(n-1)]$. For example:

   ```
   List.tabulate(5, fn x => x*x);
   ```
   val it = [0,1,4,9,16] : int list

5. Recall that in Section 5.4.5 we wrote a simple higher-order function called `filter` that takes a predicate *p* and a list *L* and returns the list of all those elements of *L* that satisfy predicate *p*. There is a function `List.filter` that is similar, but related to our `filter` as the ML function `map` (described in Section 5.6.3) is related to the simple map function of Section 5.4.2. That is, `List.filter` takes a predicate *p* and returns a function f_p. Function f_p takes a list *L* as argument and returns the sublist of elements satisfying *p*. For example, suppose we say:

   ```
   val f = List.filter(fn x => x<10);
   ```
   val f = fn : int list → int list

   We may then use *f* as in

   ```
   f([9, 10, 6, 5, 20]);
   ```
   val it = [9,6,5] : int list

6. Function `partition` is a generalized "filter" that takes a predicate and returns function g_p. The function g_p takes a list *L* and returns a pair of lists. The first list of the pair is the elements of *L* that satisfy *p*; this list is what `filter` would return. The second list is the elements of *L* that do *not* satisfy *p*. Here is an example of the use of `partition`:

   ```
   val g = List.partition(fn x => x<10);
   ```
   *val g = fn : int list → int list * int list*

   We may then use *g* as in

   ```
   g([9, 10, 6, 5, 20]);
   ```
   *val it = ([9,6,5], [10,20]) : int list * int list*

9.4.8   The Structure `Array`

Structure `Array` contains a number of functions besides the principal tools — `array`, `sub`, and `update` — that we met in Section 7.2.2. We shall mention here only a few; all but the first are analogs of functions of the same name that we have seen for lists:

1. Function `fromList` takes a list L and creates an array of the same length whose elements are the elements of L, in order. For instance:

   ```
   val A = Array.fromList [1,2,3];
   ```
   val A = [|1,2,3|] ; int array

2. Function `Array.length` returns the length of an array. Note that the function `length` in the top-level basis applies to lists, not arrays.

3. `Array.tabulate` takes an integer n and a function f whose domain is integers and produces the array whose ith element is $f(i)$ for $i = 0, 1, \ldots, n-1$. In comparison, `List.tabulate` does the same but produces a list of these values.

4. Functions `Array.foldr` and `Array.foldl` behave like the functions `foldr` and `foldl` of the top-level environment that we described in Section 5.6.4. However, these functions operate on arrays rather than lists. That is, their type is

   ```
   (('a * 'b) -> 'b) -> 'b -> 'a array -> 'b
   ```

9.4.9   The Structure `Vector`

As we have mentioned, the type constructor `vector` creates *immutable* (unchangeable) arrays of elements of a certain type. Thus, one finds essentially the same operations in the structure `Vector` that exist in the structure `Array`. The major difference is that function `Array.update` has no analog in the structure `Vector`.

Values of type T `vector` are represented by a list of elements of type T, preceded by the pound sign `#`. For instance:

```
val v = #[1,2,3];
```
val v = #[1,2,3] : int vector

Notice that the notation for vectors is available without opening or otherwise accessing the structure `Vector`.

One important operation we can perform on vectors is to extract *slices*, which are almost like substrings of a string. A slice is a triple consisting of:

a) A *base* vector v,

Slices and Substrings

Let us observe the similarities and differences between slices and substrings. First, the similarity should be expected, since a string is essentially a `char vector`, that is, a vector of characters. Both slices and substrings have a base — a vector for slices and a string for substrings. The second component is the starting position for the slice in both cases. The third component of a substring is an integer length, while for the slice the third component is an integer-option, allowing either a length or "to the end" to be specified.

We can obtain the added flexibility of the integer option for strings as well as vectors. There is a function `String.extract` that is analogous to the function `Vector.extract` that we discussed for vectors. `String.extract(s, i, SOME j)` means the same as `String.substring(s, i, j)`, while `String.extract(s, i, NONE)` produces the string beginning at position i of string s, until the end.

Moreover, there is a function `Substring.slice` that behaves like `extract` on substrings. That is, `Substring.slice` takes a substring, an integer, and an integer option and produces the appropriate (abstract) substring.

---

b) An initial position i, and

c) An integer-option, either `NONE` or `SOME` j.

If the integer-option is `SOME` j, then the slice represents the j positions starting at position i of the base vector v. If the integer-option is `NONE`, then the slice is all positions from i until the right end of vector v. As always, positions are counted starting at 0.

Example 9.14: If v is `#[1,2,3,4,5,6]`, then the slice (`v, 2, SOME 3`) is the vector `#[3,4,5]`. The slice (`v, 2, NONE`) is the vector `#[3,4,5,6]`. □

To obtain a slice of a vector, we use the function `extract`. The type of `extract` is

```
('a vector * int * int option) -> 'a vector
```

so it takes the specification of a slice as argument and returns the vector designated by that slice.

Example 9.15: Here are two examples of the use of `extract`, corresponding to the slices of Example 9.14.

```
Vector.extract(#[1,2,3,4,5,6], 2, SOME 3);
val it = #[3,4,5] : int vector
```

```
Vector.extract(#[1,2,3,4,5,6], 2, NONE);
```
val it = #[3,4,5,6] : int vector

□

The structure `Array` also has a function `extract`. This function produces a vector, not another array. That is, the type of `Array.extract` is

```
('a array * int * int option) -> 'a vector
```

9.4.10 The Structure OS

There is a structure `OS` that is designed to deal with operating systems and file systems in a machine- and system-independent way. This structure contains a new type, `syserror`, and the exception

```
SysErr of (string * syserror option)
```

which gets raised when functions in the `OS` structure or its substructures go wrong. The arguments of `SysError` are a string error message and an optional error code of type `syserror`. Here are a few examples of the substructures and functions available through the `OS` structure.

1. There is a substructure `FileSys` that allows us to manipulate files and directories. The function `getDir` in this substructure returns the path name of the current directory. For instance, as I write this chapter, I am working in directory `/dfs/sole/3/ullman/ml2/ch9`. Here is the response I get to `getDir`:

   ```
   OS.FileSys.getDir();
   ```
   val it = "/dfs/sole/3/ullman/ml2/ch9" : string

   Notice that `getDir` takes the unit as argument and returns a string.

2. Function `mkDir`, also in the substructure `FileSys`, attempts to make a new directory with the pathname specified by its string argument. For example, if I am in the directory above, I can say:

   ```
   OS.FileSys.mkDir "foo/bar";
   ```
   uncaught exception SysErr: [SysErr: No such file or directory [noent]]

   ```
   OS.FileSys.mkDir "foo";
   ```
   val it = () : unit

In the first case, there is no subdirectory `foo` of my `ch9` directory, so a system error occurs, and the `SysErr` exception is raised. In the second example, I successfully created a subdirectory `foo`. I could then reissue the first command to create a subdirectory `bar` or `foo`.

3. The substructure `Process` has functions for dealing with processes. It contains the type `status`, which is `int` in the SML/NJ implementation. There are two constants `success` and `failure`, of type `status`. In SML/NJ, `success` is 0 and `failure` is 1, as is consistent with the UNIX approach to representing success or failure of a system call. Substructure `Process` also has a number of functions for managing processes. One simple but useful example is function `system`, which interprets its string argument as an operating system command, and executes it as a side-effect. For example, the expression:

```
OS.Process.system "ls -l";
```

executed under a UNIX operating system causes the current directory to be listed as a side-effect. Assuming the execution of `ls -l` was successful, the value returned by `system` is `success` of type `status`.

9.4.11 The Structures `Time` and `Timer`

The structure `Time` contains a type `time` that represents abstract amounts of time. These times are represented in the form

$$\text{TIME } \{ \text{ sec } = <\text{seconds}>, \text{ usec } = <\text{microseconds}> \}$$

This form looks like a data constructor `TIME` applied to a record structure. However, it cannot be dissected using pattern matching or the `#` operator. Rather, we can convert to and from real numbers to create constants of type `time`. Examples are:

```
val t = Time.fromReal 4.000001;
```
val t = TIME {sec = 4, usec = 1} : Time.time

```
Time.toReal t;
```
val it = 4.000001 : real

The structure `Timer` allows us to time processes, using either wall-clock time or CPU time. There are two types provided by this structure, `real_timer` and `cpu_timer`, for real and CPU timing, respectively. A real timer produces a value of type `time`, while a CPU timer produces a record structure consisting of three fields, each of whose values is a `time`:

a) `gc` is the amount of garbage-collection time taken by the process.

b) `sys` is the amount of system time taken.

c) `usr` is the amount of user time taken; this amount includes the time taken by the garbage collector that was reported by `gc`.

We initialize and examine these timers by the following functions in the structure `Timer`:

1. `startRealTimer` takes the unit as argument and returns a real timer (i.e., a value of type `real_timer`).

2. `checkRealTimer` takes a real timer as argument and returns, as a value of type `time`, the amount of wall-clock time since that timer was started.

3. `startCPUTimer` takes the unit as argument and returns a CPU timer.

4. `checkCPUTimer` takes a CPU timer as argument and returns a record with the fields `gc`, `sys`, and `usr`. This record represents the amount of time consumed under these three categories since the CPU timer was started.

Example 9.16: In Fig. 9.10 is a function `run` that starts a real timer, runs until the timer reaches at least 10 seconds, and prints the number of times it has checked the timer. At line (1), the timer t is initialized. The response gives the current clock time, although at that point the timer t will begin to count from 0.

```
(1) val t = Timer.startRealTimer();
```
val t = RealT (TIME sec=859494139,usec=879476) : real_timer

```
(2) fun run(n) =
            let
(3)               val ct = Time.toReal(Timer.checkRealTimer t)
            in
(4)               if ct < 10.0 then run(n+1) else n
            end;
```
val run = fn : int → int

```
(5) run(0);
```
val it = 1771860 : int

Figure 9.10: Counting 10 seconds

Lines (2) through (4) are the function `run`. This function takes an argument n representing the number of calls it has made to itself. In line (3), the timer t

is checked, and the abstract time it returns is converted to a real number. This real is compared with 10.0 at line (4). If 10 seconds have not elapsed, then `run` adds 1 to its argument and calls itself recursively. If 10 seconds have elapsed since line (1) was executed, then instead n is returned and `run` ends.

In line (5) we see a call to `run(0)`. Ten seconds later, the call ends. At that time, `run` has called itself almost 2 million times. Machines are fast these days, and so is the output of an ML compiler. □

9.4.12 What If I Lose a Name?

From time to time, you may lose a function or other element of the top-level environment. For example, you may open a structure that has another function of the same name, or you may write a function of your own with the same name. You can get the name you want back, either by opening *its* structure or by using its long name. As a general rule, a function whose parameter(s) are of type T will be in the structure for type T. For example, in the structure `Real` we find functions like `trunc`, `<` on reals, and `+` on reals. There are a few exceptions, however:

- The structure `List` contains not only functions on lists like `hd`, but the higher-order functions like `map`.

- The function `str` is in `String`, not `Char`, even though its argument is a character. `String` also has the functions `implode` and `explode`, which involve both strings and character lists.

- Function `real`, from integers to reals, is in `Real`, not `Int`.

- Likewise, both `ord` and `chr`, involving both integers and characters, are in `Char`, not `Int`.

- Function `print` is in `TextIO`, not `String`.

- Function `vector` is in `Vector`, as you would expect, but its long name is `Vector.fromList`, not `Vector.vector`.

- There is a structure `General` that holds all the functions that work on values of arbitrary types, like `before` or `o`. The functions on references — `ref`, `!`, and `:=` — are in `General`. Also in `General` are all the exceptions and the functions `exnName` and `exnMessage` that operate on exceptions.

9.4.13 Exercises for Section 9.4

Exercise 9.4.1: Give the values of the following:

* a) `~14 quot ~5`.

* b) `~14 rem ~5`.

c) ~14 quot 5.

d) ~14 rem 5.

Exercise 9.4.2: Write equivalents to the following expressions on real numbers using only the `sign` function and arithmetic operators:

* a) abs(x).

!! b) if x>3.0 then x else 0.0.

Exercise 9.4.3: Find the values of the following expressions involving words. When necessary, assume that words are 31 bits long.

* a) Word.toInt 0wxABC.

b) Word.fromInt ~20.

* c) Word.toIntX 0wx40000003.

d) Word.<<(0wxFF, 0w3).

* e) Word.>>(0wxFF, 0w3).

f) Word.~>>(0wxFF, 0w3).

* g) Word.andb(0w12, 0w5).

h) Word.orb(0w12, 0w5).

i) Word.xorb(0w12, 0w5).

! **Exercise 9.4.4:** Write a function mask(w,i,j) that takes a word w and masks out (sets to 0) all positions except for the j positions starting at position i. When counting positions, start at the *right* end with position 0.

Exercise 9.4.5: Write a function $f(x, a) = a^x$, using the functions exp and ln from the structure Real.Math.

Exercise 9.4.6: Write the following functions using contains from the structure Char:

* a) A function that tells whether a character is a vowel.

b) A function that tells whether a character is an even digit.

c) A function that tells whether a character is a 1-point letter in Scrabble.

Exercise 9.4.7: Using functions tokens or fields from the structure String, write a function that breaks a string into tokens separated by:

* a) One or more white-space characters.

b) Single slashes (/), as are used to separate elements of a path name in UNIX.

Exercise 9.4.8: Use operations from the structure `Substring` to write functions that:

* a) Reverse a string.

b) Produce the odd-numbered positions of a string. For example, given `"abcdef"`, produce `"bdf"`.

Exercise 9.4.9: If L is the list `[0,1,4,9,16,25,36]`, give the value of the following:

* a) `List.take(L,4)`.

b) `List.drop(L,4)`.

* c) `List.nth(L,1)`.

d) `List.nth(L,4)`.

Exercise 9.4.10: Use the function `List.partition` to write functions that do the following:

a) Given a list of strings, divide the list into those strings that are 10 characters or longer and those that are shorter than 10 characters.

*! b) Given a list of integers, divide the list into three lists, consisting of those integers that are divisible by 3, those that leave a remainder of 1 when divided by 3, and those that leave a remainder of 2 when divided by 3.

!! c) Given a list L of integers and an integer m, produce the list of lists $[L_0, L_1, \ldots, L_{m-1}]$, where L_i consists of those integers on list L that leave a remainder of i when divided by m.

! **Exercise 9.4.11:** Using functions from the structure `Array`, write functions to do the following:

* a) Produce an array of 26 elements initialized to the characters `#"a"` through `#"z"`.

b) Find the largest element of an integer array.

Exercise 9.4.12: Let V be the vector `#[0,1,4,9,16,25,36]`. Give the values of the following expressions:

* a) `Vector.extract(V, 1, SOME 5)`.

b) `Vector.extract(V, 1, NONE)`.

c) `Vector.extract(V, 3, SOME 2)`.

! Exercise 9.4.13: Write a function that operates on vectors, performing the analog of the function `Substring.getc` on substrings. Then, use your function to write another function that finds the maximum element in an integer vector.

Exercise 9.4.14: Find the value of the following:

* a) `Time.fromReal 1.234`.

  b) `Time.fromReal 10.5`.

* c) `Time.toReal {sec=3, usec=200}`.

  d) `Time.toReal {sec=0, usec=123456}`.

9.5   Additional Features of SML/NJ

All implementations are expected to provide the "required" structures, the most important of which we surveyed in Section 9.4. Implementations may also provide optional structures that conform to the ML97 standard for those structures. Beyond that, implementations are free to provide nonstandard structures to support features that are not part of the standard. SML/NJ provides one structure, called `SMLofNJ`, in which are found several additional capabilities.

The most important of these features are ways to create executable programs. When we develop a program in any language, we need to compile the program and store the compiled program in an executable file. By so doing, we avoid having to waste time recompiling the program every time we run it. The structure `SMLofNJ` provides two functions that allow us to create such executable files: `exportFn` and `exportML`.

9.5.1   Exporting Functions

The function `exportFn` takes two arguments:

1. The name f of a file in which to write the compiled program.

2. A function F.

When executed, the file f does exactly what the function F would have done if executed in the environment that existed when `exportFn` was called. The type of function `exportFn` is

```
fn :  string * (string * string list -> OS.Process.status) -> 'a
```

That is, the first argument, the file name, is a string. The second argument, the function F, has to be of the type that takes a string and a list of strings as arguments and returns a process status. Function `exportFn` may be deemed to return a value of any type, but some type must be specified.

To understand what the arguments of the function F are, we have to recall how UNIX handles commands. When you type a command in response to the UNIX prompt, the system treats the first string on the command line as the name of the file to be executed. Any other strings on the command line are arguments to be passed to the executing program. The main program of each file executed by UNIX has an array parameter `argv` that is the list of strings on the command line. The first of these, `argv[0]`, is the name of the file being executed, and the remaining strings, `argv[1]` through `argv[`n`]`, are the n arguments to the command.

In the function F, its first argument is the string `argv[0]`, i.e., the name of the file being executed. Usually, this argument is ignored, but there are some applications that need to know it. The second argument of F, the list of strings, is `argv[1]` through `argv[`n`]`, the list of arguments to the command.

Example 9.17: Let us take a simple example of the use of `exportFn`. In Fig. 9.11 we see an ML program that, when executed, will create a file called `combfile`. When executed, `combfile` computes $\binom{n}{m}$ for the integers n and m that appear on the command line. For instance if in response to the UNIX prompt we type,

```
combfile 10 5
```

`combfile` will be executed. It will print the value of $\binom{10}{5}$ and halt.

Lines (1) through (7) contain the definition of the combinatorial function we have seen several times before. The only difference is that we have renamed the function `comb1`.

Lines (8) through (14) define the function `comb`, which is the function we actually export. Function `comb` must take its arguments from the UNIX shell, so its first argument is the name of the executing file, which we ignore, and the second argument is the list of two strings received from the shell, such as `["10", "5"]` in the command line illustrated previously.

- Note that `comb` is written in such a way that if the exported file is called from UNIX with anything but two arguments, there will be no matching pattern, and the exception `Match` will be raised.

- A more careful design would have a second pattern for `comb`, say pattern `comb(_,_)`, with an associated action to print an error message. Alternatively, we could handle the `Match` exception by printing the error message.

On lines (9) and (10) `comb` converts each of the character strings n and m to the equivalent integer using `Int.fromString`, a convenient function in the standard basis that we have not previously discussed. This function converts

```
(1) fun comb1(n,m) =
        let
(2)         exception BadN;
(3)         exception BadM;
        in
(4)         if n <= 0 then raise BadN
(5)         else if m < 0 orelse m > n then raise BadM
(6)         else if m=0 orelse m=n then 1
(7)         else comb1(n-1,m) + comb1(n-1,m-1)
        end;
```

*val comb1 = fn : int * int → int*

```
(8) fun comb(_,[n,m]) =
            let
(9)             val nInt = valOf(Int.fromString(n));
(10)            val mInt = valOf(Int.fromString(m));
(11)            val answer = comb1(nInt, mInt)
            in
                (
(12)                print(Int.toString(answer));
(13)                print("\n");
(14)                OS.Process.success
                )
            end;
```

*val comb = fn : 'a * string list → ?.OS.Process.status*

```
(15) SMLofNJ.exportFn("combfile",comb) : unit;
```

Figure 9.11: Exporting the comb function

a string that represents an integer into an integer-option; for example, `"123"` would be converted into `SOME 123`. A string that doesn't represent an integer would be converted to `NONE`. In lines (9) and (10) we take a chance that the strings on the command line really do represent integers by applying the `valOf` operator to extract the integer from the option. Should m or n not represent an integer, the exception `Option` would be raised.

Having made these conversions, `comb` then applies `comb1` to the integers n and m at line (11). The result is printed at line (12) and followed by a newline at line (13). Finally, line (14) returns the status `success`.

Line (15) is the export statement. It takes two arguments:

1. The file name `combfile` into which the executable code is to be placed, and

2. `comb`, the ML function that constitutes the program in the file `combfile`.

After SML/NJ executes the program of Fig. 9.11, we shall find, in the same directory from which ML was called, a file named `combfile`. As mentioned previously, if in response to the UNIX prompt we type

```
combfile 10 5
```

then the result 252, which is $\binom{10}{5}$, will be printed. What actually happens is that a compiled version of the function `comb` is called with first argument equal to `"combfile"` and the list `["10","5"]` as second argument. □

9.5.2 Exporting the ML Environment

SML/NJ also allows us to create executable files with the function `exportML`. This function takes one argument, a string that names the file into which the compiled program is written. The difference between `exportFn` and `exportML` is that the former produces code to execute a particular function. The latter reproduces the ML system with its environment equal to whatever it was when the `exportML` function was executed.

If we export the ML system into a file `foo` and execute `foo` at the UNIX level, the ML system is called with the environment that existed when file `foo` was created. We then get the ML prompt, `-`, and may proceed to execute ML code in the existing environment.

Example 9.18: Figure 9.12 shows a simple use of `exportML`. We begin with our usual definition of the combinatorial function; we have returned to calling it `comb`. The definition of `comb` is now part of the environment.

At the last line, we export the ML environment into the file `newsml`. Note the response of the system. The function `exportML` is of type `string -> bool`. It returns `false` when it is called with a file it did not previously create, in which case it actually creates the file `newsml` that will serve as an ML environment.

When we execute `newsml` in response to the UNIX prompt, we get the response

---

Invoking Executable Files in SML/NJ Version 109.30

There is, in Version 109.30, a somewhat different mechanism for executing an exported file than the straightforward, command-line approach described in the body of the text. A later version will allow direct command-line execution as suggested by Example 9.17. However, in Version 109.30 one must say:

```
sml @SMLload=<exported file> <command-line arguments>
```

For example, using a SUN workstation and executing the program of Fig. 9.11, the actual name of the executable file is `combfile.sparc-solaris`. To execute this file and compute $\binom{10}{5}$, we issue the UNIX command:

```
sml @SMLload=combfile.sparc-solaris 10 5
```

The same modification must be made in Version 109.30 for the function `exportML`. For example, the exported file `newsml` from Example 9.18 is actually executed on a SUN workstation by:

```
sml @SMLload=newsml.sparc-solaris
```

> *val it = true*

The value `true` tells us that we are running a file created by `exportML` rather than creating such a file. We get the ML prompt and are now able to write top-level expressions in an environment where `comb` is defined. For example, we may type

```
comb(10,5);
```
> *val it = 252*

We may also type any definitions or expressions we wish, just as we can when we invoke `sml` from UNIX. □

9.5.3   Exercises for Section 9.5

! Exercise 9.5.1 : Modify the program of Fig. 9.11 to handle all exceptions, e.g. command arguments that are not integers, or arguments that are integers but raise exception BadN or BadM. Print an appropriate error message and have `comb` return the status `failure`. Remember that local exceptions, such as BadN and BadM cannot be handled outside their scope.

```
fun comb(n,m) =
    let
        exception BadN;
        exception BadM;
    in
        if n <= 0 then raise BadN
        else if m < 0 orelse m > n then raise BadM
        else if m=0 orelse m=n then 1
        else comb(n-1,m) + comb(n-1,m-1)
    end;
```
*val comb = fn : int * int → int*

```
SMLofNJ.exportML("newsml");
```
val it = false

Figure 9.12: Exporting the ML system with a loaded `comb` function

* **Exercise 9.5.2:** Write and export a function that takes a list of any number of integers on the command line and computes their sum.

Exercise 9.5.3: Write and export a function that takes on the command line

1. A real number x represented by digits with a decimal point somewhere in the middle, followed by

2. An integer y,

and prints x^y.

9.6   Summary of ML Syntax

We shall now summarize the structure of the ML language. We begin with the lexical features — the way identifiers, constants, and other simple classes are formed. Then, we give the syntax of the language, using the grammatical notation that was introduced in Section 5.7. In this notation, we use capital letters to indicate syntactic categories; these are either lexical concepts like ID (identifier), or syntactic concepts defined by a graph like that of Fig. 5.24.

9.6.1   Lexical Categories

In our description of ML, we shall refer to the following classes of character strings without giving a grammatical description.

1. *Identifiers* (ID). The alphanumeric and symbolic identifiers were described in Section 2.3.1. However, we exclude from the class ID those identifiers that begin with an apostrophe and therefore represent types, per item (5) below.

2. *Constants* (CONST). These are integers, reals, character strings, characters, booleans, and the unit (). Their legal forms were described in Section 2.1.

3. *Labels* (LABEL). These are either identifiers or positive-integer constants, as described in Section 7.1.

4. *Infix operators* (INFIX). These are the usual arithmetic and other operators that we mentioned in Section 9.1.2, plus any other identifiers defined to be infix by the `infix` or `infixr` declarations that we described in Section 9.1.4.

5. *Type variables* (TYVAR). These are identifiers that begin with an apostrophe and stand for types.

6. *Integers* (INT). There is a context where only an integer constant is permitted, and we indicate that constraint by the class INT.

9.6.2   Some Simplifications to the Grammatical Structure

To eliminate some of the complexity in describing the syntactic structure of ML, we begin by establishing some understandings about identifiers. These modifications to the possible forms of identifiers will then be omitted from the grammatical description throughout this chapter.

1. We shall not distinguish between long identifiers (those with a sequence of one or more structure names and dots) and ordinary identifiers introduced in Section 2.3.1.

2. An infix identifier can be made to have the syntax of a normal function application by preceding it by the keyword `op` as mentioned in Section 5.4.4. The use of `op` binds tighter than any other symbol, so it applies only to the identifier that follows. We shall speak only of identifiers in what follows; the reader should understand that if it makes sense to do so, the identifier may be preceded by `op`.

3. An identifier, expression, or pattern can be followed by a colon and a type. This colon acts like an infix operator, but its precedence is lower than that of any of the operators listed in Fig. 9.1. It is, however, higher than the precedence of `andalso` or `orelse` or of other keywords that appear in expressions. Thus, for example, `x+y:int` is grouped `(x+y):int`, but `x andalso y:bool` is grouped `x andalso (y:bool)`.[3]

---

[3]Note, however, that in these examples ML can infer the types of `x` and `y` regardless of how the grouping is done.

9.6.3 Expressions

Figure 9.13 presents the grammatical diagram for expressions (EXP) in ML. As a general convention, we list the alternative forms for a syntactic category in order of highest precedence first, from the top of the diagram. Since many of the forms are more complex than infix operators applied to two expressions, the notion of precedence is not precise. However, as a rule, to parse an expression, we form the subexpressions of the higher paths in the diagram before the lower paths.

Example 9.19: Because the expression form EXP orelse EXP is above the form while EXP do EXP in Fig. 9.13, we group an expression like

> while E_1 do E_2 orelse E_3

as

> while E_1 do (E_2 orelse E_3)

not as

> (while E_1 do E_2) orelse E_3

□

The paths through the diagram of Fig. 9.13 represent the following forms of expressions, from top to bottom of the diagram. The numbers in the following enumeration are keyed to path numbers along the left edge of Fig. 9.13.

1. An identifier.

2. A constant.

3. A label preceded by a pound sign. This type of expression produces a record selector, which is a function for extracting the value of the field with this label from records, as discussed in Section 7.1.2.

4. A record, consisting of curly brackets surrounding one or more fields; each field consists of a label, an equal sign, and an expression. The fields are separated by commas. Record expressions were discussed in Section 7.1.

5. A parenthesized, comma-separated list of expressions, representing a tuple. As a special case, if there is only one expression in the list, then we have an ordinary parenthesized expression, rather than a tuple. As a special case, zero expressions is the unit. Tuples were discussed in Section 2.4.1.

6. A comma-separated list of expressions, surrounded by square brackets. These are list-expressions as discussed in Section 2.4.3.

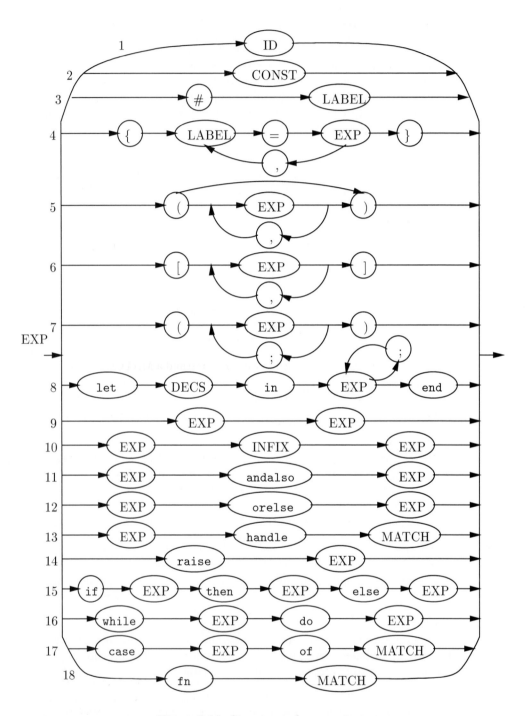

Figure 9.13: Structure of expressions

7. A parenthesized, semicolon-separated list of expressions, which is a sequence of "statements" as discussed in Section 4.1.3.

8. A let-expression, consisting of the keyword `let`, a DECS — that is, a list of declarations of a form to be described in Section 9.6.6 — the keyword `in`, a semicolon-separated list of expressions, and the keyword `end`. The form of this expression was introduced in Section 3.4, but the most general form is as given in Fig. 9.13.

9. A pair of expressions, juxtaposed with no intervening symbol. This form represents function application. The first expression must denote a function, and the second is its argument. Recall all ML functions have only one argument, although this argument may be a tuple (i.e., of form 5 described above).

10. Two expressions separated by an infix operator. This form represents the "main sequence" of operators that appeared in Fig. 9.1, along with any other identifiers declared to be infix operators.

11. Two expressions separated by the keyword `andalso`.

12. Two expressions separated by the keyword `orelse`.

13. An expression, followed by the keyword `handle` and a MATCH. The meaning of this expression form, whereby we "handle" an exception, was described in Section 5.2.3. We shall give the grammar for the syntactic category MATCH in Section 9.6.4, but the intuitive structure was described in Section 5.1.1.

14. An expression preceded by the keyword `raise`, which is an expression that raises an exception. The value of the expression following `raise` must evaluate to an exception, as discussed in Section 5.2.

15. An if-then-else expression, as described in Section 2.1.6.

16. A while-do expression, as described in Section 7.3.4.

17. A case-expression, as described in Section 5.1.4.

18. The keyword `fn` followed by a MATCH. The result is a value that is a function, as discussed in Section 5.1.3.

9.6.4   Matches and Patterns

We discussed the notion of a match in Section 5.1. Its formal structure is described by the lower diagram of Fig. 9.14. A match consists of one or more groups of the form PAT => EXP, where PAT is a pattern and EXP is an expression. Each group is separated from the next by a vertical bar.

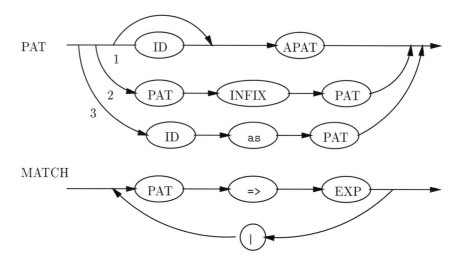

Figure 9.14: Structure of matches and patterns

The syntactic category PAT is defined recursively with the related syntactic category APAT, or *atomic pattern*. We see from the upper diagram in Fig. 9.14 that a PAT has one of the following three forms, keyed to the numbers of the paths in that diagram.

1. An atomic pattern optionally preceded by an identifier. This form represents any atomic pattern as defined in Fig. 9.15. It also represents a data or exception constructor preceding an atomic pattern. For example, if Node is a data constructor that takes two arguments, then Node(t1,t2) is a pattern. Here, (t1,t2) is an atomic pattern and node is a single identifier preceding this atomic pattern.

2. Two patterns connected by an infix operator. Most of the common infix operators, such as arithmetic or comparison operators, cannot appear in patterns because they make no sense. However, the infix operator could be ::, and as we have seen, patterns like x::xs are very common. It could also be a data or exception constructor that has been defined to be an infix operator.

3. An identifier x followed by keyword as and a pattern P says that identifier x must be bound to any value matched by the pattern P. The pattern P is interpreted according to the rules for PAT.

Atomic patterns include most of the pattern forms we have seen. Note that a PAT can be an APAT, and an APAT can be a parenthesized PAT, so the only real difference between the two is in the use of parentheses that they require. Here are the forms of atomic pattern, in order of highest precedence. The numbers of the forms are keyed to the numbers on the diagram of Fig. 9.15.

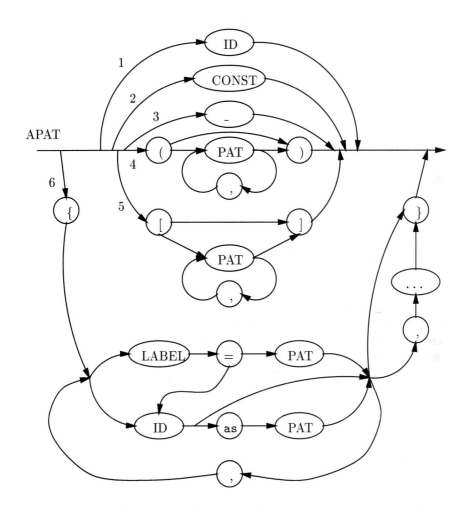

Figure 9.15: Structure of atomic patterns

1. An identifier, which matches anything.

2. A constant, which matches only itself.

3. The wildcard symbol _ that matches anything. The difference between an identifier and the wildcard is that the latter cannot be referred to elsewhere, and every use of the wildcard represents a different, anonymous identifier.

4. A list of one or more patterns separated by commas and surrounded by parentheses. This form represents a tuple pattern. In the special case that there is one pattern only, it is simply a parenthesized pattern.

5. A list of zero or more patterns separated by commas and surrounded by square brackets. This form represents a list pattern.

6. A comma-separated list of one or more elements, surrounded by curly braces. This form of pattern is a record pattern. Each element represents a field in one of several forms:

    (a) The usual form is LABEL = PAT, that is, a label representing a field, followed by the pattern that the value of this field must match.

    (b) Another possible form is a single identifier. Recall from Section 7.1.5 that identifier x in this context stands for x=x; that is, x is both the label and the pattern for that field.

    (c) An identifier x may be followed by keyword as and a pattern that the field value must match. Such an identifier x may also be preceded by a label and equal-sign, or x may be both the label and a pattern, as in case (6b).

   We also see from the complicated sixth group of paths in Fig. 9.15 that this list of elements may optionally be followed by a comma and the wildcard for fields ... .

9.6.5 Types

Another essential element of ML programs is an expression that denotes a type. Types can be concrete like int, or parameterized like 'a list. They can be built into types of arbitrary complexity using the grammar of Fig. 9.16.

    The forms of a type expression are as follows, from highest to lowest precedence. Again, the numbers below are keyed to the numbers on paths in Fig. 9.16.

1. A type variable, that is, an identifier beginning with an apostrophe.

2. A record type consisting of a comma-separated list of elements, surrounded by curly brackets. Each element defines the type of a field. The field name, a LABEL, is followed by a colon and the type expression describing the field.

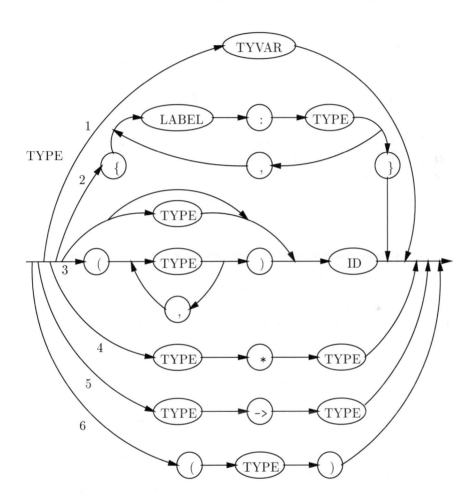

Figure 9.16: Structure of types

3. An identifier, which is a type constructor, optionally preceded by one or more type expressions. If there are two or more preceding type expressions, they must be surrounded by parentheses. If there is only one type expression, the parentheses are optional. This form includes concrete types like `int`, where the identifier (`int`) is not preceded by any type expressions. It also includes forms like `'a list`, `('a) btree`, and `(int, real) mapping`.

4. Two types separated by `*`'s. This form represents product types. Recall that grouping of components of tuples is significant. For instance, a type like `int * int * int` should not be confused with `(int * int) * int`. We can create either form by using rules (4) and (6) in the proper order. Rule (6) introduces whatever parentheses are desired.

5. Two types separated by the operator `->`. This form allows us to construct function types; it defines a type that is a function from the first type to the second. Recall that `->` is right-associative. Also, `*` takes precedence over `->`, as we can infer from the fact that the path for `*` is above the path for `->` in Fig. 9.16.

6. A parenthesized type.

9.6.6 Declarations

Let us now take up the structure of declarations in ML. Because this structure is complex, we shall first look at four important kinds of *value bindings* defined in ML. In general, a value binding associates a variable or variables with values of the appropriate kind(s). A value binding is preceded by a keyword such as `val` to form a *declaration*.

In Figs. 9.17 and 9.18 we see the diagrams for the four most complex forms of value bindings; simpler forms are included in Fig. 9.19, where we define the syntactic category DEC of declarations.

The top diagram of Fig. 9.17 shows value bindings that can follow the keyword `val`, and at the bottom of that figure is a diagram of the value bindings that may follow `fun`. One surprising point is that it is permissible to follow `val` or `fun` by one or more type variables; two or more need to be parenthesized, as usual. Any type variables placed there have a scope that is limited to this statement alone, which occasionally prevents an error because the type variable used has a scope extending beyond the statement. For example, we may say

```
fun 'a makeNil x = nil: 'a list;
```

and be sure that `'a` is a local variable and not the same as any other use of `'a` elsewhere. The body of the value binding for a val-statement consists of a pattern, an equal-sign, and an expression. This declaration binds the variables appearing in the pattern to whatever values they acquire by matching the pattern with the expression in the manner described in Section 3.3.5. Several

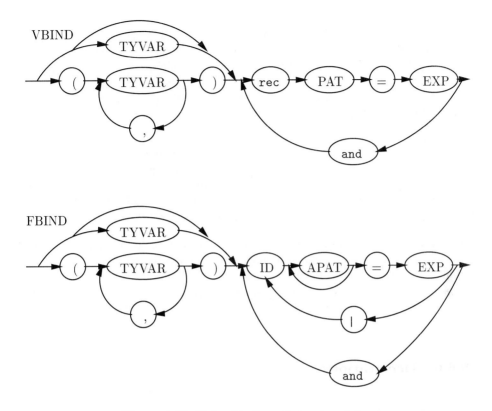

Figure 9.17: Value bindings for `val` and `fun`

value bindings can be made with one val-declaration if they are separated by
`and`. Also, the word `rec` (recursive) optionally may appear before a pattern; it
is essential if the value being described is a recursive function.

The lower diagram in Fig. 9.17 is the *function binding*. This form follows the
keyword `fun`. The binding for a single function with optional type variables,
consists of one or more groups separated by |. In each group is an ID (the
function name), followed by one or more atomic patterns, an equal-sign, and
an expression.

The atomic patterns are the arguments of the function. It is common for
there to be only one atomic pattern and for this atomic pattern to be a parenthesized pattern representing all the arguments of the function. However, as
discussed in Section 5.5, it is possible to write a function definition in Curried
form, where the function name is followed by each of its arguments with no
parentheses or commas. In this case, each argument is an atomic pattern by
itself.

Following the atomic patterns is the equal sign and an expression. The
expression is the definition of the function for those arguments that match the

given pattern (and do not match a previous pattern).

The groups separated by | form the definition of one function, and the name of this function must be the ID in each group. However, several functions may be defined in one function binding, and if so, these definitions are separated by and.

Now, let us consider the diagrams of Fig. 9.18. At the top is the diagram for *type bindings* (TBIND). These value bindings, which were described informally in Section 6.1, must be preceded by the keyword `type` to define a new type. The simplest form of binding consists of an identifier (the name of the new type), an equal sign, and a type expression. An example is `ilist = int list`. Here, `ilist` is the ID, and `int list` is the type expression.

As with the value bindings in Fig. 9.17, a type binding can have one or more type variables as parameters preceding the identifier that names the type. Two or more type variables must be surrounded by parentheses, although parentheses are optional for a single type variable. Additionally, a type binding may be a sequence of type bindings of the above forms, separated by the keyword and.

The lower diagram of Fig. 9.18 shows *datatype bindings* (DTBIND). These are preceded by the keyword `datatype` or `abstype` to describe a datatype. The informal description of this ML feature is in Section 6.2. The simplest form consists of an identifier, the name of the datatype, and an equal-sign, followed by one or more elements separated by vertical bars. Each element defines a data constructor for this datatype and is an ID optionally followed by the keyword `of` and a type expression. Here, the ID is the data constructor, and the TYPE describes the type of the values to which the constructor is applied.

Example 9.20: The binding `tree = Leaf | Node of tree * tree` is of this form. Here, `tree` is the datatype name, and `Leaf` and `Node` are two data constructors. The latter has an optional `of` followed by the type of nodes, which is a pair of trees. □

Datatype bindings may also be preceded by one or more type variables as parameters. The form of these parameters is the same as for the other value bindings; parentheses around one type variable are optional, but they are required for two or more type variables. Finally, it is also possible for a datatype binding to be several datatype bindings of the type described above, separated by keyword and.

In Fig. 9.19 is the structure diagram for declarations (DEC). This syntactic category is mutually recursive with the category DECS, or list of declarations, which has the simple definition shown in Fig. 9.20. That is, a list of declarations is zero or more declarations separated by optional semicolons. (Nothing separates declarations if the semicolon is not there.)

The forms of declarations given in Fig. 9.19 are as follows. Again, the numbers below are keyed to the numbers on the paths of Fig. 9.19.

1. *Value declarations.* The keyword `val` is followed by a VBIND, as described in the top of Fig. 9.17.

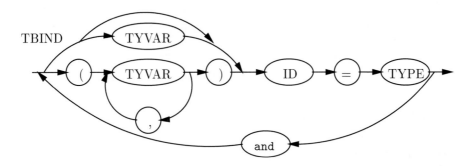

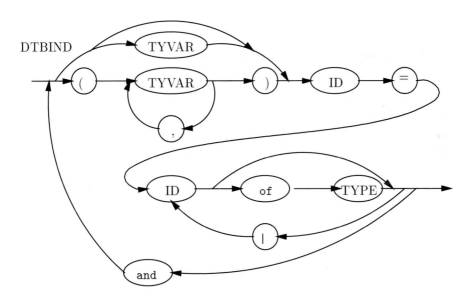

Figure 9.18: Type and datatype value bindings

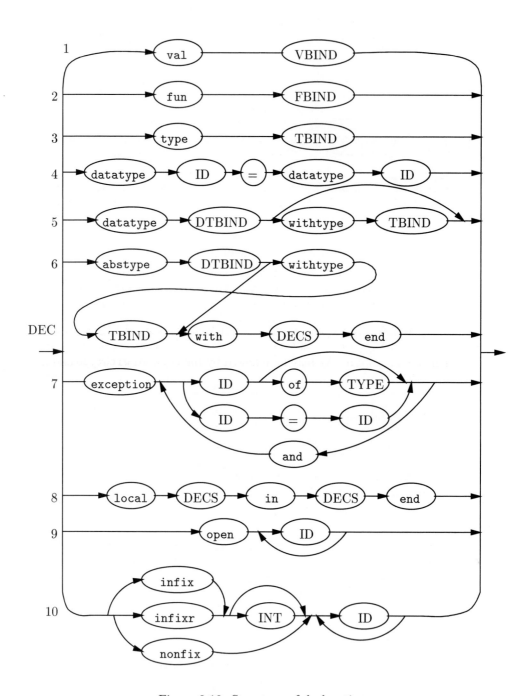

Figure 9.19: Structure of declarations

2. *Function declarations.* The keyword `fun` is followed by a function binding. The latter is the structure described in the bottom of Fig. 9.17.

3. *Type declarations.* The keyword `type` is followed by a type binding. The latter was described in connection with the first diagram of Fig. 9.18.

4. *Datatype synonyms.* This declaration, has not been discussed previously. The keyword `datatype` and an identifier may be followed by an equal sign, another occurrence of the keyword `datatype`, and another identifier. Only the second of the identifiers may be a long identifier, and a common purpose of this declaration is to give a datatype defined in some structure a local name. For instance, if you need the datatype `dt1` in the structure `Struct`, then instead of opening `Struct`, with its possible unexpected consequences regarding accessibility of names, you can say:

   ```
   datatype myDT = datatype Struct.dt1;
   ```

   and henceforth `myDT` will be a synonym for `Struct.dt1`, even in contexts where `Struct` itself is not accessible.

5. *Datatype declarations.* The keyword `datatype` is followed by a datatype binding as described in connection with the second diagram of Fig. 9.18. This binding optionally may be followed by the keyword `withtype` and a type binding. The latter clause, which we have not previously discussed, allows us to define some types as abbreviations and use them in the definition of the datatype itself. For example, the following datatype has values consisting of one or two string-integer pairs, and we use the type `pair` as an abbreviation for `string * int`.

   ```
   datatype oneOrTwoPairs = One of pair |
   Two of pair * pair
   withtype pair = string * int;
   ```

6. *Abstract type declarations.* The keyword `abstype` is followed by a datatype binding and an optional withtype-clause, just as for datatype declarations described in (5) above. Recall that the abstract type, described in Section 8.5.3, is like a datatype but with the possibility that functions on this type are used to encapsulate the type. These functions are defined following the datatype definition. They are preceded by the keyword `with` and followed by `end`.

7. *Exception declarations.* The keyword `exception` is followed by the declaration of one or more exceptions. The simplest form of an exception binding is an identifier, which becomes the name of the exception. We can also add the keyword `of` and a type expression to give the exception a parameter of a particular type. Another form of exception binding is

ID = ID, where the first identifier is defined to be a synonym for the second identifier, which must be an exception. There is occasional purpose to this definition, because the scopes of the two identifiers may be different as discussed in Section 5.2.5. Finally, several exception bindings may be connected by **and**.

8. *Local declarations.* The keyword **local** is followed by some declarations, the keyword **in**, more declarations, and the keyword **end**. As discussed in Section 8.5.4, this construct allows information hiding.

9. *Structure opening.* The keyword **open** is followed by one or more names of structures that are opened. Opened structures allow their identifiers to be used without the dot notation as discussed in Section 8.2.4.

10. *Fixity declarations.* An identifier can be declared to be an infix operator, associating from the left or right, by the keywords **infix** and **infixr**, respectively. An integer precedence level is optionally specified after either of these keywords. We can also remove the infix property by the keyword **nonfix**.

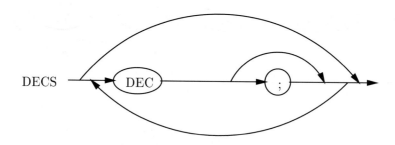

Figure 9.20: Structure of a declaration list

9.6.7 Signatures

The signature is a description of the form of a structure; both structures and signatures were introduced in Section 8.2. A signature is essentially a list of *specifications* (SPEC's). Each specification (SPEC) has one of the forms shown in Fig. 9.21. Many specifications describe an identifier, perhaps a function or a datatype, that are part of a structure with this signature. Specifications are mutually recursive with SPECS, whose simple form — a sequence of specifications separated by optional semicolons — is illustrated in Fig. 9.22.

The possible forms of a specification are the following. They appear from top to bottom in the diagram of Fig. 9.21, keyed as usual to the numbers of the paths in the diagram.

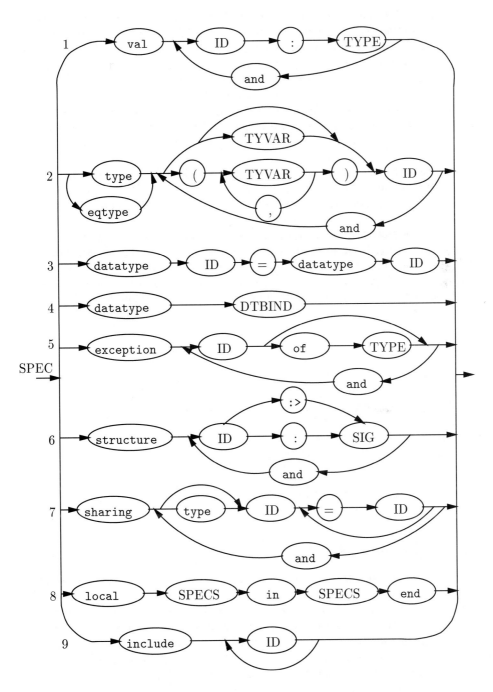

Figure 9.21: The structure of specifications

1. *Variable descriptions.* The keyword `val` followed by one or more groups, separated by `and`. Each group describes the type of one identifier, and the form of a group is ID : TYPE.

2. *Type descriptions.* One of the keywords `type` or `eqtype` is followed by an identifier that is the name of some type. If `eqtype` is used, then in the structure described, this type must be an equality type (one that allows tests for equality between values; see Section 5.3.4). The type may have parameters, in which case it will be preceded by one or more type variables. If there is more than one type variable, the list of type variables must be surrounded by parentheses. Several types may be specified at once if they are separated by `and`.

3. *Datatype aliases.* One datatype can be an alias for a second. Usually, the second is a datatype defined in some substructure of the signature, so the alias can be used even in contexts where the substructure is not accessible.

4. *Datatype descriptions.* The keyword `datatype` is followed by a datatype binding, an expression whose form is given by the DTBIND diagram in Fig. 9.18.

5. *Exception descriptions.* The keyword `exception` is followed by one or more identifiers that are the names of exceptions. The identifiers are separated by `and`, and each has an optional `of` TYPE clause describing the type of its argument.

6. *Substructure descriptions.* A signature can specify that one of the elements of a described structure is another structure. This specification consists of the keyword `structure`, the name of the nested structure, a colon or the `:>` operator for opaque signatures, and the signature of the nested structure. Several structures may be specified at once if their descriptions are separated by `and`.

7. *Sharings.* A signature may specify that certain of its identifiers must refer to the same thing in any structure described by this signature. This specification consists of the keyword `sharing`, the optional keyword `type` (used if the identifiers being equated are the names of types), and a list of two or more identifiers separated by equal-signs. When the specification begins `sharing type`, then the identifiers in the list are asserted to stand for the same type. If the keyword `type` is missing, then the equated identifiers are structures, and the assertion is that the types within these structures are the same.

8. *Local specifications.* For information hiding, some specifications may be local, indicated by a `local-in-end` construct.

9. *Inclusion of other signatures.* With the keyword `include`, followed by a list of identifiers that are the names of signatures, we can include within one signature the specifications of others.

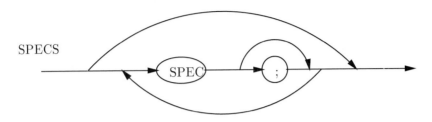

SPECS

Figure 9.22: Structure of a specification list

Figure 9.23 completes the grammatical structure of signatures. The syntactic category SIG (signature) is shown to be of one of two forms. Either it is a list of specifications surrounded by the keywords `sig` and `end`, or it is an identifier that has previously been declared to be a signature using a "signature declaration," whose form is described in the bottom diagram of Fig. 9.23.

Either of these forms of signatures is optionally followed by one or more clauses introduced by the keyword `where`. These clauses define a type name mentioned in the signature to have a particular value. For instance, having previously defined the signature MYSIG with a type t, we might later see the definition:

```
signature NEWSIG = MYSIG where type t = int;
```

to create a new signature that looks like MYSIG, but with type t specified to be `int`.

In the second diagram of Fig. 9.23 we see the structure of a *signature declaration* (SIGDEC). It consists of one or more groups separated by `and`. Each group equates an identifier to a signature; that signature can either be described explicitly by `sig`-SPECS-`end` or by a name, as we saw when we examined the diagram for SIG in Fig. 9.23.

9.6.8 Structures

We also studied in Section 8.2 the notion of a structure, which is the actual description of the collection of types, functions, and other elements whose general form is specified by a signature. The syntax for structures is found in Fig. 9.24. There are three mutually recursive syntactic categories:

a) STRUCT, a structure, analogous to SIG for signatures.

b) STRDEC, a structure declaration, analogous to a combination of SPEC and SIGDEC for signatures.

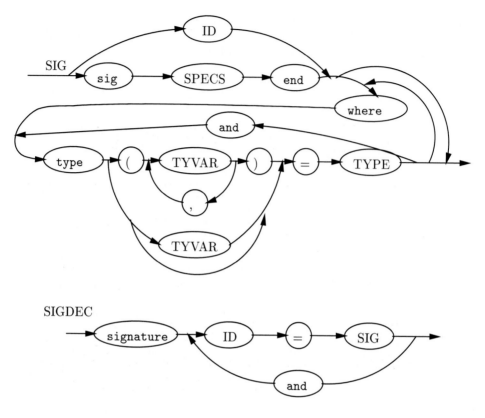

Figure 9.23: The structure of signatures

c) STRDECS, a list of structure declarations.

In the first diagram of Fig. 9.24 we see the four possible forms of a STRUCT.

1. Zero or more structure declarations surrounded by keywords `struct` and `end`. This form is the common, explicit way to describe a structure.

2. An identifier that has previously been defined to be the name of a structure.

3. A functor application as was described in Section 8.3. This form consists of an identifier — the functor name — and a parenthesized argument for the functor. The argument of a functor may be a single structure, following the simple form as in Example 8.14. Alternatively, the argument may be zero or more structure declarations, using the more general form illustrated by Example 8.17.

4. A structure defined with the help of some local definitions, using the `let-in-end` construct.

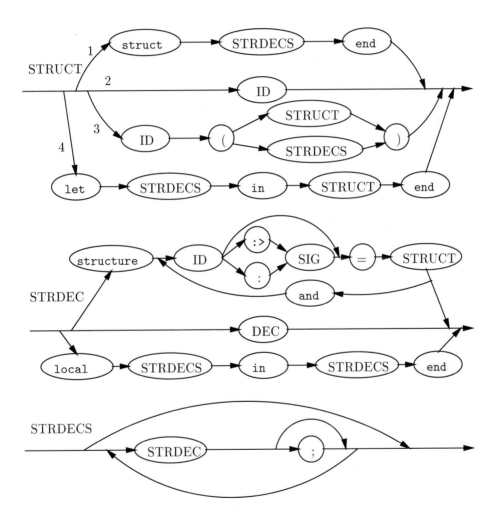

Figure 9.24: Grammatical diagrams for structures

Now let us consider the form of a structure declaration (STRDEC), as in the second diagram of Fig. 9.24. One common form of a declaration within a structure is a DEC, that is, one of the ordinary kinds of declaration that were described in the diagram of Fig. 9.19. This form is the middle path of the diagram for STRDEC.

The upper path describes the declaration of a structure, which is not among the "ordinary" declarations of Fig. 9.19. This type of declaration consists of the keyword `structure`, an identifier (the name of the structure), an optional colon or `:>` and a signature describing the structure, an equal-sign, and the structure itself. The lower path in the second diagram describes the possibility of using some local declarations to help make a structure declaration using the `local-in-end` construct.

The third diagram in Fig. 9.24 defines the syntactic category STRDECS. These are zero or more structure declarations separated by optional semicolons.

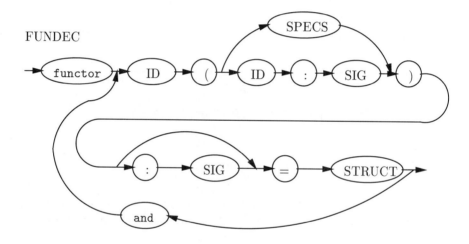

Figure 9.25: The structure of functors

9.6.9   Functors

Figure 9.25 gives the form of a functor declaration (FUNDEC). It consists of the keyword `functor` followed by one or more groups, separated by `and`. Each group defines a functor by the elements:

a) An identifier, the functor name.

b) A parameter for the functor, surrounded by parentheses. A functor parameter may have the simple form of a structure name, a colon, and a signature. For example, this form was illustrated in line (1) of Fig. 8.7. The more general form of functor parameter is a list of zero or more specifications; these are the elements used in signatures. We saw some examples of this type of functor parameter in Example 8.16.

c) An optional colon and a signature describing the structure that is the result of applying the functor.

d) An equal-sign and a structure. This structure is the expression that describes the result of the functor in terms of the argument of the functor.

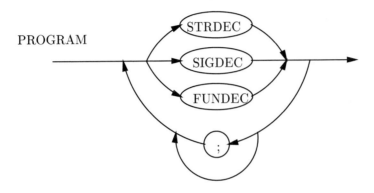

Figure 9.26: The structure of programs

9.6.10   Programs

Finally, the structure of an ML program is given by Fig. 9.26. A program is a list of declarations of functors, structures, and signatures. The elements of this list are separated by optional semicolons. Note again that common declarations — of functions, datatypes, and so on — are included in the syntactic category STRDEC, so all the usual kinds of ML program elements are included in the diagram of Fig. 9.26.

The reader may note that expressions, which are a common example of a program element when we write code at the top level, appears to be missing. In practice, the ML compiler turns an expression E at the top level into the declaration

```
val it = E;
```

Thus, expressions are included as a special kind of STRDEC. This convention also explains why the value of identifier it is given in the ML response to an expression.

Index